ISSUES OF THE DAY

100 Commentaries on Climate, Energy, the Environment, Transportation, and Public Health Policy

Ian W.H. Parry and Felicia Day, editors

RESOURCES FOR THE FUTURE

Washington, DC, USA

Resources for the Future
1616 P Street NW
Washington, DC 20036–1400
USA
www.rff.org

EDITORS:
Ian W.H. Parry, series editor
Felicia Day, managing editor
Adrienne Foerster, assistant editor

CONTRIBUTING EDITORS:
John Anderson
Sally Atwater

COVER AND BOOK DESIGN:
Ellen A. Davey

Distributed by RFF Press, an imprint of Earthscan

9781933115887 (hardback)
9781933115870 (paperback)

TABLE OF CONTENTS

EDITORS' INTRODUCTION

Every week, we post short commentaries on the RFF website, www.rff.org/weeklycommentary, that provide our readers with an easy means of learning about how policies work to control, to better and worse extents, some of the most challenging climate, energy, environmental, transportation, and public health problems of our time. Written mostly by economists, the commentaries serve to disseminate important research findings and expert judgment. They are nontechnical and enable the reader to quickly grasp the key points and background about a particular policy topic and learn from the insights of a leading expert.

We decided to collect the commentaries in book form not just for the old-fashioned pleasure of seeing them in print, but also for the most 21st-century reason: to deal with the information overload we all face and the lack of an easy place to turn to for answers. We may be well versed or even experts in our given fields, but there are many gaps in our knowledge about related fields and useful insights can often be gleaned from policy experience in other contexts.

Professors looking to update their course syllabi, students and reporters looking for background information, and business and policy professionals just trying to stay ahead of the curve should find these commentaries valuable. We also hope our readers share our intellectual curiosity; time and again, we came away edified about a problem or an idea we'd never considered before.

We cast a global net, looking at how congestion pricing works in London, malaria control is achieved in Africa, and emissions allowance auctions are designed in the United States. Some of the commentaries deal with international or transboundary policy problems, such as stratospheric ozone, and others dwell on national policy issues that are common to many countries, such as overharvesting of fish stocks.

Some commentaries are specifically focused on the United States, though they still provide useful insights for other countries. These offer an overview of various federal regulatory programs and how they might be reformed, including the Endangered Species Act, control of hazardous wastes and power plant emissions of sulfur dioxide, management of flood insurance and forest fires, and food safety regulation.

Rather than evaluating specific programs, some commentaries provide background on the seriousness of policy problems, broad trends in the form of policy interventions over time, or technologies that might be developed to help address them.

KEY THEMES

A key theme of the commentaries is the potentially critical role of careful economic analysis in helping to understand complex policy questions and hence aid in policy reform.

Some essays confirm a case for a particular policy or policy change on cost–benefit grounds. For example, the economic case for higher fuel taxes is well established. However, an alternative approach—specifically, policies to encourage automobile insurance companies to offer premiums that vary in direct proportion to vehicle mileage (in place of the current system of lump-sum insurance premiums)—would also generate substantial economic benefits, but without a large transfer of revenue to the government.

In other cases, economic analysis is valuable in informing about the extent of unintended policy consequences. For example, restrictions in the number of days vehicles can be driven in city centers appear to be an ineffective way to improve urban air quality, at least in Mexico City, because any gains in pollution are offset by increased use of secondary vehicles, as people attempt to circumvent driving restrictions. And advisories warning about mercury levels in fish have public health benefits from reduced consumption of contaminated fish, but these benefits appear to be offset because alerts lead to reduced consumption of all fish (rather than just high-mercury fish alone), thereby forgoing some of the health benefits from moderate fish consumption.

Understanding about the wide-ranging issues covered in this book is not just interesting for its own sake. Increasingly, issues in different fields are becoming related in one way or another. For example, it is useful for the climate economist to understand policy issues affecting the transport sector, like congestion pricing, fuel taxes, and fuel economy standards, as these policies have implications for the effects and costs of national-level greenhouse gas control programs. In the same light, biologists grappling with natural resource management issues can gain insights from innovative land management programs, voluntary pollution control efforts, and the use of satellite data.

ACKNOWLEDGMENTS

We owe a huge debt of gratitude to a number of our RFF colleagues for assistance with the web series and production of the book. In particular, we thank Adrienne Foerster for helping to manage the series on a week-by-week basis and for carefully editing many of the commentaries. Sally Atwater and John Anderson helped prepare many of them, and their contributions are very much appreciated. We also thank Peter Nelson and Don Reisman for their guidance during the book development process. Ellen Davey designed and produced the book. Tiffany Clements and Scott Salyer, of our web team, and David McLaughlin and Michael Eber also provided valuable support. Finally, we thank all of the 134 authors for their willingness to contribute to our series. We hope this book, and the commentary website, will help to provide them with access to a broader audience for their valuable work.

Ian W.H. Parry is an RFF senior fellow and holds the Allen Kneese chair. He dedicates this book to his late grandfather, William H. Skelton, in appreciation of support for his education.

Felicia Day is RFF's managing editor. She dedicates it to her "office" grandfathers, John Anderson and Joel Darmstadter, for their wise counsel and friendship over the years.

PART 1

Global Environmental Challenges

It is difficult to imagine a more challenging policy problem than global climate change. The appropriate goals of climate policy, and which countries should be held the most responsible for reducing greenhouse gases, are highly contentious. On top of this, there are many complicated issues in the design of domestic climate policy for a country like the United States.

The commentaries in this first section touch on a variety of climate policy issues. At the international level, these include the implications of delayed participation by developing countries in international emissions control agreements, the design of globally efficient policy architectures that take into account political constraints, incentives to comply with international agreements, the monitoring of climate-related trends, lessons from emissions trading to date in Europe, and the successful phasing out of ozone-depleting chemicals.

At the domestic level, issues covered include design provisions in prospective U.S. climate legislation, the choice among emissions control instruments, to what extent supplementary policies to promote clean fuels and clean technology innovation are warranted, how allowance auctions in a cap-and-trade system might be designed, and measures to deal with the risk that energy-intensive capital will migrate to countries with no emissions controls.

Additional issues include the case for, and practicality of, incorporating the forestry sector into climate programs, and the possibility of allowing firms to offset their carbon dioxide emissions by funding projects to reduce greenhouse gases in other sectors of the economy or in other countries. Two commentaries discuss one of the most important issues in assessing the economically efficient stringency of climate policy, namely the rates at which future damages from climate change should be discounted. Also included is a discussion of the expected risks posed by sea-level rises and how to adapt to them.

1. STABILIZING ATMOSPHERIC CO_2 WITH INCOMPLETE INTERNATIONAL COOPERATION

Jae Edmonds

is the chief scientist and a laboratory fellow at the Pacific Northwest National Laboratory's Joint Global Change Research Institute. His research focuses on long-term global, energy, technology, and climate change issues.

Leon Clarke

is a senior research economist at the Pacific Northwest National Laboratory's Joint Global Change Research Institute. His current research focuses on the role of technology in addressing climate change, scenario analysis, and integrated assessment model development.

Marshall Wise

is a senior research engineer at the Pacific Northwest National Laboratory's Joint Global Change Research Institute. His expertise is in the economic modeling and analysis of energy systems.

The urgency of bringing large emitters in the developing world into an international agreement to control greenhouse gases critically depends on the ultimate goals of climate policy. Under modest, rather than aggressive, climate stabilization targets, early participation is less critical as there is much greater scope to offset delayed participation through greater abatement in wealthy countries and more global abatement later in the century.

Most policymakers concerned about global warming have in mind some ultimate objective for limiting the amount of projected climate change, or atmospheric carbon dioxide (CO_2) accumulations. Much of the debate has focused on climate stabilization targets consistent with limiting CO_2 concentrations to either 450 parts per million by volume (ppmv) or 550 ppmv (currently, CO_2 concentrations are 385 ppmv, compared with preindustrial levels of about 280 ppmv). According to the Intergovernmental Panel on Climate Change, these stabilization targets are consistent with keeping eventual mean projected global warming to about 1.5°C and 2.5°C above current levels, respectively (this would be on top of temperature rises of about 0.75°C over the last century).

Economists and climate scientists have developed a number of models to estimate global emissions prices that are consistent with ultimately stabilizing atmospheric CO_2 concentrations at these target levels and minimizing the global burden of mitigation costs over time. To carry this out requires a uniform price on emissions from different regions within a given year (to equalize marginal abatement costs across different countries). The emissions price must also rise at roughly the rate of interest (about 5 percent) over time (to equate the discounted marginal abatement costs at different points in time).

However, it is unlikely that the world will address climate change in this wholly cooperative fashion—more likely, it will be years before developing countries are willing to comprehensively price their emissions, and even when they do, it may be at a lower rate than prevailing in the European Union and United States. How much of a problem is delayed participation by developing countries in terms of raising the overall burden of global mitigation costs, and what does this imply for appropriate near-term emissions pricing goals for the United States, if eventual targets for global stabilization are still to be met?

To explore these questions, we used our MiniCAM model and the following assumptions: that industrialized countries impose a common emissions price in 2012, China joins the agreement at a later date, and other countries join whenever their per capita income reaches that of China at the time of China's accession into the emissions control agreement. In one scenario, countries entering into the control regime would immediately price emissions at the same level as in industrialized nations, while in another case the emissions price for late entrants into the agreement converges gradually over time to the price in industrialized countries.

The model is designed to examine long-term, large-scale changes in global and regional energy systems in response to carbon policies. Given the many uncertainties—such as the costs of future emissions-reducing technologies (for example, nuclear power, carbon capture, and storage technologies) and emissions growth in the absence of controls (which is highly sensitive to assumed population and productivity growth)—the predictions should not be interpreted literally. But the results do provide some flavor for the proportionate increase in global abatement costs, and in required U.S. emissions pricing, due to delayed developing country participation.

We started with the more moderate climate stabilization target for CO_2 of 550 ppmv. In the ideal case, with full and early emissions pricing by all countries, global emissions and emissions in the United States rise above current levels before peaking around 2035 to 2050, and progressively decline thereafter. Global emissions prices rise to about \$6 per ton of CO_2 (in current dollars) in 2025 and to about \$20 per ton by 2050. By midcentury, annual global gross domestic product (GDP) losses are 0.2 percent (most other models also suggest global GDP losses of less than 1 percent by midcentury under this stabilization target).

With delayed participation, even if China joins between 2020 and 2035, the implications for emissions pricing in developed countries can be significant but are not that dramatic under the 550 ppmv stabilization goal. Compared with the globally efficient policy (with a globally harmonized emissions price at all times), near-term emissions prices in developed countries rise from between a few percent and 100 percent under the different scenarios, and discounted global abatement costs are higher by about 10 to 70 percent.

Emissions pricing policies implied by the 450 ppmv target are far more radical. Under globally efficient emissions pricing, CO_2 prices rise to about \$35 per ton by 2025 and about \$130 per ton by midcentury, while global and U.S. emissions are roughly 5 percent and 40 percent below 2000 levels in 2025 and 2050, respectively. Global GDP losses approach 2 percent by midcentury.

Moreover, the 450 ppmv concentration is so close to present-day levels, and demand for fossil fuels is rising so rapidly in developing nations, that delayed participation has severe consequences for early participants in this case. Developed countries would have to achieve a reduction of more than 85 percent (relative to 2005 emissions) in 2050 to stabilize CO_2 at 450 ppmv if developing countries don't begin participating until 2020. Even more drastic reductions would be required if the delay is longer. Discounted global abatement costs are anything from about 30 to 400 percent higher than under globally efficient pricing in most cases, and near- and medium-term emissions prices can be 10 times larger with China's accession delayed until 2035.

Why does delayed participation matter so much in one stabilization scenario, but not the other? Under the less stringent concentration target, there is much greater flexibility for offsetting delayed emissions reductions in developing countries through greater abatement by all countries later in the century. In contrast, to prevent CO_2 concentrations from rising above 450 ppmv (present levels are already more than 380 ppmv), the remaining emissions that can be released by all countries in the world, without exceeding that limit, are so limited that forgone emissions reductions in nonparticipating countries must be largely made up by far more aggressive reductions in participating nations. In other words, there is little opportunity to catch up later. The problem is compounded by emissions leakage as rapidly declining fuel demand in developed countries exerts downward pressure on global fuel prices, which in turn makes fuel use and emissions an economically more attractive option in countries without mitigation policies.

Perhaps not surprisingly, the urgency of widespread participation in international emissions agreements hinges critically on the appropriate long-term climate stabilization target. Unfortunately, there are also strong incentives for countries to be "free riders," to benefit from others' emissions mitigation efforts without undertaking their own mitigation.

In the globally efficient policy, developing countries bear about 70 percent of discounted abatement costs out to 2100 (as their emissions in the absence of controls expand rapidly relative to those in developed countries). However, developed countries bear "only" about 20 to 35 percent of global abatement costs when China's accession occurs in 2035 and new entrants face lower starting prices. Side payments and other types of compensation could create incentives for earlier actions in developing regions. However, agreeing on who gets what level of compensation will, almost certainly, be highly contentious.

Further Reading

Edmonds, J., L. Clarke, J. Lurz, and M. Wise. 2007. Stabilizing CO_2 Concentrations with Incomplete International Cooperation. Richland, WA: Pacific Northwest National Laboratory. www.globalchange.umd.edu/publications/493.

2. A PRAGMATIC GLOBAL CLIMATE POLICY ARCHITECTURE

Valentina Bosetti
is a senior researcher at Fondazione Eni Enrico Mattei, Milan, Italy. She specializes in environmental resource economics, particularly climate policy modeling.

Jeffrey Frankel
is the James W. Harpel Professor of Capital Formation and Growth at Harvard Kennedy School. His research interests include international finance, currencies, monetary and fiscal policy, commodity prices, regional blocs, and global environmental issues.

This commentary summarizes a proposed international architecture for global climate policy that takes into account a variety of likely political constraints. These include, for example, limits on the burden borne by individual countries and the reluctance of developing nations to make commitments without aggressive action to cut emissions in the United States.

Before the 15th Conference of the Parties took place in Copenhagen, many observers questioned the likelihood that much of substance would happen, much as they have many times before.

In fact, a key weakness of the first attempt to coordinate international climate policies was its lack of credible emissions targets—most countries failed to commit to emissions targets under the 1997 Kyoto Protocol, and many of those that did ratify are expected to exceed their targets for the first commitment period, 2008–2012. These considerations underscore the critical need to develop a global climate policy architecture that takes political realities into account.

Although there are many ideas for developing a successor to the Kyoto Protocol, the existing proposals are typically based on just one or two of the following factors: science (capping global carbon dioxide [CO_2] concentrations at 450 parts per million [ppm]); equity (allocating equal emissions per capita across countries); or economics (weighing the economic costs of aggressive short-term cuts against the, albeit speculative, long-term environmental benefits). Our proposal for emissions reductions takes these considerations into account but is more practical because it is based heavily on politics. Although it accepts the framework of national targets for emissions and tradable permits, it also attempts to solve the most serious deficiencies of the Kyoto agreement: the need for long-term targets, the absence of participation by the United States and developing countries, and the incentive for countries to fail to abide by their commitments.

POLITICAL CONSTRAINTS

In our judgment, any future climate agreement must comply with six important political constraints.

- First, aggressive targets to cut U.S. emissions will not be credible if China and other major developing countries do not commit to quantitative targets at the same time, due to concerns about economic competitiveness and the movement of energy-intensive industries to countries without emissions caps ("carbon leakage").
- Second, China and other developing countries will not make sacrifices different in character from those made by richer countries that have gone before them, taking due account of differences in per capita income, per capita emissions, and baseline economic growth.
- Third, in the long run, no country can be rewarded for having ramped up its emissions high above the levels of 1990 (the baseline year for emissions targets embodied in the Kyoto Protocol).
- Fourth, no country will agree to participate if the present discounted value of its future expected costs exceeds a threshold level, which, for illustration, we assume is 1 percent of GDP.

- Fifth, no country will abide by targets that cost it more than, say, 5 percent of GDP in any five-year budget period.
- Sixth, if one major country drops out, others will become discouraged and the system may unravel.

HOW IT WOULD WORK

Under our proposal, rich nations would begin immediately to make emissions cuts along the lines that their political leaders have already committed to (consistent with emissions targets in the European emissions trading scheme or in recent U.S. legislative proposals). Developing countries would agree to emissions caps that maintain their projected business-as-usual emissions in the first decades but, over the longer term, commit to binding targets that ultimately reduce emissions below business as usual. This approach prevents carbon leakage and gives industries a more even playing field. However, it still preserves developing countries' ability to grow their economies; they can also raise revenue by selling emissions permits. In later decades, the emissions targets asked of developing countries would become stricter, following a numerical formula. However, these emissions cuts are no greater than those made by rich nations earlier in the century, accounting for differences in per capita income, per capita emissions, and baseline economic growth.

Future emissions caps are to be determined by a formula that incorporates three elements. First is a progressivity factor that requires richer countries to make more severe cuts relative to their business-as-usual emissions. Second is a latecomer catch-up factor that requires nations that did not agree to binding targets under Kyoto to make gradual emissions cuts to account for their additional emissions since 1990. This prevents latecomers from being rewarded with higher targets, or from being given incentives to ramp up their emissions before signing the agreement. Finally, the gradual equalization factor addresses the fact that rich countries are responsible for most of the carbon dioxide currently in the atmosphere. From 2050 onward, this factor moves per capita emissions in each country in each period a small step in the direction of the global average of per capita emissions.

FINDINGS

We analyzed the numerical targets using an energy/climate model that represents emissions mitigation opportunities for different regions at different future time periods. Some of the main results include the following:

- The world CO_2 price reaches \$20–\$30 per ton in 2020, \$100–\$160 per ton in 2050, and \$700–\$800 per ton in 2100.
- According to the economic simulations, most countries sustain economic losses that are under 1 percent of GDP in the first half of the century, but then rise toward the end of the century.
- Atmospheric concentrations of CO_2 stabilize at 500 ppm in the last quarter of the century, implying a projected increase in world temperatures above preindustrial levels of about 3°C.

We have not been able to achieve year-2100 concentrations of 450 ppm or lower (to limit projected warming to about 2°C) without violating the same political-economic constraints.

CONCLUSION

The proposal calls for a successor international agreement that establishes a global cap-and-trade system. The emissions caps are set using formulas that assign quantitative emissions limits to countries in every five-year period from now until 2100. Three political constraints are particularly important in specifying the formulas. First, developing countries are not asked to bear any cost in the early years. Second, even later, developing countries are not asked to make any sacrifice that is different from the earlier sacrifices of industrialized countries, accounting for differences in incomes. Third, no country is asked to accept targets that cost it more than 5 percent of GDP in any given year.

The framework here allocates emissions targets across countries in such a way that every country is given reason to feel that it is only doing its fair share. Furthermore, the framework—a decade-by-decade sequence of emissions targets determined by a few principles and formulas—is flexible enough that it can accommodate major changes in circumstances during the course of the century.

Further Reading

Frankel, Jeffrey. 2009. An Elaborated Proposal for Global Climate Policy Architecture: Specific Formulas and Emission Targets for All Countries in All Decades. Discussion paper 08-08. Cambridge, MA: Harvard Project on International Climate Agreements, Belfer Center for Science and International Affairs, Harvard Kennedy School.

Bosetti, Valentina, and Jeffrey Frankel. 2009. Global Climate Policy Architecture and Political Feasibility: Specific Formulas and Emission Targets to Attain 460PPM CO_2 Concentrations. Discussion paper 09-30. Cambridge, MA: Harvard Project on International Climate Agreements, Belfer Center for Science and International Affairs, Harvard Kennedy School.

3. THINKING BEYOND BORDERS

Why We Need to Focus on Global Public Goods

Scott Barrett

is a professor in the School of International and Public Affairs at Columbia University. His research focuses on interactions between natural and social systems, especially at the global level. He is best known for his work involving international environmental agreements, such as the Kyoto Protocol.

Under what conditions has the international community dealt effectively with certain global problems, like smallpox eradication? The international response to other global problems—most notably climate change—has been ineffective so far; treaties cover only a limited number of countries, and even for those countries, incentives for complying with the agreement are too weak.

In Copenhagen in December 2009, governments met to discuss a road map for controlling global greenhouse gas emissions as a successor to the Kyoto Protocol, which expires in 2012. As we continue to contemplate a post-2012 future, it's worth reflecting on some basic economic concepts in order to better understand what it will take for that map to truly show us a way forward.

Global climate negotiators try to provide what economists call a public good. To prevent atmospheric greenhouse gas concentrations from rising, a substantial number of countries must act together. It is the total sum of emissions that affects concentrations, not the amounts emitted by individual countries. So each country has an incentive to let others act—one of the reasons so little has been achieved so far.

If each country's climate were shaped only by its own emissions, and not by the total of every country's emissions, the incentive would be different.

For example, national defense is a national public good. It is public in two senses. First, "consumption" of the good by one person does not reduce the amount available to others. Second, no citizen can be excluded from enjoying the benefit of national defense. This second attribute is particularly important: if beneficiaries do not have to pay, then why should they pay? But if no one pays, the good won't be provided—and everyone will be worse off.

This, then, is why government exists—to get around the free-rider problem and to supply public goods. Other examples of domestic public goods include clean air and water and the preservation of unique natural wonders.

But what about global public goods like climate change mitigation, nuclear nonproliferation, and disease eradication? These are harder to supply for the simple reason that there is no world government but, instead, 192 nation states. To supply these public goods, a different approach must be tried.

Imagine that we learn that Earth will be hit by a massive asteroid 25 years from now. If nothing is done to avert the collision, *Homo sapiens* will almost certainly become extinct. Engineers tell us that there are a variety of ways in which the asteroid's orbit could be altered. All it would take is a single best effort. Could we be confident that the money needed to deflect the asteroid would be raised?

The answer, fortunately, is yes. The incentives to act are so strong that we can be sure that the only real constraint on our ability to supply the global public good of asteroid protection is technical feasibility. Indeed, it would be in the interests of a single country to supply this global public good all by itself. International cooperation would not even be needed.

Perhaps the greatest global public good ever provided was the eradication of smallpox. When the world began this audacious effort, over a million people died every year from smallpox. Almost all of these people lived in poor countries, but the rich countries also gained from eradication. This is because the vaccine that offers protection from smallpox is costly and dangerous. Once the disease was eradicated, the need to vaccinate evaporated. Everyone gained.

What is novel about this global public good is that its supply requires the active cooperation of every country; success depends on the weakest link. The last case of endemic smallpox occurred in Somalia in 1977. Had this person not been isolated, had the people with whom he had come into contact not been vaccinated, and so on, smallpox would still be with us today.

Back then, Somalia had a government that could help in this effort. But in 1991, that government fell in a coup, and ever since, Somalia has been a "failed state." It is interesting to speculate whether smallpox could be eradicated today. I think the chances are good that it could not happen. Indeed, one of the reasons polio eradication has yet to succeed is that wild polioviruses still reside in trouble spots like the border region shared by Afghanistan and Pakistan.

Climate change mitigation is the hardest global public good to supply. In contrast to asteroid protection, it cannot be addressed by one huge project. Unlike eradication, it is not in the interests of each country to contribute, so long as all other countries do so. For climate change, the incentives are more challenging: success depends on the aggregate efforts of all countries.

An agreement to reduce greenhouse gas emissions must do three things. First, it must attract wide participation. Even the United States and China, the two largest emitters, are each responsible for no more than a quarter of the total problem. Also, should only a few countries act, carbon-intensive industries will likely shift production to other countries, causing their emissions to rise.

Unfortunately, the Kyoto Protocol failed to attract wide participation. True, China is a party; but China is not required to reduce its emissions. The United States, of course, is not a party. Kyoto is a failure if only because it has not provided incentives for both countries to change their behavior.

Second, the treaty must also provide incentives for compliance. Canada's emissions currently exceed the Kyoto limits by over 30 percent and are expected to rise even further. When a country like Canada, a Kyoto signatory and an upstanding member of the international community, fails to comply, then you know there are problems with the agreement itself. Kyoto provides no incentives for Canada to comply, just as it provides no incentives for the United States to join.

Finally, the treaty must get all countries to reduce their emissions by a very substantial amount—eventually by half and soon after that by much more. Even if Kyoto were implemented to the letter—if the United States were to ratify and all parties were to comply perfectly—global emissions would keep on rising.

Efforts may be made to get the industrialized countries to accept much tougher targets. This would go some way toward meeting the third requirement, but it will make no difference at all if the first two requirements are not also met. This has been the problem with the climate negotiations so far: they have avoided the hard but essential challenge of enforcement. Without that, targets are meaningless.

Lacking a world government, global public goods must usually be provided by international cooperation. The world has succeeded before—in eradicating smallpox, in vanquishing the Axis powers, in preventing nuclear war, and in protecting the ozone layer. There are reasons for this. They have to do with incentives and the ability of international institutions to change them. Climate change is a harder problem, but we will not make any progress in addressing it until we understand this. That is the main lesson to be learned from the study of global public goods.

Further Reading

Aldy, Joseph E., and Robert N. Stavins, eds. 2007. *Architectures for Agreement: Addressing Global Climate Change in the Post-Kyoto World*. New York: Cambridge University Press.

Barrett, Scott. 2005. *Environment and Statecraft: The Strategy of Environmental Treaty-Making*. Oxford: Oxford University Press.

Barrett, Scott. 2007. *Why Cooperate? The Incentive to Supply Global Public Goods*. Oxford: Oxford University Press.

Schelling, Thomas C. 2007. Climate Change: The Uncertainties, the Certainties and What They Imply about Action. *The Economists' Voice* 4(3): Article 3. www.bepress.com/ev/vol4/iss3/art3.

4. THE VALUE OF CLIMATE-RELATED SATELLITE DATA

William Gail

is the director of strategic development within Microsoft's Public Sector Product Group. He was a member of the National Research Council's recent Decadal Survey of Earth Sciences and is on the advisory board for NASA's Earth Science Applications Program.

Satellite-based climate-related data play a critical role in monitoring the impacts of climate change, perhaps giving early warning of possible instabilities in the climate system, and in validating emissions reduction policies, especially in regard to forest carbon sequestration.

Earth observations data collected from satellites (which include readings of atmospheric chemistry and temperature, in addition to Earth imagery) play a unique and critical role in supporting policy decisions related to global climate change. Perhaps surprisingly, our process for planning future capabilities of these satellites addresses only a limited aspect of the diverse policy needs society will have when these satellites become operational.

Satellite observations complement climate-related data collected from ground-based monitoring systems. Satellite data improve our ability to monitor and understand how atmospheric accumulations of greenhouse gases (GHGs) change over time, as well as reveal trends in global average and regional temperature. In this way, the data refine the forecast accuracy of scientific models that tell us how atmospheric GHG concentrations will change in response to future GHG sources, what portion of these gases might be absorbed by the oceans and other carbon sinks, and the sensitivity of global temperature to changes in GHG concentrations.

Equally important, the data provide critically needed knowledge about the risk of possible instabilities or "tipping points" in the climate system. Even though the risks might be very small, the potential for globally catastrophic outcomes is among the greatest concerns about warming the planet. One possibility is that higher temperatures could lead to emissions of methane (a potent GHG) from the melting of permafrost or from beneath the ocean floor, causing substantially greater warming than we currently forecast. Satellite observations of methane concentrations in the atmosphere can help us monitor the mechanisms by which these releases of underground methane might occur, allowing us to anticipate and respond to the problem.

Sea-level rise is a widely reported consequence of global warming. A significant portion is expected to come from the melting of ice sheets and glaciers. However, the extent to which higher temperatures will lead to melting is poorly understood. Empirical measurement, provided by satellite data, has already proven essential to understanding how ice sheets and glaciers are changing over time. Earth observations data also facilitate the monitoring of many other potential consequences of climate change, such as expansion of deserts, disappearance of freshwater sources, harm to sea life through acidification of the oceans as they absorb more carbon, biodiversity loss, and alterations to forests.

Beyond climate science, satellite data play a potentially critical role in the implementation of policies that address climate change. The trend to include forest carbon and land use within emissions trading programs for reducing GHGs is a particularly strong motivation for a robust satellite monitoring program. Satellite data are needed to measure changes in forest cover and are important, in particular, for monitoring issues such as emissions "leakage" (in which planting of forests in one region is offset by accelerated deforestation elsewhere).

Earth observations even play a role in the establishment of baselines by which to measure emissions reductions programs, as well as assist in evaluating the effectiveness of these programs. In particular, regional emissions of non–carbon dioxide (CO_2)

GHGs, like methane and nitrous oxides, are easier to track with satellite technologies than ground-based systems. Even space-based measurements of a country's CO_2 emissions are useful as a check on estimates built up from a country's fuel consumption (which may not be reliably measured for poorer countries with limited accounting systems).

Furthermore, by providing a picture of how resources and natural systems at the local level are impacted by climate change, satellite-based data help to pinpoint where adaptation policies are most needed. Examples include policies to promote the transition to hardier crops in areas at greater risk of drought and construction projects for valuable coastal regions most threatened by rising sea levels.

USING SATELLITE DATA TO ASSIST CLIMATE POLICY

Earth-based observations of climate-related phenomena are a public good. As the private market for this information is presently limited, its collection must be largely funded by the government. NASA is the only U.S. government entity with a portfolio of satellites capable of generating new scientific understanding of climate issues. Over the last 20 years, the United States has invested around $1 billion a year in expanding, maintaining, and operating satellites for climate-related monitoring. The most recent congressional stimulus package (as of this writing, HR1, The American Recovery Act of 2009) allocates a further $400 million to fund environmental satellites identified as vital by a 2007 National Academy of Sciences study.

NASA's data collection over the last two decades has laid the groundwork for understanding how Earth's complex natural variability—and human influence on it—impacts society. However, the next step is to ensure that this accumulating scientific knowledge is fully applied to improve critical policy and economic decisions. At present there is a fundamental and puzzling disconnect between those parties engaged in crafting domestic climate policy legislation and those responsible for choosing how to allocate NASA funding among alternative priorities so as to inform policy issues. Legislative proposals provide little detail on how information will be collected and used to monitor emissions control programs, particularly with regard to crediting of forest sequestration and reductions in non-CO_2 GHGs. NASA representatives need a more prominent place in deliberations over climate policy design, to ensure both that the best use is made of satellite information and that NASA focuses on the most pressing priorities for Earth observation.

Further Reading

Gail, William B. 2007. Sustainable Climate Policy and NASA. *Space News*. September 9.

Macauley, Molly K. 2009. Climate Change and Policy Considerations: New Roles for Earth Science. Issue brief 09-02. Washington, DC: Resources for the Future. www.rff.org/News/Features/Pages/New_Roles_for_Earth_Science.aspx.

Macauley, Molly K., and Daniel F. Morris. 2009. The Policy Relevance of Science. *Space News*. January 12.

National Research Council. 2007. *Earth Science and Applications from Space: National Imperatives for the Next Decade and Beyond*. Washington, DC: National Academies Press.

5. THE SUCCESSFUL INTERNATIONAL RESPONSE TO STRATOSPHERIC OZONE DEPLETION

James Hammitt
is a professor of economics and decision sciences and the director of the Harvard Center for Risk Analysis at the Harvard School of Public Health. He specializes in the development and application of quantitative methods—including cost–benefit, decision, and risk analysis—to health and environmental policy.

In what may have been the first successful international response to a global environmental threat, after the national spray can bans of the 1970s proved inadequate and the Antarctic ozone hole was discovered in the 1980s, the world community came together to limit, and ultimately eliminate, production of ozone-depleting substances.

An international agreement dealing with climate change remains elusive, but as negotiators seek consensus, we can look back to the resolution of an earlier global environmental challenge: ozone. Although the ozone layer is not yet fully recovered, the international response to the discovery of stratospheric ozone depletion has been a remarkable success.

Chlorofluorocarbons (CFCs) were synthesized in the 1930s and initially used for refrigeration. By the 1970s, CFCs were used in aerosol spray cans; air-conditioning; foams for insulation, cushioning, and packaging; and as cleaning solvents. Although the number of firms using CFCs was large, production was restricted to a small number of firms, mostly in industrial countries.

Scientific studies in the mid-1970s suggested that CFCs might deplete stratospheric ozone. Because the compounds are chemically stable, they do not break down until they waft into the stratosphere and are exposed to intense ultraviolet radiation. The released chlorine catalyzes a reaction that converts ozone (O_3) to molecular oxygen (O_2). With less stratospheric ozone, more ultraviolet light penetrates to ground level and damages crops and plastics, causes skin cancer and cataracts, and harms phytoplankton, other plants and animals, and ecosystems.

North America and Europe took the lead in developing a global system to control CFC emissions, particularly after the surprise discovery of the Antarctic "ozone hole" in 1985. U.S. industry eventually supported international controls, partly because it feared that in the absence of international rules, new domestic rules would weaken its competitive position. The Montreal Protocol, signed in September 1987, set up an international framework to reduce CFCs and other ozone-depleting substances (ODS). Subsequent amendments nearly eliminated production of CFCs and similar compounds by the mid-1990s. HCFCs, which substitute for CFCs in some applications but are less potent ozone depleters, are regulated as transitional chemicals. Their use will be phased out by 2030.

ODS REGULATORY SYSTEMS

Although ODS are dangerous only if they are released to the atmosphere, the protocol regulates production and consumption because these are more easily monitored than emissions. Consumption is not measured but defined as production plus imports minus exports. For the United States, the limits apply at the national level; for the European Union, member states' production and consumption are not limited if the union as a whole complies.

U.S. implementation relies on tradable production and consumption permits, supplemented by excise taxes and end-use controls. The U.S. Environmental Protection Agency (EPA) issues annual permits for production (or import) and consumption to firms that manufacture or import ODS. Allocation is based on historical production or import shares. Permits are defined for each ODS, but intercompound trades based on ozone-depletion potential are allowed within ODS classes. The permits are tradable among firms without restriction and can be banked (saved for later use).

The U.S. command-and-control measures include prohibitions on ODS in certain applications, required equipment and training for refrigeration-service personnel, and prohibitions on selling small quantities of ODS. The "significant new alternatives policy" (SNAP) prohibits the replacement of an ODS with certain substitutes if alternative choices would better reduce overall environmental or health risk.

The initial EU regulation imposed a system of tradable production or import permits, similar to the U.S. system. These permits are tradable among firms within or between countries. A further regulation prohibits import of ODS and products containing ODS from countries outside the protocol and includes many end-use restrictions. Some EU member states adopted additional restrictions and economic incentives, such as taxes and deposit-refund schemes to encourage recovery of ODS in certain products.

ASSESSING THE RESULTS

EPA analysis of the rules implementing the Montreal Protocol in the United States estimated that the benefits of fewer fatal skin cancers alone would dwarf compliance costs. How well did the regulations work?

Effectiveness. Substantial reductions in CFC consumption were achieved with limited economic disruption. The concentration of ODS in the stratosphere peaked in the 1990s and is expected to fall to its prior level by midcentury, with ozone likely recovering to its prior levels around then.

Compliance costs. For the United States, compliance costs were comparable to EPA's estimates. The market price of CFCs appears to have been lower in the EU, suggesting smaller marginal compliance cost or more stringent command-and-control regulations there. The EU may have had lower costs because the Montreal Protocol required equal percentage reductions from a 1986 baseline. The United States had eliminated most of its aerosol use by then, but the EU had not and could achieve part of its compliance by limiting aerosol use at relatively low cost.

Administrative burden. Economic-incentive instruments make fewer information demands on regulators than command-and-control instruments. Ensuring compliance with the Montreal Protocol through end-use restrictions alone would have required information on the magnitude of ODS use and technological alternatives for reducing it in each application. EPA estimated that a traditional command-and-control approach would require 32 staff to administer and cost firms \$300 million per year in reporting and recordkeeping. In comparison, the tradable-permit system required only 4 staff and cost firms just \$2.4 million annually. Illegal imports, however, revealed limitations in monitoring and enforcement.

Burden on industry. U.S. tradable permits were allocated without charge to producers and importers based on their historical market shares. Because the permits were valuable, the allocation was a direct benefit, partially offsetting losses from restrictions on future sales. (Congress later imposed excise taxes, in part to capture some of these rents.) In contrast, ODS-user industries faced higher ODS prices.

Innovation. Information exchange among industries, governments, and international organizations helped minimize compliance costs and disruption. Producer and user industries collaborated internationally in safety and performance testing, and diffusion of alternatives was encouraged through trade shows, sometimes with government sponsorship.

Adaptability. The U.S. and EU tradable-permit systems easily incorporated changes each time the Montreal Protocol was amended. The permitted quantities could be reduced more easily and quickly than end-use restrictions could be tightened. In the United States, rulemakings to implement these amendments were completed within a year, substantially faster than most command-and-control rules.

PARALLELS WITH CLIMATE CHANGE

The issue of CFCs and stratospheric ozone shares some parallels with the problem of greenhouse gases. The effects of CFC emissions on stratospheric ozone are the same, regardless of which country releases them. Moreover, ODS and some of their substitutes are themselves greenhouse gases with long atmospheric lifetimes. Hence the benefits of reducing emissions span many future years, while control costs are borne up front. In contrast, negotiating an international regime to control CFCs was immeasurably easier than for greenhouse gases, given the small number of firms and countries involved.

Experience in resolving stratospheric ozone depletion shows that nations can work together to confront a global environmental threat, taking costly actions even before significant environmental damages result. The cap-and-trade mechanisms used in the United States and European Union proved effective and could be easily modified as international agreements required more stringent controls. Information sharing between producer and user industries accelerated and reduced the costs of transition.

While the response to ozone depletion provides a salutary model for how to respond to global warming, global warming is a much harder challenge: sources of greenhouse gases (notably fossil fuels) account for a vastly larger share of the world economy than did CFCs, and the number of firms and countries that contribute to global warming is far greater.

Further Reading

Andersen, S.O., and K.M. Sarma. 2002. *Protecting the Ozone Layer: The United Nations History*. London: Earthscan Publications.

Hammitt, J.K. 1997. Stratospheric-Ozone Depletion. In *Economic Analyses at EPA: Assessing Regulatory Impact*, edited by R.D. Morgenstern. Washington, DC: Resources for the Future, 131–169.

Parson, E.A. 2003. *Protecting the Ozone Layer: Science and Strategy*. New York: Oxford University Press.

World Meteorological Organization (WMO). 2007. *Scientific Assessment of Ozone Depletion: 2006*. Global Ozone Research and Monitoring Project—Report No. 50. Geneva, Switzerland: WMO.

6. EVALUATING EUROPE'S PLAN FOR REDUCING GREENHOUSE GASES

Dallas Burtraw

is a senior fellow at Resources for the Future. His research interests include the costs, benefits, and design of environmental regulation and the regulation and restructuring of the electricity industry.

The centerpiece of the European Union's effort to reduce greenhouse gases is the emissions trading scheme (ETS). As discussed in this commentary, plans for Phase 3 of the program resolve some serious design flaws that have characterized the ETS to date.

The European Union (EU) has mapped out its plan for the third phase of its carbon dioxide (CO_2) emissions trading scheme (ETS), which will begin in 2013. It is evident that lessons have been learned from the first two phases of the program. The EU has embraced a regulatory design that should enable substantial emissions reductions in the future, at least for the roughly 50 percent of total emissions covered by the trading program. This was not the case in the earlier design of the ETS.

The EU began a cap-and-trade program covering the power sector and major industrial sources in 2005, and the first phase of the program stretched through 2007. The program excludes transportation, small businesses, and direct fuel consumption by firms and households. The first phase has been maligned because after all the attention it received, in the end only minor emissions reductions were achieved, and the price for a tradable emissions allowance fell to near zero. But I see the situation somewhat differently. Much of the problem was that, when accurate inventories were taken for the first time, actual country emissions turned out to be lower than expected. The development of data systems, monitoring, and enforcement mechanisms form the infrastructure for subsequent phases of the program. Because the trading program is expected to last for decades, the initial emissions reductions will be relatively unimportant in the long run, when very substantial emissions reduction targets are possible.

More important than the emissions reductions that are achieved in the near term is the architecture of the program itself, specifically the incentives created under the program. The fact that the emissions cap in Phase 1 required few reductions should not be fatal in a well-designed program, because ideally the program would enable allowances to be banked for use in future compliance periods. This would provide firms with an incentive to harvest low-cost emissions reductions in the near term, because the allowances saved would have value in the future and the number of new allowances issued could be reduced accordingly. This approach also would provide a clear price signal to guide innovation and investment into the future. Unfortunately, the program did not allow for banking of allowances into Phase 2, but going forward, emissions allowances from Phase 2 can be carried over until Phase 3, so they will retain value and firms have an incentive to overachieve in the near term.

The weak environmental performance that characterized Phase 1 should not obscure the fact that there were important measures of success. The program was put together at a breakneck pace to demonstrate a commitment to the world that the EU would pursue climate policy goals. The first phase constituted a learning period for policymakers and stakeholders, with the introduction of emissions inventory and electronic reporting of environmental statistics in many of the 27 countries covered by the program.

Phase 2 of the program, which runs from 2008 to 2012, fixes two important problems. The cap is tightened, ensuring that meaningful emissions reductions will be achieved, and banking of allowances into the future is allowed. These changes create better incentives for innovation by supporting a higher allowance price, allowing investors to capitalize on low-hanging fruit in the near term, and by curbing allowance price volatility in the long run. In late 2009, the allowance price hovers around 14 euros per metric ton of CO_2 (about $21 per ton). Whether this is a reasonable price or not is not the question I mean to address here, but it is sufficient to provide meaningful incentives for reducing CO_2 emissions.

The major problem in Phase 1, however, also remains in Phase 2—namely, the initial distribution, or allocation, of allowances. In Phase 1, 99 percent of allowances were given away for free to emitters, and in Phase 2, this figure dropped slightly to 96 percent. But free allowances to emitters were not free to consumers—the regulated firms that received allowances for free increased the price of their products to reflect the opportunity cost of allowances (for example, their market value) because this is the value firms have to surrender in order to produce their goods.

Typically, firms have charged customers for allowances that they received for free, thereby leading to windfall profits, especially in the electricity sector, where power prices rose to incorporate allowance values. In the EU, those windfalls totaled many billions of euros, coming at the expense of consumers. Just as important, this revenue was not available for other purposes that would help reduce program costs, and the overall economic cost of the program was much higher as a consequence.

Phase 3 promises several important changes. First, the EU now embraces the principle of auctioning allowances rather than giving them away for free. The power sector will have to rely on auctions to obtain a majority of its allowances beginning in 2013. By 2020, the power sector will rely on full auctioning, and other covered sectors will have to rely on auctions for a majority of their allowances. Second, the compliance period lengthens to eight years, 2013 to 2020, providing a better planning horizon for investors. Third, the program's emissions targets are tighter and would ramp up significantly if there is expanded commitment from other nations to reduce emissions. Finally, there is a well-conceived effort to achieve equity among the EU member states by redistributing allowance allocations from wealthier states to poorer ones, which should help maintain support for the program.

The plan for the EU is part of an overall package of measures to implement climate and energy policy for Europe. The central aim is to reduce EU emissions by 20 percent from their 1990 levels by the year 2020 and by 30 percent if other industrialized countries agree to do the same. The policy governing sectors outside the trading program proposes a broad array of regulatory policies. These sectors are not directly covered by an emissions cap, and consequently the emissions target for these sectors is not as convincing as for those sectors covered by the trading program.

The intended reform for Phase 3 of the trading program addresses a variety of concerns head are on. Most significant of these the extended compliance period and the transition to auctioning. The result is a regulatory design that should enable substantial emissions reductions in the future in those sectors of the European economy. The encouraging result should attract the attention of U.S. policymakers.

Further Reading

Symposium: The European Union Emissions Trading Scheme 2007. *Review of Environmental Economics and Policy* 1(1). reep.oxfordjournals.org/content/vol1/issue1/index.dtl.

7. U.S. CLIMATE CHANGE POLICY

Previewing the Debate

Daniel S. Hall
specializes in environmental policy evaluation, with a focus on climate policy. This commentary was completed while he was a full-time research associate at Resources for the Future.

The United States may soon adopt limits on emissions of greenhouse gases (GHGs), particularly carbon dioxide (CO_2), most likely by putting an indirect price on emissions through marketable emissions allowances—a cap-and-trade program. This commentary reviews the five main policy design issues.

EMISSIONS TARGETS

Most policymakers think in terms of a target that would stabilize atmospheric GHG concentrations at some "safe" level. Many recent proposals aimed to reduce 2050 emissions by 50 to 80 percent below current levels, which could—given coordinated global action—achieve atmospheric stabilization at around double preindustrial levels. Energy models suggest that near-term emissions prices need to be about $5 to $50 per ton of CO_2 (rising at about 5 percent a year) to be consistent with such targets.

In contrast, economists typically think in terms of balancing the cost of additional emissions mitigation with the benefits of avoided future damage from climate change. This requires putting a price on emissions equal to an estimate of marginal benefits. The "right" price is considered to be between $5 and $30 per ton of CO_2 in the near term, although some say these studies give insufficient weight to distant future benefits and inadequately account for extreme risks.

ALLOWANCE ALLOCATION

How allowances are allocated—or how revenues from auctioning allowances are spent—will significantly influence the distributional effects of climate policy. Given the enormous wealth at stake—the value of allowances has been estimated at around $100 billion a year—it would be preferable for the government to auction all allowances and then make explicit, transparent decisions about how to use the revenues. Giving allowances away for free, on the other hand, would represent a large transfer of wealth to regulated firms.

Recent congressional proposals move toward auctioning a larger portion of allowances. But whether auction revenues will be used judiciously or fall prey to pork-barrel politics is another question. Some proposals would simply auction all allowances and return revenues to consumers through per capita rebates, an approach called "cap-and-dividend," that would make climate policy more equitable because the dividend, relative to income, would be higher for lower-income households. Alternatively, revenues could be used to cut taxes on labor and capital income and thereby reduce the economic distortions these taxes create. A typical estimate is that recycling $100 billion of revenue in income tax cuts would generate economic efficiency gains of around $25 billion or more.

COST CONTAINMENT

Cost containment is the fulcrum on which legislators hope to balance the ambition of emissions reductions with the economic impact. Cost containment itself, however, is not well defined. In practice, it conflates two issues: minimizing short-term allowance price volatility, and managing the long-term level of allowance prices. Several policy mechanisms have been proposed to accomplish one or both of these goals.

Banking and borrowing provide intertemporal flexibility and prevent allowance prices from being driven by year-to-year fluctuations in weather, economic growth, and other unrelated factors.

Allowance reserves are essentially institutionalized long-term borrowing by the government. The government brings some allowances forward from far-future caps and distributes them in the present.

Escalators and off-ramps kick in if allowance prices move outside a defined range. If prices are low, the emissions cap declines more quickly, but if prices are high, the cap stops declining or increases.

Price floors and ceilings allow legislators to select a range within which allowance prices will remain. Price floors can be implemented by incorporating a reserve price in allowance auctions. Price ceilings—often called a safety valve—are controversial, particularly among environmentalists, because the government's willingness to sell additional allowances at a prespecified price could compromise the emissions cap.

Independent oversight bodies would have authority to intervene in allowance markets with various policy mechanisms, much as the Federal Reserve oversees monetary policy.

Which policies merit enactment? Banking of allowances is uncontroversial and will certainly be included in legislation. Borrowing is likely to be allowed but limited in both volume and duration. Triggered mechanisms, which could abruptly cycle on and off or create odd incentives, are less than ideal. Price floors—minimum auction prices—should certainly be used. A price ceiling could increase the efficiency of a cap-and-trade program but may not be politically viable, making the idea of a reserve pool of allowances potentially attractive. A reserve might not alter long-term expectations, but in the short run it indicates a commitment to climate policy that may make a program more credible. To function well, independent oversight bodies need clear objectives combined with instrumental independence—characteristics largely lacking in the proposals to date.

More generally, Congress may find it useful to focus the discussion of cost containment on the question of short-term volatility, to help separate the question of good policy design from the broader scientific, economic, and political debate about emissions targets.

COMPETITIVENESS

Climate policy will raise the price of energy-intensive goods, perhaps disadvantaging domestic producers and shifting production and emissions to unregulated regions overseas. Policies to address competitiveness concerns must either lower the cost of domestic goods and exports or raise the cost of imported goods.

One proposal supported by some domestic industries would raise the cost of imports through border taxes on the "embodied emissions" in manufactured goods. Some argue that border adjustments would prompt trading partners to adopt climate policies of their own; others warn of poisoning multilateral negotiations and sparking retaliatory trade policies. Whether such policies would pass muster with the World Trade Organization is uncertain, and accurately determining embodied emissions would be challenging.

Other proposals would weaken regulatory requirements for domestic manufacturers, typically by exempting certain industries from the cap-and-trade program and instead using product standards to regulate the carbon intensity of manufactured goods. This would be good for exempted manufacturers but distortionary for the economy as a whole, pushing economic activity into lightly regulated sectors.

This leaves the option of subsidizing manufacturers' production costs by allocating some emissions allowances for free but (unlike grandfathering) updating them based on some metric of production. This implicit rebate keeps the playing field level at home (vis-à-vis imports) and abroad (vis-à-vis competitors in export markets). Around 15 percent of allowance revenues, provided on the basis of output, would compensate energy-intensive industries for abatement costs and mitigate leakage. An important question for competitiveness policies is how they respond as major trading partners take on comparable actions—for example, accelerating phaseout of free allocation to energy-intensive industries if developing countries enact their own climate policies.

INCORPORATING STATES

So far, the states have led on climate policy: California passed GHG legislation in 2006, and 10 northeastern states instituted the Regional Greenhouse Gas Initiative (RGGI), a cap-and-trade program for electricity sector emissions, in January 2009. Will the federal program give credit to states for early actions or convert their allowances into federal allowances? Will states be allowed to go beyond the federal program? These considerations may become salient as political negotiations proceed; consider that 22 senators represent California and the RGGI states.

Further Reading

Burtraw, D., R. Sweeney, and M. A. Walls. 2008. The Incidence of U.S. Climate Policy: Where You Stand Depends on Where You Sit. Discussion paper 08-28. Washington, DC: Resources for the Future.

Fell, H., I.A. MacKenzie, and W.A. Pizer. 2008. Prices versus Quantities versus Bankable Quantities. Discussion paper 08-32-REV. Washington, DC: Resources for the Future.

Ho, M., R.D. Morgenstern, and J.S. Shih. 2008. The Impact of Carbon Price Policies on U.S. Industry. Discussion paper 08-37. Washington, DC: Resources for the Future.

Murray, B.C., R.G. Newell, and W.A. Pizer. 2008. Balancing Cost and Emissions Certainty: An Allowance Reserve for Cap-and-Trade. Discussion paper 08-24. Washington, DC: Resources for the Future.

8. WHICH IS THE BETTER CLIMATE POLICY?

Emissions Taxes versus Emissions Trading

Ian W.H. Parry
is the Allen V. Kneese Chair and a senior fellow at Resources for the Future. He specializes in quantifying the costs and benefits of environmental, transportation, and energy policies.

William A. Pizer
specializes in environmental policy evaluation, with a particular focus on climate policy. This commentary was completed while he was a full-time senior fellow at Resources for the Future.

Whether the principle instrument to reduce greenhouse gases should be an emissions tax or a cap-and-trade system has been the subject of intense debate. Both instruments actually have considerable merit, though this hinges critically on key design features.

In many ways, tax and cap-and-trade systems to reduce carbon dioxide (CO_2) from fossil fuel combustion appear to be equivalent policy instruments. Either instrument can be levied upstream in the fossil fuel supply chain to encompass all potential emissions sources, with the tax or permit requirement proportional to a fuel's carbon content. In either case, the tax or allowance price is passed forward into higher fuel and energy prices, encouraging the adoption of energy-saving technologies, substitution away from high-carbon fuels to other fuels, and so on. However, the instruments may differ in two potentially important regards.

FISCAL ISSUES

One important way in which CO_2 taxes differ from "traditional" permit systems (where allowances are given away for free to firms) is that taxes raise revenue. For example, a \$20 CO_2 tax would initially raise around \$100 billion in revenue per year for the U.S. federal government. One way of using this revenue would be to finance a reduction in individual federal income taxes of around 10 percent, which would (moderately) alleviate various tax distortions in the economy. For example, by taxing away some of the returns to working and saving, income taxes deter some people from joining the labor force and encourage others to consume too much of their income. Income taxes also induce a bias away from ordinary spending toward items that are deductible or exempt from taxes (for example, owner-occupied housing and employer-provided medical insurance). Although subject to some dispute, research suggests that the economic efficiency benefits from recycling the revenues from a \$20 CO_2 tax are as high as \$40 billion a year, representing a substantial cost savings that would not be possible under a traditional permit system.

However, the answer to the question of whether a strong fiscal argument exists for CO_2 taxes over cap-and-trade lies in the details. If legislation accompanying the tax does not specify that revenues offset other taxes, then the new revenue sources might end up being wasted in special-interest spending. Alternatively, revenue might finance deficit reduction, but it is not clear whether this will ultimately lead to lower taxes in the future, or increased public spending.

Moreover, auctioning off the allowances in a cap-and-trade system, rather than giving them away for free, would generate the same amount of government revenue as an emissions tax for a given CO_2 price. So what matters is not so much the choice of emissions control instrument, but rather whether that instrument raises revenue (as both auctioned allowances and emissions taxes do) and uses that revenue productively.

PRICE VOLATILITY

A second potential argument for a CO_2 tax is that it fixes the price of emissions. In contrast, under a pure cap-and-trade system, emissions reductions are certain, but the CO_2 permit prices would vary over time with changes in energy demand, fuel prices, and so on. Volatility in permit prices may deter large investments in carbon-saving technologies (for example, carbon capture and storage) or major research and development programs (like hydrogen or plug-in hybrid vehicles), as it makes the long-term payoffs from these investments uncertain. Moreover, it makes economic sense to allow firms to produce more emissions in years when the costs of meeting a given emissions cap would otherwise be very high (a year of particularly high energy demand, for example), while encouraging extra abatement effort in years when the costs of meeting the cap are lower. An emissions tax provides this flexibility, and studies show that over time the expected environmental benefits, minus emissions mitigation costs, may be much greater than those under a fixed emissions cap.

But again, the distinction between taxes and permits may be more apparent than real, as cap-and-trade systems can be designed to limit the price volatility. For example, "safety valves" eliminate disruptive price spikes as the government steps in to sell extra allowances if permit prices reach a certain trigger point. Alternatively, allowing firms to borrow permits from the government during periods of high permit prices and bank permits when there is downward price pressure would help to smooth out sharp price fluctuations. In fact, some limited price flexibility might be desirable as it allows new information to be instantly reflected in market prices and abatement decisions. For example, if global warming occurs faster than expected, speculators would expect a tightening of the future cap, forcing permit prices both in the future and in the present higher; in contrast, it could take years to get a change in emissions tax rates enacted in response to new scientific information.

PRACTICAL ISSUES

In short, the key distinction is not really between CO_2 taxes and emissions trading schemes per se. Rather, it is between policies that raise revenues—and use revenues to enhance economic efficiency—and have limited price volatility (as with CO_2 taxes or auctioned permits with safety valves and emissions trading over time), versus non-revenue-raising instruments with no provisions to limit price variability (as in a traditional permit systems).

However, what would be the point of developing an elaborate emissions trading system if its main purpose is largely to mimic the effects of a (simpler) CO_2 tax?

One possibility is that policymakers may prefer the certainty of progressive emissions reductions over time provided under a cap-and-trade system. But this is no reason to reject the CO_2 tax out of hand, as the tax rate could always be raised in the future if targets for emissions reductions are not being met, perhaps due to unexpectedly rapid economic growth.

Another possibility is that policymakers may wish to provide temporary compensation for industries adversely affected by the emissions control program. Under a cap-and-trade system, granting some free allowances to those industries, which they might then sell to other firms, is a natural mechanism for such compensation, though at the cost of scaling back the potential efficiency benefits from recycling allowance auction revenues. However, compensation is also possible under a tax regime, perhaps by taxing firms only for their emissions over and above some threshold level that is exempt from the tax, or providing them temporary relief from, for example, corporate tax liabilities.

MOVING FORWARD

Broad-based, and appropriately scaled, federal action to begin a progressive transition away from a carbon-intensive economy is to be welcomed. However, achieving that with the best climate policy is also important, not just for minimizing transition costs, but also for increasing the prospects that the policy will be effective and sustained over time. Aside from the overall level of policy stringency, the two most important issues are the potentially large dividends to be reaped from raising and recycling revenue, and from containing emissions price volatility. Whether either emissions taxes or cap-and-trade systems are well designed in these regards is truly in the details of the legislation accompanying the policy.

Further Reading

Goulder, Lawrence H., and Ian W.H. Parry. 2008. Instrument Choice in Environmental Policy. *Review of Environmental Economics and Policy* 2: 152–174.

Hepburn, Cameron. 2006. Regulating by Prices, Quantities or Both: An Update and an Overview. *Oxford Review of Economic Policy* 22: 226–247.

Nordhaus, William D. 2007. To Tax or Not to Tax: Alternative Approaches to Slowing Global Warming. *Review of Environmental Economics and Policy* 1: 26–44.

Parry, Ian W.H., and William A. Pizer. 2007. Combating Global Warming: Is Taxation or Cap-and-Trade a Better Strategy for Reducing Greenhouse Emissions? *Regulation* 30: 18–22.

9. SHOULD CAP-AND-TRADE SYSTEMS BE SUPPLEMENTED WITH RENEWABLE PORTFOLIO STANDARDS?

Christoph Böhringer

is a professor of economic policy at the University of Oldenburg, Germany. His research focuses on impact analysis of environmental, energy, and trade policies.

Knut Einar Rosendahl

is a senior research fellow at the Research Department of Statistics Norway. His research focuses on climate policies and energy market analysis.

Cap-and-trade proposals to reduce greenhouse gas emissions are often supplemented with renewable portfolio standards (RPS) that regulate the share of renewables in power generation. How do RPS affect the costs of emissions control programs, is there an economic justification for these policies, and if implemented, how should they be designed?

Cap-and-trade systems have become a central pillar in existing and proposed U.S. and European policies to control carbon dioxide (CO_2) emissions. But that's not the only regulatory scheme being pursued both here and abroad: many policymakers are pushing for ambitious increases in the production of renewable energy. Are there any synergies between the two? Maybe, maybe not.

Federal production tax credits for renewable power have recently been expanded in the United States, and more than half of the states have established renewable portfolio standards (RPS). These require a certain share of power generation to come from renewable sources, providing a potential basis for a future federal RPS. The EU is even more ambitious, promising to increase its share of renewables in overall energy use to 20 percent by 2020, together with a 20 percent reduction in greenhouse gas emissions. Individual member states typically rely on either RPS or feed-in tariffs (which provide temporary subsidies to encourage market penetration of new technologies), or both, to stimulate renewable power production (in Europe, RPS is usually termed tradable green certificates).

RENEWABLE POLICIES AND THE COSTS OF CAP-AND-TRADE

If the only objective were to reduce CO_2 emissions, and there were no other market imperfections, then an appropriately scaled cap-and-trade system alone would be sufficient. The price on emissions would promote cost-effectiveness by equalizing the marginal costs of abatement through different options for reducing emissions, such as switching from coal to renewables and other low-carbon energy sources, adopting carbon capture and storage technologies at coal plants, reducing overall electricity use, reducing consumption of transportation fuels, and so on.

Under these conditions, supplementing a cap-and-trade system with an RPS would be counterproductive. If the emissions cap were binding, the RPS would have no effect on emissions (unless they become so stringent that the renewable policy standalone caused emissions to fall below the emissions target). At best, the RPS would be redundant if the renewable constraint is already met by the cap-and-trade system. But the more likely result would be to raise the overall costs of the emissions cap by inducing excessive abatement from expansion of renewables and too little abatement from other mitigation opportunities.

In a recent paper, we examined the implications of implementing RPS in addition to a cap-and-trade system in the context of the German electricity market. Using a numerical model of this market, we considered a cap-and-trade system that imposes a 25 percent emissions reduction below the business-as-usual level. An RPS that progressively forces up the share of renewables in the generation mix by 10 percentage points above the share with no RPS roughly doubles the overall costs of the emissions cap.

Under a binding emissions cap, an RPS benefits not just renewable producers but also the most CO_2-intensive power producers, while other low and zero carbon sources (like nuclear and coal with carbon capture and storage) lose out. The explanation for this presumably unintended effect of renewable policies is that the price of CO_2 allowances falls, which is especially beneficial for the most emissions-intensive power plants. According to our results, when emissions in the German power sector are reduced by 25 percent through a cap-and-trade system alone, lignite power production (the most CO_2-intensive power plants in Germany) falls by around 40 percent. Then, when the share of renewables is raised by 10 percentage points, production of lignite power increases by 17 percent (that is, to a level around only 30 percent instead of 40 percent below the business-as-usual level).

RATIONALES FOR RENEWABLES POLICIES

So is there a definitive case against portfolio standards and other renewables policies? The answer is not entirely clear, as there are other possible "market failure" arguments that might justify the use of these policies as a complement to a CO_2 cap-and-trade program.

One possibility is that the market penetration of renewable fuels, even under a cap-and-trade system, may otherwise be too limited, due to technology spillovers. In particular, an early adopter of a new technology may find ways to lower the costs of using that technology through "learning by doing." Later adopters benefit from the knowledge created through earlier learning by doing at other firms, but they do not have to pay for it. Correspondingly, early investment in a technology may therefore be too low, because early adopters do not take into account the knowledge spillovers to other firms. In principle, this market imperfection may justify the use of a technology-forcing policy like an RPS.

However, at present there is little evidence available on the magnitude of these knowledge spillovers for relatively new technologies like wind and solar, so it is difficult to judge to what extent, if any, an RPS is justified as a complementary measure. A similar example would be the tax credit for hybrid cars in the United States; the question of whether that credit made sense on the grounds of learning-by-doing spillovers has never been thoroughly studied either.

Another possible rationale for using RPS is energy security interpreted as reduced import dependence for oil and gas. Increased production of renewable power will typically suppress gas power production, and therefore reduce the demand for imported gas from "unstable" sources like Russia. This is presumably a more important issue in Europe than in the United States. With a cap-and-trade system in place, this effect might be strengthened because, as noted above, introducing RPS will expand both renewable and coal power production, partly at the expense of gas power. The effect of RPS on oil imports is more modest and indirect, because oil is only marginally used in the power sector. Again, it is difficult to translate energy security in terms of reduced import dependence on fossil fuels into monetary economic benefits that may offset the additional cost of RPS.

DESIGN ISSUES

The economists' case for cap-and-trade has largely been made, but the jury is still out when it comes to renewables policies. Given that these policies are becoming increasingly prevalent for many other reasons, it behooves us to recommend design features to contain the costs of these policies.

With a cap-and-trade system in place, designing renewable policies should focus on other issues than CO_2 emissions, such as the potential market failures referred to above. If these are supposed to be equally important across renewable technologies, a market-based RPS, where firms are allowed to trade credits derived from renewable production, may be a proper instrument. It stimulates the cheapest renewable options, and so the renewable target is reached in a cost-effective way. As long as RPS are implemented at the state and not the federal level, overall costs can be further contained by also allowing trade in credits across states. Banking and borrowing can reduce costs even further, and also help smooth the price of credits, and consequently the price of electricity. Broadening the coverage of RPS to include large-scale hydro power (which is often excluded), nuclear, and coal power with carbon capture can also bring down costs. However, the choice of technologies covered by the RPS as well as the specific design should be driven by the market failure(s) it is supposed to confront.

In the case of import dependence, for example, it is reasonable to consider the market failure to be of equal importance for all renewables. The answer is less clear when it comes to technology spillovers. If these are believed to be largest for the most immature renewable technologies, which are often the least competitive ones, other instruments than RPS may be more appropriate. This could, for instance, be technology-specific subsidies that are reduced over time as the technology matures.

Further Reading

Böhringer, Christoph, and Knut Einar Rosendahl. 2009. Green Serves the Dirtiest. On the Interaction between Black and Green Quotas. Discussion paper 581. Oslo, Norway: Statistics Norway.

Dimas, Starvos. 2008. Winning the Fight against Climate Change: An EU Perspective. European Commission Speech 08/333. June 2008, Cambridge, UK. europa.eu/rapid/pressReleasesAction.do?reference=SPEECH/08/333&format=HTML&aged=0&language=EN&guiLanguage=en (accessed October 20, 2009).

Fischer, Carolyn. 2006. How Can Renewable Portfolio Standards Lower Electricity Prices? RFF Discussion paper 06-20-REV. Washington, DC: Resources for the Future.

10. INDUCING INNOVATION FOR CLIMATE CHANGE MITIGATION

Richard G. Newell

was an associate professor at Duke University, specializing in energy and environmental policies with a particular focus on technological innovation, and an RFF university fellow when this article was written.

Stabilizing global climate change at acceptable levels will require the development and wide diffusion of transformative technologies to substantially lower the emissions intensity of economic activity. What is the best long-term strategy for promoting such technological change?

Fossil fuels provide for over 80 percent of U.S. and global energy use, but unfortunately also contribute the majority of greenhouse gas (GHG) emissions. Achieving the very significant reductions in GHGs that are now widely regarded as necessary would require innovation and large-scale adoption of GHG-reducing technologies throughout the global energy system. Alongside policies aimed directly at mandatory GHG emissions reductions—such as a cap-and-trade system or a carbon tax—much discussion has surrounded policies targeted at technology R&D activities and technology-specific mandates and incentives. The resulting debate is therefore not so much over the importance of new technology per se, but rather over which policies and institutions will be the most effective and efficient for achieving the technological changes and associated emissions reductions necessary for stabilizing GHG concentrations.

When considered alongside policies that impose mandatory GHG-reduction requirements, additional technology policies may not seem necessary or desirable. After all, the point of market-based approaches is to establish a price on GHG emissions. Just as people will consume less of something that carries a price than they will of something that is given away for free, attaching a financial value to GHG reductions should induce households and firms to buy technologies with lower GHG emissions the next time they are in the market (for example, a more efficient car or appliance). This market-demand pull should in turn encourage manufacturers to invest in R&D efforts to bring new lower-GHG technologies to market, just as they do for other products and processes. That is why many experts and most economists—including this one—think that establishing a market-based price for GHG emissions is the single most important policy for encouraging the innovation and adoption of GHG-reducing technologies.

But is a GHG price the *only* useful policy, or should we have other arrows in our quiver? There are, in fact, several motivations for including additional R&D policies as complements to a pricing policy in a comprehensive strategy to address climate change. The economics literature on R&D points to the difficulty firms face in capturing all the benefits from their investments in innovation, which tend to "spill over" to other technology producers and users. This market reality can lead to underinvestment in innovative efforts—even given intellectual property protection—potentially warranting policies that directly target R&D. The problem of private-sector underinvestment in technology innovation may be exacerbated in the climate context, where the energy assets involved are often very long-lived and where the incentives for bringing forward new technology rest heavily on domestic and international policies rather than on natural market forces. Put another way, the development of climate-friendly technologies has little market value absent a sustained, credible government commitment to reducing GHG emissions.

If more stringent emissions constraints will eventually be needed, society will benefit from near-term R&D to lower the cost of achieving those reductions in the future. An emissions price that is relatively low in the near term may be inadequate to induce such innovative efforts absent very credible expectations that the policy will indeed be tightened in the future. If the politically feasible near-term emissions price (or the expected long-term emissions price) is lower than what would be best for society, market inducements for R&D on GHG-reducing technologies will also be insufficient. These motivations provide compelling rationales for public policies targeted at the R&D phases of the technology innovation process, including efforts that lower the cost and expand our options for low-GHG renewable energy, energy efficiency, nuclear power, and carbon capture and storage.

What specific policies might be useful in this regard? The R&D tax credit against corporate income has been the historical means for encouraging greater private sector R&D—in general, not just for energy or climate. Making the R&D tax credit permanent would help to further strengthen private-sector incentives that would be induced by a price on GHG emissions—currently the credit expires and then is extended every few years. Targeting the tax credit specifically at GHG-reducing technologies would be difficult, however. Another worthwhile option is to use innovation-inducement prizes to encourage GHG-reducing innovation, by offering financial or other rewards for achieving specific technology objectives that have been specified in advance.

While increased private-sector R&D is an essential part of the solution, private R&D tends to be focused on applied research and especially development. Publicly funded contracts and grants for clean energy R&D—which focuses on strategic basic research and precommercial applied research—are therefore important additional parts of the overall strategy. By virtue of its critical role in the higher education system, public R&D funding will continue to be important in training researchers and engineers with the skills necessary to work in both the public and private sectors to produce GHG-reducing technology innovations. This linkage has led to a recent increase in political support for expanded spending—particularly on physical sciences and engineering.

Overall, public funding for research tends to receive widespread support based on the significant positive spillovers typically associated with the generation of new knowledge. Many experts have advocated at least doubling relevant energy R&D over the next several years in order to help accelerate climate technology innovation. Translating this support into real increases in funding is more of a challenge—a challenge that could potentially be met through funds arising from a carbon tax or from a cap-and-trade system with allowance auctions.

Agreement over the appropriate role of public policy in technology development tends to weaken, however, when it comes to directed technology support for widespread technology deployment. Most economists and many other experts think that a broad-based, technology-neutral emissions price stands the best chance of guiding deployment among the wide variety of technological options at the lowest possible cost. To date, however, almost all technology-focused funding in proposed climate legislation is targeted at deployment rather than R&D.

In sum, climate technology policies are best viewed as a *complement to* rather than a *substitute for* an emissions pricing policy. But they are an important part of the climate policy portfolio, particularly if we hope to lower the cost and expand the options for significant future GHG reductions both in the United States and abroad.

Further Reading

Jaffe, A.B., R.G. Newell, and R.N. Stavins. 2002. Environmental Policy and Technological Change. *Environmental and Resource Economics* 22(1): 41–69.

Jaffe, A.B., R.G. Newell, and R.N. Stavins. 2005. A Tale of Two Market Failures: Technology and Environmental Policy. *Ecological Economics* 54(2–3): 164–174.

Newell, R.G. 2007. Climate Technology Research, Development, and Demonstration: Funding Sources, Institutions, and Instruments. In *Assessing U.S. Climate Policy Options,* edited by R.J. Kopp and W.A. Pizer. Washington, DC: Resources for the Future, 117–132.

11. HOW SHOULD EMISSIONS ALLOWANCE AUCTIONS BE DESIGNED?

Karen Palmer

is the Darius Gaskins Senior Fellow at Resources for the Future and the director of the Electricity and Environment Program. She specializes in environmental and public utility regulation.

Policymakers are increasingly interested in auctioning at least some of the emissions allowances in cap-and-trade systems, rather than giving them all away for free. What considerations should be taken into account for the efficient design of allowance auction markets?

As more and more governments, both here and abroad, start to implement cap-and-trade programs to reduce emissions of carbon dioxide (CO_2), interest in emissions allowance auctions is growing. Several of the states involved in the Regional Greenhouse Gas Initiative (RGGI) are auctioning 100 percent of their allowances under this cap-and-trade program. And the European Commission is now proposing that a majority of the CO_2 allowances allocated to electricity generators be sold in an auction, starting in 2013, with a phase-in to 100 percent auctioning by 2020. Auctioning is also a central component in the national cap-and-trade proposals currently before the U.S. Congress. The Kerry-Boxer bill (S. 1733), includes a provision to auction over 20 percent of the allowances initially, growing to over 70 percent by 2030. Several other federal bills envision a similar increasing reliance on auctions over time.

Policymakers are seeking an approach that will achieve a number of policy objectives, including a competitive market with no collusion and good price discovery, an efficient allocation of emissions allowances, minimal interference with operation of the secondary allowance market, minimal price volatility, and low administrative and transaction costs. Maximizing revenue—a common goal in most government auctions of public assets, like drilling rights for oil—is not a priority here.

Given these diverse needs, what's the best approach to designing an auction? Research, including economic experiments conducted to guide the design of the RGGI allowance auction, suggests that the most effective design is a sealed-bid, uniform price auction where all winning bidders pay the first rejected bid. This way, auction participants who place a high value on allowances can feel free to bid their true value, knowing that they will only have to pay the highest rejected bid (the market-clearing price) for the allowances that they win. Uniform price auctions do a better job at tracking changes in market conditions and revealing the true market price. Simplicity also suggests that a one-round auction is preferable to a more complicated multi-round approach, which is both time-consuming and more susceptible to collusion.

However, this approach could yield inconsistent prices. If allowances from more than one year are auctioned at the same time, the price of the later vintage (for example, 2010) could potentially exceed the price of the earlier one (2009). (The vintage of an allowance defines the first year or time period when it can be used for compliance with the emissions cap.) One possible solution is a combined vintage auction, based on the idea that allowances are bankable and that a bid for a later vintage should be treated as a request to purchase either that vintage or an earlier one, whichever is less expensive.

Allowance auctions should be held frequently enough to maintain liquidity in the allowance market, but not so often as to raise administrative and transaction costs unnecessarily. Having large infrequent auctions could pose a financial challenge to firms that need to acquire large quantities of allowances at each auction and consequently must put up substantial amounts of capital to participate. Such auctions also could disrupt secondary market trading because large quantities of allowances would be introduced at the time of the auction.

Well-designed auctions should include a minimum, or reserve, price below which no allowances would be sold (reserve prices are common in auctions like those on eBay). This feature helps to limit the gains to bidders from collusion and could be used to prevent allowances from being sold for less than the minimum value that regulators or society places on a ton of CO_2 emissions. Reserve prices must be backed up by a commitment not to sell allowances for less and a rule about whether and how unsold allowances could be reintroduced into the market. Reserve prices could be set at some absolute level that would presumably grow over time as CO_2 caps grow tighter or, after a secondary market has developed, at some fraction of a well-established index of recent prices in the secondary market.

Auctions should be open to all qualified participants, namely any entity that can provide assurance of the financial resources to follow through on its bid to purchase allowances. Restricting participation will limit competition in the auction and could help facilitate collusive behavior, driving a wedge between prices in the auction and the true market price of allowances.

Contrary to the open auction principle, some have tried to argue that restricting participation in allowance auctions to entities that are required to comply with the cap-and-trade regulation will have several beneficial effects. For example, advocates of this line of thinking suggest that restricting participation would prevent a large bidder with no CO_2 emissions from hoarding allowances in the auction. Limiting auction participation is also seen as a way to prevent outside entities from purchasing allowances for use as CO_2 emissions offsets in other voluntary or regulatory programs.

However, this line of argument is not sufficient. Restricting access to the auction will not by itself limit access to the allowance market, and hoarding behavior could be effected in the secondary market as well. Opportunities for hoarding can be reduced through other design features, such as frequent small auctions, and limits on the proportion of allowances in a single auction that can be purchased by a single entity. The fact that hoarding or cornering the market is likely to be an expensive and risky strategy is perhaps the greatest deterrent.

On March 17, 2008, the states participating in RGGI released a synopsis of the design elements for their allowance auctions, and the first auction took place in September 2008. The RGGI auction design is largely consistent with that recommended here. That historic event began the real world test of how well the auction design elements adopted by RGGI work in practice for CO_2 allowances. Stay tuned for the rest of the story.

Further Reading

Holt, Charles, William Shobe, Dallas Burtraw, Karen Palmer, and Jacob Goeree. 2007. *Auction Design for Selling CO_2 Emissions Allowances under the Regional Greenhouse Gas Initiative.* Washington, DC: Resources for the Future. www.rff.org/rff/News/Features/Auction_Design_RGGI.cfm.

12. COMPETITIVENESS, EMISSIONS LEAKAGE, AND CLIMATE POLICY

Carolyn Fischer
is a senior fellow at Resources for the Future. Her research focuses on environmental policy design and technological change, international trade and environmental policies, and resource economics.

Richard D. Morgenstern
is a senior fellow at Resources for the Future. His research focuses on the costs, benefits, evaluation, and design of environmental policies, especially economic incentive measures.

One of the obstacles to implementing climate policy in the United States has been the worry that domestic firms competing in global markets will be disadvantaged. How serious are these concerns?

In the debate over mandatory federal carbon pricing policies, the potential for adverse effects—on energy-intensive, import-sensitive industries, on domestic jobs, and on the nation's trade balance—consistently emerges as a significant concern. Equally important is the potential for erosion of the environmental benefits if an increase in domestic production costs shifts production to nations with weaker climate mitigation policies, or none at all.

COMPETITIVENESS

With regard to competitiveness issues, recent analyses by Ho et al. (2008) have considered the kinds of adjustments to climate policy that firms can make over different time scales.

- In the very short run, firms cannot adjust prices or production techniques, and profits fall accordingly.
- In the short run, firms can raise prices to reflect higher energy costs but lose sales as a result of product or import substitution.
- In the medium run, in addition to changing output prices, firms can change the mix of energy, labor, and other inputs in their production processes, but capital remains in place; economywide effects are considerable.
- In the long run, capital may also be reallocated across the economy.

Based on modeling results using an assumed carbon dioxide price of $10 per ton, several findings emerge. Measured by the reduction in domestic output, several industries are at greatest risk of contraction over both the short and the long terms: chemicals and plastics, primary metals, and nonmetallic minerals. Another hard-hit industry, petroleum refining, will likely be able to pass along most cost increases. Output reductions shrink over time, however, as firms adjust inputs and adopt carbon- and energy-saving strategies. Industries that continue to bear the impacts are generally the same ones affected initially, albeit at reduced levels. As profits drop in the short term, competitive markets adjust to ensure market rates of return in the longer run.

In the near term, the largest cost increases are concentrated in particular segments of affected industries: petrochemical manufacturing and cement see very short-run cost increases of more than 4 percent, while iron and steel mills, aluminum, and lime products see cost increases exceeding 2 percent.

Overall production losses also decline over time in most nonmanufacturing sectors, although a more diverse pattern applies. The initially significant impact on electric utilities does not substantially change, whereas mining experiences a continuing erosion of sales as broader adjustments occur throughout the economy. Agriculture faces modest but persistent output declines due to higher prices for fertilizer and other inputs.

Short-term losses in employment are roughly proportional to those of output. Over the longer term, however, after labor markets adjust, the remaining, relatively small job losses are fully offset by gains in other industries, leaving no net change in employment.

POLICY TOOLS

The best solution to addressing climate change, most experts agree, involves binding international agreements that create parity in carbon markets. But in the interim, unilateral actions must be taken. A consequence is emissions "leakage"—domestic reductions are offset by increases abroad as production, demand, and energy supplies are reallocated globally. Over the long term, the leakage rate for the few most vulnerable industries could be as high as 40 percent in the case of a unilateral $10 per ton CO_2 price.

Displacement of production through lost competitiveness is not the only source of carbon leakage—and may not even be the main source. A large-scale drop in U.S. demand for carbon-intensive energy will drive down fossil fuel prices globally and expand consumption elsewhere. Coal and oil will become cheaper, making electricity and steel in China less expensive and more carbon intensive. The only way to address such leakage is to ensure that all major countries adopt comparable carbon policies and prices.

Climate policy must be cost-effective: it must ensure access to inexpensive mitigation opportunities throughout the United States (and potentially around the world), minimizing the expense of achieving the emissions target. Beyond that, policymakers have several options.

A weaker overall policy—less stringent emissions caps and/or lower emissions prices—would offer relief to all industries, not just those facing increased competition. But environmental benefits and incentives for technology innovation would be smaller. Exempting certain sectors provides more targeted relief but eliminates incentives to deploy even inexpensive measures. Traditional forms of regulation, such as emissions standards, could deliver some emissions reductions while avoiding the added burden of allowance purchases (under auctioned cap-and-trade programs) or taxes on remaining emissions. However, the overall cost to society will tend to be higher than under an economywide pricing policy.

Trade-related "border adjustment" policies would require importers to purchase allowances based on actual or estimated embodied emissions, leveling the playing field at home between imported and domestic consumer goods. It would have the same effect on our exports and foreign goods, by adding an export rebate based on average emissions payments in the sector. Such adjustment policies may raise concerns within the World Trade Organization, however.

An allocation policy that keeps domestic costs from rising in the first place would also do the same thing. Allowance allocation would need to be updated in accordance with output, and the value of that allocation would function like a domestic production rebate. This type of benchmarking with ongoing adjustments stands in contrast to the fixed allocations used in Title IV of the Clean Air Act.

Fischer and Fox have examined the options and found different economic trade-offs. Although all the options promote domestic production to some extent, none would necessarily be effective at reducing leakage because while they reduce emissions abroad, they expand the emissions of domestic firms. The net effects depend on the relative responses of domestic and foreign producers to carbon price changes and on the relative emissions intensity of production at home and abroad. It seems likely that for most U.S. sectors, a full border adjustment—combining an import adjustment based on actual embodied carbon emissions with an export rebate—is most effective at reducing global emissions. But if for reasons of avoiding trade disputes import adjustments are limited to a weaker standard, the domestic rebate can be more effective at limiting emissions leakage and encouraging domestic production.

QUALIFICATIONS

Now, some caveats. First, although an emissions cap can limit domestic emissions, awarding additional allowances to certain sectors to compensate for competitiveness concerns will tend to raise allowance prices overall and shift costs among sectors. For energy-producing sectors like electricity or petroleum refining, a production rebate undermines incentives for cost-effective conservation efforts. Second, border adjustments risk providing political cover for unwarranted protectionism and may provoke trade disputes. Third, many of our largest trading partners—including the European Union—are implementing emissions pricing. And for most energy-intensive manufacturing, these partners represent a quarter or more of the leakage from lost competitiveness. Thus, actual leakage is less of a concern, and any allocation scheme must consider how preferential treatment will be phased out.

Overall, sector-specific policies are more difficult to implement than economywide approaches and can require hard-to-obtain data. Furthermore, they create incentives for rent seeking as industries seek special protection without necessarily being at significant competitive risk. Nonetheless, a unilateral or near-unilateral domestic carbon mitigation policy could in fact cause adverse impacts on certain energy-intensive, import-sensitive industries, particularly in the short to medium term, justifying some kind of policy response.

Further Reading

Fischer, Carolyn, and Alan K. Fox. 2009. Comparing Policies to Combat Emissions Leakage: Border Tax Adjustments versus Rebates. Discussion paper 09-02. Washington, DC: Resources for the Future.

Ho, Mun, Richard D. Morgenstern, and Jhih-Shyang Shih. 2008. The Impact of Carbon Price Policies on U.S. Industry. Discussion paper 08-37. Washington, DC: Resources for the Future.

Morgenstern, Richard D. 2007. Addressing Competitiveness Concerns in the Context of a Mandatory Policy for Reducing U.S. Greenhouse Gas Emissions. In *Assessing U.S. Climate Policy Options*, edited by Raymond J. Kopp and William A. Pizer. Washington, DC: Resources for the Future, 107–116.

13. ADDRESSING BIODIVERSITY AND GLOBAL WARMING BY PRESERVING TROPICAL FORESTS

Roger A. Sedjo

is a senior fellow and the director of the Forest Economics and Policy Program at Resources for the Future. His research includes climate, biofuels, and land use, as well as a variety of forest resource issues.

Environmentalists have long been exasperated by the loss of biodiversity from the progressive destruction of tropical forests. Global warming policies at last offer some hope of slowing deforestation, as firms in developing countries have incentives to partly offset their emissions mitigation obligations through the purchase of credits to maintain the carbon stored in tropical forests. Tropical forests have long been recognized as providing habitat for a huge share of the world's wildlife and plant species. For decades, however, concern has been mounting that these sensitive ecosystems, which constitute over 50 percent of the planet's forested area, are in peril. The clearing of large tracts of tropical forests and conversion of that land for other uses destroys habitats and threatens many species with extinction.

Why should tropical forests be protected? One long-standing argument is that governments should protect these areas, rich in biodiversity, because of their untapped potential for the pharmaceutical industry. For example, a plant currently undiscovered, deep in the forest, could one day prove helpful in the fight against HIV/AIDS. However, this reasoning has not held up over time. A famous project saw Merck & Co., Inc., one of the world's largest pharmaceutical companies, providing $1 million dollars to Costa Rica in return for 1,000 plants collected from its forests. Although the Merck project successfully raised money for Costa Rican biodiversity research, few, if any, drugs have been developed, and the model has not been transferred elsewhere.

However, a new justification is emerging. Real hope lies in the idea of protecting forests for their value in the fight against global warming. Forests contain huge amounts of carbon, and are often referred to as carbon "sinks," for they absorb and store carbon dioxide from the atmosphere. As concerns about the consequences of global warming grow, and as more people understand how carbon dioxide contributes to that warming, it is possible not only to estimate the value of a forest for sequestering carbon, but also to provide landowners with incentives to avoid deforestation. Simply put, by controlling deforestation we can significantly affect our carbon emissions. Studies suggest that halting deforestation in the tropics and other judicious uses of forestland for carbon control and storage could substantially reduce the costs of mitigating global warming.

Recent market transactions on the European Climate Exchange place the value of carbon somewhere between $10 and $100 per ton (the price of carbon dioxide = 12/44 the price of carbon). Furthermore, the exchange provides a vehicle to allow landowners to capture the value of the carbon benefits. Even if we use what seems like a fairly conservative price of $80 per ton, that means that the almost two billion hectares of tropical forests currently hold captive a whopping 300 billion tons of carbon, worth about $6 trillion.

If we add the 140 billion tons of carbon in the dead wood, litter, and soils on the forest floor, the additional value is $2.8 trillion, meaning an impressive total value of $8.8 trillion for the globe's tropical forests.

Sorting out the value and benefits of these forests is one thing. Next we need to work out how much we're willing to pay to keep them intact.

For a landowner, one study suggests the value of cleared land works out to $300 per hectare, on average (Pearce 1996). So let's assume that governments will need to pay $500 per hectare to stop them from felling their trees. That adds up to a $1 trillion cost across all of the world's tropical forests. Yet the benefits of sequestered carbon in those forests, even at modest prices, are about 8.8 times as great as the costs.

The difficult question remains, however, as to who will pay to sustainably maintain these forests. Until now, no one has come forward with the requisite large amounts. However, with carbon credits selling for up to $100 per ton, tropical countries may find it in their interest to take heed. The concept is that countries that can reduce or eliminate high rates of deforestation could receive carbon credits that would be recognized and could be transacted in the carbon markets. Countries that found it difficult to meet their carbon emissions targets under the Kyoto Protocol or subsequent climate agreements could purchase the credits generated by avoided deforestation to meet those targets. Thus, benefits would accrue to both buyers and sellers of carbon credits, and the benefits of tropical forests could be preserved for humankind. Another approach would be to focus on the tropical lands that are particularly subject to deforestation. Most of the world's tropical deforestation takes place in eight countries, with 50 percent occurring in Brazil and Indonesia. So, in order to maximize efficiency at the start, an initial approach might be to focus "avoided" deforestation strategies and funds on these countries. Studies estimate that in order to substantially reduce tropical deforestation, annual expenditures of $2.2 to $5 billion would be needed for an extended period.

Protecting tropical forests will not be easy. Measurement, monitoring, and an administrative and regulatory structure would be required. Efforts would need to be made to ensure that deforestation activities are not simply deflected to other regions or countries with less stringent governance. Such enforcement would be complicated, but is possible if satellites and density-measuring lasers are employed (DeFries et al. 2007). The compensation costs and outlays for monitoring would still be far less than the economic benefits of carbon capture, even without considering the other environmental benefits of the forests. Even though a system of forest protection might not be easily implemented, the potential total benefits of protection are great. Halting deforestation would be a powerful tool to help humans effectively address the peril of climate change.

Further Reading

Costanza, R., R. D'Arge, R. de Groot, S. Farber, M. Grasso, B. Hannon, K. Limburg, S. Naeem, R.V. O'Neill, J. Paruelo, R.G. Raskin, P. Sutton, and M. van den Belt. 1997. The Value of the World's Ecosystem Services and Natural Capital. *Nature* 387: 253–260.

Costello, C., and M. Ward. 2006. Search, Bioprospecting, and Biodiversity Conservation. *Journal of Environmental Economics and Management* 52(3): 615–626.

DeFries, R., F. Achard, S. Brown, M. Herold, D. Murdiyarso, B. Schlamadinger, and C. de Souza Jr. 2007. Earth Observation for Estimating Greenhouse Gas Emissions from Deforestation in Developing Countries. *Environmental Science & Policy* 10: 385–394.

Pearce, D. 1996. Global Environmental Value and the Tropical Forests: Demonstration and Capture. In *Forestry, Economics and the Environment*, edited by W.L. Adamowicz, P.C. Boxall, M.K. Luckert, W.E. Phillips, and W.A. White. Wallingford, UK: CAB International, 11-48.

14. FORESTS IN A U.S. CLIMATE PROGRAM

Promising, but the Key Is Implementation

Kenneth R. Richards is an associate professor at the Indiana University's School of Public and Environmental Affairs. He specializes in climate change and environmental policy implementation.

Ideally, the forest sector would be included in a domestic program to reduce greenhouse gases, as studies suggest there is potential to sequester in trees a substantial amount of carbon at relatively modest cost. Unfortunately, however, there are challenging design issues that need to be overcome before an effective forest sequestration policy can be implemented.

As the U.S. government develops a program to reduce the country's net emissions of greenhouse gases, it will be important to consider the role that forests and the forestry sector can play. Through photosynthesis, trees act as biological scrubbers for carbon dioxide, removing the gas from the atmosphere, storing the carbon as biomass, and returning the oxygen to the atmosphere.

Many forestry practices contribute to this carbon sequestration, including preventing deforestation, modifying harvest practices to reduce soil disturbance, reforesting harvested timberland, implementing new management methods such as extended rotations, and managing fire more effectively to avoid catastrophic loss. Perhaps more important, converting marginal or abandoned cropland and pastureland to forest stands can contribute significantly to increased carbon sequestration.

Although carbon sequestration alone will not drastically mitigate our carbon emissions, it can serve as a significant and cost-effective component. A 2005 study by the Pew Center for Climate Change reviewed nearly a dozen studies of the cost of carbon sequestration in the United States. Once the individual studies were adjusted for comparability, the results suggested that as much as 500 million tons of carbon per year—about 30 percent of national emissions—could be sequestered at a cost of $25 to $75 per ton of carbon ($7 to $21 per ton of carbon dioxide). With carbon capture and geological storage costs approaching $150 per ton, forest carbon sequestration appears quite cost-effective.

Several of the climate change bills introduced in Congress over the past few years have addressed various aspects of forest carbon sequestration. Most prominently, the 111th Congress passed HR 2454, commonly known as the Waxman-Markey bill, which includes provisions for substantial forest carbon offset projects and programs, both domestic and international.

The challenge for promoting forest carbon sequestration is designing a program that reliably induces landowners to protect and expand their forest carbon inventories. There are two basic approaches to encourage forestland owners to sequester more carbon: results-based programs and practice-based incentive systems. Each has its virtues and limitations.

RESULTS-BASED APPROACH

The results-based approach focuses on the amount of carbon actually sequestered by individual landowners and allows for innovative strategies customized to local circumstances. It would create incentives that closely coincide with the sought-after outcomes. The incentives might take the form of payments or subsidies from the government or offset credits under a cap-and-trade program.

Under a results-based approach, the government and program participants must employ some mechanism to estimate, report, and verify the actual carbon sequestration achieved by forest management changes. To win popular and political support—

particularly if credits that can be used to meet obligations under a cap-and-trade program are allocated to individual landowners—it will be necessary to develop procedures that assure the public that estimates of carbon gains are accurate.

The first and perhaps most challenging element of estimating the impact of a carbon sequestration project is developing a reference case—that is, estimating how much carbon would have been stored on a site in the absence of the program. Most of the practices that increase forest carbon sequestration are familiar activities that are already integral to land-use management. For a particular area of land, it can thus be difficult to say which practices would have been used anyway, even if government policy had not influenced management decisions. The requirement that the project go beyond the reference case is sometimes referred to as "additionality." Since the reference case cannot be observed—after all, it did not happen—sequestration project evaluators have to rely on professional judgment to estimate business-as-usual carbon sequestration.

Project evaluation is also vexed by problems with leakage—that is, countervailing off-site effects that decrease the true carbon sequestration gains of a project. For example, a project developer might protect a particular area of forest from harvest to reduce the release of carbon from the site. But if, in response to market demand, a timber company simply cuts elsewhere instead, the carbon sequestration gains of the project have been lost. Also problematic is the fact that forest carbon can be released back into the atmosphere if the wood decays or burns; it is not necessarily as permanent as other kinds of emissions reductions.

Yet another problem involves verification. Project evaluation is hard enough when the professional has no financial or personal interest in the project. But when the individual developing the sequestration project is also charged with evaluating it, as is often the case, there is an inherent conflict of interest.

The methods used to evaluate carbon offsets are supposed to lead to results that are additional, verifiable, permanent, and enforceable. Although this may sound like a demanding standard, it is not enough. What is really needed is an approach that is independently reproducible—that is, the results of the analysis do not vary with the analyst. None of the current protocols or estimation procedures has been tested to see whether it complies with this standard. Senator Boxer's bill from the 110th Congress, S 3036, is the only one introduced in Congress to require that the methods used to assess offsets be tested and verified by teams of independent experts before the methods can be used to earn allowances.

PRACTICE-BASED APPROACH

An alternative to the results-based approach is a practice-based incentive system, similar to the programs that have been used for environmental stewardship under the Farm Bills. Under this scheme, landowners are paid for adopting specific practices that are thought to be correlated with high levels of carbon sequestration—for example, converting highly erodible cropland to forest stands. The advantage of this approach is that it avoids potentially costly and contentious carbon measurement issues. The disadvantage is that the incentives for carbon sequestration are dulled; landowners' first priority is implementing the practice, not sequestering carbon.

GOVERNMENT PRODUCTION APPROACH

A more radical option that has received virtually no attention is for the government (federal or state) itself to acquire land and adopt carbon-sequestering practices. This is what the government has done in many hazardous waste cleanups. Although there may be substantial political resistance to the government's expanding its holdings of land, the "government production" approach offers the advantage of practicality. It reduces problems of asymmetry of information, makes it easier for the government to pursue multiple objectives such as biodiversity and recreation, and allows the government to adjust its practices without extensive renegotiation of terms with private parties. The disadvantage, of course, is that a government production approach dulls incentives for efficiency and innovation.

We have been working for a decade and a half to overcome the challenges of a results-based offset program, but the issues persist. While we may be able to overcome these difficulties with additional experience and experimentation, it is likely that policymakers should consider alternatives. Further developing programs that use the input-based and government production approaches may well prove more fruitful in the long run. In any case, forest carbon sequestration is so promising, we must make a continued, diligent effort to find workable systems.

Further Reading

Richards, K., and K. Andersson. 2000. The Leaky Sink: Persistent Obstacles to a Forest Carbon Sequestration Program Based on Individual Projects. *Climate Policy* 1: 41–54.

Richards, K., N. Sampson, and S. Brown. 2006. *Agricultural and Forestlands: U.S. Carbon Policy Strategies.* Arlington, VA: Pew Center on Global Climate Change.

Stavins, R., and K. Richards. 2005. *The Cost of U.S. Forest-Based Carbon Sequestration.* Arlington, VA: Pew Center on Global Climate Change.

15. EMISSIONS OFFSETS IN A GREENHOUSE GAS CAP-AND-TRADE POLICY

Brian C. Murray

is the director for economic analysis at Duke University's Nicholas Institute for Environmental Policy Solutions. His experience lies in economics, climate change, ecosystem services, land use, forests, and agriculture.

A key issue in the design of a cap-and-trade (or tax-based) system to reduce U.S. greenhouse gas emissions is to what extent covered sectors may offset some of their abatement obligations by paying for lower-cost emissions reductions in other countries, or in domestic sectors (such as agriculture) that might not be formally regulated. Some important pitfalls need to be addressed if offset provisions are to work effectively, without undermining overall emissions reduction targets.

Emissions offsets have received much attention, both positive and negative, as a policy option to mitigate climate change. Simply put, an offset is an agreement between two parties under which one party voluntarily agrees to reduce its emissions (or increase carbon storage in forests or agricultural soils) in exchange for a payment from another party. For this discussion, the paying party is mandated via regulation to reduce emissions, but the selling party is not. The underlying premise is that the offset seller can cut emissions less expensively than the offset buyer can, and will do so if paid more than the action costs.

The most well-known climate policy offset program is the Clean Development Mechanism (CDM). Under that arrangement, countries that have agreed to binding greenhouse gas (GHG) reduction commitments under the UN's Kyoto Protocol can meet their commitments through focusing on internal emissions reductions, trading emissions rights with other countries facing Kyoto emissions targets, or relying on the CDM itself, obtaining emissions reductions credits generated through offset projects in developing countries not bound by Kyoto targets.

One of the newest programs is the Regional Greenhouse Gas Initiative, which recently launched a mandatory program to reduce GHGs from the electric power sector in 10 northeastern states with offsets from the uncapped sectors allowed as a compliance option. In mid-2009, the U.S. House of Representatives passed cap-and-trade legislation to cut GHG emissions approximately 80 percent by 2050, with domestic and international offsets as a significant component of the policy's cost containment design. As of this writing, the legislation is now being considered by the U.S. Senate.

WHY OFFSETS?

The economic argument in favor of offsets is straightforward to anyone familiar with emissions trading principles. Rather than designate which parties must undertake which reductions to achieve a collective target, it is more efficient to allow parties to contract among themselves to find who can achieve these reductions at the lowest cost. This is true for emissions trading in general and for offsets in particular. Empirical evidence bears this out. A recently published study by EPA of the cap-and-trade bill that passed in the House of Representatives in 2009 found that allowing offsets even subject to quantitative limits on their use reduces marginal compliance costs by about half. In addition to cost containment, offsets are seen as a potential source of economic stimulus, delivering much-needed resources and efficient technologies to sectors and countries outside the cap that are economically disadvantaged. They can also be a source of environmental cobenefits through the deployment of less-polluting technologies and protecting forests and other ecosystems that sequester carbon.

POTENTIAL PROBLEMS

Two common criticisms of offsets are that they deflect effort from abatement in the capped sectors and generate credit for reductions that may not be real. But the former criticism is misdirected. Deflecting abatement from the capped sectors is exactly how offsets work to reduce costs. It should be the overall reductions we are interested in, not where they occur. However, if offset credits are being given for reductions that do not actually occur, the transaction and the cap are illusory.

The validity of offset reductions is called into question because they are generated from sources that do not face an emissions mandate. This makes it difficult to determine how to give credits for emissions reductions—reductions compared to what? The answer typically comes in the form of a baseline that captures what the emissions level would be under a "business-as-usual" scenario. Reducing emissions below this baseline can be considered additional to reductions that would have occurred anyway.

"Additionality" is a necessary condition for the reductions to be real. Additionality may be more readily apparent in some cases such as methane capture from livestock operations or afforestation of cropland because these are not prevalent practices for farmers under business as usual. But in practice it can be difficult to determine additionality because once a project starts, the baseline is a counterfactual event that is unobservable. This can become a matter of guesswork that varies in sophistication—from complex data analysis to simply asking the party to provide evidence the project is additional. If a party has too much freedom to set its own baseline, there is legitimate concern about its validity and whether the reductions are therefore truly additional.

Another potential problem with offset transactions is "leakage," which occurs when emissions reductions generated by the project simply lead to emissions being shifted to some ungoverned source, such as another uncapped entity not engaged in an offset project, thereby counteracting the project's reductions. A third problem, "permanence," comes specifically from offsets generated by biological sequestration of carbon in forests and agricultural soils, which have the highest physical and economic potential in a domestic U.S. program. These projects create value by removing CO_2 from the atmosphere and storing it in biomass and soils. The stored carbon, however, can be re-emitted by natural disturbances, such as fire, or intentional management actions. If this occurs, the original benefits of the project have been negated and the offset accounting shortfall needs to be addressed.

POSSIBLE SOLUTIONS

Offset policy has focused on addressing additionality, leakage, and permanence issues in two ways.

Quality standards. Each of the problems identified here can be dealt with by imposing standards to protect offset quality. This follows the CDM approach, which restricts the activities eligible for offsets and requires an executive board to approve all projects. All CDM projects must meet standards for additionality, address leakage, and require all biological sequestration projects to accept temporary payments rather than risk impermanence. This was deemed necessary to get political buy-in from parties who were skeptical of offset integrity. The results have been mixed. Indeed, it has been challenging to get many CDM projects approved, thereby restricting supply. But the logjam is loosening, and some projects that have been approved have been criticized for generating dubious reductions despite quality standards.

Quantitative restrictions. Policymakers have tended to couple quality standards with quantitative restrictions on the use of offsets for compliance. For example, the EU limits the share of compliance commitments that can be met with offset credits to approximately 10 percent (with some variation across countries within the EU). The U.S. House bill would have similarly placed compliance limits on offsets. These restrictions implicitly suggest that policymakers are lured by the appeal of offsets, but they only trust them so far.

SUMMARY

Offsets are neither a panacea nor a pox. Done well, they expand emissions reduction opportunities and lower the cost of achieving the cap, but they create a number of accounting problems for a cap-and-trade program. Rigorous standards for their inclusion are essential if the system is to have integrity. Nonetheless, some flexibility is necessary to ensure that high-quality offsets are not left out of the system because of overly burdensome requirements. This trade-off is as much art as science. Quantitatively limiting offsets for compliance is not an ideal solution, but it may be necessary, at least at first when offset quality is highly uncertain. Even with quality standards and quantitative restrictions in place, the CDM has generated a substantial flow of potential credits (3.8 billion tons in the pipeline) redeemable in the Kyoto system. Clearly, the current system, warts and all, has at least passed the first test of viability. Whether or not offsets are a critical element of the post-2012 Kyoto framework and the U.S. compliance market remains for policymakers to decide.

Further Reading

Burtraw, D., J. Goeree, C. Holt, K. Palmer, and W. Shobe. 2007. *Auction Design for Selling CO_2 Emission Allowances under the Regional Greenhouse Gas Initiative.* Albany, NY: New York State Energy Research and Development Authority (NYSERDA).

Murray, B.C. 2008. Offsets Improve Flexibility. *Environmental Forum* (November–December): 39.

Olander, Lydia et al. 2008. Designing Offsets Policy for the U.S. Report NI R 08-01. Durham, NC: Nicholas Institute for Environmental Policy Solutions, Duke University.

Trexler, M.C., D.J. Broekhoff, and L. Kosloff. 2006. A Statistically-Driven Approach to Offset-Based GHG Additionality Determinations: What Can We Learn? *Sustainable Development Law and Policy* 6(2): 30–40.

16. ETHICS AND DISCOUNTING GLOBAL WARMING DAMAGES

Cameron Hepburn

is a senior research fellow at the Smith School of Enterprise and the Environment at the University of Oxford. He specializes in environmental economics, climate policy, and long-term decisionmaking.

One of the most contentious issues in assessing what price to put on greenhouse gas emissions is the rate at which global warming damages to future generations should be discounted. How can we think about the discount rate, and is there any possibility for reconciling different views?

Over the past few years, great debates have erupted over discounting, stimulated by the economic analysis of climate change. One of the more controversial, the 2006 report by Nicholas Stern, *The Economics of Climate Change: The Stern Review,* employed a much lower discount rate—around 1.4 percent—than had previously been used. Partly for this reason, the *Stern Review* recommended more rapid reductions in greenhouse gas emissions, with carbon dioxide (CO_2) concentrations peaking at 450–550 ppmv (parts per million by volume). Stern's implicit carbon price along a business-as-usual pathway was roughly $85 per ton of CO_2, though the damages from today's emissions (and hence the appropriate price on CO_2) would be substantially lower if atmospheric stabilization targets were achieved.

In contrast, much (but not all) previous economic analysis had used market interest rates of well above 2 percent, with concentrations reaching around 700 ppmv and carbon prices of considerably less than $20 per ton of CO_2, and often single digits. By way of comparison, current carbon prices in the European greenhouse gas emissions trading scheme are around $20 per ton, and have been as high as around $40 per ton.

The discounting debate is certainly a critical issue for all of the economists now engaged in climate change policy discussions. But before engaging with the debate, it is helpful to clarify some key ideas. To start with, a discount rate is a rate of change of the price of one good relative to another. Under idealized circumstances, the discount rate for all goods could be identical. But the world is not ideal, so different goods have different appropriate discount rates. So when economists refer to "the" discount rate, we are referring to a general, economywide discount rate, which can roughly be applied to aggregate consumption in the economy. This general discount rate represents our collective willingness to trade off aggregate present for future consumption. The discount rate reflects changes in real, not just nominal, prices and is not merely an adjustment for inflation.

Economists make an important distinction between the discount rate for consumption versus utility (or well-being). We might discount expected utility in the future because, for instance, there is a risk of dying beforehand. We might discount future generations because we care less about their welfare than we care about our own. In addition to discounting utility, a further discount component is applied to future consumption, if higher living standards are anticipated in the future. This reflects the rate at which the value of additional consumption declines as consumption increases—represented by a parameter called the "elasticity of marginal utility" with respect to consumption. In total, the consumption discount rate comprises two parts: the utility discount rate and the elasticity of marginal utility multiplied by the consumption growth rate. Even with a zero utility discount rate, if aggregate consumption is expected to keep growing, then a positive consumption discount rate is appropriate.

The discount rate is a function of how we expect consumption to change in the future. Greater optimism (pessimism) about future consumption growth implies a higher (lower) consumption discount rate. In rare cases, where large-scale investment changes consumption growth, the investment will also change the appropriate consumption discount rate. Climate change, and/or our response to it, may be large enough to change the underlying growth rate, and hence also the discount rate.

So why is there such a difference between the *Stern Review* and most previous research? Stern adopts a "prescriptive" approach, explicitly considering the ethics of climate change, and his modeling treats the utility of everyone equally: individuals are not discounted just because they are born in the future. The average global per capita consumption growth was set at around 1.3 percent (although consumption growth varies from region to region and from each of the many thousand model runs to the next). With an assumed elasticity of marginal utility equal to one, this implied a global average consumption discount rate of 1.4 percent. As noted, Stern's carbon prices were higher than in earlier work, and his recommendation is to reduce emissions rapidly.

In contrast to Stern's prescriptive approach, previous research tended to be "descriptive" in assumptions about discounting, focusing on what we actually do, rather than what we ought to do from an ethical point of view. The focus was on market interest rates, which reflect the sum of many individual choices. Historic market interest rates (ignoring past and present financial crises) have averaged around 6 percent, so most previous research applied consumption discount rates at roughly this level. As such, utility discount rates were around 1–3 percent, the elasticity of marginal utility was set at 1–2 percent, and consumption growth rates were around 2 percent. With these higher discount rates, much more gradual emissions reductions are recommended, with atmospheric concentrations reaching or exceeding 700 ppmv.

TOO STERN ABOUT STERN?

Several arguments have been advanced against Stern's approach. We consider two of the more powerful. Stern's utilitarian ethics is not the only, or even the predominant, ethical outlook. For instance, "agent-relative" ethical ideas advanced by philosopher David Hume in the 18th century suggest that it is legitimate to care about those closer to us (by genetic proximity, or space or time) than those farther away. Also, if our ancestors had adopted Stern's perspective, they would have had to devote more resources (by way of savings and investment) for our benefit, reducing their own consumption, and hence also their welfare. This seems unfair given that our ancestors were significantly poorer than we are today.

There are two corresponding replies. First, it is true that utilitarianism is not the only viewpoint. But for a global issue like climate change, our analysis should be impartial, not favoring the Chinese over the Americans, say, or people alive today ahead of those alive in 2050. Many of the greatest economists and philosophers have specifically endorsed an impartial approach, and recommended a zero utility discount rate, which implies a low consumption discount rate, as in the *Stern Review*. Furthermore, the "prescriptive" school argued that there are at least three reasons for being cautious about using market prices to reveal ethical attitudes: markets do not always work properly, as we have seen in recent years; market interest rates can aggregate the choices only of those alive today, and do not represent the wishes of future generations; and interest rates reveal only one discount rate—yet, as discussed, in the real world different goods will have different discount rates.

Second, lower discount rates would indeed have compelled our ancestors to have saved more, but not ruinously so, once we account for the fact that we are so much better off than our ancestors were (as a result of impressive technological progress).

SO, WHAT TO DO?

There are several pragmatic routes to reconciling the approaches. One is to explicitly take into account uncertainty over the discount rate. For example, suppose we crudely assume that Stern is as likely to be correct as his critics, such that a 1.4 percent discount rate is as likely to be correct as a 6 percent discount rate. In this case, over a 100-year period, the discount rate that yields global warming damages equal to the average of damages under a 1.4 percent rate and under a 6 percent rate is 2 percent. In other words, the logic of uncertainty makes the arguments about ethics less significant.

Accounting for "unknown unknowns," by assuming the probabilities are themselves uncertain, further bridges the divide between the discount rate of the *Stern Review* and higher market interest rates. Also, it may be consistent to apply high discount rates for aggregate consumption, and low discount rates for (increasingly scarce) natural capital. If climate change disproportionately damages natural capital, a lower discount rate may be justified.

Finally, social institutions, beyond the market for government bonds, might be investigated with a view to backing out implicit long-term ethical preferences. This would avoid the need for a priori ethical assumptions, such as those made in the *Stern Review*, and would also avoid the problems with relying on market prices to derive ethical positions. Such research may reveal that the apparent chasm between prescriptive and descriptive approaches is narrower than it seems.

Further Reading

Beckerman, W., and C. Hepburn. 2007. Ethics of the Discount Rate in the Stern Review on the Economics of Climate Change. *World Economics* 8(1): 187–210.

Pearce, D., B. Groom, C. Hepburn, and P. Koundouri. 2003. Valuing the Future: Recent Advances in Social Discounting. *World Economics* 4(2): 121–141.

Stern, Sir Nicholas. 2008 *The Economics of Climate Change: The Stern Review.* Cambridge University Press: Cambridge, England.

Sterner, T., and U.M. Persson. 2008. An Even Sterner Review: Introducing Relative Prices into the Discounting Debate. *Review of Environmental Economics and Policy* 2(1): 61–76.

Weitzman, M.L. 2007. The Stern Review of the Economics of Climate Change. *Journal of Economic Literature* 45: 703–724.

17. CLIMATE CHANGE ABATEMENT

Not "Stern" Enough?

Dallas Burtraw

is a senior fellow at Resources for the Future. His research interests include the costs, benefits, and design of environmental regulation and the regulation and restructuring of the electricity industry.

Thomas Sterner

is a professor of economics at the University of Gothenburg, where he established and directs the Environmental Economics Unit, as well as an Resources for the Future university fellow. His main research interests lie in the design of environmental policy instruments.

If the value of environmental resources potentially at risk from climate change is rising over time relative to the value of ordinary market consumption, the future nonmarket impacts of climate change should be discounted at a lower rate. Accounting for this possibility increases the likelihood that more aggressive near-term actions to cut greenhouse gas emissions are justifiable on economic grounds.

That Earth is undergoing anthropogenically induced climate change is no longer in dispute, yet uncertainties abound—concerning cloud formation, feedback from methane in melting permafrost, and ecosystem responses to rapid change, to mention just a few. There are also economic uncertainties: what will the physical effects of climate change mean for the global economy, and how will that affect the world's societies?

As the nations of the world consider actions to mitigate a changing climate, the crucial policy issue boils down to this: what level of investment in climate change abatement should we make today to avoid costs associated with climate change in the future?

The Economics of Climate Change: The Stern Review recommended that 1 percent of global GDP be invested each year to avoid the economic consequences and the unprecedented risks from climate change. That was in 2006. In June 2008, looking at faster-than-expected climate change, Nicholas Stern doubled the estimate, to 2 percent of GDP.

Critics are divided, some calling it too pessimistic or too optimistic, depending on one's proclivities. A central issue in the debate has been the discount rate that Stern used to calculate the future benefits and costs of climate change. Because the impacts of climate change will continue to be felt in the distant future, the rate at which we "discount" the future critically affects the level of emissions reductions that is economically warranted today. For example, at a discount rate of 1 percent, the discounted value of $1 million 300 years hence is around $50,000 today. But if the discount rate is 5 percent, the discounted value is less than a mere 50 cents.

Economists disagree about what value to choose for the discount rate when determining an appropriate level of investment in climate change abatement. Stern used an unusually low rate, motivated by ethical arguments, uncertainty, and the exceptionally long time horizon. This leads to very high damage figures. Hence, his call for a high level of investment in climate change abatement today.

Among the most prominent economists studying the costs and benefits of climate change is William Nordhaus, who has argued for using a higher discount rate and therefore arrives at less startling results with respect to an economic estimate of the damages from climate change, and with respect to the measures we should take in the near term to mitigate negative impacts.

We would point out that most previous investigations (including the *Stern Review* and those by Nordhaus and others) do not consider the effects of the changing composition of economic well-being and changing relative prices. These changes can have an effect on the calculation of the present value of costs of climate change that is as substantial as the choice of discount rate.

Any discount rate assumes a growing economy. But it is unrealistic to assume constant, unwavering growth, equal for all sectors. Both logic and history indicate that growth tends to be concentrated in some sectors, depending on resources, technical innovations, and consumer preferences. If the output of some material goods (such as mobile phones) increases, but the availability of environmental goods and services (like clean water and biodiversity, or rain-fed agricultural production) declines, then the relative prices (or willingness to pay) for the environmental amenities should rise over time, a fundamental point first made by John Krutilla some 40 years ago.

Because of rising relative prices, the environmental sector could see its share of the economy grow in value even as it becomes physically smaller relative to a growing conventional sector. This has consequences for discounting itself that have been overlooked. In a multisector model, discount rates will not generally be constant—nor will they be the same for each sector. There will be a change in the relative prices for goods and services from sectors that grow at different rates.

Accounting for relative price changes can dramatically increase the abatement necessary to mitigate climate change. Using Nordhaus's integrated assessment model for climate change, Sterner and Persson show that even with the relatively high discount rate parameters assumed by Nordhaus but also modeling changes in relative prices yields results that are similar to the conclusions of the *Stern Review* and differ greatly from previous work by Nordhaus and others. If one were to use both low discount rates and changing relative prices, one would find even stronger support for strict and immediate abatement measures than did the *Stern Review.*

We also have a second concern with the *Stern Review*—that it may not give sufficient weight to nonmarket damages.

The nonmarket impacts of climate change are at center stage, because it is precisely the prices of these goods and services that we expect to rise over time. Nonmarket impacts from climate change include biodiversity and ecosystem loss, the effects of air pollution on human health, and damage from extreme hurricanes, droughts, and floods. The *Stern Review* does a great job of presenting many of these, the costs of which could be very high over the coming century: billions of people could suffer water shortages, and tens to hundreds of millions are at risk of hunger, diseases like malaria, and coastal flooding.

Those impacts could also have extreme social consequences if droughts force mass migrations, coastal inundation drives environmental refugees inland, and conflicts erupt over increasingly scarce resources. Such social problems have the potential to make the already serious climate damages much worse. However, social impacts are not included in the Stern analysis, nor have they been included in most other economic analyses. To give a full picture of the costs of climate change and the benefits of mitigation, these impacts should also be taken into account, together with their expected increase in relative value over time.

We believe that it is exactly the nonmarket effects of climate change that are the most worrisome. Given the risk of catastrophes, the main effect of climate change will be not to stop growth in conventional manufacturing, but rather to damage some vital ecosystem services, making them relatively scarcer and raising their relative prices.

In a thorough evaluation of the effect of relative prices, one would assess changes by sector. Clean water, rain-fed agriculture, and some other ecosystem services have particular importance for the very poor, and the climate change damages suffered by the poor are particularly important for human welfare. The extent of the price effect depends heavily on the elasticity of substitution, which measures the change in the composition of willingness to pay for goods and services when relative prices change.

In the meantime, analyses of abatement costs and benefits need to take into account the content of future growth. Future scarcities, whether caused by the changing composition of the economy or by climate change, will lead to rising prices for certain goods and services. Escalating prices for environmental goods and services raise the estimated damage of climate change, counteracting the effect of discounting.

Future scarcity values for nonmarket environmental assets are likely to generate high damage figures, even assuming high discount rates. Combining the low discount rates in the *Stern Review* with rising relative prices could lead to support for even higher levels of abatement than Stern recommended. This would mean that society should consider atmospheric greenhouse gas concentration targets that Stern deems unrealistic: a target below 450 ppm of CO_2 equivalents and consequently even more restrictive stabilization scenarios.

Further Reading

Krutilla, John. 1967. Conservation Reconsidered. *American Economic Review* 57(4): 777–786.

Nordhaus, W.D. 2007. A Review of the Stern Review on the Economics of Climate Change. *Journal of Economic Literature* 45: 686–702.

Stern, Sir Nicholas. 2008 *The Economics of Climate Change: The Stern Review.* Cambridge University Press: Cambridge, England.

Sterner, T., and U.M. Persson. 2008. An Even Sterner Review: Introducing Relative Prices into the Discounting Debate. *Review of Environmental Economics and Policy* 2(1): 61–76.

18. EVALUATING CLIMATE RISKS IN COASTAL ZONES

Gary Yohe

is the Woodhouse/Sysco Professor of Economics at Wesleyan University and a senior member of the Intergovernmental Panel on Climate Change (IPCC). His research interests include adaptation and the potential damage of global climate change..

Rising sea levels as a result of climate change pose complex risks for developed and developing nations alike. Local policies for adapting to higher sea levels need to be crafted, even if the international community is successful in controlling greenhouse gas emissions.

Coastal zones around the world have already experienced some of the most adverse consequences of climate change. Global sea-level rise over the last century has, for example, contributed to increased coastal flooding and erosion as well as widespread ecosystem loss. Extreme weather events have done much of the damage. About 120 million people were exposed to tropical cyclones between 1980 and 2000, and more than 250,000 of them died as a result. The U.S. State Department estimated that close to 100,000 people died as a direct result of the cyclone that stuck Myanmar in May 2008.

Future climate change will produce more of the same over the coming decades. We can expect increased risks from coastal storms, higher sea surface temperatures, altered precipitation and runoff patterns, and more acidic oceans. It is important to note that these impacts will vary considerably across regions—and with increasing unpredictability. Consider the plight of corals scattered around the globe. They are all vulnerable to thermal stress and most have low adaptive capacity. This is not really news, but the increased pace at which corals around the globe have been affected is surprising.

Coastal wetland ecosystems, such as salt marshes and mangroves, are especially threatened where they are sediment starved or constrained on their landward margin by development; here we are learning more about these systems' amplified vulnerabilities as they face multiple stresses from humans and other natural sources. Changes to coastal ecosystems also have serious implications for the societies whose welfare and livelihoods depend on the services that they provide. Indeed, we are only now beginning to understand the degree to which the associated socioeconomic costs will escalate as a result of climate change.

To be sure, the impact of climate change on coasts is exacerbated by elevated pressures from human activities, especially when they are concentrated in populated deltas (and even more so in Asian megadeltas), other low-lying urban areas, and narrow atolls. The enormous loss of life in Myanmar can, for example, be attributed in large measure to degraded mangroves that could have provided some protection from the enormous storm surge. While physical exposure can significantly influence vulnerability for both human populations and natural systems, diminished or nascent adaptive capacity is often the most important factor in creating a hot spot of human vulnerability.

The traditional view holds that adaptive capacity is largely dependent upon development status. However, there are many other underlying determinants of adaptive capacity that are only now being explored: the availability of social and political capital, the ability to manage risk, the ability to separate signal from noise in support of response decisions. Developing nations may have the political or societal will to protect or relocate people who live in low-lying coastal zones, for example, but their vulnerabilities could be much greater without the necessary financial and decision-support capacities, as well as widespread recognition of a causal link between human activity and climate-borne risk.

Adaptation costs for climate change are much lower than the damage costs that would result if no adaptive measures were taken for most developed coasts. Indeed, coastline protection decisions in developed countries can, if exercised properly, reduce economic risk by as much as 75 percent. Conversely, high-end sea-level rise scenarios, combined with other climate changes (like increased storm intensity) and insufficient adaptive capacities, will make some islands and low-lying areas completely uninhabitable. Over the long term, unmitigated climate change could overwhelm the adaptive capacities of even the wealthiest coastal communities.

Coastal vulnerabilities clearly make the point that risk can increase over time for one of two reasons (or both). On the one hand, assessed risk may grow over time because evolving scientific knowledge supports increased confidence that an impact will occur. On the other, even if science has nothing new to say about relative likelihood of a particular impact or manifestation of climate change, risk can also grow because recent research and experiences have shown that consequences have heretofore been understated. Take, for example, the Fourth Assessment Report of the Intergovernmental Panel on Climate Change on increased risk from coastal storms. The natural science community was, in 2006 (and still is, for that matter), debating whether or not a warming planet will mean an increase in the intensity and frequency of extreme storms. The social science community meanwhile learned from Hurricane Katrina (among others storms) that the assessed consequences of such storms have grown, because multiple stresses have been recognized and because even potentially strong adaptive capacity (such as that available to a big city in a wealthy country) is not always utilized to even a fraction of its full potential. Clearly, the risk of coastal storms can be assessed even higher than when the Third Assessment Report was released in 2001.

Our growing understanding of coastal vulnerabilities also supports the inclusion of "sustainability, equity, and attitudes to risk" in the iterative climate response plan described above. Development pathways matter because they dictate in large measure potential progress in building adaptive capacity and placing sustainability on par with economic growth in the calculus of development planning. But like everything else in the climate game, these connections do not work in only one direction; sustainability can affect climate impacts, and climate impacts can affect sustainability. Nor are they "linear"; these associations can have kinks and curves that cause abrupt disconnects, or at least alter the strength of the connection. And they always work together; sometimes good ideas on one side of the connection are counterproductive when their effects are evaluated on the other.

Finally, the research and policy communities are now coming to grips with the notion that increased risks associated with coastal vulnerabilities are not confined to the developing world. Even absent any change in storm frequency, sea-level rise can portend dire consequences for major cities in the developed world. For example, the likelihood that the current "every 100 years" flooding event in New York City will become the "every 25 years" event by 2035 is now assessed to be greater than 50 percent.

It is practically impossible to understate the climate risks that coastal zones will face as the future unfolds, almost irrespective of global mitigation efforts over the short to medium run. That said, the research and assessment communities continue to see them as nearly perfect laboratories within which to study the complexity of the interactions of human beings with their environments.

Further Reading

IPCC (Intergovernmental Panel on Climate Change). *Climate Change 2007: Synthesis Report. Contribution of Working Groups I, II, and III to the Fourth Assessment Report of the Intergovernmental Panel on Climate Change,* edited by Core Writing Team, R.K. Pachauri, and A. Reisinger. Geneva, Switzerland: IPCC.

Kirshen, P., C. Watson, E. Douglas, A. Gontz, J. Lee, and Y. Tian. 2008. Coastal Flooding in the Northeastern United States due to Climate Change. *Mitigation and Adaptation Strategies for Global Change* 13(5): 437–451.

Nichols, R.J., P.P. Wong, V. Bukett, J. Codignotto, J. Hay, R. McLean, S. Ragoonaden, and C.D. Woodroffe. Coastal Systems and Low-Lying Areas. In *Climate Change 2007: Impacts, Adaptation and Vulnerability. Contribution of Working Group II to the Fourth Assessment Report of the Intergovernmental Panel on Climate Change,* edited by M.L. Parry, O.F. Canziani, J.P. Palutikof, C.E. Hanson, and P.J. van der Linden. Cambridge, UK: Cambridge University Press, 315–357.

Yohe, G., and M. Schlesinger. Sea Level Change: The Expected Economic Cost of Protection or Abandonment in the United States. *Climatic Change* 38(4): 447–472.

PART 2

Energy Policies

The political pendulum in the United States has swung away from the highly interventionist role governments played in energy markets following the oil price shocks of the 1970s toward deregulation in the 1980s and 1990s, and back toward much greater intervention in recent years. The latest shift reflects renewed concerns about energy security and the emerging threat of global climate change.

Naturally, there is some overlap between energy policy and some of the issues discussed in the sections on climate and transportation policy. This section covers various issues related to the economic implications of oil dependence, development of alternative energy technologies, specific energy policies, and the workings of energy markets.

A central concern about U.S. dependence on oil is the potential for future oil price shocks to disrupt the economy, to what extent (if any) taxation of oil is warranted to reduce vulnerability to price risks, and the possible causes of recent price spikes. A related issue is whether or not any military burden associated with protecting supplies from the Persian Gulf should be factored into energy taxes.

New technologies are affecting energy markets, and one of the most dramatic has been the rapid development of oil sands in Canada. With this new resource, Canada now has more oil reserves than any country other than Saudi Arabia. The future viability of the coal industry in a carbon-constrained world critically hinges on another emerging technology discussed here—carbon capture and storage. And much deeper into the future, is there any potential for satellite-collected solar power to supply electricity generation?

Specific energy policy issues that are discussed include the possibility for oil drilling in Alaska's Arctic National Wildlife Refuge; the design of policy to reduce the incidence of oil spills; the extent of, and case for removing, energy subsidies in the income tax code; whether there is a rationale for subsidizing solar photovoltaic installations; and practical obstacles to the siting of new energy infrastructure. Also discussed are market or other incentives for green building design, the functioning of markets for natural gas, and current issues in restructuring the power sector.

19. REFLECTIONS ON THREE DECADES OF U.S. ENERGY POLICY

Phil Sharp

has been president of Resources for the Future since 2005. His career in public service includes 10 terms as a member of the U.S. House of Representatives from Indiana and a lengthy tenure on the faculty of the John F. Kennedy School of Government and the Institute of Politics at Harvard University.

Written from the perspective of someone heavily involved in crafting energy legislation for many years, this commentary describes how the political pendulum first swung toward, then away from, and then back toward an interventionist role for government in energy markets.

Often the statement is made that America lacks an energy policy. In truth, we have a plethora of policies intended to reshape energy markets. What people really mean is that we lack a coherent vision, with policies that are strong enough to generate major, sustained changes in the ways energy is produced and consumed.

Over the past several decades, we have periodically engaged in intensive policymaking, usually in association with disruptive swings in energy prices. Each time, we have struggled to achieve a national consensus.

That struggle has focused on both ends and means. Essentially, there are four different goals that differing political factions have argued must be addressed.

The first is economic, namely, assuring that we can afford to fuel our homes, schools, industries, and commercial activities. All sorts of policy interventions to stimulate oil production, ethanol production, and so on have been defended on the grounds that they are important to our economic prosperity. Many of us have argued that efficiency and conservation additionally serve this purpose.

The second is protection of our national security. A host of concerns have been articulated: the threat of disruption of international oil and natural gas supplies by governments or terrorists; the pressure on our foreign policy to accommodate oil-producing states that are hostile to our values; the flow of wealth from U.S. consumers to rogue nations; and terrorism.

The third is guarding our environment—mitigating or preventing damage to our air, water, and land from the production and use of energy, such as burning coal in power plants, combusting gasoline in vehicles, and disposing of nuclear waste. Given federal ownership of massive land acreage and the outer continental shelf, major disputes arise over access for drilling and mining. Today, of course, climate change represents the mother of all environmental concerns, with calls for a radical overhaul of our energy systems in order to dramatically cut greenhouse gas emissions in the decades ahead. This issue had been identified by RFF scholars back in the 1970s.

A fourth goal has been addressing equity or fairness issues: concern for the poor and concern for regional impacts such as rising fuel oil prices for home heating in New England or gasoline prices for long-distance drivers in the West. When prices spike, political fights invariably erupt over how to protect the consumer from the producer. The intensity of equity fights rises and falls with prices.

Thus far, our political system has not been able to set priorities among these goals in a strong and sustained way. In the 2008 presidential campaign, the two major candidates essentially argued that we could serve all these goals, blurring the fact that policy that serves one goal may undercut another, such as support for "coal to liquids."

We have seen a significant ebb and flow in government efforts to redirect our energy markets. Following the Arab oil embargo of 1973, there was a major drive to cut oil imports and shield the economy from expected disruptions and price spikes. Independence was the mantra. Price controls had long been in place for natural gas; oil-price controls were adopted in the 1970s as part of an economywide anti-inflation program of wage and price controls. Such controls proved to be counterproductive to reducing oil imports. They deterred conservation and discouraged domestic production, and, further, they disrupted the internal shipment of fuels to consumers. We appear to have learned the lesson of such failure: during the recent run-up in oil prices, no political leaders called for price controls.

During the 1970s, there were other major market interventions, including mandates, public investment, loan guarantees, and tax incentives. Auto manufacturers were required to meet fuel economy standards, utilities were required to purchase electricity from other industries that cogenerated power, and utilities were prevented from building new natural gas facilities. On the public investment front, huge sums were appropriated for basic research into advanced energy technologies and for direct investment in large-scale demonstration projects meant to show, for example, that liquid fuels could be produced efficiently from coal. The tax code was reconfigured to provide incentives for a host of production and conservation activities, from installing solar panels to insulating homes, and taxes were levied on windfall profits from oil and on gas-guzzling vehicles.

Energy policy was radically overhauled during the 1980s: price controls on oil and natural gas were lifted; some mandates were ended; many tax incentives were repealed or allowed to expire; investment in large new demonstration plants ceased; and spending on research was cut back. Many of these changes derived from the Reagan administration's belief that energy developments should be left to the private markets, that the tax code should not be used for social engineering, and that government's role in research should be limited to advancing basic science. But change also resulted from the dramatic fall in oil prices in 1986 and the reversal in the conventional wisdom that had held that prices were only headed upward. Investors, consumers, and political leaders in both parties lost interest in the development of unconventional and renewable fuels, energy conservation, and efforts by government to intervene in the markets.

In the 1990s, policymaking was reenergized. On the heels of the Iraqi invasion of Kuwait came bipartisan passage of the Energy Policy Act of 1992. In the act, market liberalization continued with the drive to bring competition into electricity wholesale markets. (Several states also moved toward competitive retail markets—a movement substantially set back by the California electricity crisis in 2001.) In the 1992 act, tax incentives were again adopted, including the production tax credit, which was viewed as an improvement over the old investment tax credits as a technique for promoting renewable power. Energy efficiency standards for select household appliances were also enacted. But the Democratic Congress and the Bush administration had no appetite for upgrading auto fuel economy standards or for public investment in large-scale technology projects.

With the passage of comprehensive energy bills in 2005 and 2007, we saw, on a bipartisan basis, the greatest market intervention since the 1970s. Mandates were imposed to promote ethanol production, to ban incandescent lightbulbs, to improve fuel economy, and to upgrade household appliances. A host of tax provisions were adopted to entice changes in investor and consumer practices, including speeding the purchase of hybrids and all kinds of energy equipment in the commercial and industrial sectors and pushing production of conventional and advanced fuels. Loan guarantees were reintroduced for advanced nuclear plants, advanced coal systems, and biofuel refineries. And there was a return to appropriations for big demonstration projects like the FutureGen coal plant.

In recent years, rising prices and policy initiatives by federal and state governments have heightened investor interest in unconventional fossil fuels and in renewable fuels. As gasoline prices reached previously unimaginable levels, consumers sharply shifted their vehicle purchases away from SUVs and even curbed their driving habits. In multiple ways, investors and consumers showed renewed interest in a host of energy-efficient technologies.

Recently, with a Katrina hitting Wall Street, the economy turning terribly sour, and oil prices plunging, all of these developments may be in jeopardy. Past experience suggests that investors, consumers, and political leaders will lose interest in greater efficiency and cleaner fuels.

This time, however, may be different. If the scientific community sustains and/or intensifies the latest assessment by the Intergovernmental Panel on Climate Change (IPCC), there should be greater motivation for action to curb greenhouse gas emissions. The stage was set by both presidential candidates calling for mandatory controls that would transform the energy sector. Indeed, both candidates connected that transformation to economic growth and to greater energy security. These connections are easier to make in rhetoric than in reality, but they represent a significant shift in the public discourse. Ahead remains the tough intellectual and political work to design, adopt, and sustain the policies that can meet the climate challenge and deliver economic growth, not only in the United States but around the globe.

20. THE OIL SECURITY PROBLEM

"Déjà Vu All Over Again"

Hillard Huntington

is the executive director of Stanford University's Energy Modeling Forum. His current research interests include modeling energy demand, energy price shocks, and energy market impacts of environmental policies.

What is the likelihood of a future oil price shock, and if a price shock does occur, how much damage might it cause to the U.S. economy?

Today, three of every five barrels sold on the world petroleum market originate from relatively insecure regions: the Persian Gulf, North Africa, Nigeria, Angola, Venezuela, Russia, and the Caspian states. Political, military, or terrorist events could disrupt oil markets and quickly double oil prices. If these events happen at a time when monetary authorities find it difficult to control inflationary expectations, a trend much more likely today than just two years ago, the world could return to the 1970s and stagflation.

Reducing our vulnerability to such events is the main task for oil security policy. Curtailing imports from our major oil trading partners (Canada and Mexico) is unlikely to benefit us, because these sources are relatively secure. But reducing our imports is important only if we can reduce the market share of vulnerable supplies in the world market. Doing so would mean that disruptions will remove less oil from the market and therefore cause less severe price shocks.

Our vulnerability also depends upon how closely our infrastructure is tied to petroleum use. When disruptions cause oil prices to double, the higher price applies to any oil used in the U.S. economy. It does not matter whether we are relying on imports, domestic supplies, or even close substitutes, like ethanol and other biofuel options. For this reason, efforts to reduce oil demand may be more valuable than efforts to simply replace vulnerable imported supplies with domestic supplies of oil or ethanol.

Pursuing energy security is relatively simple in conceptual terms. The nation is buying an insurance policy against future recessions caused by unanticipated oil price shocks. Today's insurance policy should cost no more than the value of avoiding these possible damages. Higher avoided damages could be due either to a greater probability of a disruption happening somewhere in the oil market or to more serious economic impacts from such a disruption.

Since experts disagree on both issues, it is often difficult to implement this principle empirically. For example, a recent Oak Ridge National Laboratory study computed the hidden social costs attributable to oil based upon a range of different views. Their estimates ranged widely from $6 to $23 per barrel, with a midpoint estimate of about $13 per barrel.

Stanford University's Energy Modeling Forum recently completed two studies that may help resolve some of the uncertainties related to damage estimates associated with oil insecurity.

In the first effort, a working group of geopolitical and oil-market experts assembled to provide expert judgment on the risks of one or more disruptions at some point over the next 10 years. The experts identified specific disruption events and the conditions that could make them more or less likely. From there, they evaluated the probability that a certain set of events could happen and estimated the amount of oil removed from the market in each case. Four separate oil-producing regions were considered: Saudi Arabia, other Persian Gulf nations, Russia and the Caspian states, and a set of heterogeneous countries including Libya, Nigeria, and Venezuela.

The experts concluded that another disruption, given today's conditions, is very likely. At some point over the next 10 years, there is an 80 percent chance that at least one disruption of 2 million barrels per day (MMBD, or 2.4 percent of the total market) or more would last one month or longer. Those familiar with playing with a well-shuffled deck of cards will immediately recognize this probability as exceeding the chances that you would draw a club or a red suit.

Compared to previous periods, the risks today are greater for smaller disruptions below 7 MMBD than for larger ones. Not only are there more insecure regions today than in the past, but fewer opportunities exist to reduce the size of any disruption with offsets from excess oil production capacity in undisrupted regions. These offsets tend to be highly concentrated in Saudi Arabia and hence are unlikely to be available if oil is disrupted in that country.

In the second study, macroeconomic experts gathered to discuss the likely economic impacts resulting from oil price shocks. An important distinction concerns the nature of an oil price increase. During the 1970s and early 1990s, oil supply disruptions caused prices to rise suddenly and sharply. These price shocks were fundamentally different from the price elevation occurring over recent years, when oil prices have been rising more gradually than during the 1970s. Price shocks are likely to create great uncertainty, forcing firms and households to delay their investment, producing spillover effects throughout the economy. Price elevation, on the other hand, may anger the car owner who fills his or her gasoline tank, but it is unlikely to delay investment and lead to a recession.

The other unknown is how economic policymakers will respond to disruptions. Over the last few years, inflationary fears around the world have been very low, which has allowed monetary authorities to ease the money supply to offset lost economic output without creating additional inflationary pressures.

Over the last two years, however, inflationary fears have grown and may become more intense yet. These developments would make it much more difficult for governments to intervene and offset lost output without exacerbating future inflation.

If inflationary fears tie Mr. Bernanke's hands, does the nation have a fallback position? Yes, although the political process will adopt these policies very slowly. First, the U.S. Congress has finally tightened fuel economy standards, reducing both vulnerable supplies and our economy's reliance upon oil. Second, policymakers are considering larger public oil stockpiles, but these expansions will have limited value without a more explicit "trigger" mechanism for releasing oil during emergencies. Third, domestic ethanol or Alaskan oil supplies could replace more vulnerable supplies, but these approaches do nothing for our infrastructure's oil dependence. And finally, automobile insurance rates could discourage excessive driving by being based partly on the miles driven by each person.

More than a half century ago, the very possibility of oil vulnerability shocked the Western world with the closure of the Suez Canal. Despite other major disruptions since that explosive event, there has been little evidence of "learning by doing" in current oil security policy.

Further Reading

Beccue, Phillip, and Hillard G. Huntington. 2005. *An Assessment of Oil Market Disruption Risks.* Energy Modeling Forum Special Report 8. Stanford, CA: Stanford University.

Bohi, Douglas R., and Michael A. Toman. 1996. *The Economics of Energy Security.* Norwell, MA: Kluwer Academic Publishers.

Huntington, Hillard G. 2005. *The Economic Consequences of Higher Crude Oil Prices.* Energy Modeling Forum Special Report 9. Stanford, CA: Stanford University.

Leiby, Paul N. 2007. *Estimating the Energy Security Benefits of Reduced U.S. Oil Imports.* ORNL/TM-2007/028. Oak Ridge, TN: Oak Ridge National Laboratory.

21. REASSESSING OIL SECURITY

Stephen P.A. Brown

is a nonresident fellow at Resources for the Future. He previously served as the director of energy economics and microeconomic policy at the Federal Reserve Bank of Dallas.

Oil security might be defined in multiple ways. To what extent might consumption of domestic and imported oil by individuals impose broader costs on the economy, thereby warranting some level of oil taxation?

World oil prices rose rapidly from 2002 before reaching an all-time high in mid-2008. As prices rose, they were punctuated by sharp swings resulting from supply disruptions. Although oil prices have since declined, expectations that prices will rebound and once again be unstable raise concerns about oil security. Past oil supply disruptions have resulted in sharply rising oil prices and reduced economic activity. Ten of the 11 post–WWII U.S. recessions—including the one we're in now—immediately followed episodes of sharply rising oil prices.

Politicians and scholars regularly emphasize the costs of U.S. dependence on imported oil, but oil's fungibility means that consumers cannot distinguish between domestic and imported sources. All oil prices move together on an integrated world oil market, and regardless of the source, the global price for a barrel of oil ultimately determines the price at the local gas pump. But the critical security difference between domestic and imported sources of oil, namely the instability of foreign suppliers, is what creates conflict in world oil markets and where policy can be used to good effect.

The desirability of promoting oil security arises only to the extent that the potential economic losses associated with reliance on insecure oil supplies are externalities—costs that are borne by society as a whole, rather than by the parties directly involved in a transaction.

DIFFERENTIATING BETWEEN DOMESTIC AND IMPORTED OIL

Although domestic and imported oil look very much the same to the consumer, a disruption of foreign supplies would mean higher oil prices in the United States—even if it were importing no oil from the country whose production is disrupted. The reason why is that rising oil prices elsewhere in the world would divert secure supplies from the United States to other markets. Because no oil supplies are secure from price shocks, the increased consumption of either domestic or imported oil increases the economy's exposure to oil price shocks.

Nonetheless, the U.S. economy's exposure to oil price shocks does differ for domestic oil and oil imported from countries whose production is unstable. Rising U.S. oil imports reduces energy security by increasing the share of world oil supply that comes from those countries. Conversely, expanding U.S. oil production enhances energy security by increasing the share of world oil supply that comes from stable suppliers.

OIL SECURITY EXTERNALITIES

To the extent that the economic losses associated with oil supply disruptions are negative externalities that are not taken into account in private actions, they become a concern for economic policy. A number of other costs may arise from potential oil price shocks, but not all of them may be externalities. Negative externalities occur only when a market transaction imposes costs or risks on an individual who is not party to the transaction. (Of course, oil use creates other externalities—such as air pollution and greenhouse gas emissions—that are not associated with energy security.)

Oil security externalities include increases in GDP losses arising from oil supply disruptions and the expected transfers paid to foreign oil producers during disruptions. Other costs typically associated with oil imports—such as increased prices for oil imports during periods of stable supply, limits that oil imports place on U.S. foreign policy, and the defense spending and other government expenditures designed to reduce the effects of oil supply shocks—are not security externalities.

GDP losses. The increase in expected GDP losses resulting from increased oil consumption is likely an externality. Increased oil consumption ups the exposure of economic activity to disruptions. Moreover, individuals buying oil are unlikely to understand or consider how their own oil consumption affects others by amplifying the effects that oil supply disruptions have on overall economic activity—particularly because the GDP losses associated with an oil price shock are well beyond the possible increase in costs that an individual might expect as part of an oil purchase.

Increased transfers. An increase in U.S. oil imports increases the expected transfers to foreign oil producers during a supply shock, but only part of that increase should be regarded as an externality. When buying oil products, individuals should recognize the potential for oil supply shocks and higher prices. So, the expected transfer on the marginal purchase is not an externality. On the other hand, individuals are unlikely to take into account how their purchases may affect others by enlarging the size of the price shock that occurs when there is a supply disruption. So the latter portion is an externality.

Increased prices for imported oil during periods of stable supply. A rise in U.S. oil imports increases the price paid for all imported oil, and that means greater costs for those purchasing imported oil. Such an increase is considered a normal market development that does not result in market inefficiency, and it is not a security issue.

Increased government expenditures. Government actions—such as military spending in vulnerable supply areas and expansion of the Strategic Petroleum Reserve—are possible responses to the economic vulnerability arising from potential oil supply disruptions. Sound policy requires that these expenditures be balanced against the externalities of greater oil use rather than used as a measure of the externalities.

Limits on U.S. foreign policy. An overall dependence on imported oil may reduce U.S. foreign policy prerogatives. These limitations may not be greatly affected by marginal changes in oil consumption, nor is it readily apparent how to quantify such effects. Therefore, they are omitted in quantitative estimates of the security externalities associated with increased oil consumption.

Uses of oil revenue. Americans may be unhappy with the uses to which some oil-producing countries put their revenue, but that does not mean the sale creates an externality. The oil purchase itself does not create the unwanted behavior. The absence of a direct foreign policy instrument may make it desirable to use policies that reduce world oil prices, but the use of such a blunt instrument will hurt all oil producers, not just those unfriendly to the United States.

ESTIMATED OIL SECURITY PREMIUMS

In recent research, Hillard Huntington and I estimated the external security costs of U.S. oil consumption. The external security cost of the consumption of domestically produced oil has a mean value of $2.81 per barrel in a range of $0.19–8.70. (All dollar figures are in constant 2007 dollars.) The external security cost of the consumption of imported oil has a mean value of $4.98 per barrel in a range of $1.10–14.35.

These estimates suggest only a moderate oil policy is necessary to respond to the security issues associated with oil use. They are based on projections made by the U.S. Energy Information Administration that show oil prices rising from about $40 per barrel in 2009 to more than $130 per barrel in 2030. In comparison to these oil price projections, the estimated security externalities are relatively modest.

Further Reading

Beccue, Phillip, and Hillard G. Huntington. 2005. *An Assessment of Oil Market Disruption Risks.* Energy Modeling Forum Special Report 8. Stanford, CA: Stanford University.

Brown, Stephen P. A., and Hillard G. Huntington. 2009. Estimating U.S. Oil Security Premiums. Energy Modeling Forum Occasional Paper 68. Stanford, CA: Stanford University.

Deutch, John, James R. Schlesinger, and David G. Victor. 2006. *National Security Consequences of U.S. Oil Dependency.* Council on Foreign Relations Independent Task Force Report number 58. Washington, DC: Council on Foreign Relation Press.

Leiby, Paul N. 2007. *Estimating the Energy Security Benefits of Reduced U.S. Oil Imports.* ORNL/TM-2007/028. Oak Ridge, TN: Oak Ridge National Laboratory.

22. THE 2008 OIL PRICE SHOCK

Markets or Mayhem?

James L. Smith
is the Cary M. Maguire Chair in Oil and Gas Management at the Edwin L. Cox School of Business at Southern Methodist University. His current research covers international oil markets, auction theory, real options, and energy finance and risk management.

World oil prices rose from $50 per barrel in early 2007 to $140 per barrel in the summer of 2008, before falling to $40 per barrel by the end of that year. Can this dramatic price shock be explained by market fundamentals—shifts in worldwide demand and supply for oil—or were speculative forces at work?

Why did oil prices spike in 2008, and what role (if any) did speculators play? Perhaps a useful starting point is to observe that, while 2008 exhibited an extraordinarily large price swing, volatility in oil prices is ordinarily quite high because the underlying demand and supply curves are so inelastic. Demand is inelastic due to long lead times for altering the stock of fuel-consuming equipment. Supply is inelastic in the short term because it takes time to augment the productive capacity of oil fields. Price volatility provides incentives to hold inventories, but since inventories are costly, they are not sufficient to fully offset the rigidity of supply and demand.

The steep ascent in the price of oil between 2004 and 2008 coincided with the first significant decrease in non-OPEC supply since 1973 and an unprecedented surge in global demand. Although OPEC members responded by increasing their production, they lacked sufficient capacity after years of restrained field investments to bridge the growing gap between global demand and non-OPEC supply.

Even seemingly small shocks may have large effects. Can they help explain the spike in oil prices in the first half of 2008? It was definitely a time of significant upheavals, some with the potential for sustained disruption of supplies. In February 2008, Venezuela cut off oil sales to ExxonMobil during a legal battle over nationalization of the company's properties there. Production from Iraqi oil fields, of course, had still not recovered from wartime damage, and in late March, saboteurs blew up the two main oil export pipelines in the south—cutting about 300,000 barrels per day from Iraqi exports. On April 25, Nigerian union workers went out on strike, causing ExxonMobil to shut in production of 780,000 barrels per day from three fields. Two days later, on April 27, Scottish oil workers walked off the job, leading to closure of the North Forties pipeline, which carries about half of the United Kingdom's North Sea oil production. As of May 1, about 1.36 million barrels per day of Nigerian production was shut in due to a combination of militant attacks on oil facilities, sabotage, and labor strife. At the same time, it was reported that Mexican oil exports (10th largest in the world) had fallen sharply in April due to rapid decline in the country's massive Cantarell oil field. On June 19, militant attacks in Nigeria caused Shell to shut in an additional 225,000 barrels per day. On June 20, just days before the price of oil reached its historic peak, Nigerian protesters blew up a pipeline, which forced Chevron to shut in 125,000 barrels per day. Each of these events clearly registered in the spot market. It is not implausible to believe that, arriving in quick succession, they contributed heavily to the rapid acceleration in the spot price of oil.

Although the rising price of trend of 2004 to 2008 is consistent with changes in market fundamentals—surging demand and falling supply—the spectacular ascent especially in the first half of 2008 created widespread suspicion that "speculators" were responsible. But neither hedging nor speculation in the futures market exerts any significant effect on current (spot) oil prices. There are two main reasons: (1) due to the law of one price, the futures price must converge to the spot price as the expiration date draws near, and (2) virtually all futures contracts are settled for cash, which means that every futures contract purchased by a trader is subsequently sold by that same trader before the contract expires. Buying pressure is offset by selling pressure and no oil ever changes hands.

The only avenue by which speculative trading might raise spot prices is if it incites participants in the physical market (for example, producers and/or refiners) to hold oil off the market—either by amassing large inventories or by shutting in production. If participants in the physical market are convinced by speculative trading in the futures market that spot prices will soon rise, their reaction could cause inventories to rise and/or production to fall. However, neither phenomenon was observed during the recent price spike.

Finally, we might ask whether price fixing, rather than speculation per se, might be responsible for the dramatic increase in price. OPEC does engage in price fixing, and oil prices would not have reached $145 per barrel if OPEC had not previously restricted investment in new capacity. But OPEC did not actually take any positive action in 2007 or 2008 that precipitated the price spike. OPEC aside, there is no evidence of price fixing on the part of anyone else, which includes both speculators and the oil companies.

What combination of factors then explains the collapse in oil prices that occurred during the second half of 2008? Surely the primary factor is that demand for oil dropped sharply around the world due to the economic decline, which in early 2008 few analysts were predicting would turn out to be so deep.

The world oil market operates subject to the familiar laws of supply and demand, and market fundamentals are the dominant influence on price. The market is subject to shocks, and when these shocks are taken together with short-run rigidities and high costs of adjustment, the resulting price volatility is largely inherent, rather than contrived by speculators, cunning producers, or anyone else.

In the longer run, the effects of shocks will average out, and the effects of structural trends are paramount. The most conspicuous trend, by far, is the rapid pace of economic development in China and other emerging nations. If that continues, oil's high income elasticity implies a proportionate increase in demand.

The long-run trend has been for OPEC to restrict the expansion of new production capacity. But many OPEC members also have a fundamental tendency to ignore the cartel's attempts to rein in surplus production. For as long as the current economic slowdown persists, it will be difficult for OPEC to boost the price of oil of its own volition.

The sustainability of oil supplies from non-OPEC producers is also of fundamental importance. Proven oil reserves of non-OPEC producers have been rising—but resource depletion puts constant upward pressure on costs. For decades, the oil industry has been able to use technological innovation to offset the impact of depletion by finding and producing oil in ways that held the marginal cost of output in check. Although we cannot expect further technical advances to prevent the supply of conventional oil from ever declining, in the longer term, ample supplies of unconventional petroleum resources and other substitutes for crude oil should prevent oil prices from surpassing the mid-2008 peak on any sustained basis. But too many technological and political uncertainties exist to permit a definite prediction.

Further Reading

Hamilton, James D. 2009. Understanding Crude Oil Prices. *Energy Journal* 30(2): 179–206.

Harris, Jeffrey H., and Bahattin Buyuksahin. 2009. The Role of Speculators in the Crude Oil Futures Market. http://ssrn.com/abstract=1435042.

Smith, James L. 2005. Inscrutable OPEC: Behavioral Tests of the Cartel Hypothesis. *Energy Journal* 26(1): 51–82.

Smith, James L. 2009. World Oil: Market or Mayhem? *Journal of Economic Perspectives* 23(3): 145–164.

23. THE COST OF PROTECTING OIL IN THE PERSIAN GULF

Mark Delucchi

is a research scientist at the Institute of Transportation Studies at the University of California, Davis, specializing in economic, environmental, engineering, and planning analyses of current and future transportation systems.

How much of the U.S. defense budget might be attributable to protecting oil supplies from the Persian Gulf is a contentious issue. To what extent should motorists pay for military spending in higher fuel taxes?

With the United States still bogged down in the war in Iraq, rancorous debate continues in the halls of Congress regarding the political and economic costs of America's involvement in the Persian Gulf. Many contend that U.S. interests center primarily, if not exclusively, on the region's huge reserves of oil, and that, as a result, U.S. military expenditures amount to a massive "hidden cost" of oil use by the United States. Some have argued that these hidden costs, estimated to range from essentially zero to upward of $1 per gallon, are, in effect, a subsidy that should be recovered by taxes on motor fuel. The figures vary widely because analysts disagree profoundly about whether military expenditures are related at all to oil use (specifically transportation fuels) and about the magnitude of any expenditures that putatively are related.

Here I examine this debate from a slightly different perspective. What might happen if U.S. consumers and companies hauling freight curtailed their oil use? Would the federal government reduce its military commitment in the Persian Gulf? To evaluate this, the first step is to look at the mechanism—if X happens, what happens to Y?—and the second is to examine the motives of the key decisionmaker, the U.S. federal government, which determines whether resources are available to address those risks and (presumably) authorizes military spending accordingly.

However, predicting how (or even whether) Congress and the president would adjust military spending is scarcely a straightforward process. There is no line item in the defense budget for protecting U.S. oil supplies in the Persian Gulf, and no official congressional formula that relates oil imports to Department of Defense (DOD) spending. Instead, the defense budget is itemized by general functional or cost areas, such as "operations and maintenance," which cover more than one region or program.

How Congress views the relationship between regional threats and defense spending is subject to wide interpretation. Some argue that all multiregional costs and all noncombat, DOD-wide "overhead" costs are essentially fixed with respect to changes in threats in the Persian Gulf, while other analysts argue that all such costs are variable. As a result, estimates of the peacetime costs of maintaining a military presence in the region have ranged wildly, from as little as $0.5 billion to over $100 billion per year.

However, there are good reasons to doubt the claim that multiregional costs and DOD-wide "overhead" costs are essentially independent of threats in a specific region. In the first place, the cost of policing several regions at once presumably is a function of the nature and number of threats in all of the regions, which means that if any one regional threat is mitigated, then generally there is less to defend. Second, in the long run there are few, if any, truly fixed overhead costs—those that are the same regardless of the size of defense forces or the magnitude of a threat—except perhaps those related to upper-level administration, like the salaries of senior DOD staff.

Assuming that fixed multiregional and overhead costs are only a small fraction of total defense costs, I estimate that the long-run variable costs of defending all interests in the Persian Gulf in peacetime are on the order of $30 billion to $75 billion per year—a substantial fraction of the roughly $300 billion per year spent by DOD during peacetime.

The next step in this policy "proof" is to determine the importance of oil among all of our interests in the Persian Gulf. Although it is not well known, numerous military planning documents and senior officials have clearly stated that our overall military objective in the region is to preserve U.S. and Western access to the oil. Given this, two specific questions need to be addressed: (1) if we start with our estimate of the total cost of defending all interests in the region, what fraction of that is related to oil interests specifically, and (2) what is the nature of the relationship? After reviewing estimates by others and considering the true "fixed" costs of defense, I estimate that over 50 percent of the total cost of defending the Persian Gulf is related to oil, and that this annual defense cost is proportional to the annual amount or value of oil produced there.

Expected wartime costs related to oil can be estimated roughly by multiplying the annual probabilities of regional wars of various magnitudes by the estimated annualized cost of such wars and the fraction of wartime costs that are "attributable" to oil. Considering that the current Iraq war will end up costing on the order of a trillion dollars, and that there is evidence that the desire to protect our access to oil is a major factor in the U.S. response to conflicts in the region, I estimate that if there were no oil in the Middle East, the United States would reduce wartime military spending by up to $10 billion per year. Note that this is specifically an estimate of monetary costs; it does not include the very real costs of lives lost and catastrophic injuries, which perhaps could add billions of dollars per year to the total. It also does not include the virtually impossible to quantify geopolitical costs of wars and U.S. Persian Gulf policy in general.

Finally, after accounting for the portion of the oil defense cost that is not related to the consumption of highway fuels in the United States (roughly half), the bottom line is that oil used by all motor vehicles in the United States (light-duty and heavy-duty) carries a modest premium: the price of peacetime plus wartime defense spending comes to somewhere between $3 billion and $30 billion per year, over the long haul. This amounts to about $0.02 to almost $0.20 per gallon of all gasoline and diesel motor fuel used in 2004. While not necessarily trivial, this range is lower than other analysts have estimated, and lower than other environmental- and energy-related external costs of motor-fuel use.

Further Reading

Bilmes, Linda, and Joseph E. Stiglitz. 2006. The Economic Costs of the Iraq War: An Appraisal Three Years after the Beginning of the Conflict. NBER Working Paper No. W12054. http://ssrn.com/abstract=885651.

Davis, Steven J., Kevin M. Murphy, and Robert H. Topel. 2006. War in Iraq versus Containment. Prepared for the CESifo Conference on Guns and Butter: The Economic Causes and Consequences of Conflict. December 9–10, 2005, Munich, Germany. http://faculty.chicagobooth.edu/steven.davis/pdf/weighcosts.pdf.

Delucchi, Mark A., and J. Murphy. 2008. U.S. Military Expenditures to Protect the Use of Persian Gulf Oil for Motor Vehicles. *Energy Policy* 36: 2253–2264.

24. WHAT ROLE FOR "SYNTHETIC" LIQUID FUELS?

A Look at Canadian Oil Sands

Joel Darmstadter

is a senior fellow at Resources for the Future. His research interests include energy resources and policy, climate change, natural resource sustainability, and productivity in natural resource industries.

One concern about the rapidly expanding oil sands industry in Canada is the extra energy required to extract oil, compared with conventional oil sources. Would oil sands remain commercially viable if production costs were to rise with an aggressive program to control greenhouse gas emissions?

A vocal debate about an early peak in the global capacity to produce conventional crude oil has been going on for some time now. To some, a dramatic run-up in oil prices in recent years—in part, attributable to sharply accelerated demand by China, India, and other fast-growing economies—has given added weight to the notion of a long-run supply constraint, even though global recession has brought about a pronounced price drop from the near-$150 per barrel level recorded in 2008.

But even if worldwide oil productive capacity poses little likelihood of early decline, a steadily rising share of total output will most likely originate in regions posing geopolitical disruption risks as well as able to exercise market power in world oil. Translating that dual prospect into a future that may be subject to high and volatile oil prices makes it worth taking another look at liquid fuels for their abundance and reliability. Here I will focus on the prospective role of Canadian oil sands. (The outlook for a viable U.S. coal-to-liquids industry is far more problematic.)

Oil sands deserve attention for two reasons: their underlying resource base is vast, and they are being profitably produced in large amounts. At the same time, however, their long-term viability may depend on success in managing the significant carbon dioxide (CO_2) emissions inherent in their production.

OIL SANDS FACTS

Canada's proven recoverable reserves of some 180 billion barrels—exceeded only by Saudi Arabia's conventional oil reserves—are concentrated in the Athabascan region of northern Alberta. Oil sands, valued for their hydrocarbon content (called bitumen), occur as a near-solid, tarlike substance whose overall volume is a huge multiple of its energy content—thus creating a major waste management burden.

Oil sands extraction takes place by one of two techniques: surface mining (not unlike open-pit coal mining) or underground (in situ) extraction. For now, oil sands production is dominated by mining. But because overall reserves occur predominantly in deep deposits, in situ recovery is likely to dominate over the long run.

When mined, the stripped overburden—removed by giant shovels—must be upgraded by a complex, multistage chemical transformation process to yield a conventional petroleum-equivalent product. In situ extraction typically involves, as a prior step, the injection of steam to make the bitumen less viscous and capable of being forced to the surface for upgrading.

In either case, conversion is an energy-intensive process that accounts for one of its most problematic features—significant CO_2 release. The CO_2 emissions associated with oil sands, compared to those associated with conventional crude oil, exceed the latter by about 20 percent on a life cycle or—in more catchy terms—"well-to-wheel" basis.

TRENDS AND PROJECTIONS

Oil sands production currently amounts to well over a million barrels a day—a significant proportion of Canada's total oil production of around 3.5 million barrels a day. Over the next decade, a ramp-up in oil sands output to over 5 million barrels a day is widely foreseen. Because Canada is the leading source of U.S. oil imports—with a rising share of those imports derived from oil sands—that prospect is both reassuring, in that Canadian imports are certainly more secure, and worrisome because of the CO_2 implications just described.

The fact that, absent CO_2 emissions restrictions, oil sands production is currently competitive with conventional crude oil provides little comfort about the situation in a CO_2-constrained regime. A major thrust of a 2008 RAND report (see Futher Reading) was an effort to consider how that competitive status might play out with severe CO_2 restrictions, whether met by adoption of carbon capture and sequestration (CCS) technology or by purchase of carbon credits. Such credits can be represented by a "shadow price" of CO_2, reflecting, say, payment of a carbon tax or purchase of cap-and-trade permits.

The RAND report provides a cautiously favorable picture of the long-term ability of oil sands to remain commercially attractive even while obliged to comply with formidable CO_2 restrictions. More specifically, there are several noteworthy conclusions that emerge from the report. (Dollar figures refer to 2005 price level.)

- Even with CCS, oil sands production costs in 2025 are competitive with conventional crude at near the $60 per barrel world oil price projected in the Department of Energy/Energy Information Administration (DOE/EIA) "reference case" (published in the 2007 Annual Energy Outlook).
- A DOE/EIA "high oil price" projection, close to the recent $100 per barrel, makes the competitive advantage of oil sands still more robust.
- That advantage would prevail at a shadow carbon price from zero all the way to around $100 per ton of CO_2. (By way of context, the price has hovered around U.S. $33 per ton in the current EU carbon market.) Up to a shadow carbon price of around $60 per ton of CO_2, the economics favor paying the shadow price rather than installing CCS. Beyond that point of "indifference," CCS becomes progressively more attractive.
- It is to be noted that oil sands extraction and upgrading currently rely principally on use of natural gas. Variations in natural gas prices can therefore signify lower or higher overall unit production costs.

In its detailed and wide-ranging scope, the RAND analysis lends considerable credibility to these findings. Nonetheless, we are dealing with a number of unprecedented technological and environmental challenges whose ultimate success cannot simply be taken for granted but requires a sustained commitment to research and reevaluation as experience dictates.

Consider just one elusive goal being pursued in a major research effort in Saskatchewan: CO_2 sequestration that promises long-term geologic stability and integrity. It is frequently observed that CO_2 has routinely been injected into operating oil reservoirs so as to achieve enhanced oil recovery. But there is no assurance that such CO_2 will remain locked in place and not seep into the atmosphere over the long-term future. Thus, the "sequestration" element in CCS may prove a more formidable challenge than the "capture" phase.

Additionally, oil sands operations involve numerous non-carbon environmental challenges. Companies must comply with regulations governing land reclamation, water-use management, and extended monitoring of tailing ponds containing mining spoils. In principle, such costs are embodied in unit production costs. But unforeseen externalities have a habit of arising in many natural resource development projects.

Even with oil sands production rising to a level of over 5 million barrels a day, with a significant share of that increment destined for the U.S. market, it's useful to place that number in the wider perspective of the world oil market. True, in security terms, a marginal barrel of oil originating in Canada trumps the alternative of that marginal barrel from a politically problematic source in the Eastern Hemisphere. All the same, even an oil sands contribution in excess of 5 million barrels a day has to be seen in relation to world oil demand of 100 million barrels a day a decade or so from now. In that sense, to the extent that the U.S. energy system remains significantly oil-based, relief provided by Canadian oil sands—whether in economic or security terms—may be meager. Indeed, it is one—but only one—element within the broad-based energy strategy that is in this country's interest.

Further Reading

Energy Information Administration, U.S. Department of Energy. 2008. Canada. Country Analysis Briefs. www.eia.doe.gov/emeu/cabs/Canada/Full.html (accessed October 20, 2009).

Petroleum Technology Research Center. Weyburn-Midale CO_2 Project. www.ptrc.ca/weyburn_overview.php).

Toman, M., A. E. Curtright, D. S. Ortiz, J. Darmstadter, and B. Shannon. 2008. *Unconventional Fossil-Based Fuels: Economic and Environmental Trade-offs.* Technical report. Santa Monica, CA: RAND Corporation.

Woynillowicz, Dan, Chris Severson-Baker, and Marlo Raynolds. 2005. *Oil Sands Fever: The Environmental Implications of Canada's Oil Sands Rush.* Calgary, Alberta: Pembina Institute. http://pubs.pembina.org/reports/OilSands72.pdf.

25. FUTUREGEN

How to Burn Coal—Maybe—Without Contributing to Climate Change

John W. Anderson

is a journalist in residence at Resources for the Future. Previously he wrote editorials for the *Washington Post.*

FutureGen is a joint venture by the Department of Energy and a private consortium to develop a coal gasification plant that will capture and permanently store carbon dioxide emissions underground. If successful, it represents the type of transformational technology needed if carbon dioxide emissions are to be substantially reduced in the future at acceptable cost.

In its ups and downs, FutureGen is encountering all the policy issues that confront the hope of making electricity from coal without contributing to global warming.

In 2003, President Bush established FutureGen to build a pilot coal-fired generator, on an industrial scale, that would capture and sequester underground its emissions of carbon dioxide. In early 2008, the Energy Department abruptly suspended the project and called for its reorganization, citing soaring cost estimates.

In June 2009, the Obama administration restarted the planning and design process, promising a firm decision in early 2010 whether to proceed with construction. The signs strongly suggest that the decision will be affirmative.

FutureGen is a public-private partnership, nonprofit, between the federal government and, currently, nine big mining and power companies, both American and foreign. As it stands now, the partnership intends to build a 275-megawatt plant at Mattoon, Illinois, using integrated gasification combined cycle (IGCC) generating technology and capturing 90 percent of the carbon dioxide emissions. The cost is projected at about $1.5 billion, of which two-thirds would come from the government and the rest from the private partners.

A growing consensus now holds that the key question is not whether carbon capture and sequestration (CCS) technology can be developed, but rather how fast it can be deployed. In the words of one recent report, *The Future of Coal* (MIT 2007), CCS is the "critical enabling technology that would reduce carbon dioxide emissions significantly while also allowing coal to meet the world's pressing energy needs." Both of the world's largest emitters of carbon, China and the United States, have massive coal reserves, and it is not plausible that either will refrain from using them. It is difficult to envision truly aggressive action to reduce carbon emissions without widespread use of CCS technology.

FutureGen is not an isolated effort. A list maintained by MIT counts more than three dozen CCS projects, of which 14 are in the United States, 15 in Europe, and 2 in China. They range from small experimental operations to plants larger than FutureGen, and most are farther along than FutureGen.

Estimates of the cost of capturing carbon have risen sharply in the last several years, and at the same time they have become much less precise. In early 2007, *The Future of Coal* reported that the cost of CCS would run about $20 to $40 per ton of carbon dioxide, depending on the technologies used. Less than two years later, several MIT researchers published a paper (Hamilton et al. 2009) pointing out that, since 2004, construction costs for power plants had been rising around four times as fast as the consumer price index. The cost of capture in early 2009, they calculated, would be above $50 per ton of carbon dioxide for a plant using the supercritical pulverized coal technology. They could give no estimate for the cost using the integrated gasification combined cycle (IGCC) technology, they said, because of the "tremendous uncertainty in the true costs and performance characteristics of such new technology." In August 2009, American Electric Power, which is retrofitting an existing plant in New Haven, West Virginia, for carbon capture, estimated that it will cost about $100 a ton.

A careful review by Mohammed Al-Juaied and Adam Whitmore published in July 2009 by Harvard's Belfer Center concludes that the cost of capture would be about $150 per ton of carbon dioxide for a first plant built, a figure that with experience would drop into the range of $35 to $70 a ton for later plants—in their terminology, the "nth plant." But if construction costs were to fall back to the 2005–2006 level, they add, the cost of capture would be $90 to $135 a ton for a first plant and anywhere from $25 to $50 for the nth plant. (These calculations assume that the learning curve slopes sharply downward. Steve Mufson of the *Washington Post* has pointed out that in two cases—commercial nuclear power and the overseas transport of liquefied natural gas—that has not proved to be the case.)

The estimates by Al-Juaied and Whitmore do not include the costs of sequestration—that is, transporting the carbon dioxide to the burial site and injecting it underground. The paper by Hamilton et al. uses a figure of $10 a ton of carbon dioxide to cover transportation and storage, although that would vary widely with the location of various projects.

One obvious implication of all these estimates is that at least the early plants in the development of the capture technology will have to be subsidized heavily. A cost of $150 per ton of carbon dioxide avoided is the equivalent of 10 cents per kilowatt hour. The average price of electricity delivered to a residential customer in this country in 2008 was 11.36 cents.

Congress is well aware that the early plants would not produce power at competitive prices. The American Clean Energy and Security (Waxman-Markey) Bill, passed by the House of Representatives in July 2009, would provide bonus emissions allowances amounting to a subsidy of $90 a ton to pioneer plants that capture and sequester 85 percent of their carbon emissions, and $50 a ton to those that capture and sequester 50 percent.

Cost is hardly the only concern for FutureGen and the developers of CCS technology. Another is the reality that FutureGen can demonstrate only one solution, when there are many that need to be tested.

The methods of achieving high efficiency in coal-fired power generation fall into two groups. One burns highly pulverized coal. The other turns the coal into a gas, burns it to run a gas turbine, and then uses the hot exhaust to make steam that then runs a steam turbine. That's the IGCC technology. Several IGCC plants are in operation, but the great majority of coal generators currently use pulverized coal. The IGCC technology has a reputation for being difficult to manage reliably, and it is somewhat more expensive than pulverized coal as long as there is no constraint on carbon emissions.

But the gasification process makes the sequestration of carbon dioxide less costly than in conventional combustion and, where sequestration is required, IGCC becomes, in theory, the more economical choice. That's why FutureGen is going to use it. But there may be circumstances in which pulverized coal is preferable, and the ability to combine it with carbon capture needs to be demonstrated as well.

The further reality is that if CCS is to be a national policy, the technology will also have to be applied to plants now in operation through retrofitting, as at the AEP plant in West Virginia. A generating plant is built with a life expectancy of 60 years or more, and to apply carbon capture only to new plants would mean very slow progress in deploying the concept.

FutureGen continues to be a highly important experiment. With rising concerns about climate change and the realization that the use of coal is unavoidable, it is arguably more important now than when it was first conceived. But it is only one of many experiments, as governments and energy companies have concluded that, without successful and reliable CCS technologies, action to reduce the world's carbon emissions would be much harder to envision.

Further Reading

Al-Juaied, Mohammed, and Adam Whitmore. 2009. Realistic Costs of Carbon Capture. Discussion paper 2009-08, Cambridge, MA: Belfer Center for Science and International Affairs.

Hamilton, Michael R., Howard J. Herzog, and John E. Parsons. 2009. Costs and U.S. Public Policy for New Coal Plants with Carbon Capture and Sequestration. *Energy Procedia* 1(1): 4487–4494.

Massachusetts Institute of Technology. 2007. *The Future of Coal: Options for a Carbon-Constrained World*. Cambridge, MA: Massachusetts Institute of Technology.

Massachusetts Institute of Technology. 2009. Carbon Capture and Storage Project Database. http://sequestration.mit.edu/tools/projects/index.html.

26. THE ECONOMICS OF NEW GREEN TECHNOLOGY INVESTMENT

The Case of Satellite Solar Power

Molly K. Macauley
is a senior fellow and a director of research at Resources for the Future. She specializes in space economics, the economics of new technologies, recycling and solid waste management, climate policy, and incentive-based environmental regulation.

Jhih-Shyang Shih
is a fellow at Resources for the Future specializing in quantitative analysis of environmental and resource policy and decisionmaking.

Satellite-collected solar power is a possible technology for generating clean electricity, albeit for the distant future. This commentary describes the technology, its economics, and the difficulties in modeling uncertainty about investment in the technology.

An old but newly revisited proposal for clean electricity is to collect the sun's energy using antennas in space, then to beam the energy to Earth for distribution via the electricity grid. First proposed in the 1960s, space solar power (SSP) has since appeared occasionally in assessments of new energy technologies but was deemed not yet ready for practical use (for example, see Schurr et al. 1979). More recently, however, the governments of Japan and Germany, as well as NASA and the U.S. Departments of Energy and Defense, have funded large-scale studies of the engineering design for SSP to account for improvements in space and related technologies.

To many skeptics, SSP is yet another sci-fi, pie-in-the-sky idea. Arguably, pretty much all of today's technology was at first merely a gleam in the eye. But at some point the computer replaced the abacus, and Lindbergh's flight led to commercial aviation. Is SSP likely to cost-effectively power a lightbulb anytime soon?

The answer depends partly on whether we choose to invest in further development of the technology. Such a decision is made difficult because of the challenges in modeling and estimating investment under technical and economic uncertainty.

At the request of NASA, the National Science Foundation, and the Electric Power Research Institute, we carried out one of the few studies of the economics of SSP. We asked several questions in an attempt to quantify some of the issues. First, given that many technological hurdles remain for SSP, we asked what they are, what costs would be incurred to overcome them, and how soon they would be achieved. These questions were important particularly because in the time it may take to develop, test, and deploy SSP, innovation will have proceeded apace in competing technologies.

For example, many experts suggest that SSP could be ready for deployment in 2020 in quantities to meet growth in electricity demand. If so, then the relevant basis for comparison would be the expected generation cost per kilowatt hour of SSP compared with that expected in 2020 for its competitors. These most likely include advanced, gasified coal-based and natural gas-based combined cycle gasification technology (CCGT) and advanced (terrestrial) renewable energy. (To make a fair comparison, we used generation costs because SSP would use the existing electricity grid for transmission and distribution.)

Proponents of SSP also note its green advantages. We sought a comparison, then, of quality-adjusted generation costs by adding a carbon penalty to coal and natural gas. To do this, we used a range of values, including prices at which carbon dioxide emissions permits were selling on the European and Chicago climate exchanges and estimates by other researchers of the mean monetary values of impacts from carbon-related environmental damages. Also included were penalties for coal, natural gas, biomass, and solar thermal power due to the thermal effluent that occurs with these technologies through their use and discharge of reject heat into streams and other water bodies. This adjustment was based on how much it would cost the power plant to avoid the externality entirely. Another quality adjustment is reliability; we assumed that there would be low-cost ways to maintain and repair SSP during its operating lifetime and thus SSP could be as reliable as terrestrial power sources.

Our last set of adjustments is associated with the uncertainty surrounding projections of the cost and capability of a new technology. For instance, other researchers have shown that an optimistic bias usually leads engineers to underestimate the likely costs of new technology (Quirk and Terasawa 1986). Consequently, the "point" estimate of our various parameters are expressed together with distributions of possible values, informed by interviews with a variety of experts and review of experience in other space- and power-related technologies. Statistical methods were used to draw sample values repeatedly and randomly from these distributions. On the assumption that SSP would most likely be phased in as additions to baseload-generating capacity in response to increased demand, different rates of technology adoption were included in the simulations.

Finally, a unique attribute of SSP is that it can transmit power anywhere depending on its location in space. Therefore, we looked at the comparative advantage SSP could have in a variety of locations, including places where renewable energy could be abundant and thus give SSP a good run for its money. Our sample included California, the U.S. Midwest, Germany, and India.

What did our findings suggest? SSP could be competitive under the very stringent assumptions we have described—that is, if there are penalties for the externalities of competing technologies and rapid adoption of fully reliable SSP available at a price per kilowatt-hour (kWh) promised by engineering models. Under these assumptions, deploying SSP would provide net benefits from $27 million to $100 million, depending on the region. If any of these assumptions is relaxed, however, the net benefits from SSP are on average an order of magnitude less than those from other types of renewable energy, particularly wind and biomass. When the uncertainty of the cost of SSP is taken into account, its cost advantages are not only smaller, but negative in some cases.

The technological hurdles remain large. For example, in order to collect enough solar energy so as to have a large amount after beaming it the huge distance from the sun to Earth (depending on the efficiency of solar cells and transmission frequencies, energy is lost en route), the transmitting antennas have to be truly enormous. Their size requires multiple rocket launches and an as yet not fully developed ability to robotically assemble the array of antennas in space. The receiving antennas on the ground must also be large, covering hundreds of acres, and are likely to encounter "not-in-my-backyard" concerns.

Another possible shortcoming that is repeatedly pointed out (although not in our model) is that SSP has not been tested as a possible source of the health and environmental effects associated with concentrated amounts of electromagnetic energy—long a concern for many conventional technologies and for which, even now, long-term epidemiological data are lacking.

So, should we invest further in the next steps toward demonstrating SSP? Might it help us hedge against uncertainty about other future technologies—carbon capture and storage, for example? The decision rests much on willingness to invest in complementary technologies (low-cost launch, robotic assembly methods), satisfactory solutions to facility siting, health and environmental concerns, and of course, whether optimism about cost-reducing innovation in our conventional energy technologies in the coming decades bears fruit.

Further Reading

Macauley, Molly, and Jhih-Shyang Shih. 2007. Satellite Solar Power: Renewed Interest in an Age of Climate Change? *Space Policy* 23: 108–120.

National Research Council. 2001. *Laying the Foundation for Space Solar Power.* Washington, DC: National Academies Press.

Quirk, J., and K. Terasawa. 1986. Sample Selection and Cost Underestimation Bias in Pioneer Projects. *Land Economics* 62(2): 192–200.

Schurr, Sam H., Joel Darmstadter, Milton Russell, Harry Perry, and William Ramsay. 1979. *Energy in America's Future: The Choices Before Us.* Washington, DC: Resources for the Future.

27. OIL AND THE ARCTIC NATIONAL WILDLIFE REFUGE

Matthew Kotchen
is a professor at the University of California, Santa Barbara, and a faculty research fellow at the National Bureau of Economic Research. He specializes in public goods, program evaluation, green markets, and interdisciplinary environmental science.

Nicholas Burger
is an economist at the RAND Corporation; his ANWR research was done during his time at the University of California, Santa Barbara. His research focuses on climate policy, transportation, and economic development.

A highly contentious issue in the debate over energy policy is the extent to which domestic oil production should be enhanced by allowing drilling in the Arctic National Wildlife Refuge (ANWR) and other areas. What are the benefits and costs of drilling in ANWR, and how might the revenue from royalty taxes be used to promote environmental objectives?

To drill or not to drill? That is the question once again in Alaska's Arctic National Wildlife Refuge (ANWR). Proponents of drilling promote the advantages of a decrease in the price of oil and reduced reliance on foreign imports. Opponents argue that the only benefit would be windfall profits for oil companies, and that drilling in ANWR would destroy one of the last great wilderness areas on the planet. While advocacy on both sides of the issue is widespread, reliable information and balanced discussion are surprisingly absent.

So how much oil are we really talking about? At prices around $100 per barrel, the U.S. Geological Survey estimates the amount of economically recoverable oil in the federal portion of ANWR to be approximately 7.69 billion barrels of oil BBO)—an amount roughly equal to U.S. consumption in 2007. Accounting for uncertainty, the estimates range from a low of 4.25 BBO with 95 percent certainty to a high of 11.8 BBO with 5 percent certainty. For purposes of comparison, the estimated amount of oil beneath the outer continental shelf is approximately 86 BBO. Under any scenario, however, it would take several decades to extract all of ANWR's oil, and forecasts predict a peak around 2025, at which time ANWR would account for 3 percent of all domestic consumption.

These estimates immediately challenge the two benefits that proponents of drilling most frequently advance. Because ANWR would increase the world's proven reserves by only 0.6 percent and oil prices are determined in a world market, any effect on the price of oil would be negligible. What is more, with ANWR supplying such a small fraction of domestic consumption, even at its peak, U.S. imports of foreign oil would remain significant even if ANWR were tapped.

The real benefit of drilling in ANWR would be the revenue from selling the oil. Consider that 7.69 BBO at a price of $100 per barrel generates revenue of $769 billion. Subtracting the estimated costs of finding, developing, producing, and transporting this oil, the financial net benefit of ANWR's oil is substantial—$613 billion. And if prices continue to rise, as many analysts predict, this number could grow substantially larger.

But what about the environmental costs? There is no doubt that ANWR protects a broad spectrum of natural habitats that are unparalleled in North America. These habitats support a number of large animals—including caribou, musk oxen, wolves, wolverines, and polar bears—and some 135 different bird species. While the specific environmental effects of drilling remain uncertain, it is clear that even with minimal adverse effects, many people would feel a loss if ANWR were developed. This is because many are likely to hold substantial "nonuse" values for ANWR; that is, even people who never visit ANWR may benefit from simply knowing that it exists in a pristine state.

The challenge is to place an economic value on these nonuse benefits for ANWR in order to compare them against the financial benefits of drilling. While a large body of research suggests that the nonuse benefits for ANWR might be substantial, it is reasonable to question whether they would be large enough tip a cost–benefit analysis in favor of not drilling.

Nevertheless, when it comes to policy questions as symbolic and contentious as ANWR, cost–benefit analysis is typically—and perhaps appropriately—employed as a decision tool rather than a decision rule. Beyond economic efficiency, distributional concerns play an important role. Consider how the financial benefits of ANWR's oil would be divided. We find that the financial net present benefits of $613 billion, based on the $100 per barrel scenario, would be partitioned as follows: $271 billion in industry profits, $72 billion in Alaskan state tax revenues, and $270 billion in federal tax revenues.

These numbers obviously shape the political economy of ANWR today. It is not surprising why the state of Alaska and oil companies favor drilling. And beyond opposition from environmentalists, many people are unlikely to support policies that further increase the profitability of oil companies, which continue to earn high profits while people pay high prices. So ANWR continues to be contentious.

But perhaps the ANWR question can be recast to minimize conflict and create an opportunity. We should all acknowledge that drilling in ANWR would negligibly satisfy our addiction to oil. Nevertheless, it could provide a massive source of revenue to fund scientific innovation, renewable energy, energy efficiency, and climate change policy. The revenue could be earmarked specifically out of ANWR's tax revenue or taken out of what would otherwise be industry profit.

Consider that the president's 2008 budget for all climate change activities was $7.37 billion. This number generously accounts for all expenditures related to science, technology, international assistance, and energy tax provisions. Clearly, the scope of these programs would change dramatically if even a modest portion of ANWR's $613 billion were directed their way. But, of course, any policy that aims to accomplish this objective would need to ensure safeguards against the types of corruption and incompetence that were recently uncovered in the Interior Department's collection and spending of oil and gas royalties.

We are in serious need of new ideas for simultaneously satisfying our demand for energy and meeting the challenge of global climate change. While helping to satisfy our demand for oil, drilling and redistributing ANWR's benefits might provide a somewhat counterintuitive opportunity—one that is at least worth contemplating. It is possible the environmental community might be willing to trade off uncertain impacts of drilling in a remote area in exchange for real efforts to address other environmental concerns.

Further Reading

Hahn, R., and P. Passell. 2008. The Economics of Allowing More Domestic Oil Drilling. Reg-Markets Center Working Paper 08-21. Washington, DC: Reg-Markets Center. http://ssrn.com/abstract=1265728.

Kotchen. M. J., and N. E. Burger. 2007. Should We Drill in the Arctic National Wildlife Refuge? An Economic Perspective. *Energy Policy* 35: 4720–4729.

Lazzari, S. 2008. *Possible Federal Revenue from Oil Development of ANWR and Nearby Areas.* Congressional Research Service Report for Congress RL34547. Washington, DC: Congressional Research Service.

28. OIL SPILLS

The Deterrent Effects of Monitoring, Enforcement, and Public Information

Mark A. Cohen
is the vice president for research and a senior fellow at Resources for the Future. He also serves as a professor of management and law at Vanderbilt University and an honorary visiting professor in the Department of Economics at the University of York (UK).

Although regulations introduced following the 1989 Exxon Valdez *accident have helped reduce the number of oil spills, oil pollution in coastal waters remains an important policy problem. What are the appropriate roles of deterrence, monitoring, and targeted enforcement policies in reducing the frequency and size of oil discharges?*

A single pint of oil can spread into a film covering an acre of water surface area, degrading the environment and ultimately threatening human health. To encourage compliance with laws prohibiting the discharge of oil, government agencies can hike the penalty for a violation or increase monitoring activities to raise the likelihood that an offender will be caught and punished.

In theory, less monitoring coupled with higher penalties is always beneficial. Taking economist Gary Becker's "crime and punishment" model (1968) to its logical conclusion, the optimal penalty is arbitrarily high, and the optimal expenditure on monitoring approaches zero. In reality, however, such a policy would bankrupt any firm that spilled even a few pints and thus stifle commerce: who would take such a risk?

Consequently, we need a policy that includes a significant amount of monitoring and well-designed penalties for noncompliance. EPA and the Coast Guard both have enforcement powers and conduct monitoring to prevent oil spills. Should a spill occur, U.S. law also requires that the responsible firm report it and clean it up. In the event of an oil spill, EPA and the Coast Guard may assess administrative penalties and require remedial actions, and courts may impose civil or even criminal sanctions on responsible individuals and corporations.

Much has changed in the past two decades. The 1990 Oil Pollution Act (OPA), passed a year after the Exxon *Valdez* spilled more than 10 million gallons of crude into Prince William Sound, states that a company cannot ship oil into the United States until it presents an acceptable plan to prevent spills; it must also have a detailed containment and cleanup plan in case of an oil spill; and all vessels entering U.S. waters must eventually be double-hulled. Since then, the number and volume of spills in U.S. waters have declined considerably, primarily due to the introduction of double-hulled vessels, which have prevented many of the largest spills from occurring. For example, the Coast Guard reports the number of spills to have dropped from about 700 to 400 annually, and the volume of oil spilled reduced from about 5 million gallons to 600,000 gallons annually since OPA was enacted.

But those numbers do not tell the whole story. Not all spills are large and many are not even accidental: vessel operators have been known to clean their bilges out near a port in order to save money, and some spills simply occur through faulty or negligent transfer operations.

Aside from technological mandates such as double-hulled tankers, how effective are the various approaches—monitoring, enforcement, penalties—in deterring oil spills, and what is the best mix?

Assessing data on compliance and enforcement is not an easy task. A reported increase in enforcement activities might indicate more frequent spills, but it could also reflect better monitoring and detection, or more vigorous prosecution. Empirical studies must be carefully designed to sort out the effect that these variables have on actual spill frequency versus spill detection.

Monitoring oil transfer operations has been found effective in reducing oil spill volumes: the crew of a tanker apparently takes more care when the Coast Guard is watching. Such monitoring might also have a general deterrent effect on all vessels that transfer oil: if their captains believe they might be monitored in the future, they probably train their crews and check their equipment more thoroughly, even if they are never actually monitored. Random port patrols looking for oil sheens have a similar influence because they raise the probability of detection for all vessels entering that port. However, compliance inspections themselves have not been found to be as effective as the other two mechanisms.

ALTERNATIVE APPROACHES

Because government monitoring is expensive, three alternatives have been tested: targeted monitoring for vessels thought likely to be out of compliance or likely to spill oil; differential penalties based on prior compliance history, with higher penalties for frequent violators; and mandatory self-reporting, with higher penalties for vessel operators who do not voluntarily report their spills.

Targeted monitoring. In the early 1980s, the Coast Guard began classifying ships as low risk (to be monitored only occasionally) and high risk (always monitored). This two-tiered enforcement policy has been found to be effective in reducing the cost of enforcement without having a negative effect on the environment.

Differential penalties. A 2000 study by Weber and Crew found penalties ranging from \$.01 to \$280 per gallon, and estimated that increasing the fine for large spills from \$1 to \$2 a gallon decreased spillage by 50 percent. They concluded that the current penalty policy—relatively high per-gallon fines for small spills and very low per-gallon fines for large spills—undermined deterrence. Their results parallel mine, that the Coast Guard's statutory maximum penalty of \$5,000 was too small relative to the optimal penalty required. Under OPA, the potential penalties considerably increased, up to \$1,000 per barrel of oil (about \$24 per gallon) discharged.

Self-reporting. To increase deterrence and lower the cost of government monitoring, vessel operators are told they must report any spill, and if the government detects a spill that was not voluntarily reported, the penalty is higher and may include a criminal sanction. Firms found to be out of compliance are more likely to self-report violations in subsequent periods. This suggests that firms try to regain credibility with the government so that they will be taken off a target list.

Firm reputation. Information that a firm has been sanctioned for violating environmental laws may be of interest to shareholders or lenders if the monetary sanction reduces the expected value of the firm and therefore its share price or bond rating. It may also give lenders and insurers pause about risking more capital on that particular firm. Other costs might include future debarment from government contracts, targeted enforcement by EPA, and lost sales to green consumers. Several studies looking at bad environmental news, such as oil or chemical spills or the announcement of civil or criminal enforcement actions, have demonstrated a negative stock price effect; however, the evidence is mixed as to whether or not this price effect simply reflects the expected cost of penalties and cleanup as opposed to any additional reputation penalty.

POLICY IMPLICATIONS

Despite OPA's success in reducing oil spills, costs are still significant. A recent Coast Guard study estimated the total cost of removal and damages from oil spilled since 1990 to be \$1.5 billion. If the government's goal is to improve the environment at the least cost to society, then firms that are the most likely to cause significant harm need to be identified along with those most likely to be responsive to enforcement activities as well as compliance assistance. This kind of empirical evidence can help government agencies plan targeted enforcement measures. Additional evidence on the costs of enforcement and compliance must be gathered, however, to conduct a cost–benefit analysis.

In terms of sanctions, the evidence to date shows little deterrent effect from fines that are only a few thousand dollars. To have any real effect, significantly larger fines and/or targeting individuals instead of firms may be appropriate.

Finally, community pressure and social norms can be important factors in compliance. External market pressures may exert some influence on firm behavior and help prevent oil spills from occurring. Being known as a polluter may induce firms to take precautions, lest consumers and shareholders exact their own form of punishment.

Further Reading

Becker, G.S. 1968. Crime and Punishment: An Economic Approach. *Journal of Political Economy* 76: 169–217.

Cohen, M.A. 1987. Optimal Enforcement Strategy to Prevent Oil Spills: An Application of a Principal-Agent Model with Moral Hazard. *Journal of Law and Economics* 30(1): 23–51.

Cohen, M.A. 1999. Monitoring and Enforcement of Environmental Policy. In *International Yearbook of Environmental and Resource Economics 1999/2000*, edited by Tom Tietenberg and Henk Folmer. Cheltenham, UK: Edward Elgar, 44–106.

Weber, J.M., and R.E. Crew. 2000. Deterrence Theory and Marine Oil Spills: Do Coast Guard Civil Penalties Deter Pollution? *Journal of Environmental Management* 58: 161.

29. TAKING A CLOSER LOOK AT ENERGY SUBSIDIES IN THE FEDERAL TAX CODE

Gilbert E. Metcalf

is a professor of economics at Tufts University and a research associate at the National Bureau of Economic Research. His current research focuses on policy evaluation and design in the area of energy and climate change.

The federal government effectively subsidizes various forms of energy production, through favorable tax treatment. How large are these subsidies, what activities do they affect, and is there an economic rationale for these subsidies?

According to the Office of Management and Budget in President Bush's FY2009 budget submission, the federal government provided over $10 billion in energy-related subsidies through special tax deductions and credits in 2007. But the evidence is mixed on their effectiveness. On the one hand, an increasing share is flowing to nonpolluting energy sources, such as production tax credits for renewable electricity generation. On the other, the tax code continues to provide wasteful subsidies, many of which work at cross purposes with desirable energy policy goals; an example here would be the provision of more generous percentage depletion rather than cost depletion for oil and gas drilling. This does nothing to reduce our reliance on oil and natural gas while probably doing little to encourage increased production given current energy prices.

Tax-based energy subsidies are an increasingly important policy tool: in constant dollars, these subsidies have more than tripled between 1999 and 2007. So how do these subsidies work, and are we getting our money's worth? First, we'll look at the subsidies by fuel type.

Subsidies for renewables currently account for nearly 40 percent of the overall total, with the exemption for ethanol from the federal excise tax on motor vehicle fuels comprising a high percentage. Production tax credits for power generated from renewable sources have been important for encouraging the growing wind market, although they account for less than 7 percent of total tax-based subsidies to energy.

Coal accounts for 25 percent of tax-related subsidies, and 90 percent of that goes to refined coal. (Refined coal is a fuel produced from coal or high-carbon fly ash that is modified to increase its energy content and reduce certain emissions.) This particular subsidy, however, phased out at the end of 2008. Other coal subsidies include, among other things, capital gains tax treatment of royalty payments to owners of land on which coal is mined.

Oil and natural gas received 20 percent of the tax-related subsidies in FY2007. Expensing exploration and development costs and allowing independent producers to use percentage depletion rather than cost depletion account for over three-quarters of this total. President Obama has called for an end to these subsidies, but as of September 2009, Congress had not taken up his request.

Deductions and credits for installation of energy-efficient appliances, solar panels and fuel cells, and home improvements or construction totaled $790 million in 2007. This area is small in the grand scheme but has grown rapidly, from 3 percent of tax subsidies in 1999 to its current 8 percent share. (The remaining subsidies are non-fuel–specific subsidies for the electricity sector.)

CHALLENGING THE STATUS QUO

Three rationales are often cited to support these subsidies: externalities (in this case, the unreimbursed environmental costs) from energy production and consumption, national security, and market failures in energy conservation markets. While externalities are a significant concern, providing subsidies comes with two important caveats. First, a more efficient approach would be to tax the offending activity rather than subsidize clean alternatives, because subsidies lower the cost of consuming energy and so increase demand. Second, subsidies do not always operate on the right margin. For example, subsidizing the production of electric cars exacerbates rather than alleviates congestion on our nation's roadways.

National security concerns suggest a shift from oil and gas—increasingly being supplied by politically unstable countries—toward renewable energy sources. Subsidies for domestic oil and gas production are often touted as contributing to national security, but this ignores the fact that these fuels are priced in world markets. An oil price shock affects the domestic economy whether we are consuming domestic or imported oil. Corn-based ethanol poses an additional problem. By competing with the use of corn as feed, ethanol production drives up agricultural and meat prices, a painful reality that has been well documented in the media. In effect, we are swapping one risk for another: lower energy prices for higher food prices.

The role of market failures in discouraging energy-efficient capital investment cannot be overlooked. Consumers often lack sufficient incentives to change their behavior. Rental housing provides a good example. Tenants who pay directly for their utilities may desire more energy-efficient housing and appliances, but landlords may be reluctant to make necessary improvements out of concern that they cannot recoup their incremental investment through higher rents. And tenants who live in buildings that are not individually metered have no direct incentive to save. The appropriate policy response in this situation is to provide investment tax credits for tenants or landlords for such green investments.

We can do better than our current system of subsidies by taking a three-pronged approach. First, the United States should implement a carbon tax that—for political reasons, as I discuss elsewhere (see Further Reading)—is neutral in terms of both revenue and distribution. The tax rate should be raised gradually and predictably over the next several decades as recommended by—among others—William Nordhaus. Second, the United States should double the federal gasoline tax rate, as supported by the research of Ian Parry and Ken Small (2005), and index it for inflation. The increment over the current tax rate of 18.3 cents per gallon should be earmarked for an Energy Independence Fund and rebated to households on an equal per capita basis. Finally, the United States should double its spending on basic energy-related research and development from the current levels of roughly \$3.5 billion a year as recommended by Richard Newell in a recent Hamilton Project presentation (2007).

For the United States to move toward a carbon-free future and reduce our reliance on oil will require harnessing market forces and unleashing the creativity of our scientific and engineering community. This kind of retooling could come at less than half the cost of our current system of energy subsidies.

Further Reading

Metcalf, Gilbert E. 2007. Designing a Carbon Tax to Reduce U.S. Greenhouse Gas Emissions. *Review of Environmental Economics and Policy* 3(1): 63–83.

Metcalf, Gilbert E. 2007. Federal Tax Policy toward Energy. *Tax Policy and the Economy* 21: 145–184.

Newell, Richard, 2007. Inducing Innovation for Climate Change Mitigation. Hamilton Project presentation, October 30. Washington, DC: Brookings Institution.

Parry, Ian W. H., and Kenneth A. Small. 2005. Does Britain or the United States Have the Right Gasoline Tax? *American Economic Review* 95(4): 1276–89.

30. LEARNING BY DOING AND THE CALIFORNIA SOLAR INITIATIVE

Kenneth Gillingham
is a Ph.D. candidate at Stanford University. His research has focused on the economics and modeling of technological innovation in new energy technologies.

Arthur van Benthem
is a Ph.D. student in economics at Stanford University. His interests and research are in energy and environmental economics.

James L. Sweeney
of Stanford University is the director of the Precourt Institute for Energy Efficiency, a professor of management science and engineering, and a senior fellow at the Stanford Institute for Economic Policy Research, the Hoover Institution, and the Woods Institute for the Environment.

What are some possible rationales for California's program of subsidies for solar photovoltaic installations? In particular, a transitory subsidy is potentially warranted if, by producing a new (immature) technology, firms lower their production costs over time through "learning by doing," and this confers benefits to later producers of the technology.

California has been at the forefront of environmental policy in the United States for the past several decades, with policies like energy efficiency standards and air quality standards often preceding similar legislation at the national level. Recently, California has undertaken one of the largest renewable energy incentive programs in the world: the California Solar Initiative (CSI). The CSI provides for a significant rebate (in dollars per watt) on solar photovoltaic (PV) installations that begins at roughly $3.50 per watt and phases out progressively over the 10 year span of the policy. This ambitious program has spurred the California solar market, but, to this day, solar PV technology remains quite expensive when compared to grid electricity, leading to the question: does this significant investment make sense?

SOLAR POLICY IN CALIFORNIA

Let's first examine how solar policy has evolved in California. The state's interest in solar energy is not at all surprising—California enjoys copious sunshine and has strong environmental values, as well as an enviable base in high technology. In fact, solar policy in California is nothing new; a sizable rebate per installation was in place before 1998, and a tax credit has been in place since 2001. These have served to foster a rapidly growing solar PV industry—from under 5 megawatts (MW) installed in 2000 to nearly 198 MW installed by the end of 2006.

Nevertheless, the solar PV market in California has faced two major hurdles: cost and uncertainty. Electricity from solar PV systems is much more costly than grid-based electricity, due to the high up-front cost of PV installation. Solar PV electricity often costs roughly 20 cents per kilowatt-hour (kWh), which is much greater than the price of grid electricity—in the order of 12 to 15 cents per kWh in California. Prior to the initiative, solar subsidies were subject to renewal each year, leaving investors and solar installers with variable prospects. For these reasons, solar energy makes up only a tiny fraction of the total electricity supply in California—even today it is less than 0.5 percent.

In January 2004, Governor Schwarzenegger set in motion the plan that would eventually become the CSI, through his evocatively named Million Solar Roofs Initiative. The California Public Utilities Commission's January 12, 2006, rulemaking implemented key elements of this original vision and created the CSI, providing the assurance of incentives over 10 years, at a revenue cost of approximately $3 billion per year.

The incentives are implemented as a rebate in dollars per installed watt, paid for by an electricity ratepayer surcharge. They can be applied to residential, commercial, industrial, or even government installations, but not to central generation solar (solar thermal plants, for example). Importantly, the incentives are designed to be progressively phased out over the 10-year policy life span, corresponding to an expected decline in the cost of solar PV technology due to learning by doing, as explained below—a key element of the justification in Sacramento for the solar incentives.

RATIONALE FOR SOLAR INCENTIVE POLICIES

If solar PV technology is so much more expensive, why should California bother to subsidize it? A few primary arguments stand. The first is the most well-known: more electricity from solar will mean less electricity from fossil fuels, thereby avoiding the well-known environmental externalities. The second is that peak solar radiation is highly correlated with times of high electricity spot prices, such as in the middle of a summer day, and consumers do not take this correlation into account because they only face the mean price of electricity, namely the price for kilowatts per hour.

A third argument is more controversial, but turns out to be critical. There is evidence suggesting a learning-by-doing (LBD) effect, whereby the cost of solar installations declines as cumulative solar installations increase. On the surface, LBD may not seem to provide motivation for public policy. But if the installation of an additional solar PV system today leads to less expensive solar PV systems for all firms in the future—that is, there is a spillover effect that the individual firm cannot capture—then the profit-maximizing firm will install fewer systems today than what would result in socially optimal environmental and consumer benefits.

IS THE CSI JUSTIFIED?

We aimed to answer this question by developing a model of the California solar market. Our results suggest that LBD spillover effects that cannot be fully captured by the individual firm are critical to justifying the CSI. We find that without these effects from LBD, the CSI cannot be justified by the combination of its environmental and temporal correlation benefits alone. However, by inclusion of these LBD effects, we find an important result: the CSI can be justified on the grounds of improving economic efficiency. The consumer benefits from reduced PV installation costs in the future, resulting from additional installations today, greatly outweigh the environmental benefits—tipping the balance in favor of the CSI. Moreover, we find that the socially optimal policy may be quite similar to the CSI.

Here's why. The cost of a solar PV installation can be broken into three major components: the module made up of the PV cells, the electric inverter to convert the electricity generated by the cells, and the remainder, which covers the balance of the system—namely, marketing, management, supply chains, and the physical installation, which combined make up roughly just under half of the total cost of an installation. It is this last component of the total cost that is the most relevant here, for there is some evidence to suggest localized LBD. The idea is pretty straightforward: as installers gain more experience, some of this knowledge will spill over to other California installers. This benefit, not captured by the individual installing the system now, is large enough to justify the CSI subsidy on economic efficiency grounds. However, our key result is that without this LBD effect, the cost of the CSI cannot be justified on economic grounds.

The model quantifies these separate impacts. The present value of the decreased costs of future installations due to LBD caused by one additional installed kilowatt of solar is estimated to be $1,140; the present value environmental benefit from reduced carbon dioxide (CO_2), even if we assume a CO_2 damage of $50 per ton of CO_2, is only $192. This numerical estimate indicates that the primary motivation for solar policy in California should be LBD. If we do not believe that there are LBD spillovers, the environmental reasons alone are not sufficient to justify the ambitious CSI.

Further Reading

Borenstein, S. 2008. The Market Value and Cost of Solar Photovoltaic Electricity Production. CSEM Working Paper 176. Berkeley, CA: University of California Energy Institute.

Duke, R., R. Williams, and A. Payne. 2005. Accelerating Residential PV Expansion: Demand Analysis for Competitive Electricity Markets. *Energy Policy* 33(15): 1912–1929.

Nemet, G. 2006. Beyond the Learning-Curve: Factors Influencing Cost Reductions in Photovolatics. *Energy Policy* 34(17): 3218–3232.

van Benthem, A., K. Gillingham, and J. Sweeney. 2008. Learning-by-Doing and the Optimal Solar Policy in California. *Energy Journal* 29(3): 131–151.

31. OPPOSING THE CHICKEN OR OPPOSING THE EGG?

New Challenges in Siting Networked Energy Facilities

Shalini Vajjhala
studies and maps the social implications of environmental and economic policies. This commentary was written while she was a full-time fellow at Resources for the Future.

Meeting the ever-rising demand for electricity, as the U.S. population and real income continue to grow, implies a steady expansion in electricity transmission infrastructure and the number of power plants. For this expansion to occur smoothly, it is critical that policymakers address various obstacles to siting new energy infrastructure at the local level.

Everyone is talking energy these days. With record-high oil prices and the looming prospect of a price on carbon, citizens and policymakers alike are calling for major changes in our energy systems. Some are pushing for a large-scale shift to renewable energy resources, while others are calling for expansion of existing low-carbon technologies, like nuclear power. And still others are looking to entirely new technologies, like geologic carbon sequestration, to reduce greenhouse gas emissions and meet demand.

Change is in the air, but what is not clear is where that change will show up on the ground. Everyone seems to agree that, as a whole, our nation's energy infrastructure is in need of upgrading at minimum and complete restructuring at the other end of the scale. But the process of siting, or finding locations for specific facilities on the ground, remains a daunting challenge. There is little agreement on what the energy future should look like, especially locally, and protests continue to rage against new projects. Even if there is broad support for change, it is not certain that there will be support for any given project. Take, for example, Cape Wind in Nantucket Sound. This proposal, for 130 wind turbines off the coast of Massachusetts, has moved slowly through years of regulatory reviews and high-profile opposition.

The Cape Wind project is an extreme example of the types of siting difficulties that can plague energy projects. More commonly, there are three main causes of siting difficulty that affect a wide range of energy facilities: environmental barriers, regulatory roadblocks, and public opposition. Environmental conditions, such as inhospitable terrain, are often dealt with quietly, early on in a project's design and proposal phases. In contrast, public opposition is the siting hurdle that receives the most attention, because it frequently arises after a project proposal is submitted for regulatory approval. Moreover, opposition can extend project timelines from a few years to decades or block projects altogether.

The seriousness of the problem is evident in the acronyms that are now synonymous with public opposition and siting difficulty: NIMBY (not in my backyard) to BANANA (build absolutely nothing anywhere near anything). In the midst of this siting alphabet soup, it is often overlooked that people generally oppose a project's location, not the service it provides. In fact, we demand that electricity and transportation fuel be widely available and extremely reliable whenever we want to flip a switch or fill up the tank. We just don't want to look at the power plants and refineries that provide these services.

HINGED INFRASTRUCTURES

This is especially true for the networked infrastructures—power lines and pipelines—that support the services that everyone wants but no one wants to see. These "hinged infrastructures" face unprecedented siting challenges. As the push for energy system transformation has grown stronger, opposition to different types of energy facilities has also strengthened. Opponents of a specific project or a new technology now have the option of opposing a project itself, and then if that fails, they can oppose the power lines or pipelines that connect the project to a larger network, effectively stifling the entire project at a key choke point—the link to the network. In the case of Cape Wind, opponents of the project split their attention among the impacts of the wind turbines, the cables buried in the seabed to carry electricity to the shore, and the power lines on land.

The chicken-and-egg relationship between energy facilities and the networks that support them has evolved recently, in the wake of industry deregulation. Electric utilities are no longer vertically integrated as they once were. Now separate companies manage generation, transmission, and distribution assets. This means that large-scale generation capacity additions and upgrades to the grid as a whole are no longer evaluated jointly. Instead, additions are considered on a facility-by-facility basis. Without *existing* power lines, many projects are unlikely to cross the threshold of economic viability, and without adequate generation capacity in place to justify new transmission construction, investment in new lines also is unlikely to occur.

A HOUSE OF CARDS

This piecemeal approach to expanding and upgrading our energy networks has profound implications for making any large-scale shift to new resources or technologies. Major energy facilities are constrained by the different fuels they use, and resources are located in very different places—with different trade-offs. For example, a site that would support 100 MW of wind power will not likely be the same spot that would most effectively produce 100 MW of solar power, or the same size as one that would support most cheaply a coal plant with carbon sequestration. Therefore, developers cannot easily switch projects or sites. In other words, Cape Wind will never become Cape Coal to keep the lights on in coastal Massachusetts.

As a result, opponents to *local* energy projects are faced with few clear trade-offs: if they win, they keep their beautiful views and their reliable power, while developers find other sites or projects. But eventually, something will have to give. Before this happens, policymakers must work to realign our energy network priorities to smooth joint siting processes for primary facilities and secondary network infrastructure, ranging from power lines for renewables to pipelines for CO_2 sequestration, especially in areas that are isolated from existing grids.

The Energy Policy Act of 2005 made some encouraging early steps in this direction with mandates to develop integrated energy corridors on federal lands in the western United States and National Interest Electric Transmission Corridors across the country. However, implementation of these mandates and the resulting corridor designations have generated controversy and opposition in and of themselves. Despite setbacks, these and other initiatives to identify publicly acceptable solutions to coordinated network development are critical. Without them, the push for energy system transformation, no matter how strong, could grind to a halt with local opposition to either the chicken or the egg.

Further Reading

National Commission on Energy Policy. 2006. Siting Critical Energy Infrastructure: An Overview of Needs and Challenges. White Paper. Washington, DC: National Commission on Energy Policy.

Vajjhala, Shalini. 2007. Siting Difficulty and Renewable Energy Development: A Case of Gridlock. *Resources* 164(Winter). Washington, DC: Resources for the Future.

Vajjhala, Shalini, and P. Fischbeck. 2007. Quantifying Siting Difficulty: A Case Study of U.S. Transmission Line Siting. *Energy Policy* 35(1): 650–671.

Vajjhala, Shalini, Anthony Paul, Richard Sweeney, and Karen Palmer. 2008. Green Corridors: Linking Interregional Transmission Expansion and Renewable Energy Policies. Discussion paper 08-06. Washington, DC: Resources for the Future.

32. THE GREENING OF BUILDINGS

George S. Tolley
is a professor emeritus of economics at the University of Chicago, where he received his Ph.D. in economics. He has been a professor in the department since 1966 and is currently the president of RCF Economic and Financial Consulting, Inc.

Sabina Shaikh
is a lecturer in public policy studies and the Program on Global Environment at the University of Chicago. She also serves as a senior research economist at RCF Economic and Financial Consulting, Inc.

A quiet grassroots revolution has been taking place in the design of new buildings, which has important implications for the environment. Why do so many designers seek to obtain green building certification without any prodding from the government, and how might the current rating system for green buildings be improved?

Spontaneous actions below the federal level are emerging as a burgeoning source of efforts to improve the environment. One such trend is the growing green building movement, which encompasses many cities, educational institutions, other nonprofit organizations, and private developers.

The central idea is to focus more holistically on buildings as a source of multiple environmental effects. Design features that determine how an entire building affects environmental goals are considered. A strong case can be made for this approach: according to the U.S. Green Building Council (USGBC), the operation of buildings accounts for nearly 40 percent of primary energy use, 71 percent of electricity consumption, and nearly 40 percent of carbon dioxide emissions in the United States.

Buildings offer impressive opportunities for pollution abatement. A report by McKinsey (Creyts et al. 2007) singles out buildings as a cluster with particularly great abatement potential. Promoting green buildings conserves energy and water, reduces greenhouse gas emissions, and provides state-of-the-art modern facilities for office and residential use.

A major catalyst to the growth of the green building movement has been the green building rating system known as Leadership in Energy and Environmental Design (LEED), promulgated by the USGBC. Earning LEED certification announces to the world that a building has met strict green standards. LEED for new construction (LEED-NC) began through pilot programs in the 1990s and was established as a rating system in 2000 for new commercial buildings. Since 2000, LEED has been expanded to include existing commercial buildings and residential homes, and is now being used cooperatively in evaluating the greenness of entire communities. USGBC expects that by 2010, approximately 10 percent of new commercial construction will be LEED certified.

The green building movement offers a significant and novel advantage over traditional environmental protection efforts, in that it is essentially free. Emanating from grassroots support, it comes at no cost to the federal government, either in tax dollars or in the burden of federally mandated regulations, since LEED certification is above and beyond existing building codes. The green building movement has come so far and so quickly for several reasons.

A first, perhaps primary reason for growth is that green buildings can reduce overall building costs and therefore contribute to a builder's bottom line. In the normal course of events, architects change a variety of things over time, ranging from building layout to details of heating choices and the like, in response to changing material prices and technological developments. Organizations such as USGBC are, in part, vehicles for helping building designers keep up with the times. Claims of cost reductions that are made by green building proponents are consistent with the fact that these practices are being adopted voluntarily.

A second reason for going green is that it will appeal to potential tenants. Going green can be a good marketing strategy; a green building may command higher rents, quicker sales, and greater retention than a traditional one.

A third reason for the spread of green buildings is the influential role played by architects in shaping building aesthetics. Building styles are inevitably influenced to a greater or lesser extent by incentives to keep down costs, but final design choices are still made by architects in conjunction with their clients.

A fourth reason helping to explain why developers provide green buildings is local and governmental impetus. Some cities put LEED-certified buildings first in line in issuing permits and other regulatory matters that a builder faces. Policies such as Chicago's green permits, or Los Angeles's ordinance that requires all privately built projects over 50,000 square feet to meet a "standard of sustainability," rely on LEED ratings for implementation. U.S. government policy now states that new federally owned buildings will be LEED certified.

But the LEED system is experiencing growing pains: while now being treated as a standard for new construction, it was originally designed as a reward system and not a set of building codes with such widespread implications. LEED-NC also lacks standard operating or maintenance requirements, which raise concerns about the long-term effectiveness of the current version for reaching policy objectives. USGBC is aware of these and other issues and is actively working on more systematic rating systems for future versions of LEED.

Green building certification in its present state is not perfect, but, after all, no practical environmental tool ever is. Nevertheless, we have some recommendations.

Sort out the goals toward which green building measures are aimed. Points toward green building certification can be earned for approximately 70 different individual measures, which are categorized under six objectives: sustainable sites, water efficiency, energy and atmosphere, materials and resources, indoor environmental quality, and innovation and design. A challenge is to recognize differences in the importance of the individual measures—first, to the related objective, and second, to a balancing among objectives. For instance, reduction of greenhouse gas emissions and reduction of dependence on foreign oil might well be given explicit recognition as important objectives, in view of the fact that they are externalities from the point of view of individual behavior that need special encouragement.

Estimate the typical effect of each recommended measure in quantitative terms, and rank the measures that contribute to a given common goal by their effectiveness in contributing to the goal. As an example, among the eight measures that can earn points toward certification under the sustainable sites objective, brownfield redevelopment and light pollution reduction can both earn 1 point each, suggesting that they are of equal importance. It should be possible to choose a metric for measuring sustainability and to quantify the effects more precisely than giving each equal weight.

Rethink the weights given to different goals. The points given to each of the 70 possible measures that can earn qualification depend in part on the weights given to the overarching goals. For example, the maximum possible number of points for measures contributing to indoor environmental quality is 15, while for energy and atmosphere the number is 17. At first glance, these two goals appear equally important, though the number of possible measures under each is similar. Underlying a point system, either implicitly or explicitly, is a choice of the relative importance of different goals. While all the measures are commendable, how commendable are they in relative terms? More thought needs to be given to this dilemma.

Choose the total point requirement for certification so as to maximize program effectiveness. If the total number of points required for certification is too low, qualifying will be too easy and the certification will lose its meaning. If too high, it will be viewed as impossible to achieve and lose effectiveness as an incentive.

Estimate the contribution of the green building movement to achieving national and world environmental improvement. Suppose the United States were to make a commitment to reducing greenhouse gas emissions by 10 percent. In order carry this out, how could green buildings contribute to this goal? The answer would influence the emissions reductions to be sought from other sources.

This list is by no means exhaustive. Green buildings offer a promising approach to improving the environment. This approach deserves more attention from economic researchers and environmental policy analysts than it has yet received.

Further Reading

Creyts, J., A. Derkach, S. Nyquist, K. Ostrowski, and J. Stephenson. 2007. Reducing Greenhouse Gas Emissions. How Much at What Cost? Executive Report, U.S. Greenhouse Gas Mapping Initiative. Washington, DC: McKinsey & Company. www.mckinsey.com/clientservice/ccsi/pdf/US_ghg_final_report.pdf.

Gill, G. 2007. Designing Sustainable Buildings. *Urban Land* 66(6): 54–59.

Heinfeld, D. 2007. Putting the "Green Costs More" Myth to Rest. *Urban Land* 2(1): 56–61.

U.S. Green Building Council. 2008. *U.S. Green Building by the Numbers. Green Building Facts.* Washington, DC: U.S. Green Building Council.

33. WHY INTERNATIONAL NATURAL GAS MARKETS MATTER IN TODAY'S ENERGY AND ENVIRONMENTAL PICTURE

Steven A. Gabriel

is an associate professor at the University of Maryland. His research interests include optimization, equilibrium, and statistical modeling in energy, transportation, land use, and wastewater treatment.

What are the recent trends in natural gas markets? How vulnerable is the United States to worldwide disruptions in the supply of natural gas and possible abuse of market power by a group of OPEC-like countries?

In recent years, the environmental and economic value of natural gas has soared, making it an ever-important fuel for power generation, industrial operations, as well as residential and commercial use. Natural gas holds a favorable environmental position relative to coal and oil, all the more important given the current move toward a low-carbon world. In the United States, demand for natural gas rose over 33 percent in the period 1986–2006, driven by a multitude of factors. In Europe, geopolitical issues are more pronounced, as almost half of the European Union's imports of gas come from Russia. Additionally, there is now competition in both the Atlantic and Pacific basins for liquefied natural gas (LNG) from exporting countries. The overall picture then is one of a global competition for this important fuel source.

Two other trends have emerged over the last two and a half decades that have helped to spur both domestic and international natural gas consumption. The first was the enactment of regulations geared at liberalizing gas markets. In the United States, the Federal Energy Regulatory Commission required interstate pipeline companies to unbundle, or separate, their sales and transportation services in order to promote competition and mitigate their potential market power. Similar legislative measures were enacted in the European Union that promoted third-party access and legal splitting of gas sellers and network operators.

The second trend is the rise of liquefied natural gas trading. LNG is the liquid form of this fuel, achieved by cooling the normally gaseous substance to about –260° and removing certain components. By using specialized cryogenic tankers, natural gas can be moved much more easily around the world, but this process is costly. While there is not yet a common "world gas price" as in the case with oil, there are some very large producers. Nearly 75 percent of the world's natural gas reserves can be found in the Middle East and Eurasia, with reserves in Russia, Iran, and Qatar combined accounting for nearly 60 percent of this total, resulting in geopolitical market power. For example, the influence of Russian production and control of key pipelines was felt in Ukraine and Western Europe in the winter of 2005–2006, when Russia temporarily cut off gas to Ukraine over a price dispute, which affected downstream Europe.

In the United States, dependence on natural gas from other countries has been rising over time. Imports of natural gas as a percentage of total consumption rose from just over 4 percent in 1986 to almost 16 percent in 2006. Colleagues and I have created detailed game theoretic models of market equilibria in which producers (or their marketing arms) may withhold production in order to achieve higher profits. The resulting simulations indicate that market power can raise natural gas prices considerably. Compared with an assumption of perfectly competitive producers in Europe (that is, producers not having the ability to influence market prices by withholding production), the effects of market power raise European prices by some 27 percent. This is further exacerbated if a major supplier such as Algeria is shut down or gas from Russia is curtailed through a transit country such as Ukraine.

While the demand for natural gas is rising, this is not cause for immediate concern if you consider the reserves-to-production ratios, which give an estimate of the number of years left if current production rates hold into the future. For example, the worldwide reserves-to-production ratio is 65 years, with higher values for certain regions such as Russia (80 years) and the Middle East (more than 100 years).

Despite a number of years of available gas left, many countries are seeking to diversify their supply sources and mitigate the market power held by the major suppliers. Rather than rely on pipelines to deliver gas, several "downstream" European countries have set up and are increasing their numbers of LNG regasification (import) terminals, which convert natural gas back to gaseous form for use in regional pipelines.

The impact of building more LNG regasification terminals can be a greater choice of prices and other contractual terms for the downstream countries. More LNG terminals are in the works also for the United States. The current five LNG import terminals, accounting for just over 5.8 billion cubic feet per day, will be supplemented with four new ones being constructed in the Gulf of Mexico, which will more than double LNG import capacity. Also, Japan already is a huge LNG importer, buying over 40 percent of the worldwide share in 2005. Thus, LNG's importance is a worldwide phenomenon.

How will these global and regional factors affect international natural gas markets in the future? First, in order to satisfy growing demand, exploration efforts will need to increase, which will undoubtedly require larger amounts of capital for harder-to-reach sources and thus, all things being equal, lead to higher prices. These prices may be raised further by the effects of market power, especially in Europe, whose dependence on gas from other countries is significant. Second, the formation of a "gas cartel" like OPEC may be in the offing if major producers like Russia, Iran, and Qatar deem it economically in their interests to cooperate with each other, which could have broad ramifications for gas-consuming countries. Third, while downstream customers are looking for ways to ensure greater security of supply by building LNG facilities and additional pipelines, producers are also interested in "demand security." Specifically, they are looking for assurances that if they spend large sums of money on natural gas infrastructure, their investments will be economically viable. Producing countries could start buying stakes in downstream operations and markets to hedge their positions. Lastly, the importance of natural gas in the cap-and-trade carbon markets that are forming should not be underestimated. If the price of natural gas rises significantly, this increase affects these markets as coal then becomes more economically appealing, causing allowance prices to go up.

Further Reading

Egging, R., and S.A. Gabriel. 2006. Examining Market Power in the European Natural Gas Market. *Energy Policy* 34(17): 2762–2778.

Egging, R., S.A. Gabriel, F.Holz, and J. Zhuang. 2008. A Complementarity Model for the European Natural Gas Market. *Energy Policy* 36: 2385–2414.

Gabriel, S., A. J. Zhuang, and S. Kiet. 2005. A Large-Scale Complementarity Model of the North American Natural Gas Market. *Energy Economics* 27: 639–665.

Worldwide Look at Reserves and Production. 2006. *Oil and Gas Journal* 104(47): 22–23.

34. ASSESSING ELECTRICITY MARKETS

Prospects and Pitfalls

Timothy Brennan

is a senior fellow at Resources for the Future and a professor of public policy and economics at the University of Maryland, Baltimore County. His research interests include antitrust and regulation, particularly in electricity, telecommunications, and intellectual property.

The electricity sector is a critical piece of the U.S. economy, on which our society depends heavily. Over the past 10 to 15 years, electricity markets have been opened and restructured, and competition has been introduced. How have these changes affected prices, consumers, and reliability?

The electricity sector garners considerable attention and deservedly so. On size alone, it represented about 2.4 percent of GDP in 2005—more than we spend on motor vehicles or gasoline. Large as it is, the sheer size of the sector belies its significance to our society and economy, which literally cannot operate without it. Perhaps the most reported aspect of natural disasters such as hurricanes, following casualty figures, is the extent and persistence of power outages. It is therefore crucial to study and assess the effects of policies that, over the last 10 years, have introduced competition into the previously regulated electricity sector.

Prior to the mid-1990s, the sector was dominated by regulated private utilities that generated, transported, and sold their own electricity. Following the wave of largely successful moves from regulation to competition in other sectors such as telecommunications and transportation—finance is looking a little shaky these days—electricity markets were opened. The federal government began by setting rules for allowing independent generators access to still-regulated transmission networks. A number of states followed by opening retail markets under their control, giving consumers choice over competing retail providers, although generally leaving the traditional utilities in place.

HAS OPENING MARKETS LED TO BETTER (NOT NECESSARILY LOWER) PRICES?

Whether opening electricity markets has helped or hurt consumers is a matter of considerable controversy. From the public's perspective, the case for competition has taken three significant hits: the California market meltdown in 2000–2001, the Northeast Blackout in August 2003, and the rapid rise in electricity rates in many states. Maryland, for example, saw increases in excess of 70 percent in 2006–2007. Partly for these reasons, much of the country retains traditional regulation of monopoly utilities. Only Texas, Illinois, Michigan, and most of the mid-Atlantic and northeastern United States (except Vermont) currently have open electricity markets. Many states, including California and Virginia, have suspended their deregulatory policies.

The public controversy is matched by disagreement among researchers as to the effects of opening electricity markets. Contrary to what competition advocates might expect, a number of studies have found higher prices in areas of the country where electricity markets were opened. Such studies, however, face considerable difficulties. Among these are that the states and regions opting to open markets are likely to be those where prices would have been above average in the first place, creating a spurious correlation between competition and high prices.

Moreover, higher electricity prices under open markets aren't necessarily bad. Because electricity cannot be stored, it has to be produced exactly when needed to avoid blackouts. Consequently, generation capacity has to be in place, to be used only for those few summer hours when demand peaks to run all of our air conditioners. To cover the cost of that capacity, prices in these critical few hours have to be very high, up to 50 times the price at more normal "baseload" times.

These higher prices need not reflect dysfunctional markets or monopoly power, any more than do high summer rates for beachfront hotels. Rather, they can provide suppliers and users with the right signals, so we might turn down our air conditioners and defer optional uses when electricity becomes extraordinarily expensive to generate. A virtue of competition is not that it makes prices lower, but that it ties prices to the costs of producing the electricity needed to meet demand, whether those costs are high or low. But because every supplier gets to charge the high price, this economic virtue comes at a political cost, as electricity bills and generator profits rise. Voters may not have the patience to wait for new generators to come online and drive overall rates and profits back down to competitive levels. If regulators set ceilings on electricity prices to mitigate this effect, funds to pay for peak generation units have to come from other sources. This has led to the institution of wholesale markets in "capacity" on top of those for electricity itself.

DO CONSUMERS WANT MORE CHOICES?

Consumers may be upset about losing their regulatory insulation from facing high prices, but they may also simply not find competition worth the trouble. In most jurisdictions where residential users have been given the opportunity to choose new electricity suppliers, few have done so. A recent Maryland Public Service Commission (MDPSC) study reported that entrants supplied only about 2 percent of residential electricity use in that state.

Although residual rate regulation may have something to do with this, consumers simply may not want to be bothered. A measure of the hassle is the "helpful" assistance many states provided, which effectively told consumers that determining whether they would save money by switching suppliers was about as simple and pleasant as filling out a tax return. It is hardly surprising that most consumers would rather stick with their old utility rather than go to the trouble of switching to save a few dollars a month. That said, the rate of switching by commercial and industrial users is far higher—almost 70 percent of their load, according to that MDPSC report. On that score, the "electricity competition" glass is considerably more than half full.

HAS COMPETITION THREATENED RELIABILITY?

The biggest impediment to opening electricity markets, however, has long been the potential conflict between the independence necessary to realize the fruits of competition and the cooperation potentially needed to maintain reliability. Because electrons take all available paths to get from where electricity is generated to where it is used, the grid operates as a single entity even if different utilities own different lines. If one supplier fails to meet its customers' needs, not only will those customers lose power—the entire grid may go down.

The grid's vulnerability implies the need for some degree of central control—but how much? Ensuring reliability may need only relatively minimal rules, such as reserve requirements, enabling transmission and distribution system operators to obtain energy to get over unexpected emergencies. The challenge to competition is whether control needs to go deeper.

Fostering competition has generally led to the undoing of the traditional integrated utility structure—why opening electricity markets is called "restructuring." Both local distribution lines and regional transmission systems are monopolies. Regulation is unlikely to replace competition of those "wires" in the foreseeable future. If companies owning generation control these lines, they may be able to subvert competition by denying reasonable access to rivals. This concern has motivated regulators to limit such control by requiring separate, independent operation of transmission lines. On the other hand, needing to coordinate large-scale transmission and generation investments may undercut the entrepreneurial initiative that drives the benefits of competition.

The fundamental question in assessing electricity markets is whether they are consistent with keeping the grid efficient, growing, and reliable. The fact that today's controversies about the merits of electricity markets focus on prices, and not on repeats of the California meltdown or the Northeast outage of the early 2000s, suggests that the worst fears regarding reliability have not come to pass—so far. Whether we have been skillful or lucky remains to be seen.

Further Reading

Brennan, Timothy. 2007. Consumer Preference Not to Choose: Methodological and Policy Implications. *Energy Policy* 35: 1616–1627.

Brennan, Timothy. 2008. Generating the Benefits of Competition: Challenges and Opportunities in Opening Electricity Markets. C.D. Howe Institute Commentary 260. Toronto, Ontario: C. D. Howe Institute.

Joskow, Paul. 2006. Markets for Power in the United States: An Interim Assessment. *Energy Journal* 27: 1–36.

Taylor, Jerry, and Peter Van Doren. 2004. Rethinking Electricity Restructuring. *Policy Analysis* 530. Washington, DC: Cato Institute.

PART 3

National Environmental Policies

In the United States, air and water quality has improved considerably over the past 40 years due, at least in part, to the introduction and progressive tightening of regulations on automobile and industrial sources of particulates, sulfur dioxide, lead, and other pollutants. At the same time, there has been increasing recognition of the drawbacks of traditional forms of regulation, such as mandates stipulating technologies that must be used to control pollution. The key attractiveness of market-based approaches, like cap-and-trade and emissions taxes, is that they allow firms the flexibility to choose the lowest cost means of reducing pollution.

As the most serious national environmental challenges have, in part, been addressed, and disenchantment with traditional forms of regulation has generated interest in more novel approaches, national environmental policy issues of the day have diversified in many directions. These are discussed in the collection of commentaries in this section.

More attention is now being paid to other environmental problems, such as hazardous chemicals that are difficult to monitor and regulate, the generation of household waste and its disposal in landfills, agricultural pollution, and pollutants like nitrogen that require a portfolio of control measures. Policymakers have also become interested in to what extent voluntary programs, or businesses acting on their own to become green, may complement, or substitute, for mandatory environmental programs.

Other policy options that are evaluated in this section include how successful programs like the cap-and-trade system to regulate sulfur dioxide might be reformed going forward, to what extent cost/benefit assessments might be used in the design of environmental regulations, and how measures of gross domestic product might account for environmental trends.

Finally, there is greater interest in the distributional impacts of environmental hazards, across different racial and income groups, and how this might be factored into policy reform.

35. WHAT ARE THE BIGGEST ENVIRONMENTAL CHALLENGES FACING THE U.S.?

A broad-brush evaluation of EPA'S role in regulating pollution since its inception in 1970 leads into a discussion of the key challenges facing environmental policymakers in coming decades.

Paul R. Portney
is the dean of Eller College of Management, University of Arizona. He served on the RFF research staff for more than 30 years and as the president of Resources for the Future from 1995 to 2005.

We can pick 1970 to conveniently mark the beginning of the modern environmental era in the United States. After all, that was the year that EPA was created, and with it came significant federalization of environmental protection efforts that had until then been the province of individual states. And that same year saw the passage of amendments to the Clean Air Act, the first really dramatic assertion of power by the federal government in the environmental arena. Two years later, Congress passed what we now refer to as the Clean Water Act, and, in the decade or so to follow, a handful of other federal laws were passed dealing with pesticides, solid and hazardous wastes, and drinking water.

So, where do we stand 30 years later? It's simply beyond dispute that air and water quality have improved in virtually every part of the United States, no matter which pollutants we consider or how we choose to measure them. Moreover, in most parts of the United States today, we treat solid waste—garbage, that is—with about as much care as we handled nuclear wastes back then—a pretty low bar, I realize, though progress has been great. Not only are truly hazardous wastes today treated with even greater care, but their use has been significantly reduced, in part because of the expense of dealing with them in the modern regulatory system. This progress is all the more remarkable because our population has exactly doubled since 1970, and real GDP has tripled.

I know, I know, air quality was improving in at least some U.S. metropolitan areas before 1970, the result of state and city regulations like banning the open burning of leaves and burning household garbage in basement incinerators. And well before 1970, California took on the auto industry and required cars sold there to meet the first vehicle emissions standards in the country. Some analysts have used this to argue that we would have made the same environmental progress had we left matters to the states and not created EPA, nor passed the statutes of the 1970s.

Baloney. It strains credulity to suggest that individual metropolitan areas, or even states, could have mounted as effective a campaign to control air and water pollution from industrial facilities like electric power plants, petroleum refineries, steel mills, paper mills, and cement kilns, among others, as the new EPA did. And it's painful to imagine 50 different sets of standards governing tailpipe emissions from new cars, trucks, and SUVs. Detroit's carmakers would be in even graver condition by now had they been forced to cope with such Balkanization.

Before we bruise our backs patting ourselves too hard, let's remember two things. First, while we have made terrific environmental progress in the United States, we could have accomplished as much, if not more, at much less cost (in the tens of billions annually) had we built our initial federal regulatory apparatus using the kinds of incentive-based approaches that have become the default approach to environmental regulation today. No one likes to hear "I told you so." But economists in the late 1960s and early 1970s, like Allen Kneese, Cliff Russell, and Walter Spofford at RFF, as well as Charles Schultze at Brookings, were pointing out how much more efficient pollution taxes or tradable emissions permits would be than the clumsy command-and-control apparatus EPA was erecting at Congress's behest. The success of the sulfur dioxide emissions trading program established in the 1990 amendments to the Clean Air Act has proved they were right on the money.

Second, while we've done an exceptionally good (if also overly expensive) job of dealing with the environmental problems at which the laws of the 1970s were aimed, we neglected two problems that ought to concern us the most as we look forward in this new century. First, no federal law or regulation has required emissions reductions for carbon dioxide (CO_2) or other greenhouse gases (with the exception of chlorofluorocarbons, or CFCs, which were controlled out of concern for their ozone-depleting potential). While I think there is more uncertainty about the causes and likely consequences of global warming than most scientists suggest, we're nuts not to have instituted gradually increasing controls on CO_2 and other greenhouse gases. The worst-case scenario, especially for future generations, is too scary not to be taking some preventative measures now.

The second environmental problem we face lends itself less to federal control and is not the province of EPA, namely the steady conversion of wilderness and open space to developed uses as our population grows and spreads out. In many respects, we're lucky we're a growing country, both demographically and economically. But as we expand, the wilderness areas and open spaces we enjoy, which are home to a host of species, are getting chewed up in the process. Forget recreation and habitat for a minute. Who doesn't find it pleasing to drive from one place to the next while looking out at forest, fields, or even desert, rather than still another subdivision or shopping mall, however attractive the latter might be? We have never regulated land use very much at the federal level in the United States, and that's not all bad—the thought of social planners in Washington telling local communities who can build what and when, not to mention what it ought to look like, is not reassuring. But leaving the protection of a prototypic public good like open space *solely* to locals surely has its own set of problems. We have to do better at preserving some natural beauty and habitat while still accommodating our growing numbers.

That's how I see it, anyway. I think our environmental laws have served us reasonably well over the years, with the one qualification and two conspicuous exceptions mentioned above. Unfortunately, it is more difficult to conclude that those laws are the appropriate ones for the challenges that lie ahead. Nor am I confident that EPA still has the vitality and creativity to be as effective as it was in the early years, though that is for others to decide.

36. WHERE THINGS STAND WITH HAZARDOUS WASTE REGULATION

Sarah Stafford

is the Verkuil Distinguished Associate Professor of Economics and the associate director of the Thomas Jefferson Program in Public Policy at the College of William and Mary. Her research focuses on hazardous waste regulation and corporate environmental behavior, with an emphasis on compliance and enforcement.

One problem in hazardous waste regulation is the difficulty of ensuring regulatory compliance, not least because violations are often inadvertent. Therefore, complementary programs, such as compliance assistance, environmental audits, and voluntary compliance initiatives, can play a valuable role.

The U.S. economy generates a significant amount of waste. According to recent estimates, on average we generate about 250 million tons of trash each year, or 4.5 pounds per person per day. In addition to municipal solid waste, the United States generates 50 million more tons of hazardous waste each year.

Hazardous waste is a relatively new phenomenon and was not generated in significant quantities until we started using fossil fuels and chemicals in earnest at the beginning of the industrial age. Initially it was not considered to be any different from other waste and so was essentially unregulated. Hazardous constituents were routinely released into the environment, where they polluted groundwater, rivers, and lakes and killed people, livestock, and wildlife. As the consequences of uncontrolled management of waste became clear, the public began to call for regulations to protect human health and the environment.

FIRST, SOME HISTORY

The first environmental law that specifically addressed the generation and management of hazardous waste was the Resource Conservation and Recovery Act (RCRA), passed in 1976. RCRA's Subtitle C delineated the basic structure of federal hazardous waste regulation and required EPA to establish criteria for identifying and listing hazardous waste and to develop standards applicable to generators, transporters, and managers of hazardous waste. In 1984, Congress passed the Hazardous and Solid Waste Amendments (HSWA), which expanded the scope of RCRA by requiring EPA to develop treatment standards for hazardous waste, minimum technological requirements for hazardous waste management units, and a corrective action program for contamination at active waste management facilities. Together these two acts provide the mandate for EPA's current hazardous waste program, commonly referred to as the RCRA program, which covers hazardous waste "from the cradle to the grave."

Although hazardous waste is often referred to as toxic waste, a material does not have to be toxic to be considered hazardous. Hazardous waste includes any discarded material that is potentially harmful to human health and the environment because it is ignitable, corrosive, reactive, or toxic, as long as the material has not been specifically excluded from the definition of hazardous waste. Two major categories of waste have the potential to be classified as hazardous but have explicitly been excluded from regulation as such—agricultural and mining wastes.

Even with these exclusions, the RCRA-regulated universe is both large and diverse, including well over 600,000 facilities in the United States, ranging from large chemical manufacturers and petroleum refiners to small dry cleaners and photo finishers. Nonprofit and government entities, such as hospitals, universities, and military bases, generate hazardous waste as well.

Interestingly, perhaps the most well-known toxic waste sites—Superfund sites—are not part of the RCRA universe. The Superfund program was established separately to cover cleanup of hazardous waste at inactive or abandoned sites and hazardous waste spills that require an emergency response, whereas RCRA covers only active hazardous waste facilities.

MUCH SKEPTICISM

RCRA is a relatively mature program, and over the past decade there have been only minor changes to hazardous waste regulations. With no new regulations to implement, EPA has turned its focus toward waste minimization and improving regulatory compliance.

Waste minimization, which includes both pollution prevention and increased recycling, has been promoted primarily through voluntary initiatives such as WasteWise, the National Environmental Performance Track, and Responsible Care. The majority of these programs are cross-media and, in theory, have the potential to increase environmental performance because they encourage facilities to think holistically about their environmental impacts. Both industry and EPA have been enthusiastic about such programs, but many in the environmental community are more doubtful because of the general lack of public accountability or oversight.

Over the past few years, researchers have conducted a number of studies to analyze the effectiveness of voluntary environmental programs. Only a few have been able to show that voluntary programs can significantly improve performance for more than a limited set of facilities. This lack of evidence may be behind EPA Administrator Lisa Jackson's suspension of the National Environmental Performance Track.

Under previous EPA administrators, voluntary programs were not limited only to waste minimization efforts; during the Bush administration, the agency placed increased emphasis on voluntary compliance initiatives and self-policing. But still, neither voluntary nor command-and-control approaches appear adequate to get the job done. Many are skeptical that voluntary efforts are effective at increasing compliance, while others doubt that traditional enforcement can bring all facilities into compliance because many violations appear to be due to confusion or ignorance, rather than deliberate decisions to violate the rules.

Although a facility may knowingly violate RCRA regulations by sending hazardous waste to a nonhazardous waste landfill for disposal, it may also inadvertently violate regulations if one of its hazardous waste storage tanks leaks. Traditional enforcement measures, such as inspections and fines, can help decrease the level of deliberate violations by making violations more expensive for the facility. When EPA revised its RCRA penalty policy in 1991 by drastically increasing its fines to 10 or 20 times the previous fine levels, hazardous waste compliance increased. Similarly, increasing the probability of a compliance inspection has been shown to increase the likelihood that a facility will comply with RCRA regulations.

For inadvertent violations, however, increasing penalties and inspections may not be very effective at increasing compliance. Facilities may be noncompliant because they do not fully understand the regulatory requirements, do not fully know their facility's operations, have poor internal environmental management systems, or do not have the ability to comply. Alternative policies such as compliance assistance or environmental audits may help to increase compliance.

In my research, I have found some evidence to support the effectiveness of compliance assistance programs. In a study on RCRA compliance behavior to try to determine whether facilities were deliberately or inadvertently violating hazardous waste regulations, facilities in states with compliance assistance programs were found to be less likely to violate than facilities in states without them. Environmental auditing has not been shown to be as effective. While facilities in states with environmental audit privilege and self-policing policies are less likely to violate, a more recent study of Michigan hazardous waste facilities suggests that facilities that implement environmental audit programs are not any more likely to be in compliance than facilities that do not audit.

Although the data on the ability of voluntary compliance programs to improve environmental performance are limited, I nonetheless believe that there is an important role for such programs to play in complementing traditional enforcement and improving compliance in the future. Facilities violate hazardous waste regulations for a variety of reasons, and we must develop an equally wide range of initiatives and programs to increase compliance. Voluntary programs should not supplant traditional enforcement efforts but instead should be used in tandem.

Further Reading

Evans, Mary, Lirong Liu, and Sarah Stafford. 2009. A Facility-Level Analysis of the Long-Term Consequences of Environmental Auditing among Hazardous Waste Generators. Department of Economics Working Paper 78. Williamsburg, VA: College of William and Mary.

Khanna, Madhu, and Keith Brouhle. 2008. Effectiveness of Voluntary Environmental Initiatives. In *Governing the Environment: Interdisciplinary Perspectives*, edited by M. Delmas and O. Young. Cambridge, UK: Cambridge University Press.

Porter, Richard C. 2002. *The Economics of Waste*. Washington, DC: RFF Press.

Stafford, Sarah L. 2006. Rational or Confused Polluters? Evidence from Hazardous Waste Compliance. *Contributions to Economic Analysis and Policy* 5: Article 21.

37. REINSTATING THE SUPERFUND TAXES

Good or Bad Policy?

Kate Probst

is a senior fellow at Resources for the Future. She has conducted numerous analyses of environmental programs, focusing mainly on improving the implementation of Superfund and other hazardous waste management programs.

This discussion of the state of funding for the cleanup of polluted sites under EPA's Superfund Program adds context to the debate about whether to reinstate dedicated taxes for the program to supplement general revenue sources and, potentially, increase program funding.

With Democrats back in power in both Congress and the White House, there is a renewed effort to reinstate the taxes that once stocked the Superfund trust fund. While proponents argue that the taxes are critical to ensuring that the "polluter pays," the reality is a little more complicated. Two questions are always raised in this perennial debate: (1.) Does EPA need more money to pay for Superfund cleanups? The unequivocal answer is "yes." And, (2.) Should the taxes that once stocked the Superfund trust fund be reinstated? Here, the answer is "maybe."

While it has been nearly 30 years since the law was first implemented, there are still sites contaminated with hazardous substances that need to be cleaned up. To date, 1,596 sites have been placed on EPA's National Priorities List (NPL), all highly contaminated sites where trust fund monies can be used to pay for cleanups. While construction of the proposed remedy is completed at the majority of those sites (1,065), more work remains to be done at fully one-third (531).

Just because implementation of the remedy is complete does not mean that cleanup goals at the site have been achieved. At many sites, long-term operation and monitoring activities will continue for years, if not decades, requiring government oversight. And the percentage of sites where remedies are implemented—and paid for—directly by those parties responsible has been decreasing. For much of the 1990s, private parties paid for 70 percent of site remedies. By FY2008, this figure had fallen to 56 percent. While it would be nice to think that we no longer need the Superfund program, this simply is not the case.

But first, a little funding history. The Comprehensive Environmental Response, Compensation, and Liability Act (CERCLA)—better known as Superfund—put in place two mechanisms for ensuring the cleanup of sites contaminated with hazardous substances: broad liability provisions to require the "responsible parties" to pay for and implement cleanups themselves and a dedicated trust fund to provide funds for the government to clean up sites where those responsible did not have needed funds, had gone out of business, or were recalcitrant.

For the first five years of the program, total appropriations were $1.6 billion, and the majority of the funds came from excise taxes on petroleum and chemical feedstocks, plus additional funding from general revenues. When Congress reauthorized the program in 1986, annual appropriations were increased to $1.6 billion, thus *quintupling* the size of the program. Congress added a third tax to generate revenues for the Superfund trust fund, the corporate environmental income tax, which was based on every corporation's modified alternative minimum taxable income. Many different kinds of companies paid this tax, not just the chemical and petroleum companies subject to the excise taxes.

When authority for the Superfund taxes expired at the end of 1995, annual appropriations for the program did not decrease immediately, because of a large unobligated balance in the trust fund. Appropriations continued at approximately $1.5 billion through FY1999. Annual appropriations declined to $1.2 billion in FY2003, where they have pretty much stayed ever since.

But by the late 1990s, it was clear that EPA was experiencing a shortfall in funds needed for cleanup. Work by Resources for the Future in 2001 estimated a "best case" funding shortfall of just over $2 billion over the 10 years from FY2000 through FY2009. In the years since then, EPA's Office of the Inspector General and senior EPA officials have documented funding shortfalls that have prevented remediation from moving forward at a host of specific sites. The number of sites each year where cleanup activities are completed—which reached a high of about 80 sites per year in the late 1990s—fell to 47 in FY2001 and to an all-time low (not counting the first few years of the program) of 24 in FY2007.

While fewer sites are being added to the NPL each year—in FY2008, only 18 new sites were added—the funding shortfall is likely to continue for the foreseeable future. Just how big this deficit is, and how long it will continue, is unknown as there have been no comprehensive estimates of funding needs made public since the RFF report that was released nine years ago.

In addition, it has become clear that some of the sites that warrant federal attention—mining sites and contaminated waterways—are among the most complex and expensive types of sites to remediate. No public estimates exist regarding how many of these sites will likely be placed on the NPL in the future.

TO TAX OR NOT TO TAX?

Supporters see reinstating the expired Superfund taxes as a way to increase funding for cleanups. And when the trust fund was flush, appropriations were certainly higher. According to the U.S. Government Accountability Office, from 1981 through 1995, taxes accounted for about 68 percent of trust fund revenues. From FY1996, when the tax expired, through FY2007, however, taxes accounted for just 6 percent of all trust fund revenues.

But in these difficult economic times, it is worth asking whether it makes sense to reinstate one, two, or three distinct taxes—with their attendant transaction costs—to raise what is, in fact, a minuscule amount of funding in the overall federal budget.

What, then, about the argument that reinstating the taxes will ensure that the polluter pays? While this sounds good, it really does not hold water. It is true that the Superfund taxes are paid by private industry, and that a large percentage of the taxes are levied on corporations that produce hazardous chemicals and substances that contaminate the environment. And, in some cases, it is likely that the companies paying the taxes did contaminate sites and groundwater, and may well have sites that have been—or will be—cleaned up either through federal enforcement actions or because they are on the NPL.

But those companies that contaminated sites and are now out of business will not be paying Superfund taxes in the future. And many companies that will pay the taxes include entities already being held liable for cleanup and paying directly for site-specific activities.

Before seeking to reinstate the Superfund taxes, Congress should focus on figuring out the program's real funding needs. Sadly, the questions that need to be asked—and answered—today are much the same as those Congress asked RFF to address a decade ago:

- How much will it cost to clean up those sites already on the NPL?
- How many and what kinds of sites are likely to be added to the NPL in the near future?
- What are the likely costs of postcleanup activities for NPL sites?

With a new administration in the White House and at EPA, it is time to increase the transparency of the Superfund program. EPA should, on its own, commit to again preparing an annual progress report on the Superfund program that clearly lays out past accomplishments, future challenges, and future funding needs. To ensure the integrity of this effort, EPA should create an outside review panel to evaluate the proposed data and methodologies before the analysis is conducted, and also review the interim results and final report.

Further Reading

Probst, Katherine N., Don Fullerton, Robert E. Litan, and Paul R. Portney. 1995. *Footing the Bill for Superfund Cleanups: Who Pays and How?* Washington, DC: RFF Press and Brookings Institution.

Probst, Katherine N., and David M. Konisky with Robert Hersh, Michael B. Batz, and Katherine D. Walker. 2001. *Superfund's Future: What Will It Cost?* Washington, DC: RFF Press.

Ramseur, Jonathan, Mark Reisch, and James McCarthy. 2008. *Superfund Taxes or General Revenues: Future Funding Issues for the Superfund Program*. Congressional Research Service (CRS) Report to Congress. Updated February 4, 2008. Order Code RL31410. Washington, DC: U.S. Congressional Research Service.

U.S. GAO (Government Accountability Office). 2008. *Superfund: Funding and Reported Costs of Enforcement and Administration Activities*. July 18. Washington, DC: U.S. GAO.

38. TRASH TALK

Don Fullerton

is the Gutgsell Professor of Finance at the University of Illinois. He specializes in environmental and energy economics, public economics, and taxation.

Margaret Walls

is the Thomas J. Klutznick Senior Fellow at Resources for the Future. She specializes in environmental and energy policy and urban land use.

What are the merits of charging households by the can or bag for their garbage, and what other policies might help promote conservation of trash without encouraging illegal dumping?

An inevitable by-product of our consumer society is the generation of trash. And continued economic development combined with population growth in communities across the United States and around the world are only making matters worse.

In this country, the problem is a big one. Americans generate about 4.5 pounds of trash per person per day, 95 percent more than our neighbors to the north in Canada, 64 percent more than Australians, and 37 percent more than the French. This high per capita rate, combined with our large population, means that the United States generates far more trash each year than other developed countries. The amount is also much greater than it used to be: in 1970, the average American generated only 3.25 pounds per day.

Recycling and composting do make a dent: in 1970, composting was virtually nonexistent and only 7 percent of solid waste generated was recycled. But by 2005, the numbers had risen to 24 percent for recycling and 8.4 percent for composting. These figures have remained relatively unchanged for the past several years, however And while some materials have relatively high recycling rates—half of all paper and paperboard is recycled—others pose perennial problems. Less than 6 percent of plastics are recycled because the process is difficult and costly. Furthermore, products like cell phones and computers are creating new headaches.

What are the key problems that government officials and policymakers need to address with respect to solid waste? And what policy instruments do the best job of tackling those problems?

For local communities, three goals seem paramount: trash needs to be managed properly without the high social costs of litter and other forms of illegal disposal; the amount of legally disposed waste should be reduced to a level that accounts for its own social costs; and particularly hazardous or toxic wastes need to be disposed separately, not thrown in the landfill with other trash.

Policymaking inevitably involves trade-offs, so furthering one goal may reduce progress toward another. For the most part, developed countries have figured out how to manage solid waste to avoid extensive dumping. Local communities provide trash collection and disposal services—usually through government provision, franchises, or contracts with private companies. Although the number of landfills has fallen in the past 15 years or so, landfill capacity has remained steady. Moreover, landfills are safer than they used to be because of requirements for liners, methane control, and monitoring. What is less clear is how best to reduce the volume of solid waste in the first place. Based on economic analysis, empirical research, and years of real-world experience, our view is that no "one size fits all" solution exists. An array of policies can best make the trade-offs for different locations and different waste materials.

The economist's typical solution to an externality problem is a Pigouvian tax: charge a tax or fee per pound of trash exactly equal to the social damages imposed by that trash. That would reduce waste in landfills, but it raises two questions. The first is whether the social damages can actually be estimated. Even if policymakers know what to charge, however, the second question is whether any such fee can feasibly be administered and enforced.

Some communities charge for each can or bag of trash, under a system commonly called "pay as you throw" (PAYT). Households might be charged one monthly amount for one can a week, or a higher monthly amount for a larger can or two cans a week. But not every can gets filled every week, leaving households with no incentive at the margin to reduce waste. A better system, closer to true marginal cost pricing, requires households to buy a special bag at the grocery store, or a special tag to use on a bag of garbage of a particular size.

EPA estimates that approximately 7,100 communities in the United States use some kind of PAYT, making it available to approximately 25 percent of the country's population. The number of communities has risen over time and, in some areas of the country, is quite high. Some states (Wisconsin, Oregon, and Minnesota) even have a law requiring that communities use PAYT.

Does it work? Results from the economics literature suggest that demand for garbage collection is relatively unresponsive to prices, but PAYT towns have experienced some reductions. And it is important to keep in mind that even if reductions are small, charging the right price may result in the *right* amount of garbage disposal. Fixed monthly charges—the norm in many places—set a zero price for an additional bag or can and thus provide no incentive for households to conserve.

The big question for PAYT communities, though, is what households are doing with the garbage they no longer place at the curb. To avoid paying the fee, households can reduce their waste by recycling, composting, consuming less in the first place, or disposing illegally—burning, finding a commercial dumpster, or throwing it by the side of the road. Recycling does increase with PAYT but not enough to account for all of the reduction in trash. Clearly, municipalities can help themselves by providing free curbside collection of a wide variety of materials for recycling and yard waste collection for central composting. Towns also must choose how much to spend on enforcement and how to set penalties.

PAYT is most effective in small cities and suburban areas but has not worked so well in densely populated urban areas where apartment dwellers use chutes and dumpsters for their normal disposal (and might easily use vacant lots for everything else). PAYT is also not as well suited to very rural areas where illicit dump sites are similarly easy to find. In general, it is most feasible where we can measure and monitor individual households' weekly trash and recycling.

Even in towns where a PAYT fee works well to reduce waste amounts without increased dumping, it does nothing special for separate handling of hazardous and other troublesome items like batteries, tires, or used electronic equipment. These products, especially, are candidates for some kind of deposit refund system (DRS). Experience has shown great success with a DRS applied to certain products: beverage containers in "bottle bill" states have recycling rates that range from 60 to 95 percent, significantly higher than in states without such a program; 96 percent of lead-acid batteries are recycled; and tires in states with a DRS are recycled at a 72 percent rate. But the idea can be generalized, in a "two-part instrument," a general sales tax on everything at the store (all of which eventually becomes waste) along with a subsidy per ton of waste handled at the recycling center. Products like computer monitors could still be specifically targeted with a special fee, but most items could be treated in bulk, without time-consuming transactions to count or weigh individual items.

Thus the "best" policy is not any single policy. PAYT can successfully be employed in at least some communities, and probably in more than are currently doing so. Other towns, however, need a two-part instrument—a general sales tax on new items at the store, plus a subsidy for recycling. And products that pose special problems may need targeted deposits or refunds. Different circumstances therefore call for different policies—PAYTs, DRSs, or two-part instruments. All of these options have a key feature in common, and one that economists invariably seek in all of their policy prescriptions: they provide the proper incentives to consumers and others to generate a socially desirable outcome.

Further Reading

Calcott, Paul, and Margaret Walls. 2000. Can Downstream Waste Disposal Policies Encourage Upstream "Design for Environment"? *American Economic Review* 90(2): 233–237.

Fullerton, Don, and Tom Kinnaman. 1996. Household Responses to Pricing Garbage by the Bag. *American Economic Review* 86(4): 971–984.

Jenkins, Robin, Karen Palmer, Michael Podolsky, and Salvador Martinez. 2003. Determinants of Household Recycling: A Material Specific Analysis of Unit Pricing and Recycling Program Attributes. *Journal of Environmental Economics and Management* 45(2): 294–318.

Porter, Richard. 2002. *The Economics of Waste*. Washington, DC: RFF Press.

39. THE NEW ECONOMICS OF MANAGING THE NATION'S WASTE

Molly K. Macauley

is a senior fellow and a director of research at Resources for the Future. She specializes in space economics, the economics of new technologies, recycling and solid waste management, climate policy, and incentive-based environmental regulation.

Stephen W. Salant

is a professor of economics at the University of Michigan, specializing in industrial organization and natural resource economics, and a nonresident fellow at Resources for the Future. He previously worked at the Federal Reserve Board and at the RAND Corporation, where he served as the first editor of the *RAND Journal of Economics*.

While the development of large, state-of-the-art landfills encouraged greater interstate shipments of solid waste, regulations and taxes affecting these shipments have also proliferated. How have such policies raised the overall costs of managing waste disposal in the United States?

It's an industry worth over $40 billion dollars a year and the bane of every city mayor—managing the nation's solid waste stream.

Some 20 years ago, we disposed of most of our waste at the local dump. New environmental regulations that took effect in the 1990s as a result of the Resource Conservation and Recovery Act (RCRA) led to the closure of most local dumps and, in their place, the opening of a smaller number of large, state-of-the-art landfills. These new facilities required that waste be hauled long distances, often across state boundaries.

A funny thing happened on the way to the landfill, however. Local governments began to get involved in the waste market. Intervention took many forms, but because it affected interstate transport of waste, each gave rise to legal challenges on the basis of the U.S. constitutional provision (the "commerce clause," Article 1, Section 8) for unimpeded transport of goods and services across state lines.

For example, states that hosted large landfills began to require that their state's waste go to that landfill, even if the waste was generated in a jurisdiction for which the nearest fill was just over the border in a neighboring state. This practice arose in states for which the scale of operation of the landfill required large amounts of waste.

Other states jealously guarded their landfills and prohibited imports of waste from other states, deeming the state landfill a precious resource with limited capacity reserved for in-state waste only.

In some cases, jurisdictions levied fees on out-of-state waste. Sometimes jurisdictions justified these on the basis of needing to finance bonds issued to build the landfill. Jurisdictions also intervened to manage waste flows to achieve scale economies at recycling and incineration facilities.

In West Virginia, which, along with the state of Washington, regulates waste through state public service commissions, the commission put in place a set of licensing and other requirements for out-of-state waste haulers.

These interventions all have had the effect of restricting waste flows and impeding their least-cost management. A more cost-effective approach would take into account the distance between where the waste is generated and the nearest disposal facility, plus the cost of transportation, the remaining capacity in the disposal facility (a measure of opportunity cost), and other factors. Distorting the interplay of these factors can reduce benefits of cost-effective waste management for households. Although it can transfer benefits to owners of waste disposal facilities, the net effect on society is likely to be cost, not benefit.

Disentangling these effects on households and waste facility owners has been the subject of research we have conducted. We estimated the total loss and, given the new pattern of landfill location, the regional distribution of losses and gains across the nation under different kinds of interventions, including state and local requirements stipulating where waste must be landfilled, prohibitions on the import and export of waste across state boundaries, quantitative limits on these flows, and extra fees levied on imported waste.

In all cases, overall social welfare declines, but some geographic regions, consumers, and landfill owners bear relatively higher costs than others. For example, the discounted present value of the reduction in overall social welfare over a 20-year period if trade is prohibited is about $3.8 billion, or twice as much as volume-based restrictions capping the size of the waste flows or imposing $1 per ton surcharges. The losses are largest for consumers and producers in the Northeast, where waste exports are large, and smallest for those in the Midwest. Short of prohibiting trade entirely, the largest loss in discounted social surplus occurs under a policy that restricts the maximum volume between states and does not allow states to trade at all unless they had been "grandfathered in" because they had been trading before announcement of the policy.

In addition, and perhaps most important, some policies to restrict exports may substantially *increase* the number of interstate waste shipments as some states export smaller volumes to more destinations in order to meet limits on the size of shipments to any one state.

The courts have been extremely busy hearing the legal arguments for and against interstate restrictions. High-level courts have heard nearly 20 cases, and the U.S. Supreme Court has heard 2. By and large, most decisions, including the first of the Supreme Court findings, struck down restrictions. But the most recent decision, in 2007, found the opposite: the court held that because the waste disposal facility was owned by the local government, the commerce clause would "allow for a distinction between laws that benefit public, as opposed to private, facilities." But in the dissenting opinion, three judges held that the "public-private distinction drawn by the Court is both illusory and without precedent."

Our story is thus one of technological change (from the town dump to state-of-the-art regional landfills) in response to regulation (as set forth in RCRA) and the transformation of a local market into a national one. The recent Supreme Court decision notwithstanding, the new economics of our waste market emphasize the advantages of unimpeded trade among states.

Further Reading

Eduardo Ley, Molly K. Macauley, and Stephen W. Salant. 2002. Spatially and Intertemporally Efficient Waste Management: The Costs of Interstate Trade Restrictions. *Journal of Environmental Economics and Management* 43: 188–218.

Macauley, Molly K. 2009. Waste Not, Want Not: Economic and Legal Challenges of Regulation-Induced Changes in Waste Technology and Management. Discussion paper 09-11. Washington, DC: Resources for the Future.

Porter, Richard. 2002. *The Economics of Waste: Policy Instruments, Waste Management and Site Cleanup*. Washington, DC: RFF Press.

40. ENHANCING PRODUCTIVITY WHILE SAFEGUARDING ENVIRONMENTAL QUALITY

David Zilberman

is a professor and holds the Robinson Chair in the Department of Agricultural and Resource Economics at the University of California, Berkeley. His research interests include agricultural and environmental policy, economics of technological change, economics of natural resources, and microeconomic theory.

Steven Sexton

is a Ph.D. candidate in the Department of Agricultural and Resource Economics at the University of California, Berkeley.

Regulating agricultural use of pesticides involves complex trade-offs. For example, regulators must take into account health risks to consumers and farm workers, broader environmental damages from farm runoff, and the risk that extensive pesticide use will speed up the evolution of pest resistance. How might current policies be improved?

Calculating the benefits and costs of pesticides is highly controversial. On the one hand, they are responsible for considerable improvement in the human condition. They have increased food supply and enabled agricultural production in regions where it would otherwise be impossible. By reducing the damage pests inflict on crops, pesticides improve farm yield as much as 100 percent in some cases. They reduce the costs of agricultural inputs like labor and energy. Also, they confer environmental benefits by reducing pressure for agricultural expansion and by enabling environmentally beneficial farming practices, like low tillage, which reduces soil erosion and permits carbon sequestration in the ground.

On the other hand, chemical pesticides can be harmful to humans and the environment, potentially causing health problems in farm workers exposed to toxic materials and to consumers exposed to residues on food. They can pollute the environment by runoff and drift, contaminating ground and surface water and affecting nontarget species. In addition, excessive pesticide use can also reduce pest susceptibility, making it a resource that may suffer the tragedy of the commons. These negative side effects of pesticide use make a strong case for regulation.

The current pesticide regulatory structure in the United States does not take sufficient account of the public health benefits of pesticides (in terms of diseases prevented or reduced cost of food). And regulators are too quick to react to public opinion and do not fully acknowledge the results of the risk–benefit balancing they are required to do under law. As a result, no one is well served—not consumers, who face higher prices; nor farmers, who contend with higher costs and lower productivity; nor pesticide manufacturers, who have weaker incentives to innovate. And it is not clear whether there is an improvement in public health or environmental quality, given the problem of regulating pesticides sequentially.

First off, the process of testing potential chemicals and the criteria and standards imposed on final products should be consistent and integrated across the three government agencies that have a role in pesticide regulation: the U.S. Department of Agriculture, the Food and Drug Administration, and the Environmental Protection Agency. An essential step will be to eliminate the inevitable redundancies that exist among the agencies.

While the current system of testing and screening chemicals before they are approved for market is necessary, it is not without very real costs. It takes roughly $15 million to bring a pesticide to market in this country, certainly enough to act as a barrier to entry and lead to market concentration in the agrochemical industry. As per capita income rises, consumers are demanding ever-lower levels of human and environmental risk.

But the pursuit of safety must have its limits. Risk is inherent in all new technologies. While laboratory testing should ensure a basic level of safety, chemicals that fare well in the lab should be brought to market where monitoring in the field can provide additional validation. Should pesticides approved for market prove unsafe in some respect, domestic and international regulations permit their use to be restricted or banned altogether.

Regulators all too often respond to revelations of adverse effects by banning implicated pesticides altogether, ignoring the benefits they provide as well as the potential for narrower responses. Some pesticides may be beneficial from a social perspective despite some risks. The much-maligned DDT, for example, was banned after it was known to cause significant environmental damage and substitutes were available. However, it enabled eradication of malaria in parts of the United States and Europe, and selective use could have saved tens of thousands of lives in Africa.

The use of chemicals that have negative impacts under certain circumstances, such as in specific areas or weather conditions, should be restricted accordingly. As much as 80 percent of the benefit of some chemicals is derived from as little as 20 percent of their applications, suggesting that use restrictions dominate pesticide bans from a social welfare perspective. Bans not only eliminate the benefits of pesticide use, but also increase the likelihood of resistance by restricting the damage control portfolio of farmers and making them dependent on a small set of pesticides.

Regulatory compliance poses additional challenges. Pesticide application guidelines are far from binding and leave users with considerable latitude. Enforcement is difficult because pesticide contamination is a nonpoint-source pollutant; for example, many farmers may contribute to contamination of a watershed. However, new technologies make monitoring and enforcement more feasible. California has developed a strong regime of pesticide-use reporting that capitalizes on wireless technologies.

The value and effectiveness of pesticides can vary by chemical, crop, location, application technology, weather, and other factors. Policy must recognize this heterogeneity and aim to permit pesticide applications where the total social benefits exceed the total social costs. A pesticide fee, for example, would discourage chemical use in instances when the benefits are small. Another policy option to achieve more efficient pesticide use would be a regional cap-and-trade program (similar to the sulfur dioxide trading program under the Clean Air Act) that limits the use of pesticides in a region and permits farmers to trade allowances.

Regulators can go one step further and develop incentives that vary by location, recognizing that contamination of a certain area poses greater risk to environmental services, biodiversity, and human health than in others. In the same vein, policies should provide disincentives for application technologies that result in drift and runoff, such as aerial spraying. Incentives that account for all forms of heterogeneity may be too costly and information intensive from a regulatory standpoint, but to the extent policy can rely on new information and communication technologies and employ economic instruments, it should.

The introduction of better monitoring and traceability requirements can lead to reliance on financial incentives that penalize misuse and reward decisions that lead to environmental benefit, such as carbon sequestration. Pesticides have been essential in enhancing agricultural productivity and improving human welfare, but they have substantial negative side effects. It is crucial to develop systems that result in better products and improve pesticide use. Pesticide regulation should be an ongoing activity that takes advantage of new scientific and technical capacities, utilizes better information, and incorporates more intensively refined and enforceable incentives that result in better outcomes.

Further Reading

Laxminarayan, Ramanan. 2003. *Battling Resistance to Antibiotics and Pesticides: An Economic Approach.* Washington, DC: RFF Press.

Sexton, Steven E., Zhen Lei, and David Zilberman. 2007. The Economics of Pesticides and Pest Control. *International Review of Environmental and Resource Economics* 1(September): 271–326.

Travisi, Chiara Maria, Peter Nijkamp, and Gabriella Vindigni. 2006. Pesticide Risk Valuation in Empirical Economics: A Comparative Approach. *Ecological Economics* 56(4): 455–474.

Zilberman, David, Andrew Schmitz, Gary Casterline, Erik Lichtenberg, and Jerome B. Siebert. 1991. The Economics of Pesticide Use and Regulation. *Science* 253(5019): 518–522.

41. WHY WE NEED TO TREAT NITROGEN AS A SYSTEMS PROBLEM

Andrew Manale,
with the U.S. EPA's Office of Policy, Economics, and Innovation, has analyzed a wide range of environmental policy issues, generally from a systems perspective, for various levels of federal and state governments, nonprofit organizations, and the private sector.

A discussion of the sources and environmental impacts of reactive nitrogen is followed by an examination of why a comprehensive portfolio of policy approaches is needed to contain nitrogen pollution.

Too much of a good thing leads to a decline in our well-being.

Nitrogen is an essential element in the building blocks of life, constituting 80 percent of Earth's atmosphere. Though surrounding us in vast quantities, nitrogen exists in a biologically inaccessible (inert) form, with only about a thousandth of 1 percent biologically available. Nature—through the electrical process of lightning, biological fixation, and combustion—makes it available in a reactive form (rN), literally out of thin air. With it, life blooms because it is generally the limiting factor for growth. With too much in its reactive form, though, fragile systems within which flourish higher life forms, such as mammals and reptiles, fail.

Before the German chemist Fritz Haber in 1909 discovered a ready means for creating large quantities of rN, societies recycled it. Human "night soil" and animal manure were collected and applied to the land as fertilizer. It was scarce, hence it was valuable. Where there were virgin lands, such as in the New World, early settlers mined soils for their nitrogen, moving on when soils failed. Haber's technological breakthrough made rN abundant. Forty percent of all humans now alive owe their existence to anthropogenically created rN because of the additional food production it has facilitated. But with abundance comes waste and ever more rN lost to the environment, harming ecological systems more than it benefits them.

Excess rN causes myriad environmental problems. Atmospheric emissions that have increased fivefold since preindustrial times contribute to the formation of ozone, a major air pollutant. Atmospheric deposition rates now exceeding natural rates by more than tenfold and too much nitrogen-containing runoff from the land reduce the biodiversity of ecosystems and degrade the quality of rivers, lakes, streams, and estuaries for all uses. Severe eutrophication of 44 estuaries along the nation's coasts can be attributed to rN. The excess rN that causes hypoxia (low oxygen levels) in marine environments now accounts for over 200—and growing—dead zones around the world, doubling in just 10 years.

When overapplied as chemical fertilizer or deposited as acid rain, rN can acidify waters and soils, damaging crops and forests and lowering economic output. In drinking water, it can cause health problems in infants, such as blue-baby syndrome. And under oxidative conditions, agricultural soils, nitrate-saturated rivers and streams, and episodic dead zones become sources of nitrous oxide (N_2O), a greenhouse gas with over 300 times the warming potential of carbon dioxide, the primary greenhouse gas.

Humans have more than doubled the total annual global production of rN over natural levels, a rate that is accelerating. Fertilizer rN accounts for some 38 percent that is anthropogenically introduced. Other sources include burning of biomass, land clearing, and the draining of wetlands, all of which release stored (sequestered) nitrogen into the environment (33 percent); legumes, such as soybeans (19 percent); and combustion of fossil fuels (10 percent and growing). With economic growth in the developing world, its imbalance in ecosystems will correspondingly increase, as wealth drives meat and dairy consumption and the crops that feed livestock. Wealthier societies also consume more electrical power, generated largely through the combustion of fossil fuels. Fertilizer demand grows at over 3 percent and electricity generation at 2.9

percent a year.

The problem of the introduction of ever greater amounts of rN would not be so severe were the rate of the reverse process—the rate at which reactive nitrogen is converted back to inert nitrogen (denitrification) or the rate at which reactive nitrogen is biologically sequestered in soils and plants—growing as well. No longer can we count on natural denitrification and sequestration processes, such as those that occur in wetlands, seasonally wet agricultural soils, and marine environments, nor grasslands and forests to serve as "sinks," for tilling soil and land conversion release rN from its organic complex. There are plenty of economic incentives to increase the amount of rN introduced into the environment; few or no private incentives exist for denitrification, except where clean water is scarce.

Despite successful national regulatory programs for nitrogen, there are gaps in controls. Clean Air and Water Acts regulations cover air emissions of nitrogen oxides and water emissions of rN from large point sources, such as sewage treatment plants. However, continued economic growth—and hence industrial and commercial activity—only heightens the need to do ever better just to maintain current levels. Moreover, not all sources of rN are regulated. Agriculture, which is largely outside EPA's regulatory authority, is the primary user of fertilizer. Voluntary interventions for managing the loss of rN have had mixed success.

More importantly, interventions to date have treated rN as a conventional pollutant for which a control technology is identified and imposed. Many of these interventions simply shift reactive nitrogen from one medium to another rather than destroy or capture it in long-term storage, such as in sustainably managed soils. Nitrogen contained in municipal sewage sludge applied to the land and not managed sustainably can be released to water bodies in rainwater runoff. Thus excess rN in the environment is a systems issue where sources, sinks, and control options vary across the landscape. Economic interests, left unchanged, favor increased generation and environmental emission of reactive nitrogen.

Imbalance of rN in the air, water, and soil is perhaps the best single indicator that the environment is not being managed sustainably. Nitrogen is tied to other chemical cycles, such as carbon and water. Mismanagement of one leads to imbalances of the others.

The following example illustrates the magnitude of the problem. The great majority of nitrogen other than in its inert form is locked up in soil organic matter—1.5 million times a million metric tons (1,500 petagrams, or Pg). All plants and animals, in contrast, only contain 1 percent as much (15.2 Pg). Most of this organic nitrogen is contained in arctic and boreal soils that have, for thousands of years under permafrost conditions, accumulated both carbon and nitrogen. If ecosystems are managed unsustainably, especially given the increasing threat of global warming, that stored nitrogen could be released, overwhelming any current regulatory effort.

Just reducing fertilizer use, as economic theory has dictated in the past, will not suffice if major emissions come from broadscale land modifications and land-use changes. As developed and developing nations demand more agricultural production of food, feed, fiber, and now fuel, the problem escalates. The seemingly small changes to our ecosystems over many generations—such as the draining of wetlands, the straightening of rivers, agricultural monoculture, and confined animal feeding operations—aggregate to the very large impact experienced today.

Without a new focus on reducing excess rN in the environment, a decline in well-being, evidenced by degradation of habitat and our soils and water, will ultimately affect human health, whether through degraded water quality or increasing global temperatures or loss of biological species. A systems problem, such as rN, requires a systems solution that addresses the multiple objectives inherent in managing ecosystems and the linkages between levels of rN in soil, water, and air, and management of the carbon cycle and water resources.

How does one deal with a systems reactive nitrogen problem? Store it, through land-use and management practices that put carbon back into the soil and protect and restore wetlands, which sequester rN. Destroy it by protecting denitrifying aquatic and terrestrial systems. And, of course, what civilizations that preceded us learned through wisdom accumulated through the ages—we can recycle it, making commercial use of waste products containing rN and transforming waste into a valued commodity.

Further Reading

Energy Information Administration. 2008. Electricity. In *International Energy Outlook 2008*. Report #DOE/EIA-0484(2008). Washington, DC: U.S. Department of Energy, Chapter 5.

Galloway, James, Alan R. Townsend, Jan Willem Erisman, Mateete Bekunda, Zucong Cai, and John R. Freney, et al. 2008. Transformation of the Nitrogen Cycle: Recent Trends, Questions and Potential Solutions. *Science* 320: 889.

Hatfield, J.L., and R.F. Follett, eds. 2008. *Nitrogen in the Environment: Sources, Problems, and Management*, 2nd ed. Oxford, UK: Elsevier.

Heffer, Patrick, and Michel Prud'homme, eds. 2008. *International Fertilizer Industry Association, World Agriculture and Fertilizer Demand, Global Fertilizer Supply and Trade 2008–2009*. Summary Report. Paris, France: International Fertilizer Industry Association.

The views expressed here do not necessarily represent those of the U.S. Environmental Protection Agency or other federal entities. No EPA endorsement should be inferred.

42. THE EFFECTIVENESS OF VOLUNTARY ENVIRONMENTAL PROGRAMS

Richard D. Morgenstern is a senior fellow at Resources for the Future. His research focuses on the costs, benefits, evaluation, and design of environmental policies, especially economic incentive measures.

William A. Pizer specializes in environmental policy evaluation, with a particular focus on climate policy. This commentary was completed while he was a full-time senior fellow at Resources for the Future.

Drawing on case studies of seven voluntary environmental programs across the United States, Europe, and Japan, this commentary discusses the effectiveness of such programs, their pros and cons, and their possible role as a complement to mandatory emissions control policies.

Voluntary environmental programs have been multiplying at an explosive rate since the early 1990s in the United States and many countries abroad. The trend reflects growing optimism about the possibilities of cooperation between government and business. It also is fed by frustration with the long and expensive battles that often arise from regulatory controls. But how much actual impact are the voluntary programs having?

Our own findings, drawn from research on a number of programs, are that they are having a real but limited effect. Compared with a credible baseline, they reduce releases of pollutants by probably not more than 5 percent.

Now a 5 percent reduction is not trivial: many nations have commitments under the Kyoto Protocol that are roughly of that order of magnitude (although the United States and Canada would impose much larger requirements). In addition to near-term reductions, voluntary programs may influence corporate attitudes and management practices, leading in time to broader-scale improvements in performance.

But it is hard to argue for voluntary programs where there is a clear desire for dramatic changes in behavior, as would be required to achieve virtually any of the goals now being discussed in Congress.

Out of the thousands of these programs now in operation, which cover a wide range of environmental issues, we chose seven prominent examples (Morgenstern and Pizer 2007) for a close look, including EPA's 33/50 program aimed at toxic releases, along with energy or carbon dioxide reduction programs in the United States, Europe, and Japan. While the U.S. programs all involve participation criteria established by government, the UK, Danish, and Japanese programs we studied rely on explicit negotiations between industry and government to set emissions reduction goals and other parameters of agreement. In contrast, all the key programmatic decisions in the single German program examined were made by industry.

Even though most of the programs had extensive operating experience, our evaluation was hampered by concerns about the self-selection of participants—those firms that participated may be planning to do the relevant activities anyway, which would generate coincidental reductions—and by the absence of good emissions or energy-use data derived from a well-defined baseline.

Voluntary programs offer valuable opportunities for firms to get practical experience with new types of environmental problems without the straitjacket of mandatory regulation. In the process, firms are able to enhance their reputations with a broad range of constituents. These programs also give government agencies a similar chance to deal with new challenges and new industries, sometimes with more holistic approaches than the media-specific, end-of-pipe focus of most existing legislation.

On the other side of the ledger, voluntary programs are limited by the absence of clear price or regulatory signals to push changes in corporate or consumer action, or to stimulate demand for cleaner technologies. "Free riding," where some firms avoid making any effort while others voluntarily address a problem and keep further regulation at bay, may be an issue in some cases. Arguably, a voluntary approach may shift attention from the biggest polluters—which may be the source of both more emissions and more low-cost emissions reductions—to cleaner firms that emit less and have already taken significant action. Some in the environmental community see voluntary programs as a distraction from the real work of taking mandatory action.

Extensive work has been done on the motivation for firms to participate: doing so may help preempt the threat of regulation, influence future regulation, improve stakeholder relations, or gain competitive advantage. Several studies have shown the importance of public recognition to be a key inducement. The nature of the firm's market may also be important as well as the willingness of its customers to pay for green products.

Incentives offered by some voluntary programs to firms that join and take stipulated actions can affect the magnitude of the efforts they make. Among the voluntary programs that we studied closely, those that provide greater financial incentives or relief from other requirements seem to facilitate larger results than those without incentives, although the difference is not significant. However, incentives may draw more firms into the program and thereby increase its impact by multiplying the number of contributors. Consequently, environmental results may be enhanced by expanding participation rather than seeking deeper cuts from a limited number of firms.

Another question is whether, under voluntary cooperation, the initial gains will persist over time, both as the program is broadened and more participants come in, and as the original participants mature. Among the cases that we studied, the evidence showed that some initial gains may not persist. Typically, the most profitable gains are taken early and the most cooperative firms join first, with the result that the program may lose momentum over time. Or it may be that program participants are simply taking actions earlier than other firms would within a few years.

In designing a voluntary program, significant initial considerations must be the targeted environmental mediums and the activities being addressed. If it is a novel and unstudied area, or one that involves clear impacts on local communities—as was the case with toxic pollutants 20 years ago—there may be opportunities for more significant improvements at low cost. At the same time, if it is an area that has already been carefully scrutinized with fewer local consequences, as we believe the case to be for energy efficiency, effective opportunities are less likely.

At the end of the day, voluntary programs can indeed affect behavior and produce environmental benefits—but the limitations are clear. These programs make sense when mandatory action seems premature or lacks legal or political support. They are a useful step when mandatory programs will take a long time to implement. But we have seen no solid evidence that voluntary action can produce sharp and truly fundamental improvements in environmental protection.

Further Reading

Khanna, Madhu, and Lisa A. Damon. 2004. Effectiveness ofVoluntary Approaches: Implications for Climate Change Mitigation. In *Voluntary Approaches in Climate Policy*, edited by A. Baranzinin and P. Thalmann. Cheltenham, UK: Edward Elgar.

Maxwell, John W., and Thomas P. Lyon 2007. Public Voluntary Programs Reconsidered. papers.ssrn.com/sol3/papers.cfm?abstract_id=967490.

Morgenstern, Richard D., and William A. Pizer. 2007. Case Study Findings, in How Well Do Voluntary Environmental Programs Work? *Resources*164 (Winter).

Morgenstern, Richard D., and William A. Pizer. 2007. *Reality Check: The Nature and Performance of Voluntary Environmental Programs in the United States, Europe, and Japan.* Washington, DC: RFF Press.

43. DOES GREEN CORPORATE SOCIAL RESPONSIBILITY BENEFIT SOCIETY?

Thomas P. Lyon

is the Dow Professor of Sustainable Science, Technology and Commerce at the University of Michigan's Ross School of Business. His research interests include environmental information disclosure, corporate greenwash, voluntary environmental programs, nongovernmental organizations, and renewable energy.

John W. Maxwell

is a professor of business economics and public policy at Indiana University's Kelley School of Business. He specializes in business strategy in the nonmarket environment, with a focus on interactions among firms, government, and special interest groups.

What does corporate social responsibility (CSR) actually mean in an environmental context? The case for or against CSR from a broader social perspective is rather nuanced and calls for examining instances of CSR on a case-by-case basis to judge whether it provides overall net benefits, or net costs, for society.

Corporate social responsibility (CSR) is not a new concept, but over the past decade its focus has shifted from labor issues and local philanthropy toward environmental actions. More and more companies desire to go green and are building to Leadership in Energy and Environmental Design (LEED) certification standards, joining the Chicago Climate Exchange, and producing corporate social reports to make public their environmental performance in accordance with the Global Reporting Initiative. Numerous factors are driving this trend, including managerial altruism, cost-cutting efficiency improvements, the emergence of a new generation of green consumers, and savvier business leaders who take proactive steps to avert political conflict rather than reacting to public pressure after the fact. Despite creeping concerns that some of the resulting corporate actions may be mere "greenwash," for the most part they are welcomed by employees, consumers, investors, regulators, and the public. But is it really socially desirable for managers to take on costly environmental initiatives that are not required by law?

WHAT DO WE MEAN BY CSR?

One of the perplexing things about CSR is that it has long meant different things to different people. To some, an action only counts as true CSR if it is unprofitable and hence motivated by altruism. This was the position taken by Milton Friedman in his highly influential 1970 *New York Times Magazine* article on the social responsibility of business. In this view, socially beneficial actions that increase profits are merely strategic CSR, or in Friedman's words, "hypocritical windowdressing." However, even advocates of altruistic CSR admit that most CSR actions can be viewed through a strategic lens. Thus we take a pragmatic perspective and define environmental CSR simply as environmentally friendly actions not required by law, encompassing both possible motives.

IS CSR GOOD FOR SOCIETY?

One familiar argument against CSR is that it imposes a manager's preferences on a whole group of shareholders, who might prefer to allocate their charitable contributions in different ways. This is a powerful argument in a world where shareholders are motivated solely by maximizing the monetary earnings from their investments, the market for charitable donations is perfectly competitive, and the political marketplace efficiently internalizes all environmental externalities. If these assumptions do not hold in practice, however, the distinction between "altruistic" and "strategic" CSR blurs, and the argument against CSR weakens.

Socially responsible firms can be viewed as a vehicle for combining an investment with a charitable contribution, which can be attractive to investors since it avoids both taxation of corporate profits and the transaction costs of personal giving.

Even if investors prefer to make direct charitable donations, socially responsible firms can still survive in the marketplace, although they will trade at a discount to other firms. If investors are informed about the firm's CSR activities at the time they invest, then it is the entrepreneurs who have created the firms that bear the cost of the CSR activities, not ordinary shareholders. The entrepreneur's creation of a CSR firm is a gift to society—he or she benefits from starting the firm, investors benefit from the expanded range of investment opportunities, and the recipients of CSR benefit directly.

Even if CSR offers some benefits to investors, the question remains: is it more appropriate for altruistic managers and shareholders to work through the political system rather than through corporate voluntarism? If legislators and regulators actually pursue the public interest, there is little scope for CSR to improve on enlightened government regulation. However, many would argue that regulatory agencies are often captured by the companies they regulate, implying that the political marketplace is far from efficient. If so, then the welfare effects (or net benefits) of strategic CSR depend on the political context in which it occurs.

Even when politicians are well intentioned, government regulation can be a cumbersome and costly enterprise. As a result, CSR can be a less costly substitute for government mandates, and hence increase welfare. Industry self-regulation that preempts legislation is typically welfare-enhancing because consumer groups can intervene in the political process if they find the firm's CSR efforts unsatisfactory. Similarly, if CSR is executed through voluntary agreements with regulators, this improves welfare as long as the regulator has society's best interests at heart. However, there is no guarantee that society gains if regulators are influenced by particular interest groups with narrow agendas.

CSR activities may influence regulatory decisions in several ways. CSR can benefit society by signaling to regulators that pollution abatement is not prohibitively costly, encouraging new regulations that may produce a competitive advantage for the signaler. However, if leading firms make modest environmental commitments, this may induce regulators to eschew tough environmental standards, potentially making society worse off. A company's CSR investments may also induce regulators to shift enforcement resources toward other firms that are more likely to be out of compliance with regulations. This can be beneficial for society, but there is also a risk that firms will become overzealous in their CSR efforts as they attempt to deflect regulatory attention toward other firms.

Over the past decade, there has been a rise in direct engagement between firms and environmental nongovernmental organizations (NGOs). While sometimes hostile, this engagement can also take the form of a partnership where an NGO advises a firm and then endorses its green products and services, often through a formal certification program such as the Forest Stewardship Council for forest products or the green-E scheme for renewable energy and carbon offsets. In an unregulated market, NGO approval can increase sales of environmentally friendly products and therefore enhance social welfare when consumers switch from "brown" to green products. When there is a possibility of government regulation, however, NGO involvement does not necessarily enhance social welfare. The existence of an NGO certification scheme can induce firms to lobby against government standards that might be of even greater value to society.

Firms have multiple motives for undertaking CSR, and its welfare effects are highly contingent on the institutional context in which it is undertaken. This makes it a fascinating field for researchers but a potentially tricky one for citizens and policymakers.

Further Reading

This commentary is based on a 2008 article by the authors: Corporate Social Responsibility and the Environment: A Theoretical Perspective. *Review of Environmental Economics and Policy* 2: 240–260.

Friedman, Milton. 1970. The Social Responsibility of Business Is to Increase Profits. *New York Times Magazine*, Sept. 13.

Hay, Bruce, Robert N. Stavins, and Richard H.K. Vietor, eds. 2005. *Environmental Protection and the Social Responsibility of Firms.* Washington, DC: RFF Press.

44. THE EVOLVING SO_2 ALLOWANCE MARKET

Title IV, CAIR, and Beyond

Karen Palmer

is the Darius Gaskins Senior Fellow at Resources for the Future and the director of the Electricity and Environment Program. She specializes in environmental and public utility regulation.

David A. Evans

is an economist at the U.S. EPA's National Center for Environmental Economics, specializing in regulatory design, stated preference methods, and evaluation of federal air quality regulations.

While the sulfur dioxide cap-and-trade program has been highly successful in generating substantial pollution-related health benefits at relatively low cost, this commentary suggests ways to make the program still more efficient. Recent regulatory initiatives are also considered, as well as how they may have contributed to recent volatility in SO_2 allowance prices.

Recent congressional debates over a potential cap-and-trade program to combat global warming have brought renewed attention to the sulfur dioxide (SO_2) cap-and-trade program established in 1990 under Title IV of the Clean Air Act. This program has brought about large reductions in SO_2 emissions from the electricity sector and at a dramatically lower cost than originally anticipated, demonstrating that cap-and-trade programs can work in practice as well as in theory. However, researchers have identified potential improvements to the program, and regulatory initiatives are motivating further SO_2 reductions. These initiatives, in turn, have been subject to legal uncertainty that has influenced the market for SO_2 allowances.

TITLE IV

The primary motivation for the SO_2 program was to reduce ecological damages from acid rain—the deposition of sulfuric compounds into soils and waterways—in regions distant from emitting power plants. Under the program, firms are required to surrender one allowance for each ton of SO_2 emitted. Firms may transfer allowances to other firms and bank them for future use. While there are few restrictions on allowance transactions, there are strict emissions monitoring requirements, which provide regulators confidence in the environmental performance of the program and affected firms confidence in the market.

The goal of the program is ultimately to cap annual emissions from electricity generators to 8.95 million tons, a 10 million ton drop from the 1980 level. Reductions to achieve this goal have taken place in two phases. Phase I began in 1995 and affected the 110 dirtiest coal-fired generating facilities. In Phase II, which started in 2000, most other coal-fired facilities came under the program, and the allocation of allowances to Phase I sources was reduced by slightly over half. Emissions reductions have resulted largely from installation of postcombustion scrubbers and a shift from high-sulfur coal from the East to western low-sulfur coal, which was facilitated by lower freight prices following railroad deregulation.

While the program was motivated by concerns over acid rain, it has also reduced fine particulate matter concentrations, creating health benefits that are an order of magnitude greater than the costs of the program. Reductions in acid deposition have produced ecological benefits as well, but those estimated benefits are small relative to the human health benefits.

IMPROVING UPON THE TITLE IV PROGRAM

Despite the success of the Title IV program to date, significant improvements in SO_2 control can be made along two dimensions: the level of the cap and the location of emissions.

For the current cap, the marginal cost of reducing emissions is around \$150 to \$300 per ton, which is well below the \$1,800 to \$4,700 per ton estimates of the marginal benefit of further reductions. An annual cap that maximizes the net economic benefits of the program would be between 1 million and 3 million tons and yield a $3.6 billion to $23.5 billion increase in annual net benefits.

Requiring plants that cause more damages due to their location to surrender more allowances per ton emitted than those that cause less damage would also increase the benefits of the program. The estimated annual gains from such spatial refinement are around $310 million to $940 million.

Another potential improvement to the regulation of SO_2 would be to use an emissions tax approach. Given that the damage from an additional ton of emissions is roughly constant with respect to SO_2 emissions levels, a tax per ton equal to the additional damage is a preferable method for controlling SO_2 as the tax will always yield an emissions level that maximizes net benefits regardless of the level of control costs. This is true even if SO_2 control costs change because of the regulation of other pollutants, such as carbon dioxide.

RECENT POLICY DEVELOPMENTS AND ALLOWANCE PRICE FLUCTUATIONS

In May 2005, EPA adopted the Clean Air Interstate Rule (CAIR), which both effectively reduces the Title IV cap and treats facilities differently based on their location. In part, the purpose of CAIR is to reduce SO_2 emissions in upwind states that contribute to violations of EPA's primary ambient air quality standards for fine particulates in the eastern United States. The primary ambient standards are intended to be protective of human health. The CAIR SO_2 program applies only to facilities in 25 eastern states and the District of Columbia. Sources subject to CAIR must surrender 2 Title IV allowances for every ton of emissions from 2010 to 2014, and 2.86 allowances for every ton thereafter.

In July 2008, the DC Circuit Court of Appeals vacated CAIR in part because the trading program could not assure protection of downwind ambient air quality; however, in December 2008, the court allowed EPA to administer CAIR while it develops a replacement program. The form of the replacement EPA will adopt is unknown, but modifying a cap-and-trade approach to meet these concerns may be both more effective and less costly than a conventional approach, such as imposing emissions rate standards. Furthermore, while it is possible for the allowance market to move emissions across space, it is also possible for the electricity market to do the same with an emissions rate program.

The allowance price provides information regarding market conditions and expectations, and we see this in the market response to the CAIR rulings. For example, when CAIR was vacated, the price of an allowance that can be used this year (that is, the spot price) fell from $300 to $80, and on news of the decision to temporarily reinstate CAIR, the price rose from $140 to $210. Currently, 2010 allowances are trading at about half the $70 spot price, reflecting expectations that the CAIR 2-to-1 2010 compliance rate will hold in the near term. The long term suggests a different story. In March 2009, EPA auctioned Title IV allowances that can be used beginning in 2016. The clearing price for these allowances was $6.65, about two-thirds lower than the price suggested by a combination of the 2016 2.86-to-1 compliance rate and recent prices of allowances that can be used after 2010.

The CAIR rulings, current financial conditions, and depressed electricity demand help explain recent declines in the spot price. However, it is not clear why the recent auction price for 2016 allowances is low relative to the current spot price, although there are a few possible explanations. Notably, EPA has suggested that it will take about two years to develop a replacement for CAIR. If the replacement does not implicitly adjust the Title IV cap through compliance rates, as the court's ruling seems to prohibit, then the Title IV cap would become slack. Expectations of future carbon dioxide regulation may also be influencing the allowance price. For example, EPA climate bill analyses, which include CAIR in the baseline, forecast about a 60 percent reduction in the Title IV allowance price from capping carbon dioxide, but they also predict a decline in the spot price.

CONCLUDING THOUGHTS

The SO_2 trading program has been a success, but there is still room for improvement. The regulation of SO_2 will continue to develop over time, which is a lesson for the design of new cap-and-trade programs. An advantage of a cap-and-trade program is that the allowance price provides information about how the market views changing market conditions and the likelihood of future regulatory developments.

Further Reading

Banzhaf, Spencer, Dallas Burtraw, and Karen Palmer. 2004. Efficient Emission Fees in the U.S. Electric Sector. *Resource and Energy Economics* 26(3): 317–341.

Burtraw, Dallas, David A. Evans, Alan Krupnick, Karen Palmer, and Russell Toth. 2005. Economics of Pollution Trading for SO_2 and NO_x. *Annual Review of Environment and Resources* 30(November): 253–289.

Muller, Nicholas Z., and Robert Mendelsohn. Forthcoming. Efficient Pollution Regulation: Getting the Prices Right. *American Economic Review*.

Shadbegian, Ronald J., Wayne Gray, and Cynthia Morgan. 2006. A Spatial Analysis of the Consequences of the SO_2 Trading Program. Paper presented at the U.S. EPA's Market Mechanisms and Incentives: Applications to Environmental Policy. October 2006, Washington, DC.

The views expressed here do not necessarily represent those of the U.S. Environmental Protection Agency or other federal entities. No EPA endorsement should be inferred.

45. THE COOLING WATER INTAKE STRUCTURES RULE

Winston Harrington
is a senior fellow and an associate director of research at Resources for the Future, specializing in urban transportation, motor vehicles and air quality, and environmental policy cost assessment.

Why was EPA unsuccessful in its attempt to introduce more flexibility and cost-benefit considerations into traditional technology-based regulations governing the use of water for cooling systems?

Typically, technology-based (TB) regulation involves the Environmental Protection Agency (EPA) identifying a technology that meets some conception of "best" performance (as defined in legislation) and then establishing a standard that achieves this level of performance. The costs, expected environmental improvements, or the value of those improvements are not taken into account in setting the standard. In one recent case, however, EPA took an alternative approach, calling instead for minimization of adverse environmental impacts, which gives regulated plants more flexibility than usually permitted.

The case involved Section 316(b) of the Clean Water Act, which regulates water withdrawals for cooling purposes and the accompanying return flows. A steam-electric plant, for example, may draw millions of gallons per day and the intake flows may cause mortality among crustaceans, fish, and even diving birds, by pinning them against screens (impingement) or sweeping them into the cooling system (entrainment). In fact, these processes can affect entire aquatic ecosystems by killing eggs, juveniles, and small organisms at the bottom of the food chain. Moreover, the water itself discharged from cooling systems can further affect aquatic ecology, by eliminating species sensitive to heat and favoring more heat-tolerant species that may not be natural to the local area.

As required under the statute, EPA identified the "best technology available," closed-cycle cooling, which minimizes thermal releases, impingement, and entrainment through the use of cooling towers that draw much less water. Following executive orders mandating regulatory impact analyses (RIAs) on major rulemaking processes, however, the Office of Management and Budget recommended removing this technology requirement and suggested a compliance option based on a plant-specific comparison of benefits and costs. The final rule, issued in 2004, was a complicated but flexible approach to TB regulation, involving several components.

Among the most important of those were a baseline against which performance was to be measured, namely the estimated mortality of marine organisms at a facility with "once-through" cooling and no controls on impingement or entrainment; a performance standard requiring both an 80 to 95 percent reduction in impingement mortality (compared with the baseline) and a 60 to 90 percent reduction in mortality from entrainment; and the identification of two designated technologies that EPA felt would meet the performance standards: a closed-cycle cooling system and a special screen designed to minimize mortality from withdrawals. Unlike most TB performance standards, these standards were based not on the capabilities of the technology but directly on the estimated effect of the technologies on the natural environment. EPA's rule would allow a steam plant even further departures from the usual practice in TB regulation, including investment in ecological restoration measures that would, on net, reduce the mortality involved in water withdrawals and return flows, or a demonstration that it was entitled to a site-specific determination of compliance technology because the cost of adopting the designated technology would be significantly greater than the costs estimated in the rule or the expected benefits at the site.

INNOVATIONS

These measures were both innovative and controversial. EPA recognized that the costs and biological effectiveness of abatement technologies for cooling water intake systems depended on local configurations and conditions, and on the local aquatic environment and its species. The desire to bring environmental effects into the rulemaking led the agency to an unusual definition of performance standards. Customarily, EPA defines the performance standard in terms of the performance of the technology itself, such as percentage reduction in emissions compared with no treatment. For this rule, the standard was written in terms of the effects on natural organisms—percentage reduction in mortality from impingement and percentage reduction in entrainment.

Other features were equally novel. While the use of compensatory restoration had for years been an option for developers seeking permits from the Corps of Engineers to alter wetland environments, this was among the first attempts to use it in more traditional regulation. And the site-specific cost–benefit analyses had a rough parallel in the "footprint" approach to the CAFE regulations for light trucks promulgated in 2005. Those regulations set manufacturer-specific standards based on the expected cost to manufacturers of modifying each model in their truck fleet. This feature exceeds even the requirement for regulatory impact analyses—that the total benefits of a rule justify the total costs. Indeed, the cooling water intake structures (CWIS) rule considered the potential of not just total but marginal cost–benefit comparisons. This is much closer to economists' conception of how benefit and cost information should be used.

For EPA, estimating expected costs and benefits was complicated by the site specificity of cooling water intake systems. On the cost side, EPA was uncertain whether the lowest-cost compliance alternative would actually meet the performance standards at particular plants, so a more costly technology had to be assumed.

On the benefits side, EPA had to determine the physical and biological effects of the regulation, quantify those changes, and then estimate (in dollars) the value of those changes. Some categories of benefits resisted the final valuation step, and some could not even be quantified.

Ultimately, the only benefits valued were the benefits to commercial and recreational fishing. Costs of the rule exceeded benefits by a factor of about five. As this ratio makes clear, the nonmonetized benefits did receive consideration in the analysis, but necessarily were left out of the cost–benefit comparison.

THE LEGAL CHALLENGE

The cooling water intake structure rule was challenged by states, environmental groups, and the utility industry. The individual appeals were merged into a single case (*Riverkeeper, et al. v. U.S. EPA*), which was decided in January 2007.

The U.S. Court of Appeals for the Second Circuit ruled that EPA's use of cost–benefit analysis was an incorrect reading of the statute. The "best technology available" performance standard precluded the balancing of benefits and costs, it said; the only legitimate question here was whether the cost of meeting the performance standard was something that industry could reasonably bear (and the court observed that several plants had already installed the designated technology).

The court then called on EPA to tighten up the ranges in the performance standards so that a plant could not get away with minimum performance: the plant should do its best, not the minimum. The court also rejected the use of restoration as a compliance alternative, ruling that restoration was not "minimization" but impermissible "compensation" for environmental impacts, and in any event, restoration was not "technology." Finally, the court remanded the site-specific compliance alternatives—the cost–cost test and the benefit–cost test. Thus, most of the rulemaking innovations were either rejected outright or remanded to EPA for clarification.

EPA subsequently suspended its cooling water intake rule and has not yet issued revisions. Meanwhile, industry petitioners appealed the decision to the Supreme Court. In its decision, rendered on April 1, 2009, the court reversed the appeals court and ruled that EPA may, at its discretion, use cost–benefit analysis in the CWIS rule. The rule was remanded to EPA, which, of course, is not the same EPA that promulgated the original rule. At this writing, the agency has not indicated whether the rule will be revised.

The story of this regulation illustrates not only the legal difficulty of building flexibility and cost–benefit consideration into technology-based rules, but also the conceptual difficulty of basing regulatory decisions on the likely consequences if the knowledge base for determining those consequences is deficient. This is not to say that a conventional technology-based standard would perform any better. It is difficult to determine whether, by limiting the flexibility of plants in meeting environmental standards, the court improved matters or made them worse.

Further Reading

Harrington, Winston, Lisa Heinzerling, and Richard D. Morgenstern, eds. 2009. *Reforming Regulatory Impact Analysis*. Washington, DC: RFF Press.

Newbold, Stephen C., and Rich Iovanna. 2007. Ecological Effects of Density-Independent Mortality: Application to Cooling-Water Withdrawals. *Ecological Applications* 17(2): 390–406.

Newbold, Stephen C., and Rich Iovanna. 2007. Population Level Impacts of Cooling Water Withdrawals on Harvested Fish Stocks. *Environmental Science and Technology* 41: 2108–2114.

Riverkeeper et al. v. U.S. EPA. U.S. Court of Appeals, 2nd Cir., argued June 8, 2006, decided January 25, 2007.

46. THE FUTURE OF REGULATORY OVERSIGHT AND ANALYSIS

Susan E. Dudley

served as the administrator of the Office of Information and Regulatory Affairs (OIRA) at OMB from April 2007 through January 2009.

Art Fraas

is a visiting fellow at Resources for the Future and the former chief of the Natural Resources, Energy, and Agriculture Branch of OIRA at OMB. Much of his work has examined the federal regulatory process, with a particular focus on the impact of environmental regulations.

What is the role of the Office of Information and Regulatory Affairs (OIRA) in providing independent assessments of the benefits and costs of agency rulemakings? How might regulatory oversight and analysis be improved by creating an earlier review process for important regulations and expanding the scope of OIRA's coverage to the so-called independent regulatory agencies?

As the Obama administration advances its agenda for change, many of its most important actions will be implemented through regulations. Compared to programs financed directly through taxes, the effects of regulations—their benefits and costs—are less visible and less well understood. Particularly in today's economic climate, a careful and deliberate consideration of the effects of regulatory actions, facilitated by effective, centralized review, is important to ensure regulations are accountable to the American people.

Like presidents before him, President Obama recognizes the importance of the "dispassionate and analytical 'second opinion' on agency actions," that the Office of Information and Regulatory Affairs (OIRA) within the Office of Management and Budget (OMB) provides, and is seeking ways to improve this regulatory oversight function. Here we provide recommendations on what has worked and what could be improved.

WHAT WORKS

Centralized regulatory review has withstood the test of time. While regulatory agencies tend to shape their decisions to accommodate the interest groups most directly affected, OIRA's mandate is to advance the general public interest. OIRA currently operates under President Clinton's 1993 Executive Order (EO) 12866, which requires centralized, coordinated review of regulations and states that agencies should "adopt a regulation only upon a reasoned determination that the benefits of the intended regulation justify its costs."

Cost–benefit analysis: not perfect, but the best we've got. Presidents over the last three decades have recognized that while cost–benefit analysis (CBA) is not perfect, it is the best tool available for understanding the effects of potential regulations and determining whether regulatory alternatives will do more good than harm. CBA provides an extremely useful framework for decisionmaking by identifying the underlying problem to be solved, identifying and evaluating alternative regulatory (and nonregulatory) approaches, and organizing this information in a consistent, coherent, and comprehensive way. Though it does not serve as the sole basis for crafting regulations, it does help decisionmakers consider a wide range of possible effects. EO 12866 directs agencies to "select those approaches that maximize net benefits (*including potential economic, environmental, public health and safety, and other advantages; distributive impacts; and equity*), unless a statute requires another regulatory approach" (emphasis added).

Analyzing and understanding distributive effects is a particularly important aspect of CBA because regulatory actions are sometimes regressive, imposing net costs on lower income groups or on other specific subgroups of concern. Even in cases where it is not regressive, regulatory action generally represents a relatively ineffective way of addressing concerns about income distribution.

Critics of CBA rightly point out that it will never be capable of quantifying all the different effects of regulation, nor will any level of analysis allow government decisions to improve upon those that are best left to individuals acting on their own behalf. CBA is, however, still the best tool available for ensuring that when government action is appropriate, it is designed to make the public better off. Alternatives are bound to be less robust, less transparent, and result in decisions that are less well informed.

WHAT COULD BE IMPROVED

While the analytical framework established in EO 12866 remains generally sound, two changes to the executive order could make the review process more effective: (1) creating an explicit "early review" mechanism for major regulatory actions, and (2) subjecting independent agencies to executive oversight.

Early review. OIRA's review occurs after an agency has developed a proposed or final rule. Agencies often complete the regulatory analyses required by EO 12866 just in time for OIRA review—well after the agency has made key decisions on the draft rule. Regulatory analysis prepared after policy decisions are made often becomes an exercise in supporting the rulemaking. At this point, regardless of the merits of arguments raised during interagency review, regulatory agencies are understandably dug in and reluctant to deviate from a specific approach.

Furthermore, this end-stage review process has been susceptible to gamesmanship that undermines the purposes of the EO. Though the EO envisions up to 90 days for interagency review, reviews are often severely curtailed—sometimes lasting only a few days—because of internal agency delays combined with either an internal administration deadline or a statutory or court-related deadline. In March 2009, for example, after only one day of OIRA review, EPA published a proposed rule with estimated costs of $350 million per year and benefits of roughly $1 billion or more. The hasty review was necessitated by the obligation to meet a deadline arising from a settlement agreement.

This is not a new problem. Previous administrations have addressed it informally at the staff level, through briefings and discussions of early drafts of regulations subject to tight time frames. These informal reviews have raised questions, however, so in keeping with this administration's focus on transparency and its interest in increasing the integrity of the regulatory review process and the quality of analysis underlying its major regulatory initiatives, it should adopt a formal early review process for key regulatory issues. It would cover the administration's most significant rulemakings, including all major rules expected to have annual benefits or costs in excess of $1 billion.

Under this early review process, OIRA would formally designate key rulemakings, probably about 20 per year, after consultation with the affected agencies and other offices within the Executive Office of the President. After designating a rulemaking for early review, OIRA and the agency would form an interagency group to play an active role in both identifying issues and options and developing the associated regulatory analysis. This process would encourage broader discussion of options and issues at an early stage in the development of these rulemakings and provide greater policy consensus within the administration on regulatory decisions. In doing so, it would help to address the "endgame" confrontations between OIRA and the agencies and the resulting delays that arise under the current EO process.

Independent agencies. Some of the most highly publicized regulatory problems today stem from so-called independent regulatory agencies, such as the Securities and Exchange Commission, the Commodity Futures Trading Commission, the Federal Communications Commission, and the Consumer Product Safety Commission. These agencies have never been subject to the analytical or procedural requirements of executive oversight. Because they adopt regulations of enormous consequence to the nation, President Obama should subject their regulatory decisions to executive order review to ensure they provide net benefits to the public and do not duplicate or conflict with other government actions.

LOOKING FORWARD

As President Obama considers improvements to the regulatory analysis and oversight process, he should recognize that centralized oversight of regulatory development is essential for an accountable government, and, though not perfect, a goal of maximizing net benefits using a CBA framework provides the most transparent and robust approach to ensuring regulatory proposals make Americans better off.

While executive oversight has served presidents and the American people well for almost three decades, President Obama could improve the process by adopting a formal early review process for the most significant regulatory actions and holding independent agencies to the same analytical and oversight standards as other agencies.

Further Reading

Harrington, Winston, Lisa Heinzerling, and Richard Morgenstern, eds. 2009. *Reforming Regulatory Impact Analysis*. Washington, DC: RFF Press.

Obama, President Barack. 2009. Memorandum for the Heads of Executive Departments and Agencies on Regulatory Review, January 30, 2009, in Presidential Documents. *Federal Register* 74(21): 5977–5978, February 3.

Stigler, George J. 1971. The Theory of Economic Regulation. *Bell Journal of Economics and Management Science* 3: 3–18.

47. A PLEA FOR ENVIRONMENTAL ACCOUNTS

James Boyd

is a senior fellow at Resources for the Future and has carried out his research there since 1992. He studies the fields of environmental regulation and law and economics, focusing on the analysis of environmental institutions and policy.

This commentary discusses the case for creating a system of national environmental indices, analogous to the national income accounts. Unfortunately, however, there is much to be done in terms of both developing capacity to monitor environmental trends and developing widely accepted methods to weight or value different classes of environmental goods.

Over the last 80 years, our nation has moved from crude, limited measures of economic activity to an incredibly sophisticated system of national accounts. In the 1930s, if you wanted to know the state of the U.S. economy, you would have had to count boxcars traveling between New York and Chicago or the number of unemployed you could see in the streets. All we had was impressions of the economy, not measures that allowed for diagnosis, prediction, and cure.

We are at a similar moment today with respect to our natural economy—the environmental goods and services we don't pay for but that make all other economic activity possible. We know the natural economy is under stress and clearly in decline in some areas.

Unfortunately, we are at the "counting boxcars and breadlines" stage of seeing these changes. Our knowledge of natural systems is impressionistic, not systematic. The lack of well-documented, comparable, time-series data on environmental conditions hinders strategic efforts to address our fundamental environmental problems.

GDP allows us to see the market economy it measures. Green accounts will do the same thing. Without it, we are doomed to surprises, an inability to experiment and learn, and poor public accountability. Accounting systems exist because of a simple human truth: complexity is overwhelming, whether you're a household, business, or nation. Accounting embraces that complexity but ultimately simplifies it into a clear message.

It is upsetting to note that, by cutting off funds, Congress has for 15 years actively obstructed the development of environmental accounts akin to GDP. Madness? No, just politics. One can imagine certain industries or companies, for example, whose net contribution to society is negative once environmental losses are taken into account. For some, killing the messenger makes good political sense.

GDP: THE PROBLEM OR THE SOLUTION?

Some view our economic accounts, like GDP, as part of the problem. Even to its practitioners, GDP is unsatisfying because of what it leaves out—namely, goods and services that aren't bought and sold in markets. Household labor isn't there. Open source software isn't there. Random acts of kindness aren't there. And most of nature's goods and services aren't there.

At root, all GDP does is track the amount of things we consume, weight those things by the prices we pay for them, and add the result up. When GDP goes up, it means we are producing and consuming more things and more things of higher value. That is a reasonable way to measure things, as long as you're measuring everything.

But because of what is left out, GDP can easily deceive. GDP always goes up when we use more energy, develop more shopping centers, build more dams, and take more fish out of the sea. We know that can't be right. Read naively, GDP arguably lulls us into a false, excessively material view of our welfare.

But for all its problems, the *idea* of GDP is sound. GDP is a triumph of our political and economic system. It is systematic, objective, and politically insulated. There is nothing else like it. And the evidence that GDP matters is all around us. As it rises and falls, so do political fortunes. Capital markets move on its growth or decline. The press even pays attention.

What we need is an environmental analogue to GDP—a scientific, consistent, apolitical way to measure the health of our natural economy. Integrated accounts will allow us to pinpoint the most important adverse environmental trends and intervene accordingly.

Without objective accounts built on solid data, we will be doomed to squabbling, confusion, and manipulation by the cleverest purveyors of anecdotes and counterclaims. Imagine the quality of our economic policy debates if we first had to argue over the facts of GDP, consumer prices, and the labor market.

HOW TO DO IT?

It will be a challenge to create a set of national environmental accounts. It will require coordination among our federal and state agencies and confrontation with those whose interests are not served by a clearer view of the natural economy. Will it take a lot of money? That depends on your perspective. The 2010 census—another large data collection effort—is budgeted at $11 billion. If we spent just one-tenth of 1 percent of that sum on environmental accounts, it would be $11 million more than we currently spend (zero).

Once we find the political will to experiment with environmental accounts, the next step is practical measurement of natural goods and services. Resources for the Future (RFF) has an ongoing history of working on this exact measurement problem. If we are to create a green GDP, what should we count and how should we count it?

An economic account requires two things. First, clear definitions are needed of the goods and services to be counted. In order to avoid double-counting, GDP counts only final goods and services, not all the other inputs used to create them (though indices for inputs are also a part of our national accounts). An environmental index should have the same property: namely, we should count only *final* environmental goods and services.

What are final, public environmental goods and services? The issue is complex and one that RFF's research addresses directly. In the simplest terms, final goods are those things and qualities that individuals, households, and businesses directly make choices about. Many environmental goods and services are not final goods, but that does not mean they are not valuable. Rather, it means that their value is embodied in the value of the final goods. Consider a salmon population that is commercially or recreationally harvested. The salmon population is a final good, but the food chain on which the salmon depends is not.

Other final environmental goods and services include commodities like water supplies, timber, and open space. These commodities should be measured as place- and time-specific amounts, because their value depends on where and when they are available. Air, water, and soil quality are final environmental goods as well. We should also measure environmental services like reduced flood, fire, and disease risks because these too are valuable.

In almost all of these cases, goods and services should be measured as place- and time-specific commodities. Satellite monitoring and the growing availability of geospatial measurement will be very important to the measurement of goods and services.

Second, we need weights to attach to those final goods and services so that differences in the value of goods and services are reflected in the index. GDP uses market prices as weights. These are not ideal because market prices do not reflect the consumer surplus associated with consumption. But prices are the best practical measure because they are easily observable. Since the goal of an environmental index is to evaluate the contributions of public goods, we must find a substitute for market prices. This challenge should not be underestimated. Without the market's invisible hand to tell us the appropriate weights, the weights must be derived some other way. Economists have ways around this—that is, formal statistical derivations of willingness to pay for public goods—but the methods are more technically demanding, time-consuming, and controversial than the use of market prices that are observable to all. Moreover, once we have a goods and services "quantity index," we can use it to explore the effect different weights have on the overall index. In other words, we can show what *kinds of* weights lead to a declining versus increasing environmental index.

Further Reading

Boyd, James. 2007. The Nonmarket Benefits of Nature: What Should Be Counted in Green GDP? *Ecological Economics* 61(4): 716–724.

Boyd, James. 2008. Counting Nonmarket, Ecological Public Goods: The Elements of a Welfare-Significant Ecological Quantity Index. Discussion paper 07-42. Washington, DC: Resources for the Future.

Boyd, James. 2008. Don't Measure, Don't Manage: GDP and the Missing Economy of Nature. Issue brief 08-01. Washington, DC: Resources for the Future.

Nordhaus, William, and Edward C. Kokkelenberg. 1999. *Nature's Numbers: Expanding the National Economic Accounts to Include the Environment.* Washington, DC: National Academy Press.

48. THE POLITICAL ECONOMY OF ENVIRONMENTAL JUSTICE

Spencer Banzhaf

is an associate professor of economics at Georgia State University and a faculty research fellow at the National Bureau of Economic Research. His research focuses on the interactions among local environmental quality, real estate markets, and demographics.

Poor people and minorities are more likely to live in neighborhoods at greater risk of environmental hazards. To what extent, if any, might public policy intervention be warranted on the grounds of environmental justice, and what form should any such intervention take?

Over the years, the hard evidence, both documentary and academic, has shown convincingly that poor people and minorities are more likely than other groups to live in polluted neighborhoods. This pattern has been found again and again, in numerous places and with all sorts of pollutants. For example, disadvantaged groups live closer to hazardous waste facilities and landfills, live closer to large air polluters, and live in communities with higher measures of air pollution.

These findings have sparked the "environmental justice" movement, which has had mixed success in pushing its agenda. At the federal level, it won an important victory when President Clinton issued Executive Order 12898. Still in force, the order requires nondiscrimination in federal environmental programs and focuses federal resources on low-income and minority communities. However, the movement has failed to see an environmental justice act passed in Congress, though several have been introduced. It has also been rebuffed in its pursuit of legal action in federal courts under the Civil Rights Act. But other victories have come at the local level. Stakeholders have won a bigger voice in the approval process for new polluting facilities. And in one prominent case, local activists forced California's Southeast Air Quality Management District to settle a suit over the geographic distribution of pollution under its pollution trading program.

SOURCES OF ENVIRONMENTAL INEQUITY

But before prescribing any remedies for environmental inequity, it is essential that we understand the social mechanisms underlying it. Such mechanisms determine the nature and locus of any injustice, how a policy affects the distribution of pollution across places and population groups, and who bears the costs and who reaps the benefits of cleanups.

Consider just three of the most likely sources of the disproportionate pollution burden borne by disadvantaged groups. First, disadvantaged groups have less political power. Consequently, they may be less successful at lobbying government agencies to block polluting facilities in their neighborhoods. Likewise, they may be less successful at pressuring such agencies to monitor existing facilities for compliance with environmental regulations. Closing the circle, polluting firms therefore may seek out such communities for the very reason that they know they will not be scrutinized so closely. There is some evidence for this mechanism, with pollution increasing in areas with lower voter turnout. If the correlation between pollution and demographics lies in these mechanisms, then it arises from government failures. In this case, either governmental reforms are required or, alternatively, nongovernmental mechanisms for determining pollution patterns should be considered.

Second, disadvantaged groups may live in more polluted areas for the simple reason that to be poor means not having the resources to "purchase" the good things in life—including a clean environment. That is, the poor may not be able to afford to buy or rent a house or apartment in a clean neighborhood, which will be more expensive than one in a polluted neighborhood. The rich, on the other hand, can afford to pay this premium. In other words, firms may make their polluting decisions based on factors that have nothing whatsoever to do with local demographics, yet households will move in such a way that the poor end up living nearer pollution. In this case, the source of environmental inequity is the more fundamental inequity in the distribution of income.

But this mechanism has an important implication: the observed demographic patterns arise from decisions that individuals have made to make the best use of their limited resources. Saving money for food and clothing through inexpensive housing may be a higher priority for the poor than a clean environment. A cleanup may cause a neighborhood to gentrify, increasing housing prices. While this represents a capital gain to owners, 83 percent of people poor enough to qualify for welfare are renters. For them, these costs are out of their pockets and can make the poor worse off in the end. In effect, the cleanup often forces the poor to pay a price they cannot afford.

A third and final mechanism may be that some communities have features that are attractive to both disadvantaged households and polluting firms. For example, both may be attracted to lower real estate prices. Moreover, real estate prices may be lower near transportation corridors like highways or railroads. The poor live near them because of these lower costs; polluting facilities may locate near them because the transportation route reduces the cost of moving manufactured goods or wastes. And finally, both poorer households and polluting facilities may be mutually attracted by low-skilled labor markets. In this case, the correlation between pollution and disadvantaged groups again arises from the simple fact that these groups have lower incomes. The effect is reinforced by the unhappy coincidence that some features of the inexpensive communities affordable for the poor are actually attractive to polluters.

AVOIDING UNINTENDED CONSEQUENCES

For existing cleanup efforts such as the Superfund and brownfields programs, these mechanisms suggest guidelines that can help minimize unintended consequences like gentrification. Two recommendations stand out. First, as emphasized by the National Environmental Justice Advisory Council, projects should involve local participation. This will increase the likelihood that new amenities fit the preferences of incumbent residents rather than those of prospective gentrifiers. Second, projects might prioritize areas with high rates of home ownership, where local residents will capture the full value of the cleanup.

But there is a larger point at stake. When experiencing poor environmental quality is a consequence, rather than a cause, of poverty, then cleaning up the environment to help the poor is like treating the symptom rather than the disease. Some symptoms, like a moderate fever, represent the body's best efforts to heal itself. In such cases, treating the symptom may actually be counterproductive. This does not mean there is no role for a physician. But the best physician facilitates the body's natural healing processes. Like the body, the market is a remarkably efficient machine.

Accordingly, the best way to help disadvantaged groups may be to empower them, strengthening their position within the market system. Redistributing income to the poor, for example, would provide them with more resources to pay for those things they most want, including a cleaner environment. Encouraging home ownership would put more people in a position to truly benefit from neighborhood improvements such as environmental cleanups. Providing legal aid, facilitating conflict resolution, and otherwise helping poor residents in environmental disputes can help the legal bargaining process to function better and enable the poor to participate in it fully. These may be the more effective routes for helping the poor—and may prove to have "win–win" outcomes for society.

Further Reading

Banzhaf, H. Spencer. 2008. Environmental Justice: Opportunities through Markets. PERC Policy Series No. 42. www.perc.org/articles/article1113.php

Been, Vicki. 1994. Locally Undesirable Land Uses in Minority Neighborhoods: Disproportionate Siting or Market Dynamics? *Yale Law Journal* 103: 1383–1422.

Bullard, Robert D. 1990. *Dumping in Dixie: Race, Class, and Environmental Quality*. Boulder, CO: Westview Press.

Hamilton, James T. 1995. Testing for Environmental Racism: Prejudice, Profits, Political Power? *Journal of Policy Analysis and Management* 14: 107–132.

49. OVERCOMING DISTRIBUTIONAL OBSTACLES TO MARKET-BASED ENVIRONMENTAL POLICIES

Roberton C. Williams III
is a senior fellow at Resources for the Future. He is on leave from the University of Texas at Austin, and is a visiting associate professor at the University of Maryland. He has served as a coeditor of the *Journal of Environmental Economics and Management,* and is currently a coeditor of the *Journal of Public Economics.*

Economists have long advocated putting a price on greenhouse gas emissions and substantially raising the federal gasoline tax. One of the key obstacles to these policies has been that they would impose a larger burden on low-income groups. How can market-based environmental policies be designed to overcome their adverse distributional consequences?

The cost advantage of market-based approaches to environmental policies over traditional command-and-control regulation is widely accepted. By placing a price on emissions, environmental taxes and cap-and-trade systems provide incentives for emissions reductions in many different channels throughout the economy. For example, tightening fuel economy standards would lead to more fuel-efficient cars, whereas raising gasoline taxes would provide a similar improvement in fuel efficiency but would also provide an incentive to drive less. Consequently, a gas tax can achieve a substantially larger reduction in gasoline consumption at the same cost to the economy.

However, policymakers have shied away from market-based approaches in cases where they would have significant impacts on the prices consumers face. U.S. fuel taxes are very low by international standards; indeed, federal fuel tax rates have been constant since 1993 and have fallen since then when adjusted for inflation. Similarly, there has been strong opposition to putting a price on emissions of carbon dioxide and other greenhouse gases.

One key obstacle to more widespread use of market-based approaches is that they are often regressive: for many polluting goods, low-income consumers spend a bigger portion of their budgets on the polluting goods than do high-income consumers. Thus, the burden of a tax that raises the price of one of these goods will be borne disproportionately by lower-income households. In such cases, it may not be enough simply to show that a policy is justified on cost–benefit grounds alone; addressing distributional objections is also important.

FACTORING EQUITY INTO POLICY ANALYSIS

One possible response might be to follow a cost–benefit approach, but to count costs for different income groups differently (for example, counting \$1 of costs for a low-income person the same as \$10 for a high-income person). For a regressive policy, this procedure will raise the assessed costs and imply that the optimal policy will be less stringent. But this approach is unsatisfactory, because it makes the choice of how much to count the costs of any particular income group very arbitrary.

Another approach, included in the climate change proposals currently under consideration in the Senate, is to provide rebates that directly reduce consumers' electricity bills, offsetting the higher cost of energy. However, such rebates may substantially reduce incentives for energy conservation, depending on how they are structured and on how consumers interpret them. This raises the overall costs of the policy as greater emissions reductions must be found elsewhere (through fuel switching in the power sector, for example) to meet a given emissions cap.

A more promising approach would be to combine a change in an environmental tax, together with a change in the broader income tax and transfer system that would approximately offset any distributional effects of the environmental policy. For example, the average share of the household budget spent on gasoline is roughly twice as high among households earning $25,000 per year as it is among households earning $100,000 per year. But that cost could be offset by cutting income tax rates (and/or increasing government transfers), using some of the revenue raised by the increased gas tax in a way that would particularly benefit lower-income households. The resulting combined policy would then affect households of all income levels equally.

This approach recognizes that using the tax and transfer system to compensate for the burden of an environmental tax is a much more efficient way to address distributional concerns than is altering the regulation itself in a way that makes it less efficient. Devoting a portion of the revenues from an environmental tax to provide such compensation ensures that no income group would bear a disproportionate burden, and does so in a way that still preserves consumers' incentives to reduce consumption of polluting goods.

Moreover, even if a particular proposal does not include this type of compensation, analyzing how much compensation would be needed (and what the effect of such compensation would be) is still a valuable analytical tool, because it provides an objective way of gauging the importance of distributional objections to a given policy.

LIMITATIONS

Transfers like this might well increase the costs of environmental regulation, relative to what those costs would be if the same amount of revenue were used to cut taxes equally for all income groups. Economists typically find that the economic efficiency gains from increased work effort and savings tend to be larger for an across-the-board tax cut than for a cut specifically targeted at lower-income households.

Consequently, the estimated optimal gas tax will be lower than it would be if the tax were simply set to maximize economic efficiency without regard for distributional effects. And the same would be true for other policies that would have a similarly regressive distribution of costs and benefits.

However, there is still a strong case for higher environmental taxes. For example, in a 2007 paper, Sarah West and I estimated that the efficiency-maximizing gasoline tax rate for the United States is approximately $1.38 per gallon (in 2009 dollars). Modifying that analysis to take distributional effects into account, by analyzing a gas tax increase together with a compensating income tax change, leads to a significantly lower estimate of the optimal tax: approximately $1.22 per gallon. But even that lower estimate is still far above current U. S. gas tax rates, which average roughly 38 cents per gallon.

Similar results are likely to apply for other pollution taxes and environmental regulations, such as a tradable permit system for carbon dioxide or for local air pollutants. In many cases, the distribution of the costs of regulation is regressive, which means that regulation should be somewhat less strict than what a simple cost–benefit analysis might indicate. But this effect is modest; such regressive effects can be offset through the tax and transfer system at relatively low cost. In short, distributional effects need not pose a serious problem for environmental policy, if the political process allows adjustments of the broader tax and benefit system to compensate for higher energy prices.

Further Reading

Kaplow, Louis. 2004. On the (Ir)Relevance of Distribution and Labor Supply Distortion to Government Policy. *Journal of Economic Perspectives* 18: 159–175.

West, Sarah E., and Roberton C. Williams III. 2004. Estimates from a Consumer Demand System: Implications for the Incidence of Environmental Taxes. *Journal of Environmental Economics and Management* 47: 535–558.

West, Sarah E., and Roberton C. Williams III. 2007. Optimal Taxation and Cross-Price Effects on Labor Supply: Estimates of the Optimal Gas Tax. *Journal of Public Economics* 91: 593–617.

50. WHAT DO THE DAMAGES CAUSED BY U.S. AIR POLLUTION COST?

Robert Mendelsohn

is the Edwin Weyerhaeuser Davis Professor at the Yale School of Forestry and Environmental Studies. He specializes in valuing environmental damages including global warming impacts.

Nicholas Z. Muller

is an assistant professor of economics at Middlebury College. His research focuses on modeling the damages from local air pollutants, environmental accounting, and the design of efficient market-based pollution regulation.

How do economists measure the human health and environmental effects of local air pollution in the United States, the sources of pollution emissions, and how large environmental damages are relative to the overall economy?

The major pollutants first regulated by the Clean Air Act are still causing substantial damages in the United States, particularly to human health. Specifically, ammonia and the five criteria pollutants—fine and coarse particulates, sulfur dioxide, nitrogen dioxide, and volatile organic compounds—currently cause damages that range from $75 billion to $280 billion annually. Here we will explain how these damages are estimated, what sources are responsible for the damages, and compare them with estimates of the damages from greenhouse gases (GHGs).

Economists measure the impacts of air pollution using integrated assessment models that logically connect emissions to their final effects on society. Of primary concern are the human health effects associated with air pollution, including premature mortality, chronic illness (such as bronchitis and asthma), and several acute illnesses. However, the models also measure the damages from reduced crop and timber yields, impaired visibility, deterioration of man-made materials, and diminished recreation services.

Integrated assessment models applied to the United States begin with available emissions data and then calculate pollution concentrations across the Lower 48 states. These concentrations are then converted to "exposures," using county-level population information. Exposures, in turn, are converted into physical effects using concentration-response functions that capture the number of physical effects a certain exposure is likely to cause. Finally, physical effects are converted to dollar damages through valuation techniques.

We rely on an integrated assessment model that we developed, called air pollution emission experiments and policy (APEEP), to capture each of the steps above. APEEP resembles other integrated assessment models in the literature. However, the way we are using APEEP is innovative. First, APEEP calculates the damages due to current emissions from all existing sources. One ton of emissions is then added at a single source, and APEEP recalculates the aggregate damage. The change in the aggregate damage is the marginal damage of the additional ton of emissions. By repeating this experiment for the six pollutants and 10,000 source locations, APEEP estimates the marginal damage of all emissions of these pollutants in the United States. Multiplying the tons of emissions from each source location by the source-specific marginal damage and summing across all sources yields the gross annual damage (GAD). This is a measure of the value of air pollution damages just as GDP is a measure of the value of economic production.

We find that GAD in 2002 is between $75 billion and $280 billion (0.7 to 2.8 percent of GDP). The estimates vary so widely because of three controversial issues: the value of mortality risks, the age dependency of this value, and the relationship between exposure to air pollutants and mortality rates.

First, although the values of many damages from air pollution are known—reduced crop yields, for instance—the value of human health and longevity (and their inverse, illness and death) is contentious. One approach is to use the extra wages paid to workers in risky jobs. This is problematic, however, because mortality risk in the workplace is often associated with sudden death, whereas mortality from air pollution is usually due to long-term exposure. It is also true that people do not agree on what value to place on a small risk of death, and so any single estimate will be contentious no matter how it was estimated.

The second controversy is whether the value attributed to mortality risks should be the same for all age groups or decline with expected years of remaining life. That is, should a smaller value be assigned to older age groups? Age-specific values are rational because remaining consumption declines with age. However, American principles of equality as guaranteed by the Constitution may dictate that every person be valued the same, regardless of age. Finally, the magnitude of the physical impact of exposure to pollutants is also uncertain. Because controlled experimentation (intentionally exposing humans) is unethical, epidemiologists must rely on natural experiments and toxicologists must rely on animal experiments to learn about human sensitivity to pollution. Unfortunately, these methods are less precise, and so the estimates are "noisy." For all these reasons, the range of GAD values is wide.

Turning from aggregate damage to individual pollutants, we find that not all pollutants are equally harmful. Although emissions of fine particulate matter ($PM_{2.5}$), ammonia, sulfur dioxide, and volatile organic compounds make up only half of all emissions by weight, these pollutants cause almost 80 percent of total damages. $PM_{2.5}$, very tiny particles that can lodge in the lungs, accounts for only 6 percent of total emissions by weight, but causes 23 percent of total damages. In contrast, nitrogen oxides and coarse particulates are responsible for almost half of the total tonnage but only 20 percent of damages.

What fraction of GAD is due to different effects? We find that human health damages account for more than 95 percent of GAD. Loss of visibility is clearly one of the most palpable costs of air pollution, but its contribution to GAD is small. The same can be said for crop damage, forest damage, and material damages.

The largest source is still industrial production, which causes 50 percent of air pollution damages. The largest single industrial source of emissions is coal-fired power plants, which cause 20 percent of GAD. Mobile sources are responsible for the next largest share, 35 percent. Light-duty gasoline-powered cars and motorcycles contribute 9 percent, SUVs and light-duty gasoline trucks contribute 7 percent, diesel trucks and heavy-duty gasoline vehicles contribute 15 percent, and rail vehicles, aircraft, and marine vessels generate the remaining 4 percent of mobile source damages. Residential combustion of fossil fuels and wood, primarily for heating, produces perhaps more damage than people think—5 percent. Finally, agricultural sources also cause a surprisingly large share of damages (10 percent), from ammonia from livestock production and fertilizers, and dust from tilling cropland.

The above GAD estimates do not include GHGs. How does their impact compare to GAD? Although they have high current visibility on policymakers' agendas, we believe that current GHG emissions, at least, are not nearly as harmful as criteria pollutants. The empirical impact literature estimates that current emissions will cause future global damages of between $0.50 and $10 per ton of carbon dioxide (when future damages are discounted at market rates). So the current six billion tons of carbon dioxide emitted annually in the United States will likely cause future global damages of between $3 billion and $60 billion. Greenhouse gas emissions consequently cause from 4 to 18 percent of the total damages from air pollution. GHGs do need to be addressed, but the damages that current emissions will cause are relatively small compared to the damages from criteria pollutants. Of course, GHGs are accumulating and future emissions will cause higher damages, so they will become relatively more important to control in the future.

Tighter regulations on emissions of ammonia, fine particulates, and sulfur dioxide are needed. Important sources of these emissions include coal-fired power plants, diesel vehicles (especially marine vessels and heavy-duty trucks), and some industrial sources. Two other sources that have generally escaped attention must also be examined: residential homes and farms. Although each farm and each house contributes only a little to GAD, the net effect of all homes and all farms is substantial. Finally, pollution control efforts aimed at reducing solid waste (incineration) and water pollution (waste treatment plants) generate an inordinate amount of air pollution damage. Regulators need to think more carefully about integrated pollution management so that in the effort to reduce one pollution problem, they do not create a larger one.

Further Reading

Muller, Nicholas Z., and Robert Mendelsohn. 2007. Measuring the Damages of Air Pollution in the United States. *Journal of Environmental Economics and Management* 54(1): 1–14.

Muller, Nicholas Z., and Robert Mendelsohn. Forthcoming. Efficient Pollution Regulation: Getting the Prices Right. *American Economic Review*.

51. WHAT CAN POLICYMAKERS LEARN FROM EXPERIMENTAL ECONOMICS?

John List

is a professor in the University of Chicago Economics Department, a research associate at the National Bureau of Economic Research, and a nonresident fellow at Resources for the Future. Much of his work has focused on the use of field experiments in economics.

How does research on field experiments bear on the issue of how we might quantify the benefits of environmental policies? Such valuations are a critical ingredient for judging whether or not individual policies make sense on cost–benefit grounds.

How can we value the benefits of preserving wilderness areas and wetlands, providing the recreational benefits of cleaner lakes and rivers, and reducing the pollution in the air? Good policy requires good data on economic values, and generally economists rely on markets to provide them. But in some areas, notably environmental protection, we often need to know the worth that society assigns to incremental benefits for which there are no markets.

This need is frequently a legal requirement. Ever since President Reagan's 1981 executive order, federal agencies, including EPA, have been required to consider both the benefits and costs of regulations for economically significant rulemakings before implementation.

Economists rely on several different methods to estimate environmental benefits or damages. For example, one approach to valuing the benefits of cleaner air is to looke at compared how much extra people are willing to pay for houses in regions with good air quality, such as in Laramie, Wyoming, with houses in regions with relatively dirty air, like Los Angeles. The main challenge here is trying to separate out, statistically, the price premium for clean air from all the other factors that may cause property prices to differ across regions—including local factors such as climate, job opportunities, crime levels, school quality, and so on. Moreover, this approach is limited in that it cannot be used, for example, to value how much people would be willing to pay to know that Alaska's Arctic National Wildlife Refuge will be passed on to future generations in pristine condition, even though they may never visit the refuge themselves. As opposed to the value of clean air, which people inhale and thus "use," these other kinds of values are considered "nonuse values." They pose problems in that they generally lack markets—and therefore prices—that economists could use for analysis.

The most widely used approach to estimating the total value of nonmarket goods and services is known as contingent valuation (CV). Under this approach, the researcher uses a questionnaire to ask respondents contingent questions concerning how much they would be willing to pay in donations, taxes, or price increases to achieve a certain goal—preservation of an endangered species, perhaps, or the cleanup of a contaminated area.

Possibly the most celebrated example of CV in an environmental case arose from the 1989 Exxon *Valdez* oil spill. On behalf of the state of Alaska, a group of economists conducted a large-scale CV study of Americans' willingness to pay for the avoidance of another oil spill in Prince William Sound, and the state used the resulting figure, $2.8 billion, in court. The final settlement was $1 billion on top of the $2 billion that Exxon itself spent on restoration.

In California, in another notable case, a fight over water rights raised the question of whether it was worth diverting water into Mono Lake to ensure the survival of the lake's flora and fauna. Certain downstream parties derided it as a choice between the interests of "300 fish versus 28,000 people." But the state's Water Resources Control Board was persuaded otherwise and ordered an increase in the flows into the lake that significantly decreased the city's water rights.

Even though the CV approach has clearly influenced the policy process, it has remained highly contentious, for it is difficult to know whether people's answers to hypothetical questions provide a reliable guide to the amounts that they would actually be willing to pay in practice. Here, the techniques of experimental economics are making a significant contribution. Experimental economics sets up choices that people actually make, whether in the laboratory, under carefully controlled conditions, or in the field, where their decisions can sometimes be compared with results in real markets.

In one of the early uses of the technique, the researcher Peter Bohm, a generation ago in Sweden, compared respondents' answers to hypothetical questions about the value of admission to a sneak preview of a television show with the prices in an actual market for admission. He found that the hypothetical values were higher, but only moderately so. In a recent analysis of these kinds of studies, Craig Gallet and I found that, on average, hypothetical values are three times larger than what people are actually willing to pay in a market setting, implying that we need to be cautious in interpreting the results from CV studies. Further laboratory and field experiments should make plain the situations wherein CV might be viable.

Another complication associated with nonmarket valuation is that differences in values arise, depending on the way in which a question is posed. Sometimes people are asked what they would pay to prevent the loss of a certain environmental benefit, such as a wetland. Sometimes researchers reverse the question, and ask what their respondents would consider fair compensation for the loss of that benefit—suffering the loss of that wetland. Typically, people set a much higher figure for compensation than they are willing to pay to avoid the loss.

At first, many economists argued that the answers on compensation were unreliable and should not be taken seriously. But lab experimentation reinforced the survey evidence, confirming that the difference between willingness to pay and fair compensation is robust across a wide variety of goods. Field experiments have complemented the extant lab and survey evidence by showing the limitations of such results. For example, my own work shows that people experienced with trading ordinary private goods, like mugs and candy bars, are not subject to this value disparity. Other field evidence using public goods, such as increased environmental quality, has reinforced these results and shown that the value disparity lessens because people with experience state much lower fair compensation values. One implication is that we should look at whether CV studies carefully control for (lack of) experience when estimating fair compensation. And when inexperienced agents are important in the valuation process, willingness-to-pay statements of value should be used rather than willingness to accept, since the latter tends to converge to the former with market experience.

Experimental research now under way in the field demonstrates that there is much to be gained from designing economic experiments that span the gap between the laboratory and the world outside, with important implications for economics. Examples include developing new auction formats to distribute pollution permits, exploring compensation mechanisms in social dilemmas (such as what is necessary for many endangered species cases), and examining efficient means to provide public goods. For instance, the optimal approach to engage providers of public goods to actually give resources and what factors keeps people engaged are beginning to be better understood because of field experiments.

What has become clear in this process is that field experiments can play an important role in the discovery process by allowing us to make stronger inference than we could make from lab or uncontrolled data alone. Similar to the spirit in which astronomy draws on the insights from particle physics and classical mechanics to make sharper insights, field experiments can help to provide the necessary behavioral principles to permit sharper policy advice.

Further Reading

Bohm, Peter. 1972. Estimating the Demand for Public Goods: An Experiment. *European Economic Review* 3(2): 111–130.

Harrison, Glenn W., and John A. List. 2004. Field Experiments. *Journal of Economic Literature* 42(4): 1009–1055.

List, John A. 2003. Does Market Experience Eliminate Market Anomalies? *Quarterly Journal of Economics* 118(1): 41–71.

List, John A., and Craig Gallet. 2001. What Experimental Protocol Influence Disparities between Actual and Hypothetical Stated Values? Evidence from a Meta-Analysis. *Environmental and Resource Economics* 20(3): 241–254.

52. ENVIRONMENTAL FEDERALISM

Wallace E. Oates

is a professor of economics at the University of Maryland and a university fellow at Resources for the Future. He specializes in public finance (with a focus on fiscal federalism and state-local finance) and environmental economics (with a focus on economic incentives for environmental management).

What are the pros and cons of setting environmental policies at the state and local levels, as opposed to the federal level? Several examples are given to help answer this question, and evidence is presented on the claim that competition among state governments will result in insufficient environmental protection.

The basic principles of economics make a compelling case for environmental regulation because of the excessive use of our freely available, but scarce, environmental resources under a system of free markets—or, in the jargon of economics, as a result of "externalities." But in a federal system, with several levels of government, the next question involves the locus of regulatory authority: which *level* of government should undertake a specific regulatory responsibility?

A cursory look at U.S. policy on this issue reveals some puzzling anomalies. Under the Clean Air Act in 1970, the U.S. Congress instructed the newly formed EPA to set standards for ambient air quality in the form of maximum permissible concentrations of pollutants applicable to *every* jurisdiction in the country. Only two years later, under the Clean Water Act (1972), the states were assigned the responsibility for setting standards for water quality within their own boundaries. It is not at all clear why standards for air quality should be centrally set and uniform across the nation, while determining standards for water quality is left to the states.

Economics, as it turns out, can provide some guidance on this issue. From an economic perspective, standards for environmental quality should be tightened so long as the benefits from incremental cleanup exceed the additional costs. However, the geographic setting for applying this principle varies among different forms of pollution. In some instances, such as carbon dioxide emissions, which contribute to global climate change, all that matters is the aggregate level of emissions—the precise location of their emission into the atmosphere doesn't matter (at least for purposes of global climate change). For pollutants of this kind, what we need is a national (or, really, a global) program to restrict emissions.

In contrast, both the benefits of cleanup activities and costs of certain other forms of pollution can vary dramatically across different jurisdictions. This, for example, can be the case for various forms of air and water pollution, where one size doesn't fit all. An efficient outcome in such a setting requires different standards for environmental quality depending on how damaging the effects are and how costly it is to control the polluting activity.

A particularly interesting and provocative case in point arose in the waning days of the Clinton administration in 2000, when EPA introduced a new measure to reduce the permissible level of arsenic in U.S. drinking water by 80 percent. The "arsenic rule" applied to all jurisdictions in the nation. Careful analysis of the new provision revealed that it promised only a minuscule reduction in health risk on a national scale. EPA estimated that the tough new standard could save approximately 20 to 30 statistical lives per year (the value of a "statistical" life is typically understood by economists to be the cost of reducing the average number of deaths by one). But this estimate was subject to sufficient uncertainty that it is not unreasonable to believe that no lives would be saved under the standard.

Of special interest in this case was the enormous variation across the country in the cost per household of meeting the arsenic standard. Huge economies of scale exist in the treatment of drinking water such that the new measure could be met in a large water district like New York City for under $1 per year per household. In fact, many large districts were already in compliance with the new standard. But in very small water districts, largely in rural areas, the cost of meeting the new standard was in excess of $300 per household per annum, dwarfing any prospective gains. Indeed, far greater health benefits could be achieved if such sums were used for other public (or private) health measures, such as increasing the frequency of mammograms, colon screenings, or a host of other procedures. One size certainly didn't fit all in this case: the arsenic rule *may* have made sense for large water districts, but it was economically wasteful for smaller districts.

Critics of this approach to environmental federalism contend that it overlooks the fact that municipalities compete for new business investment and jobs. If we leave important matters of environmental regulation to state or local governments, we can set in motion a competitive "race to the bottom," with officials setting lax environmental standards as a means of reducing the cost to new (and existing) businesses. Consequently, the critics argue, it is necessary to centralize standards setting to avoid a competitive depreciation of environmental quality.

However, a closer look suggests that both in theory and in practice, the case for a race to the bottom is not very compelling. A standard theoretical model in which government seeks to maximize the well-being of its citizenry reveals no such race. People care about the quality of the environment—and a government that fails to respond to these concerns is unlikely to stay in office. Moreover, the existing evidence provides little support for this view. Under the Reagan administration in the 1980s, several measures were introduced that effectively moved the responsibility for environmental management on a number of fronts back to the states, creating a favorable setting for a race to the bottom. Three empirical studies have carefully examined this episode, however, and none found any evidence of a competitive reduction in environmental standards. On the contrary, increased state spending on environmental programs and improvements in environmental quality continued unabated through this period.

Basic economics thus suggests an important principle for the structure of environmental regulation: polluting activities that degrade environmental quality in a local jurisdiction should therefore be a local responsibility (including the setting of standards). This way, regulatory measures can be tailored to the specific circumstances of each jurisdiction. In contrast, those forms of pollution that reach beyond state or local borders require a national approach to the setting of standards. This does not, incidentally, imply that there is no role for a centralized agency with regard to local environmental issues. An agency like EPA can provide critical information and guidance on the potential damages from various forms of pollution and on the costs of pollution control. State or local jurisdictions would then be in a position, either through their own officials or, perhaps, through some kind of referendum, to establish standards and a regulatory framework that address the particular circumstances of local environmental issues.

The appropriate use of decentralized environmental decisionmaking can have further benefits. In a federal system, state and local governments have the opportunity to introduce new and innovative regulatory measures. They can serve as laboratories in which to conduct experiments that can provide valuable lessons on the potential of new approaches to public policy. Under the Clean Air Act, for example, many state and local governments introduced a variety of emissions-trading systems that both demonstrated their effectiveness and exposed certain problems in their design. I doubt that the United States would have introduced the very successful national cap-and-trade program in the 1990 Clean Air Act Amendments to control sulfur emissions to reduce acid rain without the invaluable earlier experience with this policy approach at state and local levels.

Further Reading

Oates, Wallace E. 2002. The Arsenic Rule: A Case for Decentralized Standard Setting? *Resources* 147(Spring): 16–18.

Oates, Wallace E. 2002. A Reconsideration of Environmental Federalism. In *Recent Advances in Environmental Economics*, edited by J. List and A. De Zeeuw. Cheltenham, UK: Edward Elgar, 1–32.

Oates, Wallace E., and Robert M. Schwab. 1988. Economic Competition among Jurisdictions: Efficiency-Enhancing or Distortion-Inducing? *Journal of Public Economics* 35(3): 333–354.

PART 4

Managing Natural Resources

Often, there is no obvious need for the government to regulate use of natural resources. For example, the owner of an oil well should adequately trade off the profits from extra oil extraction today against the loss in future profits from reduced availability of the oil reserve. That's not always the case, however; frequently societal costs are not fully taken into account by those who use natural resources, creating a potential role for government intervention.

An obvious example is the overharvesting of ocean and freshwater fish, where individual fishermen do not consider the costs to future generations from depleted stocks. One commentary in this section discusses various issues in the design of tradable quotas as a possible means of managing fisheries. Others discuss how political opposition to this promising policy might be overcome and the potential role for worker cooperatives to prevent overfishing.

Another class of policy problems is associated with the use of water itself. Pollution is a serious problem in many water systems, and commentaries in this section discuss existing and prospective measures to clean up the Great Lakes region and the Gulf of Mexico. Others review the effectiveness of information disclosure programs in raising water quality, legal reforms to promote more efficient water use, and policies to expand insurance against flood risk.

Use of land resources for agriculture and forestry raises further environmental policy issues that are discussed in this section, including possible perverse incentives created by laws to protect endangered species and how funds for species protection might be better spent; the reform of programs that take environmentally sensitive land out of farm production; and policies to better manage the risks of forest fires.

53. CAN CATCH SHARES SAVE FISHERIES?

Christopher Costello

is a professor of environmental and resource economics at the Bren School of Environmental Science and Management at the University of California, Santa Barbara. His research covers natural resource management, with particular focus on uncertainty and incentive-based management.

Steven Gaines

is a professor of ecology, evolution, and marine biology and director of the Marine Science Institute at the University of California, Santa Barbara. He is a marine ecologist with research interests in conservation biology, sustainable fisheries, and biogeography.

Relentless depletion of ocean fish resources has heightened interest in novel policy approaches to prevent the overharvesting of fish stocks. One promising approach is catch shares, which limit the allowable harvest each year for individual species.

The systematic decline of the world's ocean resources is well documented. Dramatic collapses in top predators, ecosystems, and over one-third of the world's fisheries reflect weak or nonexistent institutions that govern fish extraction. This widespread mismanagement squanders precious biological and economic resources; present value economic losses may exceed $1 trillion, and simple extrapolation of current trends suggests that all commercial fisheries could be unviable by the middle of this century. Yet a potential solution, grounded in economic incentives, is emerging and should be pursued more broadly. This novel and widely adaptable approach to fisheries management, known collectively as catch shares, holds tremendous promise if executed with care.

Traditional fisheries management relies on limited fishing seasons, gear restrictions, and limited licenses, which often induce a race to fish, leading to overexploitation and economic collapse. Grounded in the incentives they provide for resource stewardship, catch shares are globally rare but increasingly implemented in many countries. The most common form of catch shares in the developed world is the individual transferable quota (ITQ), by which shares of the total allowable catch are allocated to fishermen, communities, or cooperatives. Unlike cap-and-trade programs for air pollutants, ITQs are allocated on a percentage basis and are granted over a long time horizon. These features accommodate the wide natural fluctuations in fish stocks that are common around the world. The total allowable catch is optimized annually depending on the bioeconomic conditions of the fishery. Because profitability is tied to setting the total catch appropriately, catch shares may enhance the role of science and economics in fisheries management. Beyond ITQs, other common catch share forms include spatial property rights (sometimes called territorial user right fisheries, or TURFs), temporal concessions, and cooperatives. Although these forms are less common in the United States, the developing world has extensive experience with them in places such as Mexico, Chile, and many African countries. Price instruments, such as landings taxes, may also be economically viable but have been politically unpopular and are not implemented in any substantial way in large fisheries.

Widespread adoption of catch shares in the developed world began in the mid-1980s and 1990s in New Zealand, Iceland, Australia, and to a lesser extent North America. Recent evidence suggests a strong empirical link between adoption of catch shares and significant reductions in fisheries collapse, as well as enhanced profitability. While the United States is an emerging catch share leader (with over 10 catch share fisheries, and many more in development), fewer than 2 percent of the world's fisheries operate with catch shares, likely because implementation poses challenges and controversies. Contentious issues include how the rights will be initially distributed, the longevity of the rights, whether consolidation will be allowed, and what additional restrictions should be placed on shareholders (for example, must share owners be fishermen?). A related issue concerns who should capture the economic benefits generated by catch shares, which can be substantial because transferable shares are valued as assets.

The appropriateness of these design features hinges on the ultimate goals sought by the communities they are meant to serve. When economic efficiency is the sole criterion, design strives to mimic the behavior of a sole owner, and thus imposes relatively few additional restrictions. When a community desires to maintain or enhance the fishing heritage of local ports, caps on consolidation are typical, and communities or cooperatives of fishermen are often allocated initial rights. A tension sometimes exists when objectives conflict owing to the inverse relationship between the degree of control retained by the state and the strength of stewardship incentives accruing to fishermen.

Design features can also affect ecological performance. Even under catch shares, an incentive may exist to discard low-value species that are inadvertently harvested as "by-catch." This becomes a particularly salient problem when species of ecological significance have life-history traits that make them more vulnerable to fishing than the target stocks. One solution is to assign separate ITQs over each species. Quotas on target species reflect the profits from harvesting those species. Quotas on by-catch species reflect the relative difficulty of avoiding their capture. If by-catch species quotas can be traded, the market provides an incentive to avoid by-catch.

Other mechanisms exist. For example, under TURFs, cooperatives or individuals maintain exclusive access to fixed areas of ocean. In addition to enhancing stewardship incentives, TURFs may catalyze the implementation of marine protected areas (MPAs), which act like parks in the ocean. This can occur for two important reasons. First, well-designed MPAs may actually increase the profitability of certain fisheries, essentially by protecting "source" areas where larvae originate. So TURF owners may voluntarily implement MPAs to increase profits, for example, by protecting spawning sites. This kind of private sector implementation of MPAs has been observed in several fisheries around the world. Second, the profitability of TURFs is enhanced when they are sited adjacent to MPAs. The spillover of adult fish across the boundary of an MPA can become part of the adjacent TURF holder's yield. By combining catch shares with other approaches to ecosystem-based management, we are likely to enhance economic and ecological outcomes beyond what could be achieved via catch shares alone.

This optimistic recommendation notwithstanding, one substantial hurdle remains. Implementing catch shares often requires buy-in from incumbent fishermen. Despite mounting evidence in their favor, many fishermen view catch shares as the imposition of yet another costly regulation. A promising path forward is to allow subgroups of license holders to obtain exclusive spatial (or temporal) access to a portion of the stock. rather than waiting for consensus or imposing changes in the face of intense opposition from some stakeholders. Then those fishermen who opt to undertake a catch share experiment would be ensured exclusivity—a necessary condition for success—to a fraction of the stock. Those opting out would simply fish independently in the area allocated collectively to them. This approach is not without precedent or success: in the Chignik Salmon Cooperative, permit holders self-selected into either a cooperative or independent sector, and received allocations proportional to their membership.

Catch shares are not a one-size-fits-all solution. Instead, when viewed broadly, and when coupled with MPAs and other approaches to achieve simultaneous objectives for a target fishery and its ecosystem, catch shares show tremendous promise. By aligning economic incentives with desirable ecological outcomes, our use of ocean resources can shift from a story of increasing collapse to stories of recovery, sustainability, and profitability.

Further Reading

Costello, C., S. Gaines, and J. Lynham. 2008. Can Catch Shares Prevent Fisheries Collapse? *Science* 321: 1678–1681.

Deacon, R., D. Parker, and C. Costello. 2008. Improving Efficiency by Assigning Harvest Rights to Fishery Cooperatives: Evidence from the Chignik Salmon Co-op. *Arizona Law Review* 50: 479–509.

Newell, R., J. Sanchirico, and S. Kerr. 2005. Fishing Quota Markets. *Journal of Environmental Economics and Management* 49:437–462.

Worm, B. E.B. Barbier, N. Beaumont, J.E. Duffy, C. Folke, B.S. Halpern, J.B.C. Jackson, H.K. Lotze, F. Micheli, S.R. Palumbi, E. Sala, K.A. Selkoe, J.J. Stachowicz, and R. Watson. 2006. Impacts of Biodiversity Loss on Ocean Ecosystem Services. *Science* 314: 787–790.

54. THE POLITICAL ECONOMY OF ADDRESSING OVERFISHING IN U.S. WATERS

Harrison Fell
is a fellow at Resources for the Future, specializing in quantitative analysis of permit systems to regulate marine resources and pollution emissions.

James N. Sanchirico
is a professor at the University of California, Davis, and a university fellow at Resources for the Future. His research applies quantitative empirical and theoretical methods to study the conservation of natural resources.

To what extent are fish processors justified in claiming compensation when a quota system is imposed on the catch of individual fishermen? Assessing the appropriate amount of compensation is a critical component in the political dealmaking required to move forward with more effective regulation of fisheries.

Overfishing is a classic example of the tragedy of the commons. Since no one owns the fish in the ocean, it's in everyone's interest to catch them as fast as possible, regardless of present or future damage to fisheries. Overexploitation and inefficient use of marine resources are the direct result of open-access conditions. For years, regulators have attempted to solve this problem by utilizing season-length restrictions, total allowable catch (TAC) limits, and gear and vessel power restrictions. This has led to a cat-and-mouse game where fishermen adopt technologies and methods to work around these controls. The result is the infamous and wasteful race to fish, where fishermen catch the allowable limits for a season in hours rather than months.

An alternative approach to dealing with this issue—by addressing causes rather than symptoms—is to allocate shares of the TAC to individual fishermen and fishing vessels. With secured access to a portion of the TAC in a season, fishermen no longer need to race, and they also have greater stewardship incentives. Individual fishing quotas (IFQs), or dedicated access privileges (the U.S. term), are an increasingly prevalent form of fisheries management around the world, regulating more than 175 species in Iceland, New Zealand, Canada, and Australia. The United States, however, lags far behind in adopting IFQ systems.

Recent attention in the United States is focusing on how to move individual fisheries from the current regulated open-access setting to an IFQ system while minimizing the potential impact on fish processors and fishing communities. Concerns over the socioeconomic effects appear to be a barrier that may, at best, stall and, at worst, threaten to derail implementation of IFQs. For example, some fishermen may find it more economically advantageous to sell their allocations rather than fish. But such actions have consequences: communities dependent upon fishing can be adversely affected by the resulting economic disruption that occurs when there are no longer large amounts of fish to be processed.

IFQ implementation could also affect the fish processing industry. Depending on the biological, economic, and market characteristics of a marine species, a shift in processing to fresher or higher-value products that maximize the value of the catch from IFQs is likely. For example, when the North Pacific halibut fishery introduced IFQ management over 10 years ago, there was a shift from an almost exclusively frozen product to a predominantly fresh product. Such a dramatic change could require different product lines and techniques that might not be feasible with current processing equipment. As a result, existing firms or new entrants could acquire competitive advantages.

In addition, the contractual and organizational arrangements between fish processors and harvesters could change post-IFQ. One potential catalyst is the additional flexibility of fishermen to spread their trips out over time to maximize the per-trip return, rather than concentrating trips and catch in short intervals due to season-length regulations or the highly competitive fishing under TAC regulations. Consequently, fish supplies will be more spread out. This change can have both negative and positive impacts. The slower-paced fishing may result in higher fish prices paid by processors as daily supplies are reduced. On the other hand, using data from the Alaska pollock fishery, a recent study by Fell (2008) indicates that the slower-paced fishing under IFQ management may improve processors' ability to react to changing market conditions.

Fish processors also argue that the transition to IFQs exposes them to stranded capital costs. When the race to fish was on, processing facilities were designed to handle a large volume in a short period of time. Capital investments made under the old regulatory regime cannot be recovered if fishermen are going out on their own timetable. Important factors in measuring stranded costs are the potential changes to the quantity supplied, product mix, price in the future, relative share of the stranded costs, and the number of years over which the fish processors suffer said losses. The magnitude of these factors depends on the relative bargaining power of fishermen and processors. If, for example, fishermen can extract higher payments for a pound of fish post-IFQ, then the ability of processors to recover stranded costs diminishes.

IFQ implementation, however, does not necessarily mean that the returns from fishing will transfer completely to the harvesting sector. This result was highlighted in another study by Fell (forthcoming) in an analysis of fishermen's bargaining power in the Alaskan sablefish fishery post-IFQ implementation, Fell estimated that while fishermen's bargaining power did increase, the fishermen and processors of this particular fishery now appear to be evenly sharing the gains.

Regardless of these findings and other similar arguments, the U.S. processing industry wants to make IFQ implementation contingent on having some kind of mechanism in place that will give them funds sufficient to cover their *perceived* stranded costs. Even though IFQs are few and far between in U.S. waters, there is some precedent for accommodating their concerns. In the Alaska crab fishery, for example, the mechanism was the creation of individual processor quotas, in which fishers are allowed to deliver fish only to processors with processing quotas, thereby guaranteeing a fixed supply for processors who own processing quotas. Other proposed IFQ systems discuss compensating processors directly by allocating fish quotas to them that can be leased to harvesters. For instance, regulators in the West Coast inshore groundfish fishery contemplated a requirement that would give up to 50 percent of the initial allocation of fish quotas to processors. Such a demand is not uncommon these days.

Of course, the fishermen object to this allocation because it dilutes their share of the pie. Unfortunately, both parties in this debate seem to have forgotten that the IFQ instrument is meant to address the causes of overexploitation, not as a free hand-out for all sectors of the fishing industry. Because quotas based on past catch histories have been the approach to make IFQs politically viable around the world, it is easy to forget that societal benefits are maximized when the quotas are auctioned, not given away. Benefits are maximized for reasons including the quotas going to their highest valued use and the ability to recycle the revenues to offset other taxes and pay for management.

If policymakers decide to capitalize on the changes in fisheries management that go with the transition to IFQs in order to address the impacts of years of inefficient regulation on fishing communities and processors, there are policy mechanisms other than an initial allocation of quotas to processors. The list includes quota allocation to vulnerable communities, mandatory sunset contracts between harvesters and processors that guarantee fixed supplies of the product over a set length of time, and levies on quota owners for processor and community compensation funds.

Further Reading

Fell, H. 2008. Rights-Based Management and Alaska Pollock Processors' Supply. *American Journal of Agricultural Economics* 90(3): 579–592.

Fell, H., and A. Haynie. Forthcoming. Estimating Time-Varying Bargaining Power: A Fishery Application. *Economic Inquiry.*

Newell, R., Papps, K., and J.N. Sanchirico. Asset Pricing in Created Markets for Fishing Quota. *American Journal of Agricultural Economics* 89(2): 259–272.

Sanchirico, J.N., and R. Newell. Catching Market Efficiencies: Quota-Based Fishery Management. *Resources* 150(Spring): 8–11.

55. ACHIEVING EFFICIENT COORDINATION AND ACCEPTANCE IN FISHERY REFORM

Robert T. Deacon
is a professor of economics and environmental science and management at the University of California, Santa Barbara, and a university fellow at Resources for the Future. His research interests involve natural resource economics, environmental economics, and political economy.

A policy of assigning fishery harvest rights to groups rather than individuals can achieve ecological and economic gains from coordination that other rights-based management regimes fail to capture. Moreover, if individual fishers are given the opportunity either to opt into the group or to stay with the traditional regime, the oft-observed incentive to resist change can be overcome.

A highly publicized article in *Science* in 2008 made a remarkable projection: that the global collapse of all groups of marine organisms now commercially fished would occur by the year 2048. Indeed, growing evidence indicates the decline of commercially important fish stocks and stocks of large marine predators in particular. Although pollution, climate change, and habitat damage no doubt play a part, poor governance is widely believed to be the root cause. Costello et al. recommended implementation of fishery closures, restrictions on catch, effort, and gear, as well as creation of marine reserves to stave off potential catastrophe. But such prescriptions, with the possible exception of the last, have long been mainstays of traditional fisheries management, leaving little cause for optimism that the gloomy forecast can be avoided.

Traditional management applies constraints to fisherywide outcomes—by limiting the total catch, season of fishing, number of fishing permits issued, or kind of gear used. Under such rules, the harvests of an individual firm depend on its ability to catch fish before rivals do, naturally leading to a race to fish. This has led to overinvestment in fishing vessels, short fishing seasons, high processing costs, and low product quality. Many believe it has led to poor ecological outcomes as well.

Fortunately, evidence exists that regulation based on property rights, or limited access privileges, can produce far better outcomes—both economic and ecological. These systems grant fishers secure property rights to specific harvest quantities, providing stewardship incentives absent from the traditional race to fish. In New Zealand, Iceland, and Canada, the introduction of such regimes has motivated commercial fishermen to seek lower catch targets to allow stock rebuilding, promote improved enforcement of catch limits, support stricter size limits, and invest directly in replenishing stocks. Moreover, reanalysis of the data that indicated global collapse by 2048 found that trends in fisheries managed with catch rights show a strikingly different pattern—following the institution of rights-based management, previous downward trends were either halted or reversed.

So mission accomplished, right? Wrong. Almost 99 percent of the world's commercial fisheries and roughly 85 percent of the worldwide catch are either unmanaged or managed in the inefficient and ecologically detrimental traditional way. Deciding how to assign catch rights is a contentious issue, and fishers who are well suited to competing under existing regimes may fear being disadvantaged by a transition. Compounding the problem, inefficient regulation often spurs excessive investment in vessels and processing plants, and owners of such capital naturally resist any change that would impair its value. Finding a management regime that eliminates incentives to block change is therefore of paramount importance.

One interesting option—tried during 2002 to 2004 in the Chignik, Alaska, sockeye salmon fishery—assigned a portion of the aggregate catch to a group of fishers, formed voluntarily, to manage as the group saw fit. Those that chose not to join fished under preexisting rules. In Chignik, the group formed as a cooperative with members sharing profits equally, but this structure is not essential. It was essential, though, that the fishery manager could partition access to the resource and limit interference by designating different fishing seasons for the two groups.

This system offers two key potential advantages. First, a careful division of the catch between voluntary and independent sectors can yield an outcome that makes both groups better off, defusing the incentive to block a transition. Second, if the group assigned rights is empowered by contract to coordinate its members' actions, as was the case in Chignik, substantial efficiency gains are possible. Ordinary firms accomplish this every day, by carefully assigning tasks to workers and capital equipment in order to reduce costs and improve product quality. At best, this is difficult to achieve when all rights are held by independent individuals.

An examination of data from Chignik and other nearby fisheries indicates that allowing the cooperative (co-op) to form and exploit a dedicated catch share led to dramatic changes. By concentrated fishing activity among the most skilled co-op members, roughly one-third of those who joined, it was able to reduce costs. These individuals were paid an agreed-upon wage, and nonfishing members were free to pursue other opportunities. All members shared profits equally, after deducting payments to fishers. This radical consolidation was possible because, as in most commercial fisheries, fishing capacity in Chignik far exceeded that required to harvest a sustainable yield. The co-op's consolidation also slowed the rate of fishing, reducing the capital needed for processing and allowing for more careful handling of the catch, resulting in higher-quality fish that could command a higher price.

The co-op reaped additional gains because of its ability to coordinate fishing actions across space and time and provide shared inputs. For example, by purposely choosing to fish near the ultimate destination, Chignik River, it minimized costly transportation. Co-op fishers also shared knowledge about the location of fish concentrations—information typically concealed under independent fishing—allowing the group to economize on search costs. Additionally, the co-op installed stationary nets along the migration route that funneled the fish toward waiting purse seiners, sharply lowering its harvest costs.

Evidence suggests that the co-op's fishing methods substantially increased profitability. A comparison of permit prices in Chignik and other nearby fisheries indicates that values in Chignik rose while the co-op operated. Depending upon how long participants expected a co-op to operate, increases in annual profits could range from 27 to 100 percent.

The co-op's success was not without controversy, though, and some independent fishers believed they were disadvantaged, particularly by the formula used to divide the catch between sectors. Two of these independents filed suit against the state management agency, arguing that it had exceeded its authority. The Alaska Supreme Court acknowledged the efficiencies the co-op realized, but nevertheless ruled that the policy was inconsistent with existing statutes.

An important lesson presents itself in this unfortunate outcome. The Chignik management approach apparently had the potential to make all participants better off. The key to realizing this potential, however, was a very careful division of the allowed catch between sectors, to avoid imposing losses on some individuals. As the co-op gained popularity and membership rose, the catch allocation rule became far less attractive to independents, so their opposition is not surprising. Unfortunately, the substantial promise that coordinated fishing holds for enhancing efficiency remains unrealized to this day in Chignik because those disadvantaged individuals managed to block its implementation. Fisheries seeking to benefit from cooperative management systems would be wise to include, as a criterion for designing policy change, features that enable "reform without losers," with the goal of moving successfully toward enhanced efficiency and surviving the political process.

Further Reading

Costello, Christopher, Steven D. Gaines, and John Lyhnam. 2008. Can Catch Shares Prevent Fisheries Collapse? *Science* 321(September 19): 1678–1681.

Deacon, Robert T. 2009. *Creating Marine Assets: Property Rights in Ocean Fisheries.* PERC Policy Series No. 43. Bozeman, MT: Property and Environment Research Center.

Deacon, Robert T., Dominic P. Parker, and Christopher Costello. 2008. Improving Efficiency by Assigning Harvest Rights to Fishery Cooperatives: Evidence from the Chignik Salmon Co-op. *Arizona Law Review* 50(Summer 2008): 479–510.

Wilen, James E. 2005. Property Rights and the Texture of Rents in Fisheries. In *Evolving Property Rights in Marine Fisheries*, edited by Donald R. Leal. Oxford: Rowman & Littlefield Publishers, Inc.

56. RESTORING GREAT LAKES ECOSYSTEMS

Worth the Cost?

Soren Anderson

is an assistant professor of economics and agricultural, food, and resource economics at Michigan State University. His research spans a range of issues in energy and environmental economics and policy, with a current focus on the personal transportation sector.

Jennifer Read

is the assistant director and research coordinator for Michigan Sea Grant at the University of Michigan. Her research interests include U.S.-Canada institutional arrangements for resource management at all levels of government, with a focus on water quality and fisheries.

Don Scavia

is the Graham Family Professor of Environmental Sustainability, a professor of natural resources and environment, and of civil and environmental engineering, and the director of the Graham Environmental Sustainability Institute at the University of Michigan. His research includes understanding and predicting impacts of natural and anthropogenic stresses on Great Lakes and marine ecosystems, and using of models and integrated assessment in transferring knowledge to decisionmaking.

The Great Lakes region faces a wide array of environmental problems as a result of pollution, inadequate capacity for wastewater treatment, and invasive species. How can these diverse challenges be addressed, and what are the costs and benefits of these measures?

The Great Lakes are among North America's most important natural resources, spanning some 94,000 square miles and accounting for 90 percent of America's and 20 percent of the world's surface fresh water. The lakes and surrounding watersheds sustain thousands of species of plants, fish, birds, and mammals. The Great Lakes basin is also home to more than 35 million people in the United States and Canada.

Yet the Great Lakes face numerous environmental problems that are harming sensitive ecosystems and undermining human health, recreation, and commercial transport. The problems are particularly acute in areas of concern (AOCs), which suffer from habitat loss, degraded fish and wildlife populations, fish tumors and deformities, beach closings, fish consumption advisories, nutrient pollution, and undrinkable water. Many AOCs are essentially underwater toxic sites. To halt and reverse this environmental degradation, a group of 1,500 government officials and private-sector stakeholders, known as the Great Lakes Regional Collaboration, developed a program to address the underlying problems. The program strategies address four areas specifically.

PROGRAM STRATEGIES

Municipal Wastewater. In many cities, rainstorms regularly overwhelm wastewater treatment facilities. Untreated sewage then flows directly into the lakes, contaminating nearshore waters, sometimes causing waterborne disease outbreaks and forcing officials to close public beaches. *Recommendation:* Upgrade municipal wastewater treatment facilities.

Invasive Species. Invasive species can be devastating. Sea lampreys have decimated native lake trout populations; zebra and quagga mussels have clogged water pipes and severed links in fishery food chains; and an aggressive virus known as viral hemorrhagic septicemia (VHS) is ravaging fish populations. *Recommendations:* Require foreign shippers to treat or exchange ballast water before entering the lakes; prevent invaders from entering through canals and waterways (for example, by funding the Chicago Sanitary and Ship Canal barrier); and impose stricter rules for trade in live organisms.

Nonpoint–Source Pollution. Phosphorus and other nutrients from agricultural operations flow into the lakes, contributing to massive algae blooms. Decomposing algae wash up on beaches, cause problems in municipal water supplies, and create "dead zones" that threaten fish populations. Many of the region's marshes and other buffers, which would otherwise act as filters, have been destroyed to make room for development. More than 80 percent of the region's wetlands have already been lost. *Recommendations:* Protect and restore wetlands and streamside buffers; encourage farming practices that reduce runoff; and promote nutrient and manure management plans for livestock operations.

Contamination. Although toxic discharges from industrial sources have abated significantly, contamination persists at high levels, triggering fish consumption advisories. *Recommendations:* Curtail principal sources of mercury and other toxic substances; prevent new chemicals from entering the lakes; support efforts to combat global emissions of toxic substances; increase funding for research, surveillance, and forecasting to deal with chemical threats; start a public education campaign about fish consumption and the role of individuals in reducing toxic pollution; and clean up contaminated sediments.

POTENTIAL BENEFITS

This is an ambitious program, and implementing its recommendations would cost some $27 billion. What would be the expected return on this investment?

In 2007, a team of economists and scientists attempted to calculate the net economic benefits of this strategy, translating its recommendations into specific ecological improvements and then assigning values to these improvements, scaling by dollar benefits per person and the number of beneficiaries. All the estimates are conservative.

Upgrading wastewater treatment facilities would reduce beach closings and advisories by 20 percent, delivering economic benefits of $2 billion to $3 billion. The plans to restore wetlands and prevent the spread of invasive species would halt and reverse the declines in game fish populations, likely resulting in a 25 to 50 percent increase in fish stocks above a "do nothing" scenario. Greater fish abundance would yield $1.1 billion to $5.8 billion in benefits to recreational anglers. Restoring wetlands would generate moderate benefits of $100 million to $200 million for bird-watchers and $7 million to $100 million for waterfowl hunters.

The program would reduce sedimentation by 10 to 25 percent, improving water clarity at beaches and benefiting lakefront property owners by $2.5 billion in increased waterfront property values. The reduction in sedimentation would also reduce costs for municipal water treatment by $50 million to $125 million.

Cleaning up contaminated sediments would benefit aquatic ecosystems and reduce real and perceived health risks. One study found that households living in a Great Lakes watershed would be willing to pay $150 per year to clean up contaminated sediment completely over the next one to two decades. With more than 11 million households in the basin, this implies $12 billion to $19 billion in benefits.

People living outside the basin may also benefit from the strategy. To be conservative, however, the analysis was confined to Great Lakes anglers, beachgoers, shoreline residents, and others living in the basin; it did not include the "existence" value that millions of other people around the country might derive from knowing that the lakes are cleaner.

The analysis also deliberately excluded many expected benefits for which there are neither reliable calculation methods nor good studies from which to extrapolate, such as the general benefits of plant and animal health and the direct benefits of preventing future invasive species. Because the study was conservative in valuing individual ecological benefits, and because researchers were unable to quantify many benefits, the estimates of aggregate benefits are also conservative. Nevertheless, for a program that would cost about $27 billion, aggregate benefits amount to $18 billion to $31 billion.

Recognizing that this analysis most likely missed some important benefits, researchers also conducted a separate analysis, asking what would happen if the strategy increased residential property values by 10 percent in coastal census tracts and by 1 to 2 percent in metro areas adjacent to the lakes—increases consistent with exsiting estimates of the benefits of Great Lakes cleanups in terms of higher property values. Based on this admittedly speculative approach, the estimated benefits were $30 billion to $40 billion—well above the strategy's cost.

BROADER IMPACTS

The Great Lakes region is hoping to reverse its decades-long economic decline, and the restoration strategy could contribute to a broader program of revitalization. Recent research shows that people are willing to pay a substantial premium to live in Great Lakes coastal areas. By maintaining and enhancing this valuable resource, the strategy would likely make the Great Lakes basin more attractive, helping the region retain and attract workers and businesses.

Moreover, the economic stimulus plan passed by Congress in 2009 included several billion dollars for states to upgrade water treatment infrastructure and address other coastal issues, a sizable chunk of which was slated for the Great Lakes region. Research indicates that this and potential future spending on Great Lakes restoration are likely to generate substantial long-run environmental and economic benefits in addition to any short-run stimulus effect.

Further Reading

Austin, John C., Soren T. Anderson, Paul N. Courant, and Robert E. Litan. 2007. Healthy Waters, Strong Economy: The Benefits of Restoring the Great Lakes Ecosystem. Washington, DC: Brookings Institution.

Brookings Institution's Great Lakes Economic Initiative, www.brookings.edu/projects/great-lakes.aspx.

Great Lakes Regional Collaboration, www.glrc.us.

Michigan Sea Grant, www.miseagrant.umich.edu.

57. THE GULF OF MEXICO'S DEAD ZONE

Mess, Problem, or Puzzle?

Don Scavia

is the Graham Family Professor of Environmental Sustainability, a professor of natural resources and environment, and of civil and environmental engineering, and the director of the Graham Environmental Sustainability Institute at the University of Michigan. His research includes understanding and predicting impacts of natural and anthropogenic stresses on Great Lakes and marine ecosystems, and using models and integrated assessment in transferring knowledge to decisionmaking.

After a look at the causes of the Gulf of Mexico's "dead zone," a large area of water where low oxygen levels are highly harmful to aquatic life, this commentary discusses policy responses.

Issues affecting stakeholders tend to be messes, problems, or puzzles. Messes have both arguable issue definitions and arguable solutions. In problems, stakeholders agree on the issue definition, but disagree on the solution because multiple solutions exist. In puzzles, they agree with both the definition of the issue and its solution.

This is a useful framework for describing the evolution of a seemingly intractable environmental problem: the "dead zone" in the Gulf of Mexico, where on a seasonal basis, oxygen levels fall so low that most aquatic species cannot survive. "Hypoxia" is the scientific term for the 20,000 square kilometers of low-oxygen waters off the Louisiana coast, right in the middle of the most important commercial and recreational fisheries in the continental United States.

Whether this dead zone is natural or human-caused, whether the primary cause is organic carbon or fertilizer nutrients, and where those nutrients come from were questions resolved in the 1990s through a series of consensus-forming technical studies and integrated assessments, which I was privileged to lead. So we moved from mess to problem.

A solution was agreed upon when a federal-state-tribal task force called for reducing nitrogen loads from the Mississippi River basin by 30 percent through funding farmers to remove land from production, creating and preserving conservation buffers and wetlands, and using best management practices in the Corn Belt. Problem now becomes puzzle.

The puzzle—agreed-upon issue and solution—should have at least moved us in the right direction. But it has not, and little progress has been made even though all of the necessary tools have been available for years. Best management practices, including appropriate fertilizer application, are well known. The ability of streamside buffers and wetlands to keep excess nutrients out of streams, rivers, and the Gulf are demonstrably effective. But nutrient loads are up, the dead zone is as big as ever, and there is little expectation that either will decrease in the near future. So why are we moving backward?

There are two reasons: First, while the task force delivered the original action plan in 2001, it was never followed by funding, and the Bush administration took almost two years to convene subsequent task force meetings, which simply rehashed and reviewed previous work and agreements. Second, demand for corn ethanol (known around Washington as "political holy water") surged, and environmental elements of the action plan were trampled as corn prices rose to $3 and $4 per bushel and more. The market, encouraged by political operatives at all levels, pushed for more corn from both existing lands and lands set aside for conservation. As a result, in 2007 there were millions of additional acres in corn, 1.2 million metric tons of nitrogen loaded to the Gulf, and the third-largest dead zone since records were first kept over 22 years ago.

That 2001 action plan set a goal of reducing the size of the hypoxic region to less than 5,000 square kilometers by 2015 and called for a long-term adaptive management strategy—coupling management actions with enhanced monitoring, modeling, and research. The action plan also called for an assessment every five years of "the nutrient load reductions achieved and the response of the hypoxic zone.... Based on this assessment, the Task Force will determine appropriate actions to continue to implement this strategy or, if necessary, revise the strategy"—adaptive management. But the reassessment conducted under the EPA Science Advisory Board focused instead primarily on the scientific basis for the original plan. While it reconfirmed the relationship between the Mississippi nitrogen load and hypoxia, it recommended that nitrogen load reduction targets be increased from 30 percent to 45 percent, that phosphorus loads also be reduced by 45 percent, and emphasized that significant time had been lost because of a lack of implantation, meaning that the 5,000 square-kilometer target may not be possible to achieve by 2015. The panel also reported a regime shift in the Gulf that makes the system more sensitive to nutrient inputs.

There are conservation programs that can be brought to bear on these issues, but funding for them is not adequate to meet the needs, and they are not generally targeted to areas that can do the most good. The Environmental Working Group points out that within the 5 percent of the Mississippi basin supplying 40 percent of the nitrogen to the Gulf, the ratio of crop subsidies to conservation spending is 500 to 1. Even a modest change in that ratio would make a significant difference. Such targeting is consistent with the EPA inspector general's report calling for EPA to set nutrient criteria in a way to guide upstream targets.

Is there hope? I had been optimistic, but that had been based on the farm and energy bills that were recently debated. Policy decisions about environmental benefits from agriculture are incontrovertibly bound to decisions about commodity programs. Commodity production has had indisputable environmental effects, and past farm policy has invested in commodity programs to a greater degree than conservation—often trading them off against each other. This most recent round of debate could have been different, especially if it had considered some of the ideas from the closing chapter of our recent book (Nassauer et al. 2007)and elsewhere, on how conservation programs, modified in concert with commodity programs, could help breathe some life—and oxygen—back into the Gulf.

Paying farmers to set aside land can improve soil conservation, water quality, and habitat. However, keeping that land in retirement or adding additional acres can be difficult when commodity prices or price supports are high. These programs need to incorporate production as influenced by commodity programs, and they need to provide farmers with benefits beyond what they would receive from commodity-supported production. The government should not allow enrolled acres to come out of retirement to reduce commodity prices.

I underscore that it is farm policy, not farmers, that make it difficult to reach these environmental goals. For example, to understand how farmers might respond to different practices that could affect water quality, my Michigan colleague Joan Nassauer and her collaborators conducted in-depth interviews with Iowa farmers in 1998 and in 2007 completed an Internet survey of more than 500 Iowa farmers on farming preferences. Their analyses demonstrate that Corn Belt farmers understand the difference between current cropping practices and future innovations that could result in dramatically improved water quality. Given adequate technology to adopt conservation innovations, and assuming their income is unaffected, farmers prefer a more diverse landscape that shows better conservation and improved water quality.

Targeting conservation funds has been employed in a variety of ways to make efforts more effective, and studies have shown it is cost-effective. However, U.S. policy has aimed to both achieve conservation goals and get cash to rural areas, thereby subsidizing conservation practices that are broadly distributed across the nation. More efficient nutrient-load reduction benefits could be obtained if programs were targeted toward Corn Belt states that are responsible for the majority of the nutrient load flowing to the Gulf.

Most agricultural conservation programs use best management practices rather than performance standards, even though economists and natural scientists agree that the latter are more effective and efficient. For diffuse benefits like water quality and habitat, performance standards are difficult to measure; for example, monitoring runoff from individual farms is particularly challenging. However, if programs operated at larger scales—for example, focusing conservation programs on collectives of farms in larger watersheds—it would be possible to monitor performance in the streams and rivers leaving those watersheds.

When we began the integrated assessment on Gulf hypoxia, a false choice was presented to us: "What do you want—corn or shrimp?" It was posed in at least partial jest, but it is another way of suggesting that productive agriculture and a safe, healthy environment cannot coexist. Clearly they can: farmers will protect their environment as long as their livelihoods are not put at risk. Because their income will most likely continue to be determined more by federal policy than markets, shaping farm and energy policies appropriately can make enough corn shrimp chowder for us all.

Further Reading

Nassauer, Joan Iverson, Mary V. Santelmann, and Donald Scavia, eds. 2007. *From the Corn Belt to the Gulf: Societal and Environmental Implications of Alternative Agricultural Futures.* Washington, DC: RFF Press.

National Science and Technology Council, Committee on Environment and Natural Resources. 2000. *Integrated Assessment of Hypoxia in the Northern Gulf of Mexico.* Washington, DC: National Oceanic and Atmospheric Administration.

58. INFORMATION DISCLOSURE AND DRINKING WATER QUALITY

Lori Snyder Bennear

is an assistant professor of environmental economics and policy at Duke University's Nicholas School of the Environment. Her research focuses on evaluating the effectiveness of innovations in environmental regulatory policy.

Sheila Olmstead

is an associate professor of environmental economics at Yale University's School of Forestry and Environmental Studies and a visiting scholar at Resources for the Future. She focuses on water resource economics and policy.

In recent years, the traditional system of federal environmental regulations has been supplemented with a variety of programs requiring the disclosure of information on firms' environmental records. How effective has "right-to-know" legislation been in reducing the prevalence of contaminated drinking water?

In the United States, nearly 270 million people (about 95 percent of the population) obtain piped water from regulated community drinking water systems. The quality of drinking water from these community systems, which may serve anywhere from 25 to several million people, is regulated by the federal government under the Safe Drinking Water Act (SDWA). The SDWA regulates chemical, microbiological, radiological, and physical drinking water contaminants by enforcing 90 different maximum contaminant levels (MCLs), which limit the amount of contaminants that can legally be present in drinking water. For some pollutants, the SDWA also establishes treatment protocols that must be followed to reduce contamination.

U.S. taxpayers heavily subsidize compliance with the SDWA. Between 1995 and 2003, Congress appropriated $1 billion each year for grants and below-market loans to states (which then distributed funds to water supply systems) for treatment and distribution infrastructure improvements. Nonetheless, U.S. community water systems incur tens of thousands of SDWA violations each year. For example, between 1997 and 2003, U.S. water suppliers incurred about 9,900 violations per year of the total coliform rule—the main rule governing the presence of bacteria in drinking water and the most frequently violated MCL.

In 1996, the SDWA was amended, mandating, among other things, that community drinking water systems disclose information about such violations to their consumers every year, in a standard format called a consumer confidence report (CCR). This report must provide information on the source of drinking water, any detected contaminants (even if levels are within legal limits), and any violations of drinking water standards. The CCRs were first issued in 1999, reporting violations from the 1998 calendar year. While all community water systems must compile a CCR, the method of distribution to consumers varies by system size. Suppliers serving 10,000 or more people must mail their CCRs directly to households. Those serving more than 100,000 people must mail their CCRs and make them available online. In contrast, suppliers serving fewer than 10,000 households must post hard copies of the CCRs in a public place and make them available on request, but they are not required to mail them.

The CCR rule was one of many environmental right-to-know provisions enacted during the 1980s and 1990s. The primary public policy goal of these right-to-know rules is to provide the public with important information about environmental quality and health. But information disclosure requirements can be seen as de facto direct environmental regulatory instruments—that is, the requirement to disclose information about environmental performance may induce improvements in environmental performance.

Our recent research suggests that information disclosure may actually accomplish this goal. In analyzing whether community water suppliers in Massachusetts incurred fewer water quality violations when they were required to issue CCRs to their customers, we examined trends in violations separately for large suppliers that are required to mail their reports and for smaller suppliers that must only compile the data and make them available to households upon request. There is strong evidence that those water suppliers required to mail CCRs directly to customers had lower violations after the CCR rule took effect. The magnitude of this effect is quite significant. On average in Massachusetts, large water suppliers violated the SDWA about once every two years before 1998. Mailing CCRs reduced total violations for this group by between 30 and 44 percent, and reduced more serious health violations by 40 to 57 percent.

Proponents of "information as regulation" argue that there are at least three mechanisms through which information disclosure might affect environmental quality. The first is the market mechanism: if information about firms' environmental performance is known by consumers, investors, or employees who value environmental performance, firms can face market pressure to improve. The second is the political mechanism: people may use the political system to lobby for more stringent regulation or to protest particular production practices. Finally, information disclosure programs can affect the internal decisionmaking of an organization. The act of measuring and reporting data on environmental performance may itself generate internal changes at firms that lead to improvements in environmental performance.

While our research does not directly test any of those three mechanisms, our results are consistent with the hypothesis that the political mechanism is at work. Water suppliers required to directly mail CCRs may experience, or expect to experience, a political response and may respond by lowering violations. We would not expect the market mechanism to work in this case. There is essentially no market through which consumers can respond to information, aside from either moving to a different town (a high-cost response) or purchasing bottled drinking water, a substitution that would have only a minimal impact on demand, because drinking water constitutes a tiny fraction of household piped water consumption in the United States. The internal mechanism is unlikely, as well; water suppliers are already required to monitor and report any violations to the state, so compiling these data for their customers provides no new information to the supplier.

The evidence suggests that information disclosure requirements associated with the 1996 amendments to the SDWA resulted in substantial decreases in drinking water violations among regulated water suppliers. In this context, mandatory information disclosure complements, but does not supplant, existing pollution control regulations. However, recent research in developing countries suggests that consumers also respond to information disclosure, potentially improving health outcomes by substituting safer water supplies. These behavioral changes occur even in the absence of mandatory water quality standards. Information disclosure can be a useful complement to more traditional environmental regulatory instruments in some settings, but further research is necessary to determine whether it may also serve as a substitute for these regulations.

Further Reading

Bennear, L.S., and S.M. Olmstead. 2008. The Impacts of the "Right to Know:" Information Disclosure and the Regulation of Drinking Water Quality. *Journal of Environmental Economics and Management* 56(2):117–130.

Jalan, J., and E. Somanthan. 2008. The Importance of Being Informed: Experimental Evidence on Demand for Environmental Quality. *Journal of Development Economics* 87:4–28.

Johnson, B. 2003. Do Reports on Drinking Water Quality Affect Customers' Concerns? Experiments in Report Content. *Risk Analysis* 23:985–998.

Madajewicz, M., A. Pfaff, A. van Geen, J. Graziano, I. Hussein, H. Momotaj, R. Sylvi, and H. Ahsan. 2007. Can Information Alone Change Behavior? Response to Arsenic Contamination of Groundwater in Bangladesh. *Journal of Development Economics* 84:731–754.

59. WESTERN WATER LAW AND EFFICIENT USE OF WATER RESOURCES

Charles Howe

is a senior staff member of the Institute of Behavioral Science and a professor emeritus of economics at the University of Colorado, Boulder. He specializes in the economics of water markets.

In the western states, where water transfers have occurred under the priority doctrine of water law for more than a century, the law has been slow to recognize the legitimacy of important environmental uses of the resource, and some conflicts continue between water right priorities and the highest values in use. Efficient water markets with low transaction costs are needed to resolve these conflicts. "Water banks" of several forms hold promise.

While the very idea of "water law" and "water courts" may sound odd to someone on the East Coast, where rainfall is abundant, throughout the West having access to and the right to use water is both complicated and extremely political. For example, the Colorado River crosses seven states, from Wyoming to California, and is a major source for both agricultural and municipal needs all along the way.

Water laws are embedded in the constitutions of western states, and each water right has a priority attached to it. Seniority or priority ("the prior appropriation doctrine") is assigned according to the date of first use. Today, water rights can be leased or sold, and the initial priority remains part of the right. For example, in the South Platte basin of Colorado, many surface diversions for irrigation date back to the mid-19th century and are thus quite senior. If low streamflows prevent senior rights from diverting water to which they are entitled, the seniors can "put a call" on the river, requiring all upstream rights "junior" to the caller to stop diverting water until adequate streamflow is restored. River calls almost never occur during wet, high flow periods but can be continuous during a drought.

Two basic tenets of western water law are that the water claimed under the right must be put to beneficial use, and that when water rights are leased or sold for new uses, there must be no injury to other water users. In some ways, historically, these tenets have conflicted with the efficient allocation of water. For many decades, the interpretation of beneficial use did not include in-stream uses to sustain water quality, fish populations, riparian (streamside) ecosystems, or recreation. Only recently has it become possible to dedicate water rights to these purposes. The no injury requirement for transfers has been interpreted too narrowly by the courts in failing to recognize degradation of water quality as an injury. In Colorado, only in the past few years have the water courts (a division of the state judicial system) been permitted to consider water quality effects when reviewing proposed transfers.

Recent conflicts between surface-water users and groundwater users in Colorado and Idaho raise questions about the way in which water rights are administered through "river calls." In the South Platte basin of Colorado, 445 major agricultural wells were "called out" in the summer of 2006, continuing into the summer of 2007. Wells generally are junior to many surface-water users because of the late development of pumping technology. Low flows led to the call by senior downstream surface-water users while the wells failed to provide makeup water that might have allowed them to continue pumping. Many cities and irrigation districts were also called out.

The 2006 well shutdown turned out to be very costly, with the immediate loss of 30,000 productive acres. The impacts were felt throughout the regional agricultural community. The beneficiaries of the shutdown were the downstream agricultural users, who would benefit from increased streamflow only several years later. It is clear that the present value of the costs to the well users greatly exceeded the present value of downstream benefits. A very similar situation was found in the East Snake River plain aquifer in Idaho.

In addition to the agricultural losses from the call, many high-value surface-water users—including the Colorado cities of Boulder, Highlands Ranch, and Greeley—had to forgo some of their diversions from the South Platte. Their losses were quite high compared to agricultural values.

These cases suggest that, under current western U.S. conditions, river calls are likely to be economically inefficient. Calling parties are not motivated to take into account the losses of affected juniors, while it is unlikely that juniors will get organized to pay seniors to prevent calls from being made. The underlying problem is a low correlation between priorities and values in use. Many senior rights are still being applied to lower-value uses in agriculture, while the rights held by urban areas are typically junior.

This is where water markets can make a difference by moving lower-value water rights to higher-value uses on a willing-seller, willing-buyer basis. The challenge is to make these markets more efficient and less costly to use. In Colorado, water right transfers must be reviewed by the water court to guarantee no injury to other water users, usually requiring costly engineering and legal studies. In New Mexico, this review function is typically vested in the Office of the State Engineer, which has resident expertise to judge these factors.

In most western states, "water banks" are being used to facilitate water transfers. These programs, administered by each state, serve as clearinghouses or brokers, connecting prospective water buyers and sellers. There is extensive favorable experience with water banks in Arizona, Idaho, and other western states. While water banks still require some form of administrative review, they can significantly reduce transfer costs and the ongoing conflicts between the historical water uses patterns and the emerging need for greater flexibility and economic efficiency in western water administration.

Further Reading

Cosgrove, Donna M., and Gary S. Johnson. 2005. Aquifer Management Zones Based on Simulated Surface Water Response Functions. *Journal of Water Resources Planning and Management* 131(2): 89–100.

Howe, Charles W. 2008. Water Law and Economics: An Assessment of River Calls and the South Platte Well Shut-Downs. *University of Denver Water Law Review* 12(1). Fall.

Snyder, Donald L., and Roger H. Coupal. 2005. *Assessment of Relative Economic Consequences of Curtailment of Eastern Snake Plain Aquifer Ground Water Irrigation Rights.* Report to the Idaho Department of Water Resources. February.

Thorvaldson, Jennifer, and James Pritchett. 2006. *Economic Impact Analysis of Reduced Irrigated Acreage in Four River Basins in Colorado.* Completion Report No. 207, Colorado Water Resources Research Institute. Fort Collins, CO: Colorado State University.

60. A NEW APPROACH TO REFORMING THE NATIONAL FLOOD INSURANCE PROGRAM

Leonard Shabman
is a resident scholar at Resources for the Future. He specializes in expanding the contributions of economic analysis to the formation of water and related land-resource policies.

How might the problem of low take-up rates for flood insurance among residential and commercial properties located in floodplain regions be addressed? This commentary outlines a series of proposals to expand the use of locally managed group insurance programs.

In the mid-1960s, as Congress began work on a National Flood Insurance Program (NFIP), a House report described the nation's flood-risk management objective: "It seems highly probable that the total flood hazard in the United States will increase over the next several decades, even with careful weighing of the risks involved. A growing population, with higher average incomes per person, and attendant increased economic activity of many kinds will probably lead to greater use of flood prone areas. ... Increased use of these areas, in spite of flood hazard may well be economically rational if the new occupants bear the full cost of the occupancy of these areas."

Under these guidelines, a successful flood-risk management policy would ensure that a landowner's decision to locate an activity on a floodplain or coastal hazard area was informed: he or she would understand the river and land-use practices that could lead to possible flood damage and be responsible for any subsequent repair or replacement costs. (I will use the term "floodplain" to include coastal hazard areas.)However, it was recognized then, and is still the case, that individuals cannot readily understand their exposure to flood damage from rarely experienced storm events.

So requiring purchase of flood insurance where annual premiums reflect expert-determined estimates of expected property damages was a practical way to inform landowners of flood risk as well as replace taxpayer costs of postdisaster relief with insurance payouts.

With this logic in mind, in 1967, the nation instituted the NFIP. However, the NFIP as implemented today makes few floodplain occupants informed or cost-responsible, and there are several reasons why. Less than 25 percent of individual homes and businesses in areas that will experience at least one significant flood over a 30-year period actually purchase flood insurance. There have been many efforts to increase purchases, but even an NFIP requirement that mortgage lenders require flood insurance has had only limited effect. Of equal importance, insurance purchase requirements apply only to that portion of the floodplain where the chance of a flood is 1 percent in any year (a so-called 100-year flood)—ignoring floods that would be less frequent, but of possibly greater potential damage.

A REFORM PROPOSAL

Expecting properties located throughout the whole floodplain to have actuarially sound insurance remains an attractive objective for a national flood-risk management policy. One way to achieve this is for the NFIP to offer group flood insurance policies for all at-risk properties in the community. These policies would be purchased by local governments or specially designated flood-risk management districts. The costs could be recovered through special assessments (user fees or taxes) levied on each covered property as an adjunct to the regular property tax, and assessments would vary with flood risk.

Furthermore, Congress should affirm that flood-risk management is a shared governmental responsibility, authorizing and funding federal programs that create incentives for community purchase of group flood insurance. Requiring landowners to pay for flood-risk management services is not a new or radical proposal; for example, levee districts across the nation collect taxes for construction, repair, and maintenance. Offering flood insurance coverage through landowner assessments is simply building on the well-established practice of local governments taking fiscal responsibility for flood-risk mitigation.

However, providing and then charging for flood protection, which would enhance land value, would be more likely to meet with landowner approval than special assessments for flood insurance. Therefore, several actions must be taken to make this proposal practical and attractive to local governments and their citizens.

COMMUNITY FLOOD INSURANCE

The NFIP would continue to offer flood insurance to individual residences and small business, with other risks insured through the private insurance market, as is now the case. However, Congress should authorize the NFIP to develop and offer a new form of insurance—a community (group) policy—covering all properties throughout the whole area of the floodplain. The group premium cost for the community would be set by the NFIP, but in accord with the aggregate flood risk for that individual community. This approach would increase the number of policies in effect and therefore expand market penetration (increase in the pool of insured properties), spread risk, and lower premium costs. Properly designed, it should also reduce administrative costs for individual coverage and claim filing, further lowering premiums.

In the longer term, if group policy purchase proves attractive, private insurers might enter the market as an alternative to the NFIP group plan. Today, localities can purchase private all-risk insurance (including flood) for local infrastructure. Group flood coverage to homes and business insurance might be offered by private sellers as an extension of those local infrastructure policies.

Beyond NFIP offering a group policy, the federal government should finance the group premium of communities that purchase insurance from either the NFIP or private companies. This cost sharing could vary with the degree of community effort to reduce flood exposure or vulnerability, much as is now done through the community rating system under the existing NFIP. Cost sharing may be tied to the expense of providing coverage for preexisting structures or might offset high insurance costs for low-income people located in flood-prone areas.

The federal government has struggled for decades to define and execute a national flood-risk management policy, and as a result, there are myriad federal flood-risk management programs. With modest modifications, these could be redesigned to become incentives for local community purchase of group policies. As just one example, funding priorities for flood protection projects might favor communities that have purchased a group policy.

Of particular importance to encouraging group purchase, Congress should create a catastrophic disaster-aid trust fund with payments from that fund reserved for storms meeting clear, predetermined criteria. The fund would be financed by an annual on-budget allocation of general revenues and with annual fees paid by localities purchasing group insurance. If damages exceed insurance coverage (after considering deductibles), payment would be made from the catastrophic fund to the individuals in communities that were covered by the group insurance. One benefit of this approach is that group insurance premiums would be for less extreme events, lowering premiums for local communities to more attractive levels.

Those communities that might have implemented a group insurance program and paid into the catastrophic trust fund, but chose not to do so, would not be eligible for payments from this fund. Instead, they would continue to have access to the uncertain, not very generous, and red-tape-bound "off-budget" disaster-aid programs that now exist. Recognition of this program reality might place pressure on local jurisdictions to make group purchases and participate in the catastrophic loss fund.

Further Reading

For a comprehensive review of the NFIP program, see www.fema.gov/business/nfip/nfipeval.shtm.

Cooke, Roger M., and Carolyn Kousky. 2009. Are Catastrophes Insurable? *Resources* 172 (Summer).

Kousky, Carolyn, and Howard Kunreuther. 2009. Improving Flood Insurance and Flood Risk Management: Insights from St. Louis, Missouri. Discussion paper 09-07. Washington, DC: Resources for the Future.

61. PERVERSE INCENTIVES AND THE ENDANGERED SPECIES ACT

Jonathan H. Adler

is a professor of law and the director of the Center for Business Law and Regulation at the Case Western Reserve University School of Law. He specializes in environmental law.

The Endangered Species Act has a critical flaw: it may provide perverse incentives for landowners to preemptively clear habitat if they perceive a risk that an endangered species might someday be discovered on the land, resulting in stringent regulations being imposed regarding future land use.

The Endangered Species Act (ESA) is one of the nation's most powerful environmental laws, often characterized as a pit bull, because it is short, compact, and has sharp teeth and a strong grip. Yet for all of the ESA's force, it does not appear to have been particularly effective at recovering endangered species from the brink of extinction, particularly on private land.

The purpose of the ESA, which turned 35 in 2008, is to identify species that are in trouble and protect them. While it has undoubtedly helped stem the decline of some species, it is unclear how much the ESA has done to recover species from the brink of extinction. Since the law's enactment, nearly 2,000 species have been listed as "endangered" (in danger of extinction) or "threatened" (likely to become endangered within the foreseeable future). However, fewer than 50 species populations have been removed from the list. And as of July 2008, the U.S. Fish and Wildlife Service, which administers the ESA in conjunction with the National Oceanic and Atmospheric Administration, could identify only 21 species recoveries.

Indeed, more species have been delisted because of data errors or extinction than due to species recovery. Yet even this may overstate the ultimate effectiveness of the act, as some species recoveries—such as those of raptors saved by the banning of DDT or Australian kangaroo species—have had little to do with the ESA. Moreover, there is not a single species recovery that can be credited to the ESA's regulation of species habitat on private land. This is particularly troubling because the majority of listed species rely on private land for some or all of their habitat.

In the most basic terms, the ESA discourages the creation and maintenance of species habitat on private land by penalizing it. Specifically, under Section 9 of the act, it is illegal for a private landowner to engage in activities that could harm an endangered species, including habitat modification, without first obtaining a federal permit. Violations can lead to fines of up to $25,000 and even jail time.

Such regulations can reduce private land values and antagonize private landowners who might otherwise cooperate with conservation efforts. This is because Section 9 turns endangered species into economic liabilities. The discovery of an endangered species on private land imposes costs but few, if any, benefits.

Landowners have been known to destroy or degrade potential habitat on their land preemptively in order to prevent the imposition of the act's requirements. It is not illegal to modify land that might become endangered species habitat someday in the future, nor are landowners required to take affirmative steps to maintain endangered species habitat beyond refraining from actions that "harm" endangered species.

In the past, there was little more than economic theory and anecdotal accounts upon which to criticize the effectiveness of the ESA on private land. Now, however, there are empirical data on three contentious species that demonstrate how the act itself compromises species conservation on private land.

A 2003 study by Dean Lueck and Jeffrey Michael looked at whether private landowners engaged in preemptive habitat destruction when the presence of endangered red-cockaded woodpeckers placed the landowners at risk of federal regulation and a loss of their timber investment. Providing habitat for a single woodpecker colony could cost up to $200,000 in forgone timber harvests. To avoid the loss, those landowners at greatest risk of restrictions were most likely to harvest their forestlands prematurely and reduce the length of their timber harvesting rotations. The ultimate consequences of this behavior were potentially significant in that it resulted in a loss of several thousand acres of woodpecker habitat, a major loss for a species dependent upon private land for its survival.

In a second study involving the red-cockaded woodpecker, Daowei Zhang (2004) similarly found that "regulatory uncertainty and lack of positive economic incentives alter landowner timber harvesting behavior and hinder endangered species conservation on private lands." Zhang also concluded that "a landowner is 25 percent more likely to cut forests when he or she knows or perceives that a red-cockaded woodpecker cluster is within a mile of the land than otherwise."

Simply listing a species could discourage private landowners from participating in conservation efforts, according to a 2003 study by Brook et al. Surveys of private landowners within the animal's range found that as landowners became aware that their land contains Preble's meadow jumping mouse habitat, some became less likely to support conservation efforts. In addition, landowners would refuse to give biologists permission to conduct research on their land to assess mouse populations out of fear of the consequences that would follow such a discovery. This revelation is especially troubling because accurate data on species populations and their habitats are essential to successful conservation efforts.

A 2006 study by List et al. found that species listing can accelerate the development of potential habitat as landowners seek to preempt the imposition of land-use restrictions under the ESA. Specifically, land proposed to be designated as critical habitat for the endangered cactus ferruginous pygmy owl was, on average, developed one year earlier than equivalent parcels that were not identified as habitat. In addition, the value of undeveloped land identified as critical habitat fell relative to other lands in the study area.

These studies, taken together, provide powerful evidence that the ESA has the potential to discourage species conservation on private land. Worse, they suggest that the net effect of the ESA on private land could be negative.

Recent administrations have sought to offset these effects through various cooperative conservation programs designed to encourage voluntary conservation efforts and provide landowners with greater regulatory certainty. Insofar as these initiatives have been effective, however, they have effectively deactivated the ESA's regulatory provisions by providing landowners with assurances they can escape regulation in return for undertaking conservation measures. Such measures do very little, however, to discourage preemptive habitat destruction, and others could still be subject to court challenge for violating the express terms of the act.

Given that habitat loss and fragmentation represent the greatest threat to endangered species, the perverse incentives created by the ESA should be of grave concern. Most land—approximately two-thirds of the continental United States—is privately owned. At the same time, the vast majority of endangered species rely upon private land for some or all of their habitat. The relative importance of such lands for the maintenance of species habitat and critical ecological functions is perhaps even greater. Without active conservation on private lands, meaningful ecological conservation cannot be achieved—and the ESA's poor record at recovering species suggests that it may be failing.

Experiments with voluntary incentives suggest such programs hold promise. The North American Waterfowl Management Program, Partners for Wildlife, and the Wetland Reserve Program demonstrate that even modest financial incentives can produce significant ecological gains at modest cost. Were Congress to support expansion of such efforts, and authorize greater use of incentives under the ESA, it should be possible to enlist thousands of landowners in species conservation efforts.

If such efforts are to be truly successful, however, Congress must also revisit the punitive nature of the ESA's regulations. So long as the act penalizes private landowners who own undeveloped habitat for endangered species, it will create perverse incentives that work against effective habitat conservation on private land.

Further Reading

Adler, Jonathan H. 2008. Money or Nothing: The Adverse Environmental Consequences of Uncompensated Regulatory Takings. *Boston College Law Review* 49: 301–366.

Brook, Amara, Michaela Zint, and Raymond de Young. 2003. Landowners' Responses to an Endangered Species Act Listing and Implications for Encouraging Conservation. *Conservation Biology* 17(6): 1638–1649.

List, John A., Michael Margolis, and Daniel E. Osgood. 2006. Is the Endangered Species Act Endangering Species? National Bureau of Economic Research Working Paper No. W12777. December.

Lueck, Dean, and Jeffrey Michael. Preemptive Habitat Destruction under the Endangered Species Act. 2003. *Journal of Law and Economics* 46(1): 27–60.

Zhang, Daowei. 2004. Endangered Species and Timber Harvesting: The Case of Red-Cockaded Woodpeckers. *Economic Inquiry* 32(1): 150–165.

62. IMPROVING INVESTMENTS IN BIODIVERSITY CONSERVATION

Juha Siikamäki

is a fellow at Resources for the Future. His research focuses on valuing the environment and evaluating the benefits, costs, and cost-effectiveness of different environmental policy options.

Stephen Newbold

is a policy analyst at EPA's National Center for Environmental Economics. His research focuses on ecological modeling, ecosystem valuation, systematic conservation design, and estimation of benefits from climate change policies.

Many species listed under the Endangered Species Act are recovering slowly, while others continue to decline in numbers. How can we improve targeting of resources to habitats or activities that are most conducive to species protection and recovery?

Every year, large investments are made in biodiversity conservation by governments, nongovernmental organizations, businesses, and individual citizens. Federal expenditures in the United States under the Endangered Species Act (ESA)—the primary federal statute governing the protection and management of biodiversity in the United States—alone sum to more than $1 billion annually. Moreover, this figure excludes state and local efforts to protect biodiversity as well as any private costs associated with mandatory conservation of biodiversity, such as compliance costs associated with the ESA.

Nevertheless, biodiversity has been slow to recover and generally continues to decline. For example, according to the U.S. Fish and Wildlife Service, of more than 1,300 species listed under the ESA, only about 7 percent have achieved greater than 50 percent recovery, and a large majority (77 percent) have reached less than 25 percent recovery. One way to improve these and other conservation performance measures is to search for options that use the resources committed to biodiversity protection more cost-effectively—by targeting conservation investments toward projects and locations with the highest biological returns per dollar. The need to improve the prioritization of conservation expenditures is heightened by continually increasing pressures from land-use changes, invasive species, climate change, and other growing risks to biodiversity.

Could targeting conservation investments really make a difference? Because of unavoidable budgetary and other resource constraints, only a fraction of all possible conservation interventions can be undertaken. A conservation agency protecting endangered species must inevitably face trade-offs among choices to protect and restore current habitats, establish new habitats, and invest in other recovery programs. Complicating these choices, the number of target species may be large, requiring that conservation alternatives be evaluated from the perspective of how to best promote multiple endangered species.

Such choices can have remarkable impacts on conservation outcomes, a notion supported by evidence from a large body of research in systematic conservation design, an emerging subfield at the interface of ecology, economics, and operations research. Findings generally suggest that better targeting of conservation interventions could enable conservation agencies to more effectively achieve their goals.

Our own recent research indicates that enhanced prioritization of conservation investments toward the protection of endangered species can greatly improve conservation outcomes. While endangered species protections seek to recover listed species and prevent them from going extinct, present conservation efforts generally are not systematically evaluated based on explicit and quantified measures of this goal.

Several factors force conservation organizations to currently rely heavily on professional judgment when prioritizing funding. For example, sufficient biological data, such as observations on species abundances over time, often do not exist to help conduct reliable population analyses to support systematic prioritization of conservation interventions. The lack of methods to systematically incorporate species viability goals into the evaluations of conservation program designs is another constraint. One indication of this scientific gap can be seen in the National Oceanic and Atmospheric Administration's (NOAA) recent critical habitat designations, which the federal government is required to perform for any listed species under the ESA. NOAA described currently feasible approaches to prioritizing critical habitats as follows: "Given the state of the science, it is difficult to quantify the benefits of critical habitat designation reliably. It is possible, however, to differentiate among habitat areas based on their relative contribution to conservation. For example, habitat areas can be rated as having a high, medium, or low conservation value. Such a rating is based on best professional judgment."

To address this gap through a supplementary approach, we developed an integrated framework for prioritizing habitat conservation activities on the basis of their cost-effectiveness in enhancing the long-run persistence of threatened species populations. The framework combines population viability analysis for endangered species with a reserve site selection analysis to target alternative habitat improvement activities. We illustrated the framework with a case study of Pacific salmon, but the general approach could be applied to a variety of species and biodiversity protection problems. Selection of Pacific salmon for an application was natural because protecting endangered salmon populations in the Pacific Northwest is one of the highest-profile biodiversity conservation issues in this country, and an extensive body of ecological literature on Pacific salmon exists.

What are the benefits from improved prioritization? Our results suggest that integrated cost–benefit prioritization of alternative conservation investments can help create much greater biological benefits than those achieved by less systematic but commonly used approaches such as professional judgment or targeting based on only biological criteria. Generally, we find that identifying the subset of watersheds where the biological returns per dollar of conservation expenditure are highest is critical, particularly because the large majority of biological benefits from a specific conservation program may be associated with the protection of only a fraction of all potential target areas.

For example, if targeting is done optimally, spending 10 percent of the cost of restoring all upstream watersheds for salmon protection yields nearly 80 percent of the maximum possible increase in the predicted 100-year stock persistence achievable by protecting all watersheds. In this context, ad hoc prioritization methods also generate disproportional biological benefits at low budgets, but they are less cost-effective and generate only about 25 to 75 percent of the benefits achieved by more systematic cost–benefit prioritization.

How specific are these findings to the case of Pacific salmon? Though relative benefits from improved targeting will undoubtedly vary by application, there is reason to believe that they may be large in many cases. A recent review of conservation design studies suggests that better incorporation of cost–benefit considerations can generally improve conservation outcomes. Findings in a similar vein also have emerged in cases related to watershed protections and targeting of conservation activities in agricultural and forest landscapes.

Of course, no analytical model can capture all of the relevant ecological and economic dimensions of a complex conservation problem. Systematic prioritization methods are not a stand-alone recipe for targeting conservation investments, but can be potentially useful supplements to current methods including professional judgment. Nevertheless, given the amounts of resources and number of species at stake, as well as the increasing pressures on biodiversity, developing more systematic approaches to designing and evaluating conservation programs seems well justified.

Further Reading

Naidoo, R., A. Balmford, P.J. Ferraro, S. Polasky, T.H. Ricketts, and M. Rouget. 2006. Integrating Economic Costs into Conservation Planning. *Trends in Ecology and Evolution* 21(12): 681–687.

Newbold, Stephen, and Juha Siikamäki. 2009. Prioritizing Conservation Activities Using Reserve Site Selection and Population Viability Analysis with an Application to Pacific Salmon. *Ecological Applications* 19(7): 1774–1790.

Siikamäki, Juha, and David Layton. 2007. Potential Cost-Effectiveness of Incentive Payment Programs for the Protection of Non-Industrial Private Forests. *Land Economics* 83(4): 539–560.

Williams, J.W., C.S. ReVelle, and S.A. Levin. 2004. Using Mathematical Optimization Models to Design Nature Reserves. *Frontiers in Ecology and the Environment* 2(2): 98–105.

63. USDA'S CONSERVATION RESERVE PROGRAM

Is It Time to Ease into Easements?

Ralph Heimlich

is the principal and owner of Agricultural Conservation Economics, a consulting firm providing expertise in agricultural conservation policy. He retired as a deputy director from USDA's Economic Research Service in 2003.

The Conservation Reserve Program (CRP), under which environmentally sensitive land is taken out of agricultural production, was reauthorized under the 2007 farm bill. How has it evolved? What are its benefits and costs? How is it being affected by ethanol policies, and how might CRP be improved?

In the midst of the Great Depression, when farmers were failing and the Dust Bowl was swirling, Congress sought to retire land from agricultural production, both to reduce the supply of commodities (thereby increasing their price and propping up farm income) and to prevent soil erosion. The policy tool—generically known as the Conservation Reserve Program (CRP)—has taken various formal names as it evolved, but ever since that time, the United States has periodically idled crop acreage, generally when agricultural prices are low.

Buffers along streams, windbreaks between fields, and even entire farm fields are withdrawn from production under 10- to 15-year contracts in exchange for annual rental payments and assistance in establishing conservation cover. With renewals and extensions, some land has been under current CRP contracts for as long as 35 years. CRP was again reauthorized in the 2007 farm bill. It did not emerge unscathed, however: conferees cut the enrollment cap from 39.2 million to 32 million acres.

What are the benefits and costs of this long-running experiment in retiring land from commodity production? Has it promoted conservation, or is it a permanent subsidy for owners of marginal cropland? Are there alternatives?

COSTS AND BENEFITS OF LAND RETIREMENT

One of the economic benefits of CRP arises from the reduction in agricultural output, which may raise the crop prices and increase revenues for all growers; of course, this also reduces the welfare of consumers. Long-term retirement also reduces government expenditures for other programs intended to control commodity supplies, support prices, and raise farm incomes.

Retiring land from production offers ecological benefits, too, reducing soil erosion and flooding and improving wildlife habitat and water quality—all important to the general population. By protecting 25 million acres of vulnerable cropland, CRP reduced soil erosion by 470 million tons in FY2007 compared with pre-CRP erosion rates. CRP protects surface waters from sedimentation and nutrient enrichment, especially in national conservation priority areas, state water quality priority areas, and restored wetlands that filter nutrients and sediments. The U.S. Department of Agriculture (USDA) estimates that in 2007, CRP reduced agricultural runoff of sediment by 207 million tons, nitrogen by 480 million pounds, and phosphorus by 108 million pounds. A newly recognized benefit involves climate change. CRP lands serve as carbon "sinks" and in 2007 sequestered 50 million metric tons of carbon dioxide in soils and vegetation.

CRP costs over 1985–2005 were $21.8 billion, less savings in government costs for commodity programs of $11 billion, giving a net cost of $10.8 billion. A partial accounting of estimated benefits totals $23 billion in net present value over the period, resulting in a net social benefit of $12.2 billion.

ENTER BIOFUELS

Biofuels are unleashing a burst of "fencerow to fencerow" enthusiasm and threatening to undo the past 30 years of conservation effort. Alternative-energy proponents have had their eye on CRP as a source of "free" land for a decade: it is already subsidized and can be earmarked for biomass production at low cost. Now biofuel production is being encouraged by mandates and subsidies and even a federally supported pilot project on CRP land. As demand soars for alternative fuels, recropping retired land could provide feedstock without stressing traditional markets for feed grain and food. Increased demand for corn to produce ethanol and soybeans to make biodiesel has pushed up prices and drawn down stocks, creating an incentive for additional acres to leave their CRP contracts.

In July 2008, damage to crops from spring floods, spiking demand for biofuels and livestock feed, and rising consumer food prices nearly led Secretary of Agriculture Edward Schafer to release 12 million to 15 million CRP acres without penalty. Even with repayment and penalties, nearly 300,000 acres were bought out of contracts in 2008. Contracts expired on more than 2 million acres in 2008 and will expire on an additional 20.2 million acres by 2012. Unless CRP rental rates are raised to match incentives for recropping, 27 percent of the CRP land coming out of contract will be economically justified in leaving the program and being plowed up.

REFOCUSING ON THE GOALS

Of all the USDA conservation programs, CRP has the most explicit focus on efficiency, with an environmental benefits index for measuring the cost-effectiveness of each parcel. Nevertheless, greater benefits could be achieved with a clearer focus on the priorities.

CRP originally targeted highly erodible cropland but since 1990 has addressed water quality and wildlife habitat as well. The best parcels to enroll would score high in all three attributes, but in reality, any given parcel will score well on one and less well on the others. We need to ask which goals are best served by land retirement. Given today's agricultural methods, is retiring land the best way to protect water quality and reduce soil erosion?

CRP enrolls parcels whose water pollution and soil erosion could be addressed without retiring the land—by using conservation practices under other programs. Although giving equal weight to wildlife, water quality, and erosion seems superficially fair, wildlife habitat should count more because it can be increased only by retiring the land from agricultural production.

THE EASEMENT ALTERNATIVE

What, then, is the best way to take land out of agricultural production? Using 2006 dollars and adjusting for inflation, total payments for land retirement in CRP and related programs since 1933 were $48.7 billion. This is equivalent to $1,730 to $2,596 per acre, higher than the average cropland value of $1,270 per acre when the land was enrolled. Thus, repeatedly renting land in 10-year contracts costs as much as—or more than—purchasing it outright.

CRP is not a "rent-to-buy" arrangement, of course, and purchasing the lands now is not feasible, from either a cost or a management standpoint. But there is an alternative to outright purchase: conservation easements. Permanent easements remove cropping rights and allow compatible uses, like grazing or forestry, on certain acres but let the farmer use the remaining land in perpetuity while retaining ownership. In hindsight, a program of permanent easements might have avoided some of the problems now facing CRP—by guaranteeing an immediate transition to less intensive uses and costing less than the recurrent rental contracts.

Easements do face one major difficulty: the congressional budget process does not distinguish a onetime payment for a conservation easement from an annual rental expense. Because out-year expenditures do not count against deficit reduction caps, rental is preferred over funds for permanent easements that must be paid today.

Until the current recession, rents were rising, however. CRP rental rates have been periodically adjusted to bring them in line with the market. The recent rise in commodity prices has been so rapid that cash rental rates have also risen steeply. CRP rents should be updated to compete with market rates.

Recasting CRP as a smaller, tighter, permanent conservation easement program would fix the flaws in the program design and allow for better targeting of priority lands. It would probably mean paying for cropping rights that have not been exercised in at least 20 years, on top of the rents already paid. Some blending of these approaches, therefore, is probably in order.

For now, raising rents to market levels will help keep environmentally fragile land enrolled under the lower 32-million-acre enrollment cap. A revised environmental benefits index will help ensure that the most valuable land to meet today's environmental problems is retired.

Further Reading

Heimlich, R. 2007. Land Retirement for Conservation: History, Analysis, and Alternatives. In *The 2007 Farm Bill and Beyond*, edited by B.L. Gardner and D.A. Sumner. American Enterprise Institute (AEI) Agricultural Policy Series. Washington, DC: AEI Press.

Hellerstein, D. 2006. USDA Land Retirement Programs. In *Agricultural Resources and Environmental Indicators*, Keith Wiebe and Noel Gollehon, eds. EIB-16. Washington, DC: USDA Economic Research Service, 175–183.

USDA. 2008. Statement of Secretary Ed Schafer Discusses Conservation Reserve Program Decision. Release 0196.08, July 29. Washington, DC: USDA.

64. HOW SHOULD WE TACKLE THE FOREST FIRE PROBLEM?

Arun Malik

is a professor of economics and public policy at George Washington University. His research is in the general area of applied microeconomic theory, with a focus on environmental and resource regulation.

How has the management of wildfires on U.S. forestlands evolved over time, and what are the shortcomings in existing practices? More research, particularly on quantifying the benefits and cost-effectiveness of fire suppression options for different regions, would be especially valuable in guiding future policy reforms at the local level.

We're all familiar with the environmental and social costs of forest fires; in summertime—fire season in California—there are regular news stories about people losing their homes and thousands of acres ablaze. But the economic costs, who pays to put the fires out and how to contain them, are complex issues.

Severe forest fires have increased in frequency over the past decade, resulting in substantial losses of property and human lives. The years 2007 to 2008 brought two of the worst wildfire seasons in recent history; insured losses from wildfires in California alone were estimated to be over $2 billion. Though the number of wildfires has gone down since the 1960s, the number of acres burned has risen markedly in the current decade. More than seven million acres of wildlands burned in all but three of the nine years from 2000 to 2008.

The increased severity of fires, combined with continuing development in and near forests, puts many more communities at risk and has substantially increased both the difficulty and cost of fire suppression. Expenditures on fire suppression by the USDA Forest Service alone have exceeded $1 billion in recent years. And in 2009, nearly $2 billion (48 percent of the agency's budget) was targeted at fire management, up from $300 million (13 percent) in 1991.

A principal reason why the cost of fire suppression and the total number of acres affected have gone up stems from tradition. Federal agencies, including the Forest Service and National Park Service, have long pursued a policy of aggressive fire suppression; perversely, their success has contributed to the increased severity of fires in recent years. Fire suppression has led to denser forests with more flammable materials, or "fuel loadings," and has altered the structure and composition of forests, rendering many more susceptible to fire. By the late 1960s, there was a growing realization that some fires could be beneficial. A small-scale program of prescribed burning (intentionally burning portions of a forest) was initiated in the late 1960s to reduce fuel loadings and to maintain forest structure and composition. However, fire suppression continued to dominate Forest Service policy for the next three decades.

By the mid-1990s, the essential role of fires became well recognized in policy circles. The 2001 federal wildland fire-management policy deemed fire to be a critical natural process that should be integrated into land and resource management plans. The 2001 National Fire Plan authorized a large-scale, long-term effort to reduce fuel loadings, with annual funding of roughly half a billion dollars.

In addition to prescribed burning, reductions in fuel loadings can be accomplished through mechanical thinning, which entails physical removable of flammable material through activities such as selective logging and clearing of underbrush. The Forest Service also recently adopted the concept of risk-based fire suppression, which calls for prioritizing fire suppression based on the infrastructure, property, and human values at risk. In addition, the Forest Service expanded its policy of wildland fire use, which allows some naturally ignited fires to go unchecked if they do not pose threats to human welfare that cannot be readily mitigated.

While these policy reforms are generally considered to be in the right direction, they have nonetheless been subject to considerable criticism. Analysts have argued that current fuel reduction programs have a short-term focus and place undue emphasis on the number of acres treated, with limited attention given to treatment effectiveness. Also, more attention needs to be given to which forests are best treated as well as the types of fuels to be removed and the manner in which this should be done.

Fuel reduction is expensive, with costs running between $500 and $1,500 per acre for mechanical thinning, and $50 and $500 per acre for prescribed burning. Estimates of the costs of undertaking fuel reduction on high- and moderate-risk forestlands far exceed the sums budgeted for this purpose, especially when one considers that fuel reduction is not a onetime measure—it typically needs to be repeated at 5-to 35-year intervals, depending on forest type. Although there are regular calls for more funds to be allocated to fuel reduction, it is difficult to assess whether this would be worthwhile given the paucity of quantitative information on the effectiveness of fuel reduction in lowering fire frequency and severity. There is a clear need for better information on the cost-effectiveness of fuel reduction.

The sums spent on fire suppression have also come under question, with federal and state agencies still placing undue emphasis on the strategy. Existing policies restrict the ability of officials to pursue cheaper options, such as suppressing one area of a fire but allowing another area of the same fire to be managed for wildland fire use. Critics have also argued that huge sums are devoted to fighting the largest fires, even though the probability of success is often low, simply because of public perceptions and liability concerns.

The existing framework for sharing fire suppression costs between federal and nonfederal agencies also contributes to higher suppression expenditures by distorting incentives. Cost-sharing rules are inconsistent and vague, and state and local governments are responsible for only a small share of the costs of protecting communities near wildlands. This reduces their motivation to adopt building codes and land-use controls that could substantially lower spending on fire suppression. Although this failure has been recognized, it persists. The financial responsibilities of the various levels of government need to be more clearly and consistently defined, and a greater share of the burden needs to be placed on state and local governments.

Further Reading

Franklin, Jeremy F., and James K. Agee. 2003. Forging a Science-Based National Fire Policy. Issues in *Science and Technology* (Fall) 1–8.

Gorte, Ross W. 2006. *Forest Fire/Wildfire Protection*. Congressional Research Service Report for Congress RL30755. Washington, DC: Congressional Research Service.

Nazzaro, Robin M. 2007. Wildland Fire: Management Improvements Could Enhance Federal Agencies' Efforts to Contain the Costs of Fighting Fires. Testimony before the Committee on Energy and Natural Resources, U.S. Senate, GAO-07-922T. Washington, DC: U.S. Government Accountability Office.

Stephens, Scott L., and Lawrence W. Ruth. 2005. Federal Forest-Fire Policy in the United States. *Ecological Applications* 15(2): 532–542.

65. OPTIONS CONTRACTS FOR CONTINGENT TAKINGS

Improving Disaster Management

Carolyn Kousky

is a fellow at Resources for the Future. Her research interests include natural resource management, decisionmaking under uncertainty, and individual and societal responses to natural disaster risk.

Sam Walsh

is an associate at the law firm of Hogan & Hartson and focuses his practice on energy law. Prior to joining Hogan & Hartson, Walsh was a law clerk for the Honorable Judge David S. Tatel of the U.S. Court of Appeals for the District of Columbia Circuit.

Richard Zeckhauser

is the Frank Plumpton Ramsey Professor of Political Economy at the Kennedy School of Government at Harvard University. His current research addresses the performance of institutions confronted with inadequate commitment.

An innovative proposal to limit the potential damages caused by natural disasters involves up-front contingent contracting that would allow the government to seize private property in the event of a disaster. What might be the potential applicability of this type of contracting to various disaster situations, and how might obstacles to the writing of such contracts be overcome?

A major flood crest is moving down the Mississippi. Tearing down some agricultural levees and flooding the fields might well save downstream levees protecting billions of dollars of development. Cutting down trees on privately owned land might stop a forest fire from spreading. Killing a rancher's infected cattle might prevent much wider losses or a public health crisis. First responders to a hurricane could be more effective with access to private buildings, to treat injured victims or store supplies, or private vehicles, to reach those in need.

In crises, the government's ability to use, impinge upon, or take over private property can dramatically reduce costs. While the government at times forcibly commandeers property even if the owner is unwilling to oblige—when a foot patrolman takes a car to catch a criminal, for example—there are many times when the government leaves private property undisturbed, even when using it would offer substantial social benefits. The reasons why include questions about proper authority or whether the following economic or political costs would be too high.

We propose a new policy tool for situations like this: options contracts for contingent takings. These are contracts between the government and private parties in which the government pays for the right to use and possibly damage property if a low-probability event occurs that would make temporary use of it by the government highly valuable. The individual or firm would be compensated for such use through an up-front payment and an additional payment should the uncertain circumstances arise.

Without such contracts, the government might simply take the property or negotiate with private entities when the disaster occurs. Some might say that having one's property taken during an emergency is simply a risk one takes when living in an interdependent society. Given the likely political and legal costs, however, many efficient takings will not happen absent contracts. In addition, arguments of risk spreading and equity suggest that compensation is desirable. Contracts for compensation must be negotiated in advance; in emergencies, there is rarely time to bargain and negotiate a contract. And a bargain unstruck is a great loss taken. In addition, in the height of the crisis, there will be those that try to take advantage of the urgency of the situation, whereas lower prices could be arranged if determined in advance.

During a disaster, the spirit of voluntarism is high. Might contracts be superfluous? There will be some Good Samaritans, surely, but there will be others, perhaps ordinary businessmen and women, who pursue their own interests. Some good souls will find that they cannot recover payments for the use of their supplies during the disaster. For example, Walmart generously provided many supplies after Katrina, but compensation became a worry, because establishing purchasing agreements proved almost impossible in the aftermath of the storm.

The contingent contracts we envision are essentially call options. A call option is a contract that gives one party the right, but not the obligation, to purchase a particular asset from another at a particular price, what is labeled the "exercise" price. To obtain this right, the holder pays some amount up front for the option. If the private entity is risk averse, our research shows the optimal payment structure sets the exercise price equal to the loss imposed by the taking. Any surplus (the difference between the cost to the private entity and the benefits to the government) received is paid up front. When the government needs the participation of many entities, a reverse auction can be used to award the contracts to those who would suffer least from a taking. Georgia has put such contracts into practice to compensate farmers for suspending irrigation during a drought.

Moral hazard could be a problem in these contracts if the exercise price is set equal to the loss (determined after the fact) and there are unobservable actions that could be taken to reduce losses. For example, perhaps the farmer could harvest his crop early or relocate equipment. If he knew he would be compensated for any magnitude of loss, however, he might not undertake these actions. Some risk has to be placed on the farmer to induce him to do so. Another option is to base payments on a measure over which the farmer has no control but that is correlated with his losses. Payments could be based on losses to neighboring farms, thus giving the farmer the incentive to reduce his own losses as much as possible. A final possibility would set an exercise price up front, though that would do less well in reducing the farmer's risk.

Particularly for contracts related to land use, holdouts are also a potential problem. To flood an area, a cluster of farms may be needed. Individual farmers may hold out to try to extract the largest percentage of the surplus possible. One solution may be mutually contingent contracts, where the government offers a payment above opportunity costs, contingent on all the needed landowners participating. More likely, legislation will be needed to coerce holdouts. Participation might be mandatory once a certain percentage of the needed landowners is reached. This could be a form of a compulsory purchase law, only instead of the government forcing sale of the land, it would force participation in the contract at a fair price. There is U.S. precedent in some states for forcing holdouts to agree in the compulsory unitization rules that force oil companies into the most efficient extraction of a common pool of oil.

Options contracts for contingent takings can be used beyond our focus area of disaster response. For example, sea-level rise could threaten public beaches as homeowners armor the shore to protect their personal buildings. Titus (1998) has suggested rolling easements to overcome this problem; options contracts for public purchase of the property when inundated are similar in spirit. In another case, Defenders of Wildlife compensates farmers if a wolf eats their livestock to reduce opposition to reintroduction of the species.

While there are a few salient examples of these arrangements, there are likely many more cases where such contracts could improve social welfare. To test their performance, a pilot project in the area of flood damage reduction could be undertaken, as this is an area where there is already recognition of the merits of such an approach and where the experience of USDA contracting with farmers might ease implementation. Options contracts for contingent takings may prove as valuable as emergency personnel in reducing the losses from some disasters. The agricultural levee ripped down by prior agreement may save as many lives and dollars as the downstream levee sustained through recent reinforcement.

Further Reading

Kousky, C., S. Walsh, and R. Zeckhauser. 2007. Options Contracts for Contingent Takings. *Issues in Legal Scholarship*. Symposium: Catastrophic Risks: Prevention, Compensation, and Recovery: Article 2. www.bepress.com/ils/catastrophicrisks/.

Manale, A. 2000. Flood and Water Quality Management through Targeted, Temporary Restoration of Landscape Functions: Paying Upland Farmers to Control Runoff. *Journal of Soil and Water Conservation* 55: 285–95.

Titus, J.G. 1998. Rising Seas, Coastal Erosion, and the Takings Clause: How to Save Wetlands and Beaches without Hurting Property Owners. *Maryland Law Review* 57: 1279–1399.

PART 5

Transportation and Urban Policies

The transportation sector accounts for about three-quarters of all oil use in the United States and roughly a third of carbon dioxide emissions and is therefore at the crossroads of ongoing debates about energy security and climate change. Meanwhile, over 40,000 Americans continue to die in highway accidents each year, about the same level as 25 years ago. And relentless growth in demand for travel and housing from an expanding and wealthier population puts ever greater pressure on urban centers.

There are many fascinating issues of the day, covered in the commentaries in this section, that are at the nexus of transportation, energy, and climate policy, and others that are related to rising congestion of transportation infrastructure and urban sprawl.

Especially timely given funding shortfalls for transportation and large federal deficits, is whether fuel taxes should be increased. Some of the questions that arise include what effect this would have on gasoline demand, whether this would have adverse distributional consequences, and how extra revenues earmarked for transportation projects might be better spent. Of related interest is the net benefit or cost of fuel economy regulations and inducements for pay-as-you-drive automobile insurance. Over a longer time horizon, the penetration of hybrids and possibly even hydrogen vehicles have the potential to substantially reduce reliance on conventional gasoline vehicles, raising the issue of whether these technologies should be subsidized.

Policymakers are also considering new approaches to congestion management. Of particular interest are road pricing programs in California and London, and possible tolls for heavy duty trucks, congestion pricing for air travel, and privatization of airports. At the same time, decisions must be made about whether to renew previous approaches to alleviating congestion, such as telecommuting. And understanding the factors that determine auto fatality rates in different countries provides guidance on the design of highway safety policies. Finally, there is growing interest in the use of market-based policy approaches to striking a balance between urban development and preservation of open space.

66. TRIPLE CONVERGENCE TOWARD A HIGHER GASOLINE TAX

Kenneth Small
is a research professor and professor emeritus of economics at the University of California, Irvine. He specializes in urban, transportation, and environmental economics.

The United States taxes highway fuels at very low rates compared with many other countries—in fact, federal taxes have been fixed in nominal terms since 1993, despite inflation. Has the time come for a large increase in gasoline and diesel taxes?

It's rare that a single policy instrument can solve several problems at once; rarer still that the political and economic motivations to address these problems converge; and almost unheard of that lessons of history lead to the same conclusion. We are in such a situation today with respect to taxes on motor vehicle fuels. It is time for a dramatic, permanent increase in these taxes.

Problem #1: infrastructure needs. It is clear that state and federal governments, private investors, local authorities, and others have trouble keeping up with legitimate needs for spending on roads, mass transit, flood control, and other public assets. These needs include maintenance of aging capital, upgrades to accommodate newer standards for earthquakes and extreme weather, and expansion to handle continued population and economic growth. Taxes on gasoline and diesel fuel are the long-standing bedrock of funding for the surface transportation component of this infrastructure. But this bedrock has been eroded by a combination of a shrinking tax base (more fuel-efficient vehicles) and lower real tax rates (rates rising more slowly than inflation). The shrinking tax base cannot be reversed, but there is no reason why tax rates cannot be maintained and indeed drastically increased. Numerous countries already have rates several times higher than in the United States, without stifling their economies.

Problem #2: petroleum dependence and climate change. The United States is poised to embark on new programs to reduce dependence on foreign oil and emissions of carbon dioxide. This effort cannot possibly succeed if it ignores the underlying economic motivation for people to use petroleum: quite simply, it is cheaper than alternatives. Higher fuel prices could bring about significant reductions in petroleum use through reduced driving and by harnessing consumer self-interest to the cause of improving vehicle fuel efficiency. Other policies, such as higher fuel-efficiency standards or promoting green technologies, will work more effectively if there is pressure from customers to encourage rather than evade such measures.

Problem #3: federal and state deficits. Governments at all levels in this country face a fiscal climate in which revenues lag at just the time when increased spending is needed—both for programmatic goals and to kick-start a weak economy. The massive federal stimulus program relies heavily on public debt, giving pause to many thoughtful observers.

Raising fuel taxes can go a long way toward closing the financing gap without more debt. While tax-financed government spending is less stimulating than debt-financed spending, the well-known Keynesian "balanced-budget multiplier" shows that it remains a potent tool. Put simply, what government spends goes directly into the hands of producers, who mostly spend it on labor or intermediate goods, whereas the tax bite that finances it does not reduce people's spending dollar for dollar. Furthermore, the timing of a tax increase now fits nicely with the expected gradual decline in the desired role of fiscal stimulus as the economy recovers.

CONVERGENCE WITH HISTORY AND CURRENT EVENTS

Most of the current decade witnessed an apparently relentless increase in gasoline and diesel fuel prices, hitting about $4 per gallon in mid-2008. Expecting the rise to be permanent, many consumers, motor vehicle manufacturers, real estate developers, energy technology companies, and others had begun investments for a more fuel-scarce future: sales of large SUVs plummeted, development of battery and hybrid car technologies flourished, truckers invested in more aerodynamic designs, home buyers sought to shorten commutes. However, these efforts are now being undercut by the subsequent collapse in fuel prices. What better time to assure such decisionmakers of the long-term economic wisdom of fuel parsimony by raising fuel taxes?

History supports this analysis by revealing a lost similar opportunity. From 1973 through 1985, fuel prices rose sharply, instigating a 30 percent rise in the average fuel efficiency of the entire U.S. fleet of passenger cars, new and old. Some of this rise can be attributed to the Corporate Average Fuel Economy (CAFE) standards instituted in 1978; high fuel prices made those standards easier to meet because manufacturers did not have to fight consumer preferences. When petroleum prices collapsed in 1985, it did not take long for the market to respond with an unprecedented shift to large, low-efficiency vehicles (aided by a huge loophole in CAFE that treated SUVs and pickup trucks separately from and much less stringently than cars). With no end in sight to low fuel prices, the "big three" U.S. automakers bet heavily that the trend would last—a bet that has now cost U.S. taxpayers and workers dearly.

But the story is even more perverse. Since SUVs and pickup trucks caught on, several factors have maintained their popularity. First, manufacturers committed their designs, assembly lines, and dealership networks in ways not easy to reverse. Second, marketing efforts gave consumers a long-lasting positive image of large vehicles. Third, travelers learned that small cars fare poorly in collisions with large ones, and so turned to "upsizing" out of fear. So even if everyone would be better off with a fleet of mostly small cars, we became stuck with large ones; it will take a sustained policy change to get us out of this rut.

In addition to these factors, it is well established that drivers do not pay for various costs they impose on others, especially congestion, air pollution, and a substantial portion of accident costs. These costs amount to about 10 cents per mile on average throughout the United States. With motor vehicles now traveling more than three trillion miles per year, even small reductions add up to big cost savings. For example, raising fuel prices from $3 to $5 per gallon through a tax increase could be expected to reduce driving long-term by about 6.7 percent according to a conservative estimate; at 10 cents per mile, this reduction would produce $20 billion a year in fewer congestion, air pollution, and accidents.

RIGHT TOOL FOR THE JOB?

There are many policies better than fuel taxes for specific problems. An oil tax would do more for energy security by motivating conservation in industrial as well as transportation uses. A cap-and-trade system or broader tax would achieve greater coverage of greenhouse gases. For motor vehicle externalities, direct policies such as congestion pricing, mileage taxes (including on heavy trucks), and tighter pollution control measures are probably more effective. Private tolling initiatives can ease public fiscal stress. But it's hard to think of a single policy that covers all of these problems so well with a tool already familiar to the public, with administrative mechanisms already in place, and with experience abroad to assure us that an apparently draconian policy will not end life as we know it. At least until broader policies are comprehensively implemented, which may be a long way off, there is an overwhelming case for a large increase in federal fuel taxes.

Further Reading

Parry, Ian W.H., and Kenneth A. Small. 2005. Does Britain or the United States Have the Right Gasoline Tax? *American Economic Review* 95: 1276–1289.

TRB (Transportation Research Board). 2006. *The Fuel Tax and Alternatives for Transportation Funding.* TRB Special Report 285. Washington, DC: National Academy of Sciences.

Wachs, Martin. 2003. *Improving Efficiency and Equity in Transportation Finance.* Transportation Reform Series. Washington, DC: Brookings Institution.

67. THE PRICE OF GAS AND THE DEMAND FOR FUEL ECONOMY

Are There Any Links?

Thomas H. Klier

is a senior economist in the economic research department at the Federal Reserve Bank of Chicago. His work focuses on the effects of changes in manufacturing technology, the spatial distribution of economic activity, and regional economic development.

Joshua Linn

is an assistant professor in the Department of Economics at the University of Illinois, Chicago. His primary areas of research and teaching interest are energy economics, environmental economics, and industrial organization.

Many economists advocate higher fuel taxes as a means to reduce oil consumption and carbon emissions from the transportation sector. But just how effective are taxes at reducing fuel demand? Not very effective, apparently, based on the limited responses to the recent run-up in fuel prices.

In the ongoing public debate over reducing U.S. gasoline consumption for national security and environmental reasons, many economists support an increase in the federal gasoline tax as the most efficient policy. In principle, such an increase should curb gasoline consumption by reducing average miles traveled per household and by increasing the average fuel economy of vehicles on the road. But the empirical evidence shows that the elasticity of miles traveled to the price of gasoline is small (roughly –0.1), having almost no effect in the short run.

Consequently, a large increase in the gasoline tax would be needed to substantially reduce consumption—that is, unless average fuel economy of the vehicle fleet responds to the price of gasoline. That response includes many factors, such as at what age vehicles are retired, but an important component is the effect of the price of gasoline on the average fuel economy of new vehicles. Although the roughly threefold increase in the price of gasoline from 2002 to 2007 significantly affected sales of individual vehicle models, the effect on average fuel economy was quite small.

PRICE VERSUS DEMAND

Between the beginning of 2002 and the end of 2007, as the real price of gasoline doubled, the market share of SUVs, with a mean fuel economy of about 16.7 miles per gallon (mpg), decreased from 17 to 12 percent. The market share of Chrysler, Ford, and GM, which relied heavily on SUV sales during this time period, decreased from 63 to 52 percent.

After controlling for variables that affect market shares, such as consumer preferences for vehicle characteristics, about half of the decline in market shares of SUVs and U.S. manufacturers from 2002 to 2007 was due to the coinciding increase in the price of gasoline. Despite the strong relationship between gasoline prices and market shares in this one vehicle category, gasoline prices have had only a small effect on the average fuel economy of all new vehicles sold. A $1 per gallon increase in the price of gasoline is associated with an increase of only about 0.5 to 1 mpg after controlling for other factors.

In the short run, of course, vehicle characteristics are fixed. The simultaneous large effect on model market shares and small effect on fleet average fuel economy can be explained by the fairly narrow distribution of fuel economy of vehicles in the market at a particular time. For example, a sudden increase in the gasoline price could cause a dramatic shift from medium-size to small cars, but the change in overall fuel economy would be small because the average fuel economy of these two market segments is similar, at 26.6 and 30.3 mpg.

HOW MANUFACTURERS RESPOND

In principle, the long-run effect of gasoline prices on average fuel economy could be greater if producers responded by offering vehicles with higher fuel economy. Some of these adjustments can be rather quick, such as changing the mix of vehicles offered, but others take some time. When the corporate average fuel economy (CAFE) standards were implemented in the mid-1970s, manufacturers raised fuel economy by making vehicles shorter and lighter and by reducing engine sizes. Consequently, vehicle weight and power (as measured by horsepower) decreased by about 30 percent. Yet the reduction in engine power was quickly reversed as the price of gasoline declined and technology improved. By 1990, average vehicle power had returned to its pre-CAFE level.

It is technologically feasible for producers to significantly increase fuel economy through either an increase in production costs (by substituting lightweight alloys or adding a turbocharger and downsizing the engine) or a reduction in engine power. Given consumers' strong preferences for vehicle performance, firms are hesitant to compromise engine power in order to increase fuel economy.

POLICY OPTIONS

So where does this leave us? The price of gasoline has a very small effect on the fuel economy of the stock of vehicles on the road. A very large increase in the gasoline tax would be needed to reduce consumption because the price per gallon has so little effect on miles traveled and the fuel economy of the overall vehicle fleet. The political feasibility of such an increase is doubtful at best, and substantially reducing gasoline consumption solely by increasing the gas tax would not seem to be a viable policy option.

Other options do exist, including improving public transportation, increasing the CAFE standard, or offering cash or tax incentives to consumers. Examples of the last include federal and state tax incentives for purchasing hybrids and the recent Cash for Clunkers program.

Ultimately, the full costs and benefits of each policy need to be compared, although such a comparison is far from straightforward. In the case of CAFE, its costs are largely hidden from the consumers' view; it is not obvious to consumers the extent to which fuel economy standards affect new and used vehicle prices and cause an increase in driving (that is, the "rebound" effect). But perhaps more importantly, it is necessary to consider how policies and economic forces might interact with one another when comparing costs and benefits and addressing political obstacles. For example, high gas prices can increase public support for raising fuel economy standards, as in the 1970s and perhaps in the past few years, although the reverse would be true in periods of low gas prices. Multiple policies might also interact positively with one another—for example, improving public transportation could increase the sensitivity of miles traveled to the price of gasoline. In such cases, a combination of policies might prove politically and economically expedient.

Further Reading

Hughes, Jonathan E., Christopher R. Knittel, and Daniel Sperling. 2008. Evidence of a Shift in the Short Run Price Elasticity of Gasoline Demand. *Energy Journal* 29: 93–114.

Klier, Thomas, and Joshua Linn. 2009. New Vehicle Characteristics and the Cost of the Corporate Average Fuel Economy Standard. Federal Reserve Bank of Chicago working paper no. 2008-13. http://ssrn.com/abstract=1310761.

Klier, Thomas, and Joshua Linn. 2009. The Price of Gasoline and the Demand for Fuel Economy: Evidence from Monthly New Vehicles Sales Data. University of Illinois at Chicago, mimeo.

Li, Shanjun, Christopher Timmins, and Roger von Haefen. 2008. How Do Gasoline Prices Affect Fleet Fuel Economy? *American Economic Journal: Economic Policy* 1: 113–137.

68. SHOULD DISTRIBUTIONAL CONSIDERATIONS HOLD UP HIGHER GASOLINE TAXES?

Sarah E. West

is an associate professor of economics at Macalester College in Saint Paul, Minnesota. Her research analyzes optimal tax policy, with a focus on estimating behavioral responses to policies that reduce gasoline consumption.

Although gasoline taxes are the most efficient policy to reduce gasoline use, the federal gasoline tax has not been increased since 1993, and inflation has eroded its real value. One common argument against raising gasoline taxes is that they might impose a disproportionate burden on low-income families. Is this a valid rationale?

Increasing federal or state gasoline taxes would offer clear advantages: consumers would tend to buy less gasoline, thereby reducing greenhouse gas emissions and dependency on foreign oil. Households would have an incentive to drive fewer miles, reducing congestion, accidents, and emissions of local pollutants. Because households do not currently account for all of these costs of driving, gasoline tax rates (now 44 cents per gallon on average) are inefficiently low.

Someone would bear the burden of an increase in gasoline taxes—but who? Policymakers frequently argue that the gasoline tax is regressive by definition—poor households pay a higher proportion of their income in tax than do wealthy households. But is this a valid argument?

Assessing the approximate distributional burden of a gasoline tax is fairly straightforward. Nearly all gasoline is purchased directly by households, so if the gasoline tax is fully passed forward into pump prices, its distributional effect can be assessed by comparing gasoline consumption (relative to income) across different household groupings. At least in the short run, before households make major changes in the kinds of vehicles they drive or in the location of their residences, consumers seem to bear the bulk, if not the entirety, of any increase in the gasoline tax. Over the longer run, the effect might be more complicated as consumers switch between fuel-efficient and fuel-inefficient vehicles, shifting some of the tax burden onto fuel refiners, wholesalers, and gas-station owners. Still, supply is also more flexible in the long run, so a much greater share of the burden remains on the consumer.

Among those households that consume gasoline, the gas tax is indeed regressive. Gasoline-buying households with the highest annual income (in the top 20 percent) pay less than half of what poor households (in the bottom 20 percent) pay, as a proportion of annual income. One reason for this is that lower-income households are more likely to drive older, used vehicles, with relatively higher fuel consumption rates. Another is that vehicle miles traveled does not rise in proportion to income—someone with twice as much income as someone else does not typically drive twice as much.

But annual income is probably not the best measure of household well-being, as poorer households tend to have expenditures greater than their annual income, while other low-income people, like MBA students, are clearly not poor when account is taken of their future earnings potential. For these reasons, economists often prefer to proxy household well-being by the total amount they spend or consume each year, rather than their annual income. It's also important to account for the fact that many poor households neither own nor lease a vehicle, and therefore do not pay gasoline taxes at all.

When the amount of gasoline taxes paid is divided by total expenditures, rather than income, and when households that do not own vehicles are taken into account, highest-income households as a group still spend less in gasoline taxes as a proportion of total expenditures (half a percent) than the lowest-income households (0.7 percent), but the poorest households actually spend less than middle-income households, providing a murkier picture of just how regressive the gasoline tax actually is.

Another relationship between income distribution and gasoline consumption further mitigates the regressive nature of the gasoline tax: poorer households are more responsive to gasoline price changes than are wealthy households. This may be because gasoline price increases have greater relative impacts on poor households' budgets, or because the poor have less aversion to public transportation and place a lower value on the time savings from automobile travel. Whatever the reason, when gasoline prices rise, we can expect poorer households to reduce gasoline consumption up to twice as much as wealthy households, thereby escaping a greater proportion of the gasoline price increase. Care must be taken to account for the fact that gasoline price increases can make it disproportionately more difficult for poor households to get to work, but failing to account for flexible price-responsiveness can overstate regressivity.

REBATES CAN COUNTER REGRESSIVITY

Even accounting for the above factors, the gasoline tax still places a disproportionate burden on poor households. But careful recycling of the gasoline tax revenues back to households can mitigate or even completely overcome its regressive nature.

By using the revenues from the gasoline tax to reduce taxes on work hours, the policy can be made significantly less regressive. The overall effect of the gasoline tax rate increase and revenue rebate could be made more progressive by targeting these tax rate reductions toward the poor, or by increasing the earned-income tax credit (EITC). If the revenues are used to give rebates of the same amount to all households, the policy could be made progressive. With such a rebate scheme, the poorest households could actually be made better off. These lump-sum rebates are analogous to those in "cap-and-dividend" proposals for climate change policy.

While it might seem natural to use gasoline tax revenues to counter regressive impacts, this need not be the case. Public finance economists generally would recommend that policymakers set the gasoline tax at the efficient level, so that motorists face the full costs of driving, regardless of the distributional implications. Then, if they think that the gasoline tax places too much burden on poor and working-class households, policymakers can use the most efficient redistributive tools to attain equity goals, be they lump-sum rebates of gas tax revenue or modifications to the broader income tax and benefit system.

Further Reading

Burtraw, Dallas, Richard Sweeney, and Margaret Walls. 2009. The Incidence of Climate Change Policy: Alternative Uses of Revenues from a Cap-and-Trade Auction. Discussion paper 09-17. Washington, DC: Resources for the Future.

Parry, Ian W.H., Margaret Walls, and Winston Harrington. 2007. Automobile Externalities and Policies. *Journal of Economic Literature* 45: 374–400.

West, Sarah. 2004. Distributional Effects of Alternative Vehicle Pollution Control Policies. *Journal of Public Economics* 88: 735–757.

West, Sarah E., and Roberton C. Williams III. 2004. Estimates from a Consumer Demand System: Implications for the Incidence of Environmental Taxes. *Journal of Environmental Economics and Management* 47: 535–558.

69. DOES THE FEDERAL GOVERNMENT SPEND TOO MUCH FOR HIGHWAYS, OR TOO LITTLE?

Winston Harrington
is a senior fellow and an associate director of research at Resources for the Future, specializing in urban transportation, motor vehicles and air quality, and environmental policy cost assessment.

To what extent is the federal government involved in financing highway construction and maintenance? Are these decisions better left to state governments? Given the large amount spent on highways each year, Americans will bear a substantial cost if this money is spent inefficiently rather than on highway projects with favorable cost–benefit ratios.

Certainly, there is ample justification for some federal funding of highways. There is plenty of intercity and interstate travel, both commercial and personal, which means that the benefits of a well-integrated road network are not just local. Just note the number of out-of-state plates you see on interstates and other major thoroughfares. But what's the right amount?

Those who say the federal government is spending too much note that the Federal-Aid Highway Program makes grants to the states that cover 80 to 90 percent of the costs of qualifying highway projects. Can anyone claim with a straight face that out-of-staters enjoy 80 to 90 percent of the benefits of the average highway? To this group, which includes a lot of regional planners and antisprawl advocates, this is a major subsidy to build roads. With the federal government paying such a large cost share, the argument goes, local and state governments don't have to make the hard choices about whether projects are really justified.

Others say the federal funding share for specific projects seriously overestimates federal involvement in highways. In terms of total highway spending, the Federal-Aid Highway Program grants for states, which now amount to $30 billion to $40 billion, account for only about 25 percent of total spending on highways. Moreover, if federal highway subsidies are excessive, why is it that road use is growing so much faster than capacity? Between 1990 and 2003, for example, road use increased by 2.3 percent annually, compared to a 0.25 percent annual increase in highway lane-miles. One answer is that while your state may get 90 percent of the cost of a new section of interstate, it won't change the total disbursements to your state. That is, the federal subsidy gives a state incentives to change its spending plan without necessarily increasing it.

Besides, the way the question is asked almost equates federal spending with manna from heaven. These funds come from the Highway Trust Fund (HTF), which is financed primarily by federal gasoline taxes, which are, in turn, paid by private and commercial road users. Any annual allocation of HTF funds inevitably results in some states getting less funding than their citizens contribute, and others more. This reality above all others is what makes federal highway spending legislation so contentious and hard to pass. Indeed, chronic complaints from the "donor" states led to the establishment of an "equity" bonus that guarantees each state a minimum percentage of its citizens' contributions. In 2008, this percentage was 92 percent. Clearly, the equity provisions impose a serious constraint on the level of interstate transfers. In 2005, it appears that of the $37 billion in disbursements to the states, $3 billion to $5 billion was spent in a different state from where the money was collected.

However, even though most of the funds end up in the states where they were collected, the current approach to highway funding still gives much influence to the federal government over funding within states. The Federal-Aid Highway Program is really a collection of programs intended for various functions. While a few of these programs are discretionary and distributed by the Federal Highway Administration (FHWA), the vast majority of the funding is in so-called formula programs that determine how much each state will receive annually. For each subprogram, such as the Interstate Maintenance Fund or the Congestion Mitigation and Air Quality Program, there is a formula with objective factors and weights that determines each state's allocation for that program. And, of course, the funds in each program must be spent on program-relevant activities.

Unfortunately, there is another rapidly growing federal government influence on highway funding that probably has adverse consequences for efficiency—the rampant use of congressional earmarks. In SAFETEA-LU, the most recent highway authorization act, there were 6,000 line-item, named projects, valued at almost 10 percent of the total funding allocated. Half the funding was added at the last minute, during the House–Senate conference. Those of us who are not lobbyists think the use of earmarks has gotten out of hand, and no more so than in transportation. Earmarks do not increase the funding available to each state; rather, they direct the allocated funds to particular projects. No one has a clear idea how the earmarked projects are selected; they are simply inserted into the legislation at the last minute, without review or comparison with other projects. The potential for poor decisions, not to mention outright corruption, is pretty high.

So what would be a better approach? One increasingly popular option is road pricing. In the Washington, DC, area, the Dulles Greenway was built with private funds, and plans are moving forward with private funding of HOT (high-occupancy toll) lanes to be added to the Beltway and Interstate 95–395. In addition, there is talk of cities and states selling existing public roads to private operators, as Chicago is considering doing with the Chicago Skyway. On a more experimental level, debate is now under way about implementing road pricing on a large scale in the public sector. For example, New York City is considering implementation of "cordon pricing," charging stiff daily fees for driving into southern and central Manhattan.

Making users pay the full social cost of road use, including the incremental cost of adding capacity, automatically takes care of federal concerns about adequate revenue generation, as out-of-state users will have to pay. However attractive road pricing is in principle, it still faces serious political barriers and practical problems, especially as it becomes more widely used. Unless there is a carefully planned transition, it is likely to generate serious affordability concerns, not only for the poor, but also for others who just happen to face huge tolls because of previously made choices of where to live and work.

Absent comprehensive road pricing, information about both the local and national benefits of specific transportation projects would be needed to develop appropriate federal highway subsidies. A subsidy equal to the difference between the two would provide the right incentive. Perhaps there would be a way to combine estimates of the nonlocal benefits of such projects with a demand-revealing pricing mechanism. To put such a plan into action, what would be needed is a notion of the national, as opposed to the local, benefits of specific proposed road construction projects. Estimates of such benefits could come, perhaps, from the prevalence of out-of-state vehicles on roads in the vicinity of the proposed project. Federal officials could use this information to make an offer of a subsidy, leaving it up to the state to decide whether to provide the balance of funds for the project. Even without an estimate of national benefits, a fixed supply of funds could be distributed relatively efficiently by a competitive auction among local or state governments to elicit their willingness to accept certain subsidy levels to begin a project.

Further Reading

Federal Highway Administration. Safe, Accountable, Flexible, Efficient Transportation Equity Act—A Legacy for Users in 2005: A Summary of Highway Provisions. Highway Statistics Series: 2005, Part IV, Finance. Various tables. www.fhwa.dot.gov/policy/ohpi/hss/index.cfm.

Kirk, Robert S. 2004. *Federal-Aid Highway Program: "Donor-Donee" State Issues*. Congressional Research Service (CRS) report for Congress. Order Code RL31735. Washington, DC: CRS.

70. THE BENEFITS AND COSTS OF TIGHTER FUEL ECONOMY REGULATIONS

Ian W.H. Parry
is the Allen V. Kneese chair and a senior fellow at Resources for the Future. He specializes in quantifying the costs and benefits of environmental, transportation, and energy policies.

In the United States, fuel economy standards form the centerpiece of efforts to reduce oil dependence and greenhouse gas emissions from the transportation sector. To what extent can these policies be rationalized on cost–benefit grounds?

As a result of recent legislation, manufacturers in the United States will be required to meet carbon dioxide (CO_2) emissions per mile regulations that will raise the average fuel economy of new cars to 39 miles per gallon by 2016, and the average fuel economy of new light trucks (minivans, sport utility vehicles, pickups) to 30 miles per gallon. (Previous standards were 27.5 miles per gallon for cars and 24 miles per gallon for light trucks.) To many people, it seems obvious that fuel economy standards should be tightened to reduce CO_2 emissions and oil dependence. After all, passenger vehicles account for about 20 percent and 45 percent of U.S. CO_2 emissions and oil use, respectively. However, before we can conclude whether or not tightening fuel economy standards is a good idea, an economic assessment of the benefits and costs is appropriate. To think about this, it is helpful to separate out the effect of tighter standards on gasoline use, vehicle miles of travel, and the costs of automobile manufacture.

Higher fuel economy standards would reduce the demand for gasoline, thereby producing "externality" benefits (societal benefits that are not taken into account by individuals) in the form of avoided CO_2 emissions and reduced nationwide dependence on oil. Most estimates of economic damages from future global warming—agricultural impacts, rising sea levels and increased storm intensity, health effects from spreading tropical disease, and so on—are in the order of \$20 per ton of current CO_2 emissions, or about 20 cents per gallon of gasoline (burning a gallon of gasoline produces nearly 0.01 tons of CO_2). Damages are much higher if, as advocated by some economists, more weight is given to the well-being of future generations or extreme climate risks.

The broader external costs of oil dependence include the risk of macroeconomic disruption costs from oil price shocks that might not be fully taken into account by the private sector, such as some costs associated with the temporary idling of labor and capital. And while the United States as a whole has an influence on the world oil market, individual oil importers do not consider the impact of their own infinitesimal consumption on increasing the world oil price, which imposes an external cost by increasing the amount of money transferred from other oil importers in the United States to foreign oil suppliers. One recent estimate puts the that external costs from macroeconomic disruption risks and U.S. market power amount to, very roughly, 30 cents per gallon of gasoline. Dependence on oil also constrains U.S. foreign policy and possibly undermines national security. Politicians may be reluctant to challenge oil-producing countries on human rights and other issues, and oil revenues may help certain hostile governments, terrorists, and other unsavory groups. Putting an additional dollar figure on these broader foreign policy and national security costs is extremely difficult, however.

Motorists already pay, at least in part, for the external costs of fuel consumption through federal and state gasoline taxes, which add about 40 cents per gallon to the price at the pump. According to basic tax theory, reducing gasoline use produces net benefits to society only to the extent that CO_2 and oil dependence externalities exceed fuel taxes. Our discussion suggests, albeit very tentatively, that external costs that have been quantified might be largely offset by prevailing fuel taxes. However, accounting for national security and other costs would seem to imply net benefits overall from reducing gasoline use, though the magnitude of the gain is very difficult to pin down.

Critics of fuel economy standards sometimes point to the perverse effect of higher fuel economy on lowering fuel costs per mile and increasing the incentive to drive, which can increase highway congestion, accidents, and pollution. However, according to a recent study by Kenneth Small and Kurt Van Dender, less than 10 percent of the fuel savings from better fuel economy are offset by increased driving. While the costs of this "rebound effect" should be factored into an assessment of fuel economy regulations, they are less important than other factors.

Binding fuel economy regulations induce auto manufacturers to incorporate more fuel-saving technologies into new vehicles, leading to higher vehicle production costs and prices. However, a number of studies, such as one in 2002 by the National Research Council, suggest that fuel-saving benefits over the vehicle life would outweigh the up-front installation costs for many emerging technologies. Some analysts argue that these apparent "win–win" technologies may not be adopted without tighter fuel economy regulations, however, because consumers may underappreciate the benefits of better fuel economy if they are preoccupied with other vehicle attributes like power, comfort, and safety. On the other hand, others argue that forcing technology adoption may be costly if consumers would instead prefer new technologies be used to improve other vehicle characteristics, such as increased horsepower, rather than fuel economy. Another possibility is that manufacturers may meet higher fuel economy requirements by reducing vehicle weight and size; this can raise injury risks for occupants of these vehicles, though it makes the roads a little safer for other drivers.

In short, the case for tightening fuel economy regulations can be argued either way, because it is difficult to judge precisely how manufacturers will respond and how consumers will value changes in vehicle technology. But most importantly, the climate and national security benefits from reduced gasoline use are much disputed. Another policy option is to raise fuel taxes, which, unlike fuel economy regulations, would reduce congestion and other highway externalities, through reducing vehicle miles traveled. While the case for higher fuel taxes is more clear-cut, this option lacks political traction at present.

When I first began studying fuel economy regulations, the case for tightening the standards looked rather dubious to me. However, my perspective has changed somewhat as the difficulties in doing a nice, clean cost–benefit analysis have become more apparent. Moreover, colleagues of mine who have thought hard about the issue—like Carolyn Fischer, Lawrence Goulder, Winston Harrington, Richard Newell, William Pizer, Paul Portney, Philip Sharp, and Kenneth Small—are sympathetic to higher standards, if they are not ramped up too rapidly and reforms permit more trading of fuel economy credits to keep down program costs. My own view is that if the argument comes down to doing nothing or tightening fuel economy regulations, then the latter is what you do. As new technologies are developed over time, a progressive tightening of standards seems to make sense, given that the downside costs to the economy are not that huge, and 20 years from now we may be very glad that serious measures were taken during the intervening years to reduce the dependency of the transport system on conventional fossil fuels.

Further Reading

Austin, David, and Terry Dinan. 2005. Clearing the Air: The Costs and Consequences of Higher CAFE Standards and Increased Gasoline Taxes. *Journal of Environmental Economics and Management* 50(3): 562–582.

Fischer, Carolyn, Winston Harrington, and Ian W.H. Parry. 2007. Should Corporate Average Fuel Economy (CAFE) Standards Be Tightened? *Energy Journal* 28: 1–29.

National Research Council. 2002. *Effectiveness and Impact of Corporate Average Fuel Economy (CAFE) Standards*. Washington, DC: National Academy Press.

U.S. National Highway Traffic Safety Administration. 2008. Average Fuel Economy Standards, Passenger Cars and Light Trucks; Model Years 2011–2015; Proposed Rule. *Federal Register* 73(86): 24352–24487.

71. PAY-AS-YOU-DRIVE AUTO INSURANCE

Jason Bordoff
was a full-time policy director at the Hamilton Project, an economic policy initiative at the Brookings Institution, when coauthoring this commentary.

Pascal Noel
was a research analyst at the Hamilton Project, an economic policy initiative at the Brookings Institution, when this commentary was written.

Automobile use in the United States is underpriced, as motorists do not pay for the full costs of pollution, congestion, and traffic accidents when deciding how much to drive. Pay-as-you-drive insurance offers a novel approach for reducing automobile use, without raising the private costs of vehicle ownership and use for the majority of drivers.

Under the current lump-sum pricing structure for auto insurance, drivers who are similar in other respects—age, gender, location, driving safety record—pay nearly the same premiums if they drive 5,000 or 50,000 miles a year, even though the likelihood of being involved in a collision increases with each mile driven. Hardly an efficient approach, to put it mildly.

Just as an all-you-can-eat restaurant encourages more eating, all-you-can-drive insurance pricing encourages more driving because drivers don't face the marginal insurance cost for each mile driven. The extra driving that results imposes significant costs on society: more accidents, congestion, carbon emissions, local pollution, and dependence on oil.

Moreover, the current structure is inequitable. It forces low-mileage drivers to subsidize the accident cost of high-mileage drivers in each risk class, even though the former are responsible for fewer accidents. This problem is particularly disturbing given that low-income people tend to drive less on average.

A simple alternative, known as pay-as-you-drive (PAYD) auto insurance, avoids the problems of the current system. With PAYD, the price of auto insurance would be tied to the number of miles driven. Other rating factors such as location, age, vehicle type, and driving record still would be incorporated into this price, so higher-risk drivers would pay more per mile than lower-risk drivers.

BENEFITS

Switching to PAYD could yield substantial benefits, according to our recent findings, which are based on data from the 2001 National Household Transportation Survey. The average driver would face a per-mile insurance premium of 6.6 cents per mile, instead of a yearly lump-sum cost of about $800. Because drivers could save money by driving less, we estimate driving (miles traveled) would fall by about 8 percent.

Achieving a reduction on this scale would yield social benefits of about $60 billion a year, mostly from reduced accidents and congestion, but also from reduced carbon emissions, local pollution, and oil dependence.

And PAYD could achieve these gains while actually *reducing* the cost of driving for most drivers. Almost two-thirds of households would save money under PAYD, with average savings (for those households that save) totaling $270 per vehicle. Most of the savings result from the elimination of the current subsidy from low-mileage to high-mileage drivers. The high proportion of drivers that would pay less reflects the fact that a minority of high-mileage drivers is responsible for a majority of driving within each risk class. In fact, we find that the top 20 percent of drivers are responsible for 45 percent of all miles driven.

Our research also shows that low-income families would especially benefit from PAYD, because low-income people tend to drive fewer miles. Every household income group making less than $52,500 (in 2001) would save money on average. Further, the savings for low-income groups are significant as a share of their total income, whereas any losses by high-income groups are not significant.

OBSTACLES

Despite the large social benefits from PAYD, there are currently barriers to its widespread adoption. For one, insurance regulations in many states prohibit or pose significant obstacles to pricing insurance by the mile. Since regulations were always written with yearly premiums in mind, per-mile premiums are sometimes technically illegal even if that was never the intention of the regulators. California, for example, just acted to address this issue and make it easier for firms to offer PAYD.

A second problem is that, even where it is legal, certain costs reduce the likelihood that firms will independently offer PAYD insurance. In order to price insurance per mile, firms or their customers would need to incur the cost of verifying mileage, through either odometer checks or devices that fit in each vehicle. While odometer readings could be inexpensive procedures if done on a widespread basis, there currently is no infrastructure of certified providers that insurance firms can use. And technological devices that automatically monitor and transmit mileage to insurance companies can be expensive, costing as much as $100 to install. Moreover, to institute PAYD, firms must develop new billing and administrative infrastructures, retool their advertising, and develop new actuarial models to determine appropriate risk-adjusted per-mile prices.

While private firms and their customers would have to bear these costs, much of the benefits from reduced mileage would accrue to other insurance companies and to society as a whole. In our analysis, we find the social benefit to be about $250 per vehicle per year. This is a classic case of a positive externality, and in these cases the government has a clear role to play in promoting a better social outcome. To address the market failure around monitoring costs, the government could require that odometer readings be performed as part of required safety and emissions inspections or by certifying vehicle service businesses in other states to perform odometer readings.

The government could also offer a tax credit for each new mileage-based policy that an insurance company writes. We recommend a $100 tax credit, which would cover the cost of most technological devices that could easily measure and transmit mileage data. The tax credit could be phased out, once roughly five million vehicles (2 percent) are signed up, after which point PAYD is expected to take off on its own. To address the development costs, the government could increase the funding available to PAYD pilot programs.

While we believe that PAYD would be a significant improvement, it is not an adequate policy response to driving-related harms all by itself. It does not force drivers to internalize the external social costs of the congestion, accidents, pollution, and oil dependence they cause. It simply corrects a failure with the way that auto insurance is priced today and the inefficient and inequitable consequences of that pricing structure.

Ideally, PAYD would be complemented with other policies, such as carbon pricing and a congestion charge, which directly target the driving-related social harms. But many of these other policies raise the cost of driving, which is politically challenging, especially in these tough economic times. The promise of PAYD is that it can achieve some of the benefits of these user fees by creating incentives to reduce driving without raising the cost of driving in aggregate, and indeed lowering it for the majority of drivers. What is good for drivers, in this case, is also good for society.

Further Reading

Bordoff, Jason E., and Pascal J. Noel. 2008. The Impact of Pay-as-You-Drive Auto Insurance in California. The Hamilton Project. Washington, DC: Brookings Institution.

Bordoff, Jason E., and Pascal J. Noel. 2008. Pay-as-You-Drive Auto Insurance: A Simple Way to Reduce Driving-Related Harms and Increase Equity. The Hamilton Project discussion paper 08-09. Washington, DC: Brookings Institution.

Edlin, Aaron D. 2003. Per Mile Premiums for Auto Insurance. In *Economics for an Imperfect World: Essays in Honor of Joseph Stiglitz*, edited by Richard Arnott, Bruce Greenwald, Ravi Kanbur, and Barry Nalebuff. Cambridge, MA: MIT Press.

Parry, Ian W.H. 2005. Is Pay-as-You-Drive Auto Insurance a Better Way to Reduce Gasoline Than Gasoline Taxes? *American Economic Review* 96(2): 287–93.

72. WHAT MOTIVATES PEOPLE TO BUY HYBRIDS?

Shanjun Li

is a fellow at Resources for the Future. He has conducted research on a such microeconomic topics as the impact of gasoline price changes on fleet fuel economy, peer effects in group lending in developing countries, and the effect of free antibiotics programs on antibiotics usage.

The U.S. government has been supporting consumer purchases of hybrid vehicles in the form of federal income tax deductions before 2006 and federal income tax credits since then. Because these credits are set to expire in 2010, it is especially timely to consider how effective they have been in promoting hybrid sales and whether they should be renewed.

Since hybrid vehicles were introduced into the U.S. market, they have moved from being the rare status toy of green Hollywood actors to a good option for average commuters, or so the media would have us believe. Today, hybrids represent roughly 3 percent of new car sales because of—or perhaps in spite of—federal subsidies, which are due to expire across the board in 2010.

The evidence to support those subsidies is somewhat mixed. For example, while the federal subsidies for the most popular hybrid, the Toyota Prius, have ended, it has continued to gain market share. While most observers agree that federal subsidies were critical to gain market acceptance of what was then a brand-new technology, is that still true today? Or is what matters most the price at the pump?

HOW HYBRIDS WORK

The level of fuel economy and carbon dioxide (CO_2) emissions produced by a conventional gasoline vehicle is largely a reflection of the low efficiency of internal combustion engines. Only about 15 percent of the fuel energy consumed by these engines gets used for propulsion, while the rest is lost to engine and drive-train inefficiencies and idling. Hybrid vehicles combine power from both a gasoline engine and an electric motor that runs off the electricity from a rechargeable battery. The battery harnesses some of the energy that would be wasted in typical automobile operations (such as energy from braking) and provides power whenever the gasoline engine proves to be inefficient and is turned off.

A hybrid model typically costs around $4,000 more on average than its gasoline equivalent because of the battery required for on-board electricity storage and the computer control system that regulates use of the electric motor. Offsetting this is the fuel savings, due to higher fuel economy. For example, a hybrid vehicle achieving a fuel economy of 55 miles per gallon will save $2,340 over the first five years compared with an equivalent regular vehicle with fuel economy of 35 miles per gallon, assuming the vehicle is driven about 15,000 miles a year and the retail gasoline price is $3 per gallon. Hybrids are especially attractive to urban commuters who experience stop-and-go traffic on a regular basis.

Hybrids were first introduced in the United States in 2000 when the Toyota Prius and Honda Insight entered the market. Since that time, the number of hybrid models increased to 15 in 2007, and there could be as many as 40 hybrid models by 2012. Sales of new hybrid vehicles increased from less than 12,000 in 2000 to the recent peak of about 350,000 in 2007, with the most popular model, the Prius, accounting for over 50 percent. In 2008, sales of new hybrid vehicles dropped about 10 percent from the 2007 level, likely in large part due to the recent recession. In July 2009, hybrid sales as a percentage of total new vehicle sales set a record at 3.55 percent with the start of the Cash for Clunkers program.

WHAT EXPLAINS THE INCREASE IN POPULARITY?

One obvious factor is the recent run-up in gasoline prices. For example, the average gasoline price rose from $1.50 to $2.60 per gallon in 20 U.S. metropolitan areas between 2000 and 2006. Arie Beresteanu and I estimate that this increase in fuel prices accounts for 37 percent of hybrid sales in 2006. If prices had risen to $4 (rather than $2.60) and consumers had expected future prices to stay that high, we estimate that hybrid sales would have been higher still, by about 65 percent, in 2006. And of course, both gas prices and hybrid sales have subsequently risen in 2007 and the early part of 2008.

The Energy Information Administration, for example, projects the hybrid share in new vehicle sales to rise progressively to 17 percent by 2030 as retail gasoline prices rise (in real terms) to $3.80 a gallon, and consumers become more familiar with the new technology.

The second factor is tax incentives and other forms of incentives at federal, state, and local levels. At the federal level, income tax incentives were modest initially: from 2001 to 2005, purchases of hybrids were eligible for an income tax deduction of $2,000, which amounted to a subsidy of $500 for an individual in the 25 percent federal income tax bracket. In 2005, the tax deduction was replaced by an income tax credit of up to $3,400 a vehicle, with the credit varying based on the savings in gasoline per mile of the vehicle relative to its gasoline counterpart. (If, instead, tax credits were based on differences in miles per gallon, this would imply much larger subsidies for a given reduction in fuel per mile for small vehicles.)

Not surprisingly, we found that federal income tax deductions had a very minor effect prior to 2006, explaining less than 5 percent of hybrid sales. However, the more generous incentives made a bigger difference, spurring some 20 percent of hybrid sales in 2006. If tax credits had been twice as large, the average hybrid sale would have received a subsidy of about $4,700 and, according to our estimates, hybrid sales would have been 23 percent greater than their actual sales in 2006.

However, due to the small market share of hybrids at present—just 3 percent of the light-vehicle fleet—the federal incentive program has had very limited effects on overall fuel economy of new passenger vehicles. We estimate that the average fuel economy of new passenger vehicles in 2006 is barely noticeably higher at 23.2 miles per gallon with the program, compared with 23.1 miles per gallon without. Even if tax incentives had been twice as large, the average fuel economy of the new passenger vehicle fleet would have been only a further 0.1 miles per gallon higher. To induce the same level of change, a 10-cent gasoline price increase would suffice, without considering its further impact on driving.

Many state and local governments offer their own programs such as sales tax waivers, state income tax breaks, access to high-occupancy vehicle lanes, and exemptions from parking charges. These programs also likely played some role in contributing to hybrid sales. In the context of these state and local incentives, a study by Gallagher and Muehlegger (2009) shows that up-front sales tax waivers, which are immediate and automatic at the time of purchase, are much more effective than state income tax breaks, which consumers have to understand and apply for during the filing of state tax returns.

MOVING FORWARD

Federal income tax credit amounts begin to phase out for a given manufacturer once it has sold over 60,000 eligible vehicles. The credit ran out for Toyota and Honda in 2007 and 2008, respectively. In addition to the phaseout rules, the credit policy is scheduled to end after December 31, 2010. Is there still a case for retaining incentives or offering new policies for hybrid vehicle purchases? There exist several arguments for government support of hybrid vehicles, including significant economies of scale in automobile production, advantages of learning by doing on both consumption and production sides, failure to fully take into account the fuel saving of fuel-efficient vehicles by consumers, as well as the political difficulty of raising gasoline taxes in order to correct for the externalities associated with gasoline consumption.

Should the incentives for hybrid vehicle purchases be continued, current research points to several considerations to be taken into account in the future. Our analysis shows that a flat rebate, irrespective of household income tax liabilities, could be more effective than the current income tax incentives. Households with higher tax liability can take greater advantage of the income tax credits for hybrids, although they may not be as sensitive to such incentives as lower-income households with less tax liability. Moreover, a flat rebate program would eliminate the uncertainty in the amount of benefit for consumers at the time of purchase. In light of the finding by Gallagher and Muehlegger that up-front sales tax incentives are more effective than income tax incentives, the rebate would likely be more effective if it is applied at the time of purchase.

Further Reading

Beresteanu, Arie, and Shanjun Li. 2009. Gasoline Prices, Government Support, and the Demand for Hybrid Vehicles in the U.S. *International Economic Review*. Forthcoming.

Gallagher, Kelly, and Erich Muehlegger. 2009. Giving Green to Get Green? Incentives and Consumer Adoption of Hybrid Vehicle Technology. Working paper. Cambridge, MA: John F. Kennedy School of Government, Harvard University.

McConnell, Virginia, and Tom Turrentine. 2009. Technical report. Hybrid Vehicles and Policies to Reduce GHG Emissions. Unpublished.

73. THE OUTLOOK FOR HYDROGEN CARS

Joan Ogden

is a professor of Environmental Science and Policy at the University of California, Davis, and director of the Sustainable Transportation Energy Pathways Program at the campus's Institute of Transportation Studies. Her primary research interest is technical and economic assessment of new energy technologies.

Edward S. Rubin

is the Alumni Professor of Environmental Engineering and Science in the Engineering and Public Policy Department at Carnegie Mellon University. He specializes in technical, economic, and policy issues related to energy and the environment, particularly in the power sector.

What is the potential for hydrogen fuel cell cars to reduce U.S. dependence on gasoline over the longer term? What technological obstacles need to be overcome and policy actions taken before such vehicles could penetrate the U.S. market in large numbers?

The U.S. automotive fleet will be dramatically transformed over the next several decades as a result of energy and environmental policies being debated right now. Reductions in oil imports to enhance energy security and reduce trade balances will demand greater use of alternatives to gasoline, as will anticipated requirements to reduce carbon dioxide emissions linked to global climate change. Improving the fuel economy of current cars is an important first step, but achieving deep cuts in oil use and greenhouse gas emissions will require a suite of commercially viable alternatives—not just more efficient vehicles (gasoline-battery hybrids, plug-in hybrids, and those powered by fuel cells), but also "decarbonized" fuels, such as renewable biofuels, electricity, and hydrogen produced from low-carbon sources.

Thus far, we have seen a "fuel du jour" syndrome—waves of short-lived enthusiasm first for batteries, then fuel cells, ethanol, and plug-in hybrids. Now the consensus emerging among transportation energy analysts is that a portfolio strategy of options is needed to nurture both near-term and longer-term technologies. One of the most promising options is hydrogen.

The National Research Council has twice assessed hydrogen as a replacement for gasoline in light-duty vehicles. Its 2004 report showed that hydrogen could dramatically reduce oil use and greenhouse gas emissions from light-duty transport by 2050, but only if certain technical and transition barriers could be overcome. The 2008 report (in which we participated) examined a possible transition to hydrogen in detail, offering critical assessments of the timing and resources needed to bring fuel cell vehicles (FCVs) into widespread use.

Fuel cells are at the heart of the hydrogen strategy. They are electrochemical devices, akin to batteries, that combine hydrogen and oxygen (from air) to generate electricity to power a vehicle. The only tailpipe emission is water vapor from the reaction of hydrogen and oxygen. Although fuel cell technology has improved substantially in recent years, it has not yet achieved the performance and cost goals required for large-scale commercial production. The chief technical challenges are making fuel cells as durable and cost-effective as today's internal combustion engine, reducing the use of costly materials, such as platinum for catalysts, and developing a compact, low-cost hydrogen storage system capable of providing a driving range of 300 miles or more.

General Motors, Honda, Daimler, and Toyota are currently introducing precommercial FCVs and hydrogen fueling stations in limited markets, notably California and Germany. If technical progress continues at its current pace, FCVs could be ready for mass production by 2015. Initial costs would be high but should fall quickly as manufacturing volumes increase and vehicles continue to improve. Hydrogen for these vehicles can be produced from a variety of energy sources, including fossil fuels, renewables, and nuclear energy. In the near term, the most economical approach is to manufacture hydrogen from natural gas at individual refueling stations. The projected cost is about $1.50 per gallon of gasoline equivalent (figured on a mile-per-gallon basis), but actual costs would vary with natural gas prices. Eventually, hydrogen could be produced at large centralized plants and distributed to refueling stations via pipelines or trucks, much like gasoline.

Most hydrogen today is produced from fossil fuels, which release significant amounts of carbon dioxide (CO_2)—the major greenhouse gas (GHG) linked to climate change. Large central plants that produce hydrogen from coal could capture the CO_2 and permanently sequester it in deep geological formations. Such systems are currently in use at four large industrial operations in Europe, North Africa, and Canada, but their widespread use for climate change mitigation is still at least a decade away, pending further developments in technology and climate policy. Meanwhile, FCVs using hydrogen made from natural gas would still reduce overall ("well-to-wheels") GHG emissions by half compared with current gasoline vehicles, largely through gains in overall efficiency. Production of hydrogen from biomass also is advancing and could be competitive by the mid to late 2020s. In the longer term, carbon-free renewables, such as wind and solar energy, might be harnessed for hydrogen production via electrolysis of water.

Development of the hydrogen refueling infrastructure is another critical step. Current strategies, developed in close coordination with vehicle manufacturers, focus on targeted introduction of FCVs and hydrogen infrastructure in Los Angeles, New York, and Houston.

The number of hydrogen-fueled vehicles on U.S. roads by 2020 might be no more than about 2 million, out of an estimated vehicle population of 280 million. This assumes that mass production of FCVs gets under way around 2015, all technology goals are met, and FCVs rapidly gain market share, reaching 10 percent of new car sales by 2020. Under such favorable conditions—requiring government support during the transition period—hydrogen cars could become commercially competitive by about 2023. The number of vehicles could then grow rapidly, to 60 million in 2035 and 220 million in 2050—some 60 percent of the future fleet.

In this "maximum practical" scenario, after about 2035, hydrogen cars should reduce oil use and greenhouse gas emissions more than near-term technologies, like advanced internal combustion engines and hybrids, or expanded use of biofuels. The speed of deployment of hydrogen cars is uncertain, however: it depends on how soon technological obstacles are overcome, how fast competing technologies develop, and how quickly consumers embrace a new type of vehicle with an initially limited network of refueling stations.

Any significant market penetration of hydrogen vehicles in the next decade or so will require substantial, sustained, and coordinated public support. First, research and development will cost $16 billion through 2023. About a third would be government funding of basic and applied research, with the remaining funds from the private sector. Current public-private spending for hydrogen and fuel cell R&D totals about $1 billion per year.

Second—and far more challenging—is the need for government support of FCV production during the transition period, when hydrogen cars cost more than gasoline counterparts. Mass production of new vehicles is essential for lowering unit production costs, but manufacturers will not mass-produce a new vehicle unless they ultimately expect to profit. An estimated $40 billion in government support will be required for incremental vehicle costs (e.g., vehicle purchase subsidies) until FCVs become competitive, around 2023.

An additional $10 billion is needed to share the cost of initial investments in hydrogen infrastructure, mainly at existing gasoline stations. Longer-term investments in infrastructure would be more sizable but would be borne by the private sector as FCVs gain acceptance.

Overall, then, the total government investment needed to accelerate a transition to hydrogen cars is roughly $55 billion over the next 15 years. This averages to $3.7 billion per year, similar to current government subsidies for other transportation fuels, such as ethanol. Note, however, that this support for hydrogen R&D, incremental vehicle costs, and early infrastructure would not guarantee success: remaining technical and consumer acceptance hurdles must still be overcome.

Finally, to realize the long-term environmental benefits of hydrogen and reduced oil use, government policies to limit greenhouse gas emissions also are essential. These might include a carbon tax, a cap-and-trade program, or performance and portfolio standards. The point is to ensure that hydrogen is produced with minimal or no greenhouse gas emissions.

Given the uncertainties facing all automotive technologies, neither hydrogen nor any other option should be considered a "silver bullet." A portfolio approach including sustained fuel economy improvements, a rapid phase-in of renewable biofuels, plus an aggressive introduction of hydrogen fuel cell vehicles could, by 2050, reduce gasoline use to virtually nothing and cut carbon emissions by 90 percent, compared with business as usual. Hydrogen would play a major role in achieving this outcome. Clearly, a wise national strategy should include vigorous support for hydrogen cars as part of a national portfolio of promising transport options.

Further Reading

NRC (National Research Council). 2004. *The Hydrogen Economy: Opportunities, Costs, Barriers, and R&D Needs.* Washington, DC: National Academies Press.

NRC (National Research Council). 2008. *Transition to Alternative Transportation Technologies—A Focus on Hydrogen.* Washington, DC: National Academies Press.

Ogden, J. 2006. High Hopes for Hydrogen. *Scientific American* 295: 94–101.

Sperling, D., and J. Cannon, eds. 2004. *The Hydrogen Energy Transition.* Burlington, MA: Elsevier Press.

74. USEFUL LESSONS FROM CALIFORNIA'S EXPERIMENT WITH CONGESTION PRICING

Robert W. Poole, Jr.
is the director of transportation policy and Searle Freedom Trust Transportation Fellow at the Reason Foundation. Poole, an MIT-trained engineer, has advised the previous four presidential administrations on transportation and policy issues.

The world's first high-occupancy toll (HOT) lane, which allows drivers of single-occupancy vehicles to pay a toll to join high-occupancy vehicles on a fast-flowing freeway lane, was introduced on SR 91 in California in 1996. This pricing policy could be a better approach than pricing all freeway lanes.

December 2008 marked the 12th anniversary of the 91 Express Lanes, the world's first high-occupancy toll (HOT) or express toll lanes. A private consortium, operating under a 35-year concession, added four lanes to SR 91, one of Southern California's most congested freeways. Carpools with three or more passengers could use the new lanes at half price; all other cars (no trucks were allowed) would pay a toll set high enough to ensure high-volume but uncongested traffic flow at all hours.

Congestion pricing has turned out to work very well. Initially, the combination of added capacity on SR 91 and the fact that many vehicles switched to the new lanes yielded significant reductions in peak-period congestion on the regular or general purpose lanes (in addition to free-flow conditions in the express lanes). But after about five years, enormous growth in traffic in this commuter corridor led to the return of serious congestion in the general purpose lanes. The concession agreement included a rigid noncompete clause, preventing the addition of any more general purpose capacity. This was at the insistence of financiers, who saw huge risk in toll lanes that had "free" competition literally right alongside. This situation proved politically untenable, leading to the purchase of the express lanes by the Orange County Transportation Authority (OCTA) seven years after they had opened to traffic.

It was hoped by many (who didn't understand congestion pricing) and feared by others (who did) that the agency would be under irresistible political pressure to reduce the gradually escalating peak-period toll rates on the lanes. To their credit, OCTA did just the opposite. Recognizing that correct pricing was the only way the lanes could deliver the promised benefit of a reliable, uncongested trip, they depoliticized the toll-adjustment process. Planners created an algorithm that uses measured traffic density in the express lanes, hour by hour, seven days a week. For any one-hour time block during peak travel times—where set traffic conditions are at risk of becoming more congested, as measured over a 12-week period—the toll rate for that time block is increased accordingly. The adjustment process also checks for under-use and permits automatic downward adjustments.

As of this writing, the maximum morning peak toll for the express lanes is $4.20. In the afternoon peak, when demand is much heavier, the maximum rate (for a single, one-hour period on a Friday afternoon) is $10. For most of the weekday afternoon rush hour, tolls are in the $5–$9 range. The minimum charge during off-peak hours is $1.20.

The success of the well-studied 91 Express Lanes has sparked a boom in congestion pricing, encouraged by permissive language in successive federal transportation reauthorization bills and, especially recently, by incentive programs like the U.S. Department of Transportation's Urban Partnership Agreement competition. HOT lanes are in operation in six metro areas and under development in half a dozen others. Many pricing advocates argue that while express toll lanes may be a good introductory measure, the real goal should be to price all lanes on all freeways, at least during peak periods. But recent research suggests that this may not be optimal.

Kenneth Small and others (2006) have documented the enormous variation among different motorists in their willingness to pay for driving in high-speed lanes; in general, those with higher income or wages are willing to pay more to reduce their commute times and lower the risk of being late for work or other appointments. This variability in willingness to pay among drivers has important implications for road pricing policies. For one thing, it makes economic sense to charge different tolls on different lanes of a freeway, rather than imposing the same toll across all the lanes. Differentiated tolls allow motorists to choose which combination of low-toll/low-speed or high-toll/high-speed lanes they prefer.

Moreover, motorists who place relatively little value on travel time savings may be hit especially hard when their only choice is to drive on the freeway and pay a toll, or not use the freeway at all. In fact, a uniform toll imposed on all freeway lanes with no exemptions may actually do more economic harm overall than good, compared with a baseline situation with no freeway pricing at all. If policymakers are concerned about avoiding excessive burdens on low-income motorists, Small and his colleagues suggest that the best policy compromise might be to have freeway lane alternatives with high and low tolls, and with exemptions for high-occupancy vehicles in the low-price lane. Even in this case, the gains over simply pricing one lane and leaving the adjacent lanes free of charge may not be that great.

In related work, Elena Safirova and colleagues (2004) have studied the conversion of existing high-occupancy vehicle (HOV) lanes in the metropolitan Washington, DC, area to HOT lanes. This appears to represent a win–win policy in several respects. Drivers of single-occupant vehicles are better off as they can now choose to drive in the faster, premium lane, if the travel time savings more than compensate them for the toll. Drivers who choose to remain on unpriced lanes adjacent to the HOT lane also benefit from reduced congestion on that lane as some drivers switch to the premium lane. And the government benefits from obtaining a new source of transportation revenue.

Based on these results, urban transportation planners should feel confident about moving forward with politically feasible plans for networks of HOT lanes, rather than holding out for the politically difficult (and socially dubious) goal of pricing all lanes.

Further Reading

Orange County Transportation Authority. 2003. 91 Express Lanes Toll Policy. www.91expresslanes.com/generalinfo/tollpolicy.asp.

Poole, Robert W. Jr., and C. Kenneth Orski. 2003. HOT Networks: A New Plan for Congestion Relief and Better Transit. Policy Study 305. Los Angeles, CA: Reason Foundation.

Safirova, Elena, Kenneth Gillingham, Ian Parry, Peter Nelson, Winston Harrington, and David Mason. 2004. Welfare and Distributional Effects of HOT Lanes and Other Road Pricing Policies in Metropolitan Washington, DC. In *Road Pricing: Theory and Practice, Research in Transportation Economics 9*, edited by Georgina Santos. Oxford, UK: Elsevier, 179–206.

Small, Kenneth A., Clifford Winston, and Jia Yan. 2006. Differentiated Road Pricing, Express Lanes, and Carpools: Exploiting Heterogeneous Preferences in Policy Design. *Brookings-Wharton Papers on Urban Affairs* 2006: 53–96.

75. CONGESTION PRICING

Lessons from London

Jonathan Leape
is a senior lecturer at the London School of Economics.

London's area licensing program is arguably the most important pricing scheme to address urban traffic congestion to date. What lessons might be learned by policy-makers considering similar programs for other cities like New York?

Congestion is steadily increasing on city streets around the world, imposing a heavy cost on urban economies that depend on rapid, reliable movement of people and goods. In the United States alone, the Texas Transportation Institute has calculated that traffic delays cost $78 billion a year in wasted time and fuel. Taking account of the additional costs of doing business, lost productivity, and unrealized business revenue means that the overall cost of congestion is much higher, as shown in a recent study of congestion in New York City.

Theoretically, economics provides a solution: put a price on congestion paid by the people who contribute to it. There are other ways of trying to deal with congestion, such as building new roads, regulating parking, or subsidizing public transportation, each of which has its role. But only congestion pricing creates the right incentives when individuals are deciding whether, when, and how to travel. The idea has been under discussion for decades, but does it actually work in practice? Over the past several years, London has demonstrated that indeed it can.

But London's experience also makes clear the conditions that a city and its leadership must meet if congestion pricing is to be effective and, as in London, popular.

The first condition is a level of public and business concern about the costs of congestion that puts the problem well up the political agenda. By the end of the 1990s, average speeds in central London were below 10 miles per hour throughout the day and commuters into London spent almost 30 percent of their time stationary during peak periods. In public opinion surveys, public transport and congestion outranked crime as the most important problems requiring action.

Congestion pricing takes strong political leadership. Ken Livingstone, a high-profile London political figure since the 1980s, ran for mayor in 2000 on a platform that emphasized congestion charging. In the United States, New York seriously considered, though in the end rejected, a similar pricing scheme.

To maintain public support, a successful program also needs competent administration and tight enforcement. After he came into office, Livingstone spent two years on careful planning and extensive public consultation. The London Congestion Charge was designed as an area license (or "day pass") scheme. The charging zone, initially an area of eight square miles traditionally defined as central London, was almost doubled in size in early 2007, when it was extended westward to include Kensington and Chelsea. The zone is defined by a ring of roads that provide alternative routes for through traffic, at no charge. For those who cross the boundary, the cost was originally set at five pounds (about $10) a day, with zone residents entitled to a 90 percent discount on weekly, monthly, or annual payments. In 2005, the rate was raised to eight pounds (about $16).

The border is enforced by video cameras, which were already common in London. Concerns about civil liberties had been diminished by the cameras' effectiveness in reducing street crime. The cameras read vehicle license plates, and a computer matches them against a list of those who have paid and those exempt (which, in London, includes emergency services vehicles, taxis, buses, low-emissions vehicles, and all two-wheelers). Those who haven't paid are sent a penalty notice that includes a picture of their car in the charging zone. The detection rate is around 90 percent, and because the minimum penalty for violation is six times the cost of compliance, evasion is unlikely to pay.

The impact of the scheme exceeded expectations. In the first year of the charge, traffic delays in London dropped by 30 percent, journey time reliability increased by 30 percent, and average speeds rose 17 percent, reflecting a sharp fall in traffic jams at intersections (the time spent traveling at speeds less than 6 miles per hour decreased by one-third). The charge also changed who was using the roads: private car trips dropped by 34 percent and trucks and vans by 5 to 7 percent, but bus, taxi, and bike trips all rose sharply. The overall impact was a noticeable improvement in traffic conditions.

The London experience has also shown that it's possible—and important—to spread the benefits of congestion pricing widely. By committing to plow all the revenues raised by the congestion charge into public transportation improvements, London has ensured that congestion pricing didn't just improve mobility for car drivers who can pay the charge (the "Lexus lanes" problem), but also increased access to the city center for everyone. Innovative policies, such as the popular mass bike-share program in Paris, can also help to spread the benefits.

In fact, the shift from cars to buses outstripped predictions. Inbound bus passenger numbers increased 37 percent in the first year, about half of whom had previously traveled by car. This increased the bus share of incoming passengers to almost 10 percent, with most of the remaining passengers split evenly between rail and subway. A key reason for the surge in bus passenger numbers appears to be the "virtuous circle" for bus transport that can result from congestion pricing (Small 2005). The higher cost of rush-hour car trips and increased bus travel speeds, due to reduced congestion, result in increasing passenger numbers and falling average costs—which, in turn, lead to improved service levels and lower fares that stimulate further shifts to public transport and additional reductions in congestion. With one million people traveling into midtown and downtown Manhattan every day by private car, the potential for a virtuous circle in New York—should congestion pricing ultimately become a reality—is evident.

But London also offers a warning. Because congestion pricing has been more successful than Mayor Livingstone expected, it has brought in less revenue—a problem that was compounded by setup and running costs that far exceeded expectations. Tight control of costs is essential if the increased investment in mass transit and other transport alternatives necessary to make the scheme successful are to prove sustainable.

The central lesson of London's great experiment appears to be that congestion pricing will get and keep public support only if it is part of a larger congestion management strategy that improves public transportation. And it will work only if the impact of the scheme is highly visible and the benefits are spread widely.

Further Reading

Leape, Jonathan. 2006. The London Congestion Charge. *Journal of Economic Perspectives* 20(4): 157–176.

Newbery, David M. 2005. Road User and Congestion Charges. In *Theory and Practice of Excise Taxation: Smoking, Drinking, Gambling, Polluting, and Driving*, edited by S. Cnossen. Oxford, UK: Oxford University Press, 193–229.

Small, Kenneth A. 2005. Road Pricing and Public Transit: Unnoticed Lessons from London. *Access* 26 (Spring).

Transport for London. Various years. *Annual Reports*. Impacts Monitoring Programme. London: Transport for London.

76. HAS THE TIME COME FOR TRUCK-ONLY TOLL LANES?

Robin Lindsey
is a professor of economics at the University of Alberta. His research interests include traffic congestion, road pricing, and competition in transportation markets.

Policymakers are increasingly interested in the idea of charging heavy-duty trucks by the mile for road use. What are the pros and cons of these types of tolls, and should trucks have their own freeway lanes?

Traffic congestion imposes a direct cost on U.S. freight transporters of $7.8 billion per year, according to the Federal Highway Administration. Recurring bottlenecks accounted for about 40 percent of total delays; the rest can be attributed to random sources of congestion such as accidents and roadwork, which upset delivery schedules and inflict a higher cost per hour of delay than recurring congestion. Truck traffic is growing more quickly than light-vehicle traffic, and trucking is expected to remain the dominant mode of freight transport. Is it time for dedicated truck-only toll lanes?

The potential advantages of truck facilities have not gone unnoticed. Proposals for truck-only toll lanes or truck tollways have appeared in California, Florida, Georgia, Texas, and Virginia. In 2002, Texas developed a plan to build a 4,000-mile Trans-Texas Corridor comprising rail lines, utility right-of-ways, and highways with separate toll lanes for trucks and passenger vehicles. However, in the face of stiff opposition from environmentalists and private landowners, the project has been scaled back. Another proposed project, the I-70 corridor, would span Missouri, Illinois, Indiana, and Ohio. Truck-only corridors connecting the United States and Canada, and truck-only road networks in Britain, Italy, and the Netherlands have also been studied.

POTENTIAL BENEFITS AND DISADVANTAGES

Dedicated truck-only facilities have several potential benefits. By adding road capacity, new facilities will relieve congestion and make deliveries quicker and more predictable. And by drawing trucks off existing roads, light vehicles will benefit too. Segregating light and heavy vehicles on existing roads could facilitate traffic because they differ in size, acceleration, and maneuverability and therefore get in each other's way. However, on multilane highways without barrier separation, there are trade-offs among average speed, lane speed differentials, frequency of lane changes, and fuel consumption.

Similar considerations determine whether segregating cars and trucks would reduce accidents. Overall accident rates per vehicle mile traveled are lower for trucks than cars, because professional truckers tend to be better drivers, and the actions of truckers are easier to predict than those of "four-wheelers." However, the risk of a fatality is greater in multivehicle accidents involving trucks, and these fatality risks are primarily borne by light-vehicle occupants. Surveys indicate that car drivers would be willing to pay to avoid sharing the road with trucks.

Truck-only toll facilities also generate revenue, which is becoming a priority for building new capacity and rehabilitating existing roads as the Federal Highway Trust Fund goes into deficit. A final and potentially significant advantage from building dedicated truck facilities is that it could reduce long-run infrastructure costs. Trucks require higher road-design standards than do light vehicles. By restricting trucks to part of the road network, the remainder could be built to a lower standard. (For example, lanes could be restriped from 12 feet to 10 or 11 feet, increasing capacity if additional lanes can be squeezed in on urban expressways.)

Obviously, truck-only facilities also have disadvantages. Building new infrastructure is expensive, and continuous rights-of-way may be unavailable. It is impractical—if not impossible—to segregate cars and trucks on all roads leading to and from dedicated truck facilities. Perhaps most important, because capacity is imperfectly divisible, it is not generally possible to allocate it between light and heavy vehicles in ideal proportions. Even a single dedicated truck lane is not cost-effective if trucks comprise a small fraction of traffic.

ACCESS RESTRICTIONS AND TOLLS

Truck-only toll facilities embody access restrictions and tolls. To understand their respective roles, it is useful to consider a simple road network. The corridor in which truck-only facilities can be established comprises two parts, "road 1" and "road 2," each consisting of either a separate right-of-way or one or more traffic lanes (possibly barrier separated) of the same highway. Road 1 has a greater capacity than road 2. There are also untolled alternative routes that may not be designed to handle heavy vehicles.

Access restrictions and tolls can be used to pursue three goals:

- to distribute light and heavy vehicles (henceforth "lights" and "heavies") that use the corridor efficiently between road 1 and road 2,
- to distribute lights and heavies between the corridor and alternative routes, and
- to generate revenue.

These goals may be at odds; for example, imposing high tolls on the corridor to generate lots of revenue may increase congestion on alternative routes. Even in this simple setting there are many options. Lights and heavies can each be allowed to use both roads or be restricted to one. And tolls may or may not be levied on each vehicle type on each road. Access restrictions alone generally do not meet any of the three goals because they do not generate revenue and they are an imperfect instrument for allocating traffic between the corridor and alternative routes. They allocate traffic efficiently within the corridor only if it is optimal to segregate lights and heavies onto separate roads. Heavies can be allocated to either road 1 or road 2, but in either case, road capacities are unlikely to be ideally proportioned to handle the equilibrium volumes of lights and heavies.

Tolls, on the other hand, do generate revenue, although it may fall short of paying the full capital cost of new infrastructure. Tolls are also more effective than access restrictions because they offer a continuous, rather than discrete, degree of control. But they do have limitations. Tolls cannot influence all margins of driver behavior such as weaving between lanes and driving speed. And shippers may impose constraints on delivery times that prevent truckers from shifting to off-peak hours in response to peak-period tolls.

Light and heavy vehicles differ in characteristics such as size, weight, safety, and emissions, and so to price road use efficiently, tolls have to be differentiated by vehicle type and route. Today, tolls can be differentiated by number of axles. Technological advances may soon permit tolls to be set in real time according to vehicle or axle weight, emissions, and other characteristics of the vehicle or driver.

PROSPECTS

Assessing the merits of truck-only toll facilities is challenging. For new facilities, there are many design considerations: location, length, numbers of lanes and lane width, pavement thickness, entrances and exits, speed limits, services such as truck stops and refueling stations, and so on. Owner-operators and private carriers differ in the values they place on travel time and reliability and have shown different propensities to use toll roads. Toll road volumes have often been overestimated, sometimes by wide margins. Much of the trucking industry remains skeptical of road pricing as a way to relieve congestion and finance transportation infrastructure.

Nevertheless, the long-term outlook for truck-only toll facilities appears promising. Transportation planners are grappling with growing funding shortfalls for highway spending caused by improving vehicle fuel economy and the erosion of real fuel tax rates due to inflation. Truck-only toll lanes offer a new revenue source, while also complementing the increasing interest in charging motorists by the mile through GPS or other electronic metering, to better address the broader social costs of transportation from congestion, pollution, and accidents.

Further Reading

Cambridge Systematics, Inc. 2005. *An Initial Assessment of Freight Bottlenecks on Highways.* White Paper prepared for Federal Highway Administration Office of Transportation Policy Studies. Washington, DC: U.S. Department of Transportation.

De Palma, André, Robin Lindsey, and Moez Kilani. 2008. The Merits of Separating Cars and Trucks. *Journal of Urban Economics* 64: 340–361.

Killough, Keith. 2008. Value Analysis of Truck Toll Lanes in Southern California. Paper 08-0140 presented at 87th Annual Meeting of the Transportation Research Board. January 2008, Washington, DC.

Samuel, Peter, Robert Poole, and José Holguín-Veras. 2002. *Toll Truckways: A New Path toward Safer and More Efficient Freight Transportation.* Policy Study 294. Los Angeles: Reason Foundation.

77. USING THE PRICE SYSTEM TO REDUCE AIRPORT CONGESTION

Jan K. Brueckner

is a professor of economics at the University of California, Irvine. His research focuses on urban and public economics, industrial organization, and housing finance.

Kurt Van Dender

is a professor of economics at the Catholic University, Leuven. His research focuses on transportation economics, urban economics, and public finance.

Flight delays are increasingly common as growth in demand for air travel outpaces airport capacity expansion. How might pricing policies address airport congestion, and to what extent, if any, should fees be adjusted when hub airports are dominated by one carrier with market power?

Driven by the growth in demand for air transportation, flight volumes at many major U.S. airports have increased sharply in recent years. Since the flight capacity of airports has hardly changed, the increase in traffic volume has led to more and longer delays, a trend well documented in newspaper stories and the evening news. In 2007, 24 percent of flights arrived late, up from 15 percent in 2003.

What measures are appropriate for handling airport congestion? Building more capacity is one option, and some capacity expansion will surely be needed despite its high cost as traffic expands. Another response is to cut flight volumes through direct government intervention in airline scheduling decisions, as the Federal Aviation Administration (FAA) did at Chicago's O'Hare Airport. A more systematic approach relies on a "slot" system, where airlines cannot schedule flights as they please but must instead acquire landing or takeoff slots, issued by the airport, in order to operate. Such a system of "slot constraints" has been used at four major U.S. airports and is de rigueur in Europe.

A problem with such quantity controls is that, while they may relieve congestion, they do not guarantee that the available slots are used for the best purposes. For example, airlines may use peak-hour slots to operate smaller aircraft than would be desirable. While slot trading among airlines helps to achieve the highest and best use of slots, frictions in the trading process may still leave room for inefficiencies.

A better way to ensure efficient use of scarce runway capacity is to rely on the most basic economic pricing principle: make airlines pay the marginal cost of using a congested airport. If an airline decides to land under congested conditions, it incurs extra operating costs while subjecting its passengers to additional time costs, and it will take both of these costs into account. But the presence of congestion means the extra flight also increases operating and time costs for all other flights using the airport, and these impacts are also part of marginal cost. A condition for efficient use of congested runway capacity is that the full marginal cost, including the cost imposed on other airlines, must be internalized (taken into account) by the carriers.

But would an airline in fact internalize these costs in deciding whether to operate an extra flight? This question has been much debated among airline economists, leading to the usual answer: it depends. If each airline serving the airport has a relatively large presence, operating a substantial number of flights, then each carrier will understand that its scheduling decisions affect the overall level of congestion. Moreover, carriers will play a scheduling game with one another, with each airline setting its flight volumes to maximize profit, taking account of airport congestion as well as scheduling choices of the other carriers. In this situation, each airline will partially internalize congestion, taking into account the congestion it imposes on itself (additional delays for all its other flights) in deciding whether to schedule an extra flight. However, since the airline will ignore the congestion imposed on other carriers, marginal costs are only partially internalized.

The answer to the internalization question is even less favorable when the big players at the congested airport coexist with a competitive fringe, a collection of airlines that individually operate only a few flights. These airlines could be carriers that are large overall but only have a small presence at the congested airport. Rather than being equal players, the fringe carriers follow the lead of the big airlines, adjusting to their behavior while having no individual impact on the overall level of congestion.

In the presence of a competitive fringe, partial internalization of congestion is eliminated. If large carriers restrict their flight volumes to limit self-imposed congestion, the fringe carriers would simply fill the gap, leaving overall congestion unchanged. Therefore, each big carrier's incentive to take account of self-imposed congestion is neutralized, and partial internalization disappears. The FAA observed exactly this kind of "gap-filling" behavior after persuading United and American Airlines to cut their flight volumes at O'Hare Airport.

Since internalization of congestion is either partial or nonexistent in these two cases, policy intervention is required. Congestion pricing, which makes airlines pay for the congestion they fail to internalize, is an attractive option. Daniel (1995) calculated congestion charges for the Minneapolis–St. Paul airport, assuming that the competitive-fringe model (and the absence of internalization) is realistic. He found that the congestion charge for each flight should equal about $1,000 (in 2007 dollars) on average during the day. But once the charges have had their intended effect of reducing congestion by shifting flights to off-peak hours, the average charge would fall to approximately $360. With partial internalization, congestion charges would have somewhat smaller magnitudes. But regardless of which case applies, some level of congestion pricing would be required at most large airports.

Unlike pouring concrete for more runways, congestion pricing is virtually costless to implement, and by reducing peak traffic volumes, it will make our airports seem magically larger. While airlines strongly oppose congestion pricing, the industry seems not to recognize that congestion charges can replace the current weight-based system of landing fees. With fees dropping to zero in off-peak hours, reflecting the absence of congestion, the carriers' overall costs need not rise by much. In any case, peak-hour congestion charges are likely to be passed on to passengers, widening the current differential between peak and off-peak fares and generating the traffic shift toward less-congested hours.

Further Reading

Brueckner, Jan K. 2002. Airport Congestion When Carriers Have Market Power. *American Economic Review* 92(5): 1357–1375.

Brueckner, Jan K., and Kurt Van Dender. 2007. Atomistic Congestion Tolls at Concentrated Airports? Seeking a Unified View in the Internalization Debate. CESifo Working Paper No. 2033. Munich, Germany: CESifo.

Daniel, Joseph I. 1995. Congestion Pricing and Capacity of Large Hub Airports: A Bottleneck Model with Stochastic Queues. *Econometrica* 63(2): 327–370.

78. DELAYED

Is Privatizing America's Airports the Answer?

Clifford Winston
is a senior fellow in the Brookings Institution's Economic Studies Program. His research focuses on microeconomic policy and government performance.

Ginés de Rus
is a professor of applied economics at the University of Las Palmas de Gran Canaria, Spain. He specializes in transport economics, regulation, and cost–benefit analysis.

The United States relies on public ownership and heavy regulation of its airports and air traffic control system to address flight delays, carrier competition, and airline safety. How might steps to liberalize this regulatory system help passengers get to their destinations at lower cost and with fewer delays?

We all know the personal cost of flight delays and airport security: the missed connections, the hassle of going through screening, the annoyance of having to show up so far in advance of the scheduled departure time. In aggregate, in the United States alone, those costs are estimated at $40 billion annually. Meanwhile, ticket prices keep rising, and periodic reports of breaches of security—the grad student whose fake boarding pass goes undetected, the planted weapons that screeners don't see—undermine public confidence in the system. Is there a remedy?

Air travelers seek value—convenience, price, and safety. In theory, aviation infrastructure policy should reduce travel delays, facilitate competition, and keep flying safe, all at the least possible cost. What we see instead is the failure of publicly owned and managed airports and the federal air traffic control system to introduce innovation—a failure that arises from the paucity of economic incentives and the multitude of institutional and political constraints. Certainly there are lessons to be learned from the efforts of other countries to restructure their airport systems to better address these issues.

The key to reducing delays efficiently is to rid the system of its major inefficiencies and to institute policies that enhance airline system performance:

- Air travel could be safer and faster if ground-based radar systems were replaced with more accurate satellite communications. Travel time would be reduced because planes could fly closer together and take the most direct routes.
- The price of air traffic control services should reflect the marginal costs that a given flight imposes on the system, including delay costs to other users. The current ticket tax that funds air traffic control, however, bears little relationship to those costs and therefore does not reduce congestion.
- Runway pricing should be based on an aircraft's contribution to congestion instead of on its weight or arbitrary quantity controls, like takeoff and landing slots. Replacing inefficient administrative solutions with a potentially efficient market solution would redistribute traffic both temporally and spatially, reducing delays.
- Funding for new runways and terminals should be based on market-derived, rational assessments of which airports would benefit most from additional runway investment, rather than determined by political forces.
- Service could improve and fares fall if restrictions that prevent carriers from using certain airports or gates were removed. Travelers are worse off when incumbent carriers are permitted to slot new entrants into gates only at inconvenient times and locations or at excessive cost, or are able to prevent them from gaining access to gates altogether.
- Innovative solutions to thwarting terrorism may exist but are not likely to emerge in a government bureaucracy like the Transportation Security Administration. Israel has prevented problems by identifying suspicious passengers, for example, and private security firms provide effective but subtle security for millions in the Las Vegas casinos. One very cost-effective approach in aviation was installing bulletproof cockpit doors, which the airline industry did for a mere $500 million.

Although air travelers are painfully aware of the suboptimal service provided by U.S. aviation infrastructure facilities, regulations and political forces have made reform extremely difficult. The Federal Aviation Administration lacks organizational independence and is prevented by Congress and the administration from using its resources more efficiently. Peak-period pricing for air traffic control, for example, was blocked by pressure from owners of corporate jets. Political pressure is, in fact, the primary cause of misallocated FAA expenditures, and ineffective management is impeding development and implementation of the satellite tracking system, which will consolidate air traffic control facilities. Any effort to replace current funding mechanisms is seen as the first step to taking air traffic control out of the congressional funding process—and taking power away from lawmakers.

Predictions of continued growth in air travel make innovation imperative, but improvements won't happen under the current system: only privatization of the nation's aviation infrastructure is likely to result in constructive reform. Operating in a more competitive environment, privatized airports and air traffic control would have incentives to improve service and reduce the cost of operations while maintaining the nation's outstanding safety record. Privatized airports could even facilitate greater competition among airlines that would lead to lower fares.

Though privatization may appear a drastic and potentially risky solution, examples from other countries already exist—right next door, even. To increase investment in airport infrastructure without government funding, Canada quasi-privatized its airports in the mid-1980s and transferred them to locally based, not-for-profit authorities. The country's biggest airports then built additional runways and terminals, thereby reducing congestion.

Australia and New Zealand began privatizing their major airports in the late 1990s, specifically to sharpen incentives for efficiency, and lightened their regulation. Today, the prices charged to airlines are high but well below monopoly levels, and the airports are considered to perform well.

The United Kingdom's airport infrastructure is now mainly private. Although regulatory burdens persist, air traffic control services are provided by a public-private organization that took over from a public agency in 2001.

China went from a paramilitary organization to a system of local control of airports, a liberalization that contributed to dramatic growth in air traffic, raised airline productivity, heightened competition, improved air safety, and increased investment in infrastructure.

None of those systems work perfectly, but the examples prove that far from having an adverse effect on aviation system performance, privatization has much to offer. Taken together, the experiences of other countries are a playbook of potential solutions that U.S. policymakers can adapt to American circumstances. Just ask any road warrior: anything that promises better value in air travel—more convenience, lower prices, and an even higher level of safety—is worth a look.

Further Reading

Winston, Clifford, and Ginés de Rus, eds. 2008. *Aviation Infrastructure Performance: A Study in Comparative Political Economy.* Washington, DC: Brookings Institution.

79. TELECOMMUTING

What Is It Good For?

Elena Safirova

is a fellow at Resources for the Future. Her research focuses on economic modeling and policy analysis related to transportation and urban land use.

Telecommuting has never really fulfilled the hopes of its early advocates. Why has it been slow to catch on, and how might it potentially help alleviate pollution and congestion? Should the government sponsor programs to promote telecommuting?

When the phenomenon of telecommuting appeared on the horizon in the 1970s, it seemed to be a godsent panacea. For employees, it promised more time to spend with their families and lower commuting costs. For employers, it dangled the reduction of real estate costs and utility bills and an ability to retain and recruit better employees by using the telecommuting option as a fringe benefit. For society as a whole, telework promised reduced auto trips, less road congestion, lower energy consumption, and cleaner air. Telecommuting seemed to be a win–win solution to everybody, and all it required was a steady growth in information-type jobs and perhaps better phone lines. According to some estimates, by the year 2000, 50 percent of the U.S. workforce was supposed to telecommute. And all that government seemingly had to do was educate both employers and workers about telework and its benefits.

Fast forward to the 21st century. Although the percentage of workers who telecommute has been steadily increasing, it is way lower than what was predicted in the 1970s (according to different estimates, anywhere between 10 and 45 million of U.S. workers telecommute at least once a year, but only a small fraction telecommute at least once a week). At the same time, information technology has undergone significant transformation and is now far more advanced than in the wildest futuristic dreams of the past decades.

LIMITATIONS TO TELECOMMUTING

It turns out that the great virtues of telecommuting are often offset by less desirable features. Combining telecommuting and caring for small children at home frequently proved to be impractical and was opposed by most employers. For some employees, telecommuting removed the boundary between work and leisure and increased work stress levels. For others, telecommuting has lead to feelings of isolation and lack of social interaction with coworkers. Last but not least, telecommuting tends to reduce workers' visibility in the organization and is likely to decrease their promotion potential.

Employers also found that managing a telecommuting workforce can be quite challenging, especially when worker productivity is hard to measure. When a telecommuter works at home once a week or less, realizing sizable real-estate and utility savings turned out to be quite hard. Also, institutional implementation of telecommuting programs and resolving issues related to workplace safety at home place additional burdens on employers and make promoting telecommuting much less attractive.

Finally, the benefits for the society as a whole don't seem to be as desirable as hoped for. My early research has shown that in the long run, the presence of telecommuting options is likely to make our metro areas larger and more congested than before. In essence, there is an "induced demand" effect—when an opportunity to telecommute arrives and some workers in the metro area start telecommuting, roads become less congested and attract new workers to the urban area until congestion climbs up to the original levels again. Just as we cannot build our way out of road congestion, we cannot telecommute our way out of it either.

Although in the long run, the prospects for telecommuting to reduce traffic congestion are bleak, in the short run there could be some room for reduction in vehicle miles traveled (VMT), traffic congestion, and air quality. That said, the exact environmental and transportation benefits of telecommuting remain an open question. For one thing, research studies have shown that when telecommuters work at home, they are more likely to make more nonwork trips, thus eroding overall VMT reductions. Also, our research has demonstrated that telecommuters are more likely to drive newer cars than the population in general, and therefore emissions reductions from reduced commuting would be lower than expected.

GOVERNMENT INITIATIVES TO PROMOTE TELECOMMUTING

Although the majority of U.S. states have some policy regarding telecommuting, most of them concern either provision of information and educational resources to employers interested in starting telecommuting programs or telecommuting programs for state employees. With a few exceptions, such as the Oregon Department of Energy program that offers tax credits to employers with significant percentage of telecommuting workers, states do not provide additional incentives for telecommuting.

For metropolitan planning organizations (MPOs), the goal of most telecommuting initiatives these days is not fighting congestion, but improving air quality, especially in the areas of nonattainment. Many MPOs assume that some fraction of employees in their area will work from home a certain number of days per week, thus reducing the number of work trips and attained emissions. However, the U.S. Department of Transportation recently announced its new comprehensive national strategy to reduce congestion on the nation's roads. Metropolitan areas would commit to pursuit of aggressive strategies under the umbrella of "Four Ts"—tolling, transit, telecommuting, and technology. The goal is to use all strategies simultaneously to achieve the best results. How well these various measures work together is not well understood; for example, promoting telecommuting can potentially undermine other alternatives, such as public transit and carpools, and vice versa.

The most recent attempt to institute national telecommuting policy occurred in the spring of 2009, when the Telework Improvement Act of 2009 (HR 1722) was introduced in the House of Representatives. The bill would require government agencies to develop a program allowing employees to telework at least 20 percent of every two-week work period. A counterpart bill in the Senate, the Telework Enhancement Act (S 707), has won the approval of the Senate Homeland Security and Governmental Affairs Committee in May 2009, but is still pending. Unlike other policy attempts, the telework bill is driven more by national security concerns than by transportation and environmental goals and affects only federal employees.

At the same time, in order to promote telecommuting, a dedicated telecommuting policy is only one strategy among many. People's propensity to telecommute very much depends on their industry and type of work, and therefore targeting particular industries may be a better strategy. Because many telecommuters depend on communications technology that allows them to move large amounts of data between home and office, a national broadband policy would increase Internet capacity and therefore also boost telework. Telecommuting also rises with education level, and so government policies that encourage higher education, such as student loan programs, could have a corollary effect here as well.

Should the government be encouraging telecommuting through these types of programs? Although we lack the evidence to answer this question definitively, any transportation benefits from telecommuting policies are probably modest at best. If local governments are serious about reducing urban traffic congestion, there is no way around an inconvenient truth: the most effective way to do it is to charge motorists for using scarce road space during rush hour.

Further Reading

Mokhtarian, P.L., G.O. Collantes, and C. Gertz. 2004. Telecommuting, Residential Location, and Commute-Distance Traveled: Evidence from State of California Employees. *Environment and Planning* A 36(10): 1877–1897

Nelson, P., E. Safirova, and M. Walls. 2007. Telecommuting and Environmental Policy—Lessons from the Ecommute Program. *Transportation Research* D 12(3): 195–207

Nilles, J., F. Carlson, P. Grey, and G. Hanneman. 1976. *The Telecommunications-Transportation Tradeoff.* New York: John Wiley & Sons, Inc.

Safirova, E. 2002. Telecommuting, Traffic Congestion, and Agglomeration: A General Equilibrium Model. *Journal of Urban Economics* 52(1): 26-52

80. DECLINING TRAFFIC FATALITIES

Lessons for Developing Countries?

Maureen Cropper

is a professor of economics at the University of Maryland, a senior fellow at Resources for the Future, and a former lead economist at the World Bank. Her research focuses on valuing environmental amenities and health, and environmental regulations.

Elizabeth Kopits

is a senior economist for energy, environment, and natural resources on the President's Council of Economic Advisers. She is on leave from the National Center for Environmental Economics at EPA.

As countries have developed over time, they have experienced a pattern of initially rising, then peaking, then declining traffic fatality rates. What might be some possible explanations for the downturn in fatalities, and what are the lessons for poor countries currently in the stage of rising accident risks?

As industrial countries have developed over time, there has been a clear inverted-U relation between the incidence of traffic fatalities and per capita income (a similar pattern is often observed between pollution and per capita income). The initial, positive association between fatality rates and development is straightforward to explain—as motorization takes off, more pedestrians become exposed to the risk of being hit, while occupants of one vehicle are more likely to be involved in a collision as the number of other vehicles on the road rises. What causes the fatality rate to income relation to peak, and then trend downward, is more complex. It is due, in part, to a decline in pedestrian fatalities as pedestrians become vehicle occupants, but decreases in occupant fatalities are likely to require deliberate, safety-focused policies. A better understanding of what has caused the traffic fatality rate to decline in developed countries could provide important lessons for the design of effective auto safety polices in developing countries.

TRAFFIC FATALITY PATTERNS IN INDUSTRIAL COUNTRIES

We examined traffic fatality patterns among 32 high-income countries using the International Road Traffic Accident Database (IRTAD). Between 1970 and 1999, total traffic fatalities declined by an average of 35 percent among these countries. The decline in fatalities was most dramatic for pedestrians and cyclists, for whom the average fatality rate (i.e., fatalities per capita) fell some 60 percent, compared with a decline in vehicle occupant fatalities of 21 percent. These trends are even more striking given that vehicle kilometers traveled (VKT) increased by about 250 percent over the period. Thus, pedestrian fatalities per VKT declined 86 percent on average, while occupant fatalities per VKT declined by 76 percent.

EXPLAINING THE TRENDS

To explain why these trends occurred, we began by examining the relationship between fatalities and per capita income. A striking fact is that although pedestrian fatalities per capita and per VKT declined as per capita income increased within these countries, there was no significant relationship between occupant fatalities and per capita income. This suggests that reductions in occupant fatalities do not automatically accompany increases in income. What does explain the decline in occupant fatality risk? To answer this question, we examined, in addition to income, the impact of demographic factors, the number of motor vehicles and length of roads, a measure of alcohol abuse, and the availability of medical services on occupant and pedestrian fatality risks.

Demographic factors appear to be especially important: young drivers are likely to be less skilled, less experienced, and less averse to risk, while older drivers have more experience and perhaps drive more carefully (though an offsetting factor is that they may have a slower reaction time to an imminent collision). In fact, we found strong evidence that the share of drivers under the age of 24, which declined by 20 to 40 percent between 1970 and 1999, was negatively associated with occupant fatality risk. This demographic trend alone could account for nearly 30 percent of the decline in occupant fatalities. We also found that the decrease in the share of under age 24 drivers reduced pedestrian fatality risk. On the other hand, an increase in the share of drivers aged 65 and over significantly raised pedestrians' fatality risk, as did the share of the population living in urban areas.

Rising vehicle ownership rates affect fatality risk in a variety of ways. Occupant fatality rates per VKT initially increase as more vehicles on the road raise accident frequencies. However, the faster the fleet grows, the higher the proportion of recent models equipped with advanced safety features, which causes the occupant fatality rate per VKT to decline. Initially, pedestrian fatality rates rise as motorization takes off; however, this trend peaks and then reverses as the share of pedestrian trips in total travel trips declines.

Expanding the total capacity of the road system network over time (for a given vehicle fleet size) reduces occupant fatality risk, as collisions are less frequent when cars have more space. The effect is especially pronounced for pedestrians, perhaps because larger road networks include more motorways that separate vehicles from foot traffic. However, an offsetting effect is that road improvements (e.g., additional lanes, wider lanes) may encourage more risky driving behavior, leading to an increase in collision frequency.

Alcohol abuse (as proxied by a country's incidence of liver disease) is positively correlated with occupant deaths per VKT. Over the study period, the liver disease death rate decreased substantially (by 30 to 60 percent) in the United States and many European countries. These reductions in alcohol abuse contributed to about a 6 percent decline in occupants' fatality rates. Alcohol abuse has an effect that is twice as large for pedestrians as for vehicle occupants. This likely reflects not only drunk driving but also risky behavior by pedestrians under the influence. Changes in alcohol use contributed to nearly a 10 percent decline in pedestrian deaths per VKT.

Finally, increases in the availability of emergency medical care services (as measured by physicians per capita) significantly decreased occupants' fatality risk, but had no statistically significant effect on pedestrians' fatality risk. No matter how quickly accident victims are rushed to the hospital, it seems, the likelihood of death is higher for pedestrians than for vehicle occupants.

POLICY IMPLICATIONS

Our study was limited to 32 high-income countries for which we had reliable data. We believe, however, that the findings are relevant to developing countries, whose per capita incomes today are comparable to those of the poorest IRTAD countries 40 years ago. Their patterns of traffic fatalities—in particular, the high rate of pedestrian fatalities—also recall the former situation for industrialized countries.

The decline in the road death rate in industrialized countries is attributable largely to a decline in pedestrians' death rate. It appears that this decline can be attributed to increased motorization and a smaller proportion of young drivers. The factors that best explain the decline in occupant fatalities per VKT are reductions in alcohol abuse, improved medical services, and a shrinking of the young driver population.

Reductions in alcohol abuse and improved medical services are clearly the result of explicit resource allocation decisions. The importance of the demographic factor suggests that in countries where young people constitute an increasing share of the driving population, policies to improve young driver education and reduce speeds will be crucial.

Further Reading

Kopits, Elizabeth, and Maureen Cropper. 2005. Traffic Fatalities and Economic Growth. *Accident Analysis and Prevention* 37(1): 169–178.

Kopits, Elizabeth, and Maureen Cropper. 2008. Why Have Traffic Fatalities Declined in Industrialized Countries? Implications for Pedestrians and Vehicle Occupants. *Journal of Transport Economics and Policy* 42(1): 129–154.

Noland, Robert. 2003. Medical Treatment and Traffic Fatality Reductions in Industrialized Countries. *Accident Analysis and Prevention* 35: 877–83.

Noland, Robert. 2003. Traffic Fatalities and Injuries: The Effect of Changes in Infrastructure and Other Trends. *Accident Analysis and Prevention* 35(4): 599–611.

81. PRESERVATION AND DEVELOPMENT

Can TDRs Improve Land Markets?

Virginia McConnell

is a senior fellow at Resources for the Future and a professor of economics at the University of Maryland, Baltimore. She works on environmental issues related to transportation and urban land use.

Margaret Walls

is the Thomas J. Klutznick Senior Fellow at Resources for the Future. She specializes in environmental and energy policy and urban land use.

As expanding population and real income fueled demand for ever greater residential development, in many cases this has led to excessive loss of open space, as developers lacked incentives to account for lost habitat, scenic views, and other natural amenities. Transfer of development rights (TDR) programs offer some hope for striking a balance between development and conservation.

Conflicts over private and public uses of land have long been part of our history. Private land can provide myriad public benefits—such as habitat for wildlife, scenic views, and preservation of sensitive environmental resources—that are not likely to be fully valued by private landowners. Consequently, some land will be developed that should be preserved. Designing and implementing cost-effective policies to remedy this problem can be difficult.

In private land markets, owners have the right to subdivide and develop land, subject to zoning rules established by local governments that typically limit the number of dwelling units that can be built per acre of land. Some communities have tried tightening these density limits to very low levels, such as one dwelling unit per 25 or 50 acres, as a way to limit development and preserve open space. Purchase of development rights (PDR) programs is another option in which the government uses tax revenue to purchase and retire the development rights to particular parcels of land.

A private market-based alternative is known as a transfer of development rights (TDR) program. Property owners are able to sell their development rights to, most commonly, a developer, who then uses them to build in a different location. The land from which the development rights are sold is preserved from development with an easement or restrictive covenant; the land on which the rights are used is developed more densely than would otherwise be allowed.

TDRs offer several advantages. Because they are voluntary, landowners have more flexibility compared to strict mandates or changes in zoning rules. They can also be used in conjunction with downzoning—that is, reducing the number of dwelling units per acre—to compensate landowners for any lost development potential from such reductions. Another political advantage is that TDR transfers occur through a private market, and therefore no tax dollars are needed for ensuring that land is preserved. And finally, TDRs can achieve land preservation, while still accommodating growth in the region.

Current TDR programs vary widely in their designs, objectives, and outcomes. Many are designed to preserve farmland, but some attempt to protect environmentally sensitive lands and habitat. Still others have "smart growth," or antisprawl, objectives—namely, to preserve open space and channel development toward more compact, urbanized areas with existing infrastructure. Over 140 jurisdictions around the country have TDR programs on the books.

TDRs sound relatively simple on paper—density is transferred from one property to another—but in practice, they can be quite complicated. The programs create a market for development rights, and many things can affect the profitability of buying and selling those rights. For example, local governments must determine which areas of the community are allowed to sell TDRs and which are allowed to use them to develop more densely, how densely the "receiving areas" can be developed, how trades occur in the marketplace, and the kind of mechanism by which transfers are approved. The underlying zoning in both the "sending" and "receiving" areas, as well as land values when developed or used otherwise, will influence how well a TDR market works.

A continuing problem in many programs lies on the demand side of the market. Many jurisdictions allow TDRs to be used to increase density only in established urbanized areas and town centers. However, this outcome is difficult to achieve in many communities; possible reasons why include a lack of demand for higher density and opposition by existing residents to more development. Most of the programs where demand has been strong have allowed TDR use in relatively low-density, or less developed, zones.

WHAT WORKS?

A very small number of programs have effectively created a working TDR market over time and have achieved local land preservation goals. The two programs that are perhaps the most long-running and successful in the country are in Maryland, in Calvert and Montgomery Counties. Although both have focused on protecting farmland, their approaches have been quite different. Both programs were initiated in about 1980, and since that time, the Montgomery County program has protected about 49,000 acres and the Calvert program about 13,000 acres. (Montgomery County is nearly two and a half times the size of Calvert County.)

The Calvert program is unique in that it allowed the additional density from TDR sales to be placed in many different areas, including town centers, residential zones, and even some rural areas. Moreover, it allowed landowners in some of the rural areas to either sell their development rights and preserve their land or use development rights purchased from elsewhere to develop more densely. This overlap in sending and receiving areas is highly unusual in TDR programs and makes the Calvert program one of the most flexible and least restrictive programs in existence.

The Montgomery County program, in contrast, downzoned one 90,000-acre area of farmland in the western part of the county, and the development rights that were taken away by the downzoning were allowed to be transferred to other areas that were designated for higher density. The receiving areas were all designated in residential areas, but as in Calvert County, the TDRs that were actually used tended to go into the relatively lower-density areas. The Montgomery program is often held up as the best example of a successful program, but it is important to understand the key role played by the downzoning: without the option to use the development rights on their properties anymore, landowners in the sending area were obviously quite willing to sell.

TDRs cannot be expected to achieve all of a community's land-use goals. They work best when used in conjunction with other policies, such as PDRs, land purchase programs for public open space, and zoning. TDRs can help attain land preservation goals at little public cost, but targeting particular properties for preservation with TDRs is difficult as the programs are voluntary. TDR programs also retain land in private ownership and are thus not a substitute for public lands such as parks and recreation areas. Communities would benefit from considering a well-designed and implemented TDR program as one important component of an overall approach to land-use policy.

Further Reading

McConnell, Virginia, Elizabeth Kopits, and Margaret Walls. 2006. Using Markets for Land Preservation: Results of a TDR Program. *Journal of Environmental Planning and Management* 49(5): 631–651.

McConnell, Virginia, Margaret Walls, and Elizabeth Kopits. 2006. Zoning, TDRs, and the Density of Development. *Journal of Urban Economics* 59(September): 440–457.

McConnell, Virginia, and Margaret Walls. 2007. *Transfer of Development Rights in U.S. Communities: Evaluating Program Design, Implementation, and Outcomes.* Washington, DC: Resources for the Future.

Pruetz, Rick and Noah Standbridge. 2009. What Makes Transfer of Development Rights Work? Success Factors from Research and Practice. *Journal of the American Planning Association* 75(1): 78–87.

82. IS THERE AN "EFFICIENT" WAY TO ADDRESS SUBURBAN SPRAWL?

Antonio M. Bento
is an associate professor in Cornell University's Department of Applied Economics and Management. Most of his research lies at the boundaries of environmental, energy, urban, and public economics.

Development fees are potentially the best policy to curb excessive urban sprawl from the standpoint of economic efficiency. However, for practical purposes, they are also one of the more challenging policies to implement.

The predominant pattern of urban growth in the United States over the past half century has been one of low density and employment decentralization that has yielded excessive amounts of sprawl, certainly from an economist's point of view. To begin with, developers do not take into account the societal losses from the irreversible paving over of large open spaces at the urban fringe. These include the aesthetic benefits existing residents might otherwise enjoy from unspoiled views of rolling farmland, and the possible loss of ecosystems and natural habitat. Also, developers do not consider the broader societal costs of decaying inner cities (such as crime and run-down communities) caused by the flight to the suburbs.

As cities spread out, commutes get longer, leading to more traffic congestion and pollution. This would not be a problem if drivers were fully charged for their contribution to congestion and pollution through, for example, road pricing schemes, but such comprehensive pricing policies are a long way off. Moreover, urban development is frequently subsidized—typically developers do not pay for the infrastructure costs (schools, roads, sewers, and other public services) needed to accommodate residential development. Other policies, such as zoning restrictions requiring minimum lot sizes at the urban fringe may further, exacerbate the problem.

Concern about urban sprawl has led to a variety of "smart growth" initiatives including, for example, urban growth boundaries and other regulations (such as conservation easements, transferable development rights, and designation of priority funding areas) designed to limit expansion of the urban fringe. An alternative approach emphasizes pricing instruments, such as taxes on residential development and property. So how should policymakers choose among these alternatives?

PROMOTING EFFICIENT DEVELOPMENT

In terms of economic efficiency, an ideal policy instrument would trade off the benefits of land preservation at the urban fringe with the costs in terms of reducing the availability of housing, and producing denser, or more clustered, housing than residents would otherwise prefer. In principle, a tax per unit of land developed could achieve this efficient outcome, by reflecting the full costs of development in the prices of new, suburban housing lots. It would be feasible to approximately measure infrastructure costs and the costs of congestion and pollution from additional driving that should be included in the tax. Even the value of open space might be incorporated into the tax, based on studies that estimate how much extra people are willing to pay for houses in close proximity to open space amenities.

Property taxes would still be inferior to development taxes, even if it were feasible to impose differentially higher property tax rates for housing units at the urban fringe. The key problem with property taxes is that they penalize capital, or housing value, in addition to land. This creates an incentive for lower-density development, which partly undermines attempts to limit urban sprawl. Due to this perverse effect, in work with Sofia Franco and Daniel Kaffine (2006), we found that the economically efficient amount of open space preserved under property taxes is only a minor fraction of the amount that would be saved under an efficient system of development fees.

In principle, urban growth boundaries can be designed to mimic the effects of development taxes. However, this requires knowledge of how much land would be saved under the ideal tax, which is very difficult to gauge in advance.

Moreover, another difference is that development taxes generate revenues that can be recycled in ways to improve the efficiency of the local economy. For example, revenues can be used to fund city-center revitalization programs, which in turn helps to lessen pressure for land conversion at the fringe due to flight to the suburbs. Revenues might also be used to purchase conservation easements that could permanently save large open spaces at the fringe. Additionally, they can be used to cut the rate of preexisting property taxes, thus promoting density over land expansion.

PRACTICAL OBSTACLES TO EFFICIENT PRICING

On paper, development fees seem like the most efficient solution, but there are definite obstacles to putting them into practice. First, the distributional burden borne by developers is greater under the development tax than under the urban growth boundary. The development fee essentially penalizes all developers and subsidizes agricultural landowners. In contrast, an urban growth boundary only penalizes those developers at the fringe that would have converted the land in the absence of this policy. As a result, urban growth boundaries seem to get substantially more political support. Indeed, several communities throughout the United States have implemented urban boundaries, while very few have implemented development fees.

Second, successful implementation of development fees may require coordination among different governments. Currently, most smart growth programs are implemented by local governments, typically cities and counties. However, there is a concern that such programs could actually exacerbate suburban sprawl because communities can use urban growth boundaries almost as an exclusionary zoning restriction. As a consequence, housing prices tend to increase and push individuals to bedroom communities that are often located farther away from their place of work. In this case, smart growth can have a perverse effect by displacing and reallocating growth in ways that exacerbate sprawl and traffic congestion.

Coordination across local governments, to prevent spillover effects from displacing and reallocating growth across neighboring communities, is potentially important. However, this metropolitan-wide approach to managing urban growth will require local governments to, in part, give up some of their power to regulate land use as well as some of the fiscal benefits that can come with some land-use choices. Not surprisingly, this may be the greatest obstacle of all in controlling sprawl.

Further Reading

Bento, Antonio M., Sofia Franco, and Daniel Kaffine. 2006. The Efficiency and Distributional Impacts of Alternative Anti-Sprawl Policies. *Journal of Urban Economics* 59: 121–141.

Brueckner, Jan. 2001. Urban Sprawl: Lessons from Urban Economics. In *Wharton Papers on Urban Affairs*, edited by W.G. Gale and J.R. Pack. Washington, DC: Brookings Institution Press, 65–89.

PART 6

Public Health Policies

Environmental and health issues overlap in several regards. For many environmental hazards, the most serious causes of concern are risks to human health. And some key policy design issues are common to both environmental and health problems. These include how to value public health risks and to what extent these risks are internal (that is, taken into account by individuals) versus external (borne by society at large), as this determines the appropriate level of policy intervention.

Two of the commentaries in this section focus on issues in the valuation of human health: one explains why people's valuation of life expectancy (how much they would theoretically pay to live longer) has been steadily rising over time, with important implications for public policies, such as medical research, that potentially yield future improvements in longevity. Another discusses how people in different countries might value changes in mortality risks, a critical issue when evaluating policies with health benefits in those countries.

Specific public health problems are covered, including a brief history of attempts to roll back malaria, the growing threat of superbug infections that are resistant to drugs, the costs and benefits of interventions to reduce tuberculosis, modernizing the regulatory system governing the safety of the U.S. food supply, to what extent health risks warrant taxing cigarettes, and private-sector incentives to market products that help people quit smoking.

Public health programs regarding environmental problems are also evaluated: public information programs to warn about mercury contamination in fish, issues in measuring the human health benefits of reducing exposure to lead, and improving health in low-income countries through use of less polluting cooking methods.

83. THE VALUE OF HEALTH AND LONGEVITY

Kevin M. Murphy

is the George J. Stigler Distinguished Service Professor of Economics at the University of Chicago's Booth School of Business. He primarily studies the empirical analysis of inequality, unemployment, and relative wages, as well as the economics of growth and development and the economic value of improvements in health and longevity.

Robert H. Topel

is the Isidore Brown and Gladys J. Brown Professor in Urban and Labor Economics at the University of Chicago's Booth School of Business. He focuses on labor economics, industrial organization and antitrust, business strategy, health economics, national security economics, economic growth, and public policy.

The value of increased life expectancy, and health improvements more generally, has been rising over time. This trend has important policy implications, such as the amount we should be investing in medical research.

During the 20th century, life expectancy at birth for an average American increased by roughly 30 years, a remarkable increase that reflects advances against a variety of afflictions and diseases. Progress during the first half of the century was rapid and concentrated at younger ages because of reductions in infant and child mortality. Progress then shifted toward older individuals, with better prevention and treatment for heart disease, strokes, and other older-age ailments. The largest single contributor since 1950 has been reduced mortality from heart disease, which has added more than 3.5 years to the expected lifetimes of both men and women.

Rising life expectancy, and health improvements more generally, represent an important form of economic progress, and their valuation is critical for two reasons. First, traditional measures of economic growth and economic welfare, based on national income accounts, do not take into account this source of rising living standards and may therefore seriously understate improvements in well-being. Second, large portions of both medical research and medical care are publicly funded, and efficient decisions concerning the allocation of these resources require a framework for measuring the benefit of treatment and research-based medical progress.

WHY DO THE VALUE OF HEALTH IMPROVEMENTS RISE OVER TIME?

In a recent study, we developed an economic framework for understanding what factors determine how much people are willing to pay for health improvements that increase both longevity (which increases consumption of goods and leisure time over the life cycle) and quality of life (which raises the utility individuals obtain from given amounts of goods and leisure time). Some health advances (such as better surgical techniques) primarily increase longevity, others (like reduced pain from arthritis) primarily improve the quality of life, and many others (like medications that reduce blood pressure or retard the advance of cancer) improve both aspects of health.

The social value of health improvements has been increasing over the past several decades, and will increase into the future, for a number of reasons, including some simple math. The U.S. population is growing, so proportionately more people benefit from a given advance. As income grows over time, and living standards rise, people gain more enjoyment out of an additional (healthy) year of life. Furthermore, people's willingness to pay for health improvements peaks as they approach the age when they are most vulnerable to the risks of heart disease, cancer, and so on—so the aging of the baby-boom generation has raised the social value of medical advances against age-related ailments.

But most importantly, there is an increasing return inherent to medical progress: past success raises the value of new health improvements. Increases in life expectancy (from any source) raise people's willingness to pay for further health improvements. That is, people are willing to pay more for good health as the likelihood that they will be around to enjoy that health increases. This means that advances against, say, heart disease raise the value of progress against other age-related ailments, such as cancer and Alzheimer's.

ECONOMIC BENEFITS FROM IMPROVED HEALTH

In fact, the economic gains from declining mortality in the United States have been enormous. Cumulative gains in life expectancy during the 20th century were worth nearly $2 million for a newborn in 2000, or more than $1.2 million to the average-age American alive in that year. Increased life expectancy between 1970 and 2000 alone added about $3.2 trillion per year to national wealth—an uncounted value equal to about 50 percent of average annual GDP over the period. About half of this gain since 1970 was from reduced prevalence of heart disease.

Moreover, reductions in mortality since 1970 have raised the value of future health advances by almost 20 percent. Prospective gains from a 10 percent reduction in all causes of mortality in the future would have an enormous social value of almost 20 trillion dollars in present value to current and future Americans. About 30 percent of this is due to potential progress against cardiovascular diseases, and 25 percent from progress against cancer. A 10 percent reduction in mortality from infectious diseases (of which mortality from AIDS accounts for about a third) has a far lower value (about $500 billion) because of the much lower incidence of this type of disease. For women, mortality-reducing progress against heart disease would be four times more valuable than equivalent progress against breast cancer.

These estimates are conservative in the sense that they focus only on the United States and do not include the value of these same health innovations to the rest of the world. They also ignore corresponding improvements in the quality of life, which, evidence suggests, may be even more valuable than gains in longevity.

WEIGHING COSTS AND BENEFITS

Health improvements are worthwhile if their economic value offsets their additional economic costs. Some of these costs take the form of changes in consumption or behavior, such as reductions in smoking, increased exercise, healthier eating habits, and moderate alcohol consumption. Other costs are those associated with implementing new procedures and treatments, or extended provision of existing medical service.

Nonetheless, we estimated that additional medical expenditures offset only 36 percent of the value of increased longevity after 1970. Even though the United States now spends more than $50 billion a year in medical research, about 40 percent of which is federally funded, substantially greater expenditures might be worthwhile given that the returns to basic medical research may be quite large. For example, using our estimate that a 1 percent reduction in cancer mortality would be worth about $500 billion, then spending an additional $100 billion on cancer research and treatment would be worthwhile if it has a one-in-five chance of reducing mortality by 1 percent.

One significant caveat is that the presence of third-party payers (insurance companies and the government) increases incentives to spend on medical care, since at the margin the individual receiving treatment bears only a small fraction of the treatment costs. In fact, over 25 percent of all Medicare expenditures are incurred in the last year of individuals' lives, with allegedly little benefit. These pricing distortions may also skew investment in research away from cost-saving improvements in medical technologies. As a result, not all health improvements may be socially efficient.

Further Reading

Murphy, K.M., and R.H. Topel. 2006. The Value of Health and Longevity. *Journal of Political Economy* 114(4): 871–904.

84. HOW U.S. AND CHINESE CITIZENS FEEL ABOUT REDUCING MORTALITY RISKS

Alan Krupnick

is a senior fellow and a director of research at Resources for the Future. His research focuses on air pollution policies in the United States and developing countries and the valuation of health and ecological improvements.

How might a monetary value be attached to reductions in mortality risks from pollution control or other public health policies in low-income countries? This is critical for helping sort out which policies do and do not make sense from a cost–benefit perspective.

To help prioritize policies and to design better regulations, cost–benefit analyses are commonly performed in developed countries and increasingly in developing ones. When it comes to environmental priorities and policies, health effects, especially mortality risks, are often involved. For example, reducing fine particulates, a form of air pollution, has been shown to have a significant effect on reducing death rates from lung cancer and other diseases. To compare the benefits and costs of various policies, however, it is not enough to know about the mortality risks. They must be "monetized," that is, converted into monetary units, so they can be compared to costs. Indeed, how strongly the public feels about reducing their mortality risks, relative to doing all the other things we can do with our money or expect our government to do, is important, even if one were not doing cost–benefit analyses of regulatory programs.

These preferences are summarized in the term "value of statistical life" (VSL), which simply is the average amount that people are willing to pay to reduce their risks of death by a tiny amount, divided by the amount of this risk reduction. If 10,000 people are willing to pay $100 on average to reduce their risks of death by 1 in 10,000 (thereby expecting that one less among them will die prematurely), this translates into a VSL of $1 million ($100/[1/10,000]). Such a number can then be multiplied by the number of premature deaths expected to be cut by, say, a fine particulate policy, to arrive at the mortality benefits of reducing this pollutant.

Note what this number is not. It is not the amount you would pay to save your grandmother's life, nor the life of any known person. It is not a jury award that the family of a person killed in a wrongful death suit would receive. It is about using a money metric to measure how strongly people feel about reducing their risks of death by a small amount—something they do every time they push their foot down on the accelerator to get to a meeting faster, or cross in the middle of the street to save time. These time–risk trade-offs are easily converted to money terms. Indeed, some people commonly take more risky jobs, like washing windows on skyscrapers in return for a wage boost over what they could get exercising the same skills on the ground.

To date, most VSL estimates have been made in developed countries. But people's feelings about avoiding death risks are universal—although the strength of this feeling, as expressed in money will depend on many things, some of which may vary systematically across developed and developing countries. For example, wealthier people, other things held equal, are found to be willing to pay more for reducing death risks. Older and ill people may be willing to pay more or less than younger and healthy people—although how much, and even in what direction, are open questions. This difference is important because developing countries typically have a much greater proportion of younger and sicker people than developed countries. The types of risks can matter too: how large they are, what type (is it something you have control over or a risk that's unfamiliar?) and when they kick in (now or in the future).

Arguably, it is even more important to do good cost–benefit analyses in developing than developed countries because the former have such a shortage of capital and resources to devote to improving the quality of life.

There are two ways to get estimates of the VSLs. One is to actually do the studies. Here there are two credible approaches—asking people, using highly structured surveys, about their willingness to pay (that is, their "stated" preference) or examining their "revealed" preferences in labor markets (in terms of jobs chosen) and similar places where trade-offs between money and death risk may be observed. The other option is to transfer estimates of the VSL from developed to developing countries, which is the standard practice because it is so cheap to do although not without costs in terms of being inaccurate.

My colleagues and I recently carried out a revealing study in Shanghai and other cities in China, using methods and a survey nearly identical to those used in the United States, Canada, Great Britain, Japan, Italy, and France to value reductions in mortality risk. Our findings showed that in spite of the lower per capita incomes in China, the VSL was not as low as one would expect—about $700,000 (when adjusting the yuan for purchasing power parity). Further, for future risk reductions, such as one would get from reducing exposure to a carcinogen today, the VSL dropped less in China than in other countries. An inference: the Chinese people may be much more future-oriented than their counterparts in the other countries we tested (certainly savings rates are higher). At the same time, there were commonalities. Older people (over 70) are consistently shown in these surveys to be willing to pay somewhat less than younger people (40–70), although these differences are not always statistically significant. Ill people are also shown to be willing to pay more or the same, but never less than healthy people. And incomes matter within the countries; that is, richer people within a country are willing to pay more to reduce a given risk of death than poorer people in that country. However, in the case of our China study, cultural factors, possibly optimism about the future or a great fear of death, may act to push up willingness to pay even in less prosperous areas.

At the end of the day, these kinds of studies reveal more to us than simply how the VSL varies; they show how cultural differences translate into preferences for improving health and thereby result in a better allocation of our scarce resources. For example, the China results have already been applied to a major World Bank study assessing the health damages of air pollution. The study's key finding is that high particulate levels (China has 20 cities in the top 30 most polluted cities in the world) cause mortality damages equal to about 3 percent of GDP. In India, which accounts for 30 percent of the global burden of tuberculosis, the costs of interventions per death prevented are as cheap as $1,000, cluster around $10,000, and are as high as $1 million. With a VSL of, say, $1 million, all or most of these mortality risk reduction measures would deliver net benefits to society.

Further Reading

Alberini, Anna, Maureen Cropper, Alan Krupnick, and Nathalie Simon. Forthcoming. Does the Value of Statistical Life Vary with Age and Health Status? Evidence from the U.S. and Canada. *Journal of Environmental Economics and Management.*

China SEPA and the World Bank. 2007. *Cost of Pollution in China: Economic Estimates of Physical Damages.* Washington, DC: World Bank.

Krupnick, A., S. Hoffmann, B. Larsen, X-Z. Peng, G.-C. Cheng, et al. 2007. The Willingness to Pay for Mortality Risk Reductions in Shanghai and Chongqing, China. In *Costs of Pollution in China: Economic Estimates of Physical Damages.* Washington, DC: World Bank.

Symposium on Mortality Risk Valuation and Age. 2007. *Review of Environmental Economics and Policy* 1(2): 228–282.

85. A NEW CHAPTER IN THE HISTORY OF MALARIA CONTROL

Maciej F. Boni

is a research fellow at the Oxford University Clinical Research Unit in Ho Chi Minh City, Vietnam, and a fellow at the MRC Centre for Genomics and Global Health in Oxford, UK.

David L. Smith

is an associate professor in the Department of Biology and assistant director for disease ecology in the Emerging Pathogens Institute, University of Florida. He is also a visiting scholar at Resources for the Future.

This brief history of attempts to control malaria is especially timely, given the development of effective new drugs to treat the disease and the current attempts by the Gates Foundation and the global community to eradicate it.

Malaria claims the lives of more than a million victims each year, 80 percent of whom are children from sub-Saharan Africa. Causing fever, anemia, malaise, and death in its most severe forms, its greatest impact is on children who have not yet built up the immunity required to combat severe malaria infections. Compounding the devastation wrought by the disease itself, malaria is often blamed for fevers caused by other infections. By interfering with proper treatment of nonmalarial diseases, it contributes to higher death rates from other causes. Furthermore, it reduces economic growth in some African countries by more than 1 percent, costing over $1,000 a year in per capita GDP. These staggering numbers are finally seeing the light of day.

For the first time in nearly 30 years, new donor money is available to build malaria-control programs. In October 2007, Melinda Gates officially announced the Gates Foundatiz (WHO), the Global Fund, and the President's Malaria Initiative echoed the message in a surprising show of hope and unanimity about the scientific and donor communities' current capacity to eradicate malaria. The ensuing discussion broke a taboo in the malaria community—born of previous failures to eradicate the disease—and the "e-word" was again spoken openly.

The world's first attempt to eradicate malaria came after World War II. Enthusiasm was stoked by two new tools for malaria control: dichloro-diphenyl-trichloroethane (DDT) and chloroquine. Control trials in the 1950s demonstrated that DDT was very effective at lowering malaria transmission. Soon the chemical was sprayed on the interior walls of houses all over the world. Its odor repelled some mosquitoes, and the residual DDT on the walls killed those mosquitoes that landed to rest after feeding on humans. The combination of effects worked quite well: in many areas where DDT was used, malaria transmission was severely disrupted, with 80 percent annual declines in the prevalence of infection. At about the same time, mass production of the antimalarial drug chloroquine provided a cheap and effective way of treating clinical malaria and curing infections.

To control malaria successfully and ultimately eliminate it, the key epidemiological concept to focus on is malaria's "basic reproductive number," which measures the expected number of infectious mosquitoes that would be generated by a single infectious mosquito. This number describes the amplification of the infection process and provides a measure of the control effort required to eliminate malaria. Estimates of the basic reproductive number for malaria suggest that it is may be as high as 10,000 in some African populations. This means that 99.99 percent of all transmission must be prevented in these areas to eliminate malaria. While drug use is critical for treating clinical malaria, it is not an effective way to reduce transmission. Initial elimination efforts in high-transmission areas met with mixed success, while efforts in low-transmission areas were more successful at ridding these regions of malaria.

By 1970, 24 countries had completely eliminated malaria, but there were equally many places where the effort had failed. Many of these countries were in Africa, where early malaria-control programs substantially reduced malaria transmission but were not enough to eliminate the parasite completely. Early trials in East Africa reduced the fraction of infected people from more than 60 percent to less than 10 percent, but did not sufficiently interrupt transmission. In the 1970s, WHO organized a massive demonstration project in Garki, Nigeria, to eliminate malaria, but when it failed, it seemed to be the nail in the coffin for global eradication efforts. Donor fatigue, DDT-resistant mosquitoes, and emerging environmental concerns about the overuse of DDT all contributed to the cessation of malaria-control programs in the 1970s. In regions where malaria had been eliminated completely (southern Europe and the southeastern United States), it remained absent. But in areas like India and Sri Lanka, where malaria was not entirely eliminated, the disease came back and reestablished itself at its previous levels.

In the decades that followed, malaria became a neglected disease. To make matters worse, chloroquine-resistant parasites were imported into East Africa in 1978, and the subsequent spread of chloroquine resistance undermined treatment of malaria. Throughout the 1980s and 1990s, malaria mortality increased, even as other causes of mortality declined. Finally, within the past few years, rising malaria mortality has been slowed down by the mass distribution of insecticide-treated mosquito nets, and by switching from chloroquine to other, more effective drugs, most notably a new class of antimalarial drugs called artemisinins. For the current generation of research scientists and public health officials working in malaria control, the recent progress and the new flow of money have been a huge relief, and there is some evidence that control programs have begun to reverse malaria mortality in Africa.

Current research efforts at Resources for Future are focusing on methods of drug distribution, preserving the life span of artemisinin-based combination therapies, finding ways to reverse trends of increasing drug resistance, determining whether subsidies for certain drugs will allow more types of drugs to be used, and understanding if having more types of drugs in use will be beneficial to malaria-control programs. The initial answers to these questions are coming out of mathematical models that allow us to evaluate hypothetical situations of how malaria might be eliminated in a particular country or region, and how effectively particular treatment strategies or drug subsidies would work in these places.

The worldwide community of malaria researchers is optimistic about the current treatment possibilities and eradication strategies, but enthusiasm for malaria eradication must be tempered with a serious assessment of realistic costs and timelines. The actions necessary to eliminate malaria ultimately will be carried out by individual governments that must rise to the challenges. Even the best efforts can be undermined if a country continually reimports the disease from neighboring countries; if the necessary drugs, bed nets, and insecticides cannot be secured for economic reasons; and if the elimination programs put in place are not sustainable. The coming global effort to eradicate malaria will derive its success from sustainability, coordination, a generous flow of money, and the diligence and will of scientists, doctors, public health workers, and government officials who recognize malaria eradication as a permanent public health benefit to future generations.

Further Reading

Hay, S.I., C.A. Guerra, A.J. Tatem, A.M. Noor, and R.W. Snow. 2004. The Global Distribution and Population at Risk of Malaria: Past, Present, and Future. *Lancet Infectious Diseases* 4(6): 327–336.

Institute of Medicine. 2004. Saving Lives, Buying Time: Economics of Malaria Drugs in an Age of Resistance. Washington, DC: National Academies Press.

Roll Back Malaria Partnership. 2009. www.rollbackmalaria.org (accessed October 20, 2009).

World Malaria Report 2005. World Health Organization. http://rbm.who.int/wmr2005 (accessed October 20, 2009).

86. THE SPREAD OF MRSA

Antibiotic Resistance with a Name

Hellen Gelband

is a program fellow at Resources for the Future. Her work explores the growing resistance to antibiotic and antimalarial drugs, as well as access to and cost of such pharmaceuticals.

The rapid spread of the superbug MRSA in hospitals around the world, and the more recent spread of MRSA strains in the community, has heightened concern about the declining effectiveness of frontline drugs, as bacterial strains resistant to those drugs evolve. How is MRSA transmitted, why is it becoming more prevalent, and how many people are now dying because of it?

By now, almost everyone has heard of MRSA (methicillin-resistant *Staphylococcus aureus*)—variants of the ubiquitous staph bacteria that are resistant to penicillin and related antibiotics, the original "wonder drugs" that transformed the treatment of infectious diseases in the mid-20th century. Methicillin is the antibiotic named to signify bacterial resistance to the class that includes penicillins (even though bacteria are not routinely tested against it). Methicillin, no longer used because of its toxicity, was developed in 1959, a decade after bacteria resistant to pencillin arose (which occurred a mere four years after penicillin went into mass production). This is a lesson we still must heed today—that resistance is an inevitable natural phenomenon, bound to occur against every antibiotic the more it is used.

MRSA news stories tend to focus on healthy young victims who have picked up the bacteria on the football field, in school, or somewhere else in the course of daily living, and end up with an overwhelming infection that puts them into the intensive-care unit. MRSA may kill through infections of the lung, blood, or tissue (it's one of the "flesh-eating bacteria"). What has happened to these victims is shocking and tragic, of course, but their cases represent just a small part of the larger MRSA problem. Sadly, the more numerous deaths of elderly hospital patients with serious medical problems are not exactly front page material.

Both MRSA and common staph are typically harmless on the surface: they can "colonize" the skin or the nasal passages without causing any health problems. When they enter broken skin through a cut or sore, however, they "infect" the surrounding tissue and proliferate in boils, blisters, or pimples. Often these skin and soft tissue infections can just be cleaned out and left to heal. But when bacteria invade the bloodstream, causing blood infections called septicemia or bacteremia, or the lungs, causing pneumonia, the situation becomes much more serious, and quickly. When these staph infections are MRSA, they take longer to cure, about doubling the time spent in the hospital, and also doubling the hospital bill.

Septicemia and pneumonia are almost exclusively acquired in hospitals or other health-care settings, where staph bacteria are ubiquitous if no special infection control measures, such as testing new patients and isolating those who are colonized, are in force. Bacteria can enter patients' internal organs during surgery, around catheters used to infuse intravenous drugs and fluids, and around urinary catheters. The result can be deadly MRSA infections—especially in patients who are already weakened by illness or old age. Ironically, the infection vectors in hospitals are often health-care workers who become colonized and then spread the bugs around.

National and local publicity has raised public consciousness about MRSA, although it doesn't inform us about the extent of the problem. RFF researchers Eili Klein, David Smith, and Ramanan Laxminarayan analyzed data from the past few years to answer that question, as part of Extending the Cure, an ongoing research project on antibiotic resistance. What their analysis (2007) tells us is that, unlike some health-scare stories that represent only a small risk, this one is growing and worth worrying about.

The fact that the development of new antibiotics is at an all-time low could turn this into a full-scale disaster—a return to the preantibiotic era, when ordinary infections were deadly.

Here are some basic statistics from Extending the Cure: MRSA infections treated in hospitals more than doubled nationwide between 1999 and 2005, from an estimated 127,000 to 278,000. MRSA also represents a growing proportion of staph infections seen in hospitals—from 40 percent in 1999 to 60 percent in 2005. The numbers themselves are difficult to verify and are the subject of controversy. Using a different data source and other methods, other researchers estimated that the national prevalence rate of MRSA among hospital patients in 2006 was five to eight times as high as what Klein and colleagues reported for 2005. Putting these differences in perspective, it's worth remembering the MRSA phenomenon is relatively recent: in the late 1980s, resistant staph bacteria accounted for perhaps 2 percent of infections.

Counting infections in hospitals is tricky, but the question of how many people die from MRSA is even more difficult and involves judgment calls. Many people who die entered the hospital because they had a life-threatening condition and were already advanced in age. In this context, any infection is more perilous than it would be for a healthy, young person: in other words, the infirm and elderly may die in the hospital even without MRSA.

This led Klein, Smith, and Laxminarayan to create two estimates of deaths attributable to MRSA. Using stricter criteria, they estimated about 5,500 deaths per year over the seven-year period, with no suggestion of a trend up or down. Using a more inclusive definition—everyone who died and had a documented case of MRSA during their hospitalization—the estimates were higher and rose steadily. In 1999, about 11,000 such deaths occurred, and by 2005, more than 17,300. Using similar definitions and entirely different data sources, two other groups of researchers came up with very similar results for deaths in 2005: from the Centers for Disease Control and Prevention (CDC), 18,650 deaths, and from the Agency for Healthcare Research and Quality, 17,300 deaths.

Patients hospitalized with MRSA infections included both those with septicemia and pneumonia who acquired their infections during their hospital stays and those more likely to have picked up the infection in the community (skin and soft-tissue infections, mainly noninvasive). Septicemia cases increased 81 percent over seven years and pneumonias increased 19 percent. But the steepest increase by far was in the "community-associated" skin and soft-tissue infections, which nearly tripled between 1999 and 2005. Most deaths from MRSA still result from infections that take root in hospitals, but the community-associated MRSA burden is becoming increasingly important.

As important as it is to keep track of MRSA cases and count those who die from MRSA, it is even more important to institute preventive measures to reduce the spread of MRSA and other infections in hospitals, nursing homes, and other health care sites. We already know some measures that work—including testing patients (all or high-risk only) on hospital admission and isolating the ones who are colonized or infected, and implementing contact precautions for hospital workers (for example, keeping stethoscopes and other equipment in patients' rooms, promoting better hand hygiene by the staff). The other approach stems from that early lesson: antibiotics should be used to preserve health and save lives, but we should use them wisely, when they are the best course. Just knowing what works is not enough, however. The right incentives—both carrots and sticks—must be in place. That will require finding the precise mix of legislation, regulation, and economic incentives to improving infection control that will work, a hunt that cannot wait any longer.

Further Reading

Jarvis, W.R., J. Schlosser, R.Y. Chinn, S. Tweeten, and M. Jackson. 2007. National Prevalence of Methicillin-Resistant *Staphylococcus aureus* in Inpatients at US Health Care Facilities, 2006. *American Journal of Infection Control* 35(1): 631–637.

Klein, E., D. L. Smith, and R. Laxminarayan. 2007. Hospitalizations and Deaths Caused by Methicillin-Resistant *Staphylococcus aureus*, United States, 1999–2005. *Emerging Infectious Diseases* 13(12): 1840–1846.

Klevens, R.M., M.A. Morrison, et al. 2007. Invasive Methicillin-Resistant *Staphylococcus aureus* Infections in the United States. *Journal of the American Medical Association* 298(15): 1763–1771.

87. CONTROLLING TUBERCULOSIS

What Is the Benefit, at What Cost?

Ramanan Laxminarayan

is a senior fellow at Resources for the Future, where he directs the Center for Disease Dynamics, Economics, and Policy. His research deals with the integration of epidemiological models of infectious disease transmission and economic analysis of public health problems.

Eili Klein

is a Ph.D. candidate in the Ecology and Evolutionary Biology Department at Princeton University and a consultant with Resources for the Future.

Sarah Darley

completed her work on this commentary while a full-time research associate at Resources for the Future.

This commentary discusses the widespread prevalence of tuberculosis in developing countries and estimates of the highly favorable cost–benefit ratio for potential interventions to contain the disease.

After HIV/AIDS, tuberculosis (TB) is the most important cause of adult mortality due to infectious disease in low- and middle-income countries. It accounted for some 1.2 million deaths in 2004 in the 22 countries identified by the World Health Organization (WHO) as "high burden." (These countries constitute approximately 80 percent of global tuberculosis cases.) The advent of antibiotics was once thought to herald the end of TB, or "consumption," the wasting disease caused by a lung bacterium, but in many of these countries, poor sanitation, high rates of HIV infection, and drug-resistant strains of the bacterium have allowed tuberculosis to spread.

Tuberculosis is a contagious disease, spread through the air via coughing, sneezing, or even talking. In its most common form, known as pulmonary TB, the bacteria attack the lungs and can cause chronic coughing (often with bloody sputum), fever, and weight loss. WHO estimates that, left untreated, each person with pulmonary TB will infect on average 10 to 15 people every year.

Weakened and unable to work, once-productive adults who have contracted the disease must be cared for by other members of their families, putting the caregivers at greater risk of infection and lowering their own productivity. The cost of treatment can account for as much as 8 to 20 percent of annual household income, but without it, most people die within 18 months of being infected. The burden of TB is borne not just by those afflicted and their families, but also by communities and governments. Adult mortality dampens national economies by claiming productive workers. People are reluctant to invest in education or take entrepreneurial risks if they don't expect to live long enough to see the payoff, and they tend to have more children and invest less in their offspring.

Lifting the burden is one of the UN's Millennium Development Goals—specifically, reversing the incidence of TB by 2015. The Stop TB Partnership goes further and aims to halve prevalence and death rates by 2015, relative to 1990. One of the tools for reaching either target is "directly observed treatment, short-course," or DOTS, in which patients take their drugs under a health worker's supervision (to ensure that they get the recommended doses at the appropriate intervals).

Determining the benefits of achieving the goals begins with quantifying the economic costs of not achieving the goals: how much does TB cost society? What is the economic burden of not doing more than is being currently done to prevent and treat the disease?

To address these questions, we turned to a widely used concept in economics, the value of a statistical life (VSL), which puts a value not on person X's worth as a human being, but rather on measures that people are willing to undertake (such as buying safer cars or choosing safer occupations) that can reduce the statistically expected number of deaths by one. EPA recommends a VSL of $6.1 million (in 2004 dollars) for the United States, which, adjusted for differences in per capita income between the United States and low-income countries, translates into VSL estimates from $23,000 for Zimbabwe to nearly $1 million for the Russian Federation. To assess the economic burden of TB, we first must ask, how many people will die of TB in the 22 high-burden countries from 2006 to 2015? The WHO epidemiological models consider three scenarios:

- No DOTS: the program was never introduced, case detection rates are variable, rates of cure are low;
- Sustained DOTS: case detection and treatment success rates are sustained at the 2005 level to 2015; and
- Global Plan to Stop TB 2006–2015: DOTS coverage is expanded, programs address TB-HIV coinfection and drug-resistant TB, and infections are targeted with new diagnostics, medicines, vaccines, and educational efforts.

We estimated the economic cost of projected TB deaths under those three scenarios, factoring in average age of death from TB, life expectancy for TB-HIV coinfection cases, and so forth. We also calculated the costs of implementing health interventions to improve TB control (including the welfare losses associated with raising the necessary funds from national tax revenues). On the flip side, we calculated the benefits of averting deaths (saving lives) through improved TB control.

With No DOTS, we found that the economic burden of deaths associated with TB and TB-HIV between 2006 and 2015 in the 22 high-burden countries would be roughly $3 trillion, including $1.175 trillion in China and $519 billion in the African countries. This is, of course, only a hypothetical scenario because DOTS is being implemented in all TB-endemic countries, but it serves as a useful benchmark against which to calibrate our assessments of Sustained DOTS and the Global Plan.

Sustained DOTS would cost $18.3 billion to implement but deliver a dramatic economic gain of $1.6 trillion. The cost–benefit ratio of moving from No DOTS to Sustained DOTS is about 10 to 1—a very healthy return on the investment.

In the final scenario, the full Global Plan version of DOTS would cost $33.2 billion to implement and yield a gain of about $1.9 trillion compared with No DOTS. This is a relatively small incremental improvement over Sustained DOTS, but the benefits still exceed the costs in the African countries.

The economic burdens of TB deaths and the benefits of TB control are greatest in China and India, where the combination of growing incomes and high numbers of TB deaths multiplies into a significant economic effect. Although more TB deaths occur in the African countries, the economic benefit of either Sustained DOTS or Global Plan DOTS is more modest here, partly because incomes are expected to grow more slowly than in Asia, and partly because the benefits of treatment in Africa slip away when HIV claims lives that would otherwise be saved from TB. Nevertheless, the benefits of the Global Plan are highest in the African countries with high levels of HIV. Because the economic burden of TB in Africa is significant, the benefits of either DOTS strategy are large and exceed the costs by a wide margin.

While progress is being made, challenges such as funding gaps, higher-than-expected incidence rates through the 1990s, HIV coinfection, and multidrug resistance point to the urgent need for more comprehensive action to control TB. Fortunately, the state of our knowledge means that TB control is not a question of whether, but of how and how much we will commit to do. The significant economic benefits of taking action indicate that there is no reason we cannot do more to tackle this disease—the up-front costs are more than outweighed by the decades of not only health, but also productivity and prosperity that would follow.

Further Reading

Aldy, Joseph E., and W. Kip Viscusi. 2008. Adjusting the Value of a Statistical Life for Age and Cohort Effects. *Review of Economics and Statistics* 90(3): 573–581.

Dye, C. 2006. Global Epidemiology of TB. *Lancet* 367: 938–940.

Dye, C. and K. Floyd. 2006. Tuberculosis. In *Disease Control Priorities in Developing Countries.* 2nd ed., edited by D. T. Jamison. New York: Oxford University Press,289–312.

Laxminarayan, R., E. Klein, S. Darley, and O. Adeyi. 2009. Global Investments in Tuberculosis Control: Economic Benefits. *Health Affairs* 28(4):730–742.

88. BRINGING OUR FOOD SAFETY SYSTEM INTO THE 21st CENTURY

Sandra A. Hoffmann
is a fellow at Resources for the Future. Her research focuses on enhancing the contribution of economics and risk analysis to managing environmental health risks.

In recent years, foodborne illness incidents have been prominent in the news, and Congress has been holding hearings to determine what can be done. How and where does U.S. food safety policy need to change in order to ensure public safety in the face of our rapidly changing food supply system?

Over the past two years, a succession of cases of foodborne illnesses, many serious and some even fatal, has raised questions about the effectiveness of the U.S. food safety system. Our current system is based on procedures that have accumulated over the past century in response to various crises, scandals, and discoveries. Some are now seriously out of date. In other cases, new issues have emerged that the system was never designed to address.

The problem, at its root, is that hazards, foods, food sources, and food marketing are all changing rapidly, while our policies are not. Our meat inspection is governed by a 1906 act that still mandates visual inspection of every carcass processed in the country. Yet today's major hazards are microbial. New problems arise regularly and sometimes unpredictably. *E. coli* O157:H7, a potentially lethal bacterium, wasn't even recognized as a foodborne pathogen until 1982.

Changes in products and processes can create unforeseen problems. For example, a major shift has occurred in how ground meat is processed: today, meat from multiple sources is blended in large batches and distributed across the country, creating heightened potential for product contamination and illness. Another significant shift is the growing amount of food we now import. Consumers certainly benefit from flexibility in the food supply through lower prices, greater variety, and better nutrition throughout the year. But those benefits may be coming at the cost of increased risk.

The right response is to start thinking about food safety policy as a problem in modern risk management. In this context, risk management involves the ability to monitor changes in food safety risks systemwide in something like real time and the flexibility to redeploy resources to control these risks as needed. Carrying this out will involve recognizing who has least-cost access to information on how risks are generated and can most efficiently be controlled, and using this knowledge in designing policy. The United States, largely at the initiative of federal agencies and industry, has moved in this direction for the past two decades. But this effort has been seriously hampered by antiquated legislation and severe federal funding cuts.

SPECIFIC NEEDS

Better public health information. Information is the foundation for risk management. It is surprisingly difficult to estimate the rate of foodborne illness because often the link to food goes unrecognized. The most widely cited estimates date from 1999. Death estimates are highly uncertain because we do not have a good understanding of the longer-term effects of foodborne illness, such as links to heart disease. In the 1990s, significant efforts were made to establish better active surveillance of foodborne illness, but lack of funding has limited its scope to 10 states and a few localities. Passive surveillance relies both on local doctors reporting foodborne illness to local health authorities and on highly variable state and local public health funding.

Flexible, systemwide, risk-based regulation. Another positive change would be expansion of regulatory approaches that reflect the information constraints and comparative strengths of the public and private sectors. Hazard Analysis and Critical Control

Point (HACCP) regulations are a step in that direction. They require firms to identify where foodborne illness hazards are most likely to arise in their operations and to develop processes for controlling these critical points. Government's role is to verify that the firms are actually carrying out this process.

In the past decade and a half, HACCP regulations have been designed for meat, poultry, seafood, and juice. While these regulations make use of firms' informational advantages and provide firms the flexibility to adapt to changing technology and market demands, they do not adequately address the inherent conflicts of interest. Consumer groups have rightly pushed for more effective verification that these systems are not just in operation, but are actually controlling hazards. Court rulings and lack of legislative authority have prevented agencies from using product testing as a full-fledged enforcement mechanism. Third-party certification systems have also been used successfully by other industrialized countries.

Expansion of a HACCP-like approach beyond the processing and packing plant to across the full food supply chain would be helpful. Pathogen testing at retail may soon be technically feasible. Having checks on product contamination at critical junctures—like retail or the end of processing—coupled with product condemnation, recall, public information, and liability could provide powerful incentives for product safety down the supply chain. Trace-back systems are being used by private industry to identify the source of safety failures. These need broader use in public policy.

Risk management of imports. Roughly 45 percent of fresh fruit and 80 percent of seafood consumed in the United States is now imported. Globalization of the U.S. food supply poses three major challenges: volume, rapidly changing sourcing (particularly for food additives), and enforcement. Given the increasing volume of imports, border inspection alone will not assure safety. With more and more countries exporting to the United States, it is also unlikely that in-country inspection will fully address the problem. Extension of HACCP-like approaches to supply chain management for vertically integrated firms and use of third-party certification will have to play an increased role. And government needs to police conflicts of interest in these systems and to verify that certification systems are doing their job.

An end to fragmented federal governance. The pizza in your freezer complies with food safety regulations from six different federal agencies. Despite significant effort at coordination through interagency agreements, this fragmentation of authority—with the predictable turf battles, competition for budgets, and quarrels over priorities—remains a fundamental problem. But agency unification without legislative reform that authorizes modern approaches to regulation and allows flexible deployment of resources to focus on the most cost-effective opportunities for risk reduction will do little good.

Developing a risk-based food safety system, and pulling together a unified agency to administer it, would require a major reconstruction effort by the White House and Congress. That kind of effort most commonly occurs only after a disaster. The question is whether the political process can achieve a reform of such complexity without first paying the heavy price that a serious breakdown in food safety would exact.

Further Reading

Garcia, Marian, Andrew Fearne, Julie A. Caswell, and Spencer Henson. 2007. Co-regulation as a Possible Model for Food Safety Governance: Opportunities for Public-Private Partnerships. *Food Policy* 32(3): 299–314.

Golan, Elise, Tanya Roberts, Elisabete Salay, Julie Caswell, Michael Ollinger, and Danna Moore. 2004. *Food Safety Innovation in the United States: Evidence from the Meat Industry.* Agricultural Economic Report No. AER-831. Washington, DC: U.S. Department of Agriculture.

Hoffmann, Sandra. 2007. Mending Our Food Safety Net. *Resources* 166: 11–15.

Hoffmann, Sandra, and Michael Taylor, eds. 2005. *Toward Safer Food: Perspectives on Risk and Priority Setting.* Washington, DC: RFF Press.

89. TOBACCO TAXATION IN THE EUROPEAN UNION AND UNITED STATES

Sijbren Cnossen

is a professor of economics at the University of Maastricht and the Emeritus Professor of Tax Law at Erasmus University, Rotterdam.

Tobacco tax systems differ across countries with regard to not only the overall tax level, but also the mix between specific and ad valorem taxes. What does economics have to say about how governments should tax tobacco?

Both the level and the structure of tobacco taxes differ markedly between, as well as within, the European Union and United States. (The focus here is on cigarettes alone, as they constitute over 90 percent of tobacco consumption.) Within EU member states, the total tax burden (excises and value added taxes, or VAT) is around three-quarters of the retail price of cigarettes, or over 300 percent of the pretax price. The southern member states favor predominantly ad valorem taxes (that is, percentage rates on the value of a pack of cigarettes), whereas in the northern member states, specific taxes constitute more than half of the total tobacco tax burden.

In the United States, tobacco taxes are almost wholly specific. The federal government levies a tax of 39 cents per pack (of 20 cigarettes), state governments levy taxes that average about 60 cents per pack, and the Master Tobacco Settlement Agreement, concluded in 1998 (under which tobacco companies are expected to pay $206 billion to settle product liability suits) effectively added a further 30 cents per pack. Nonetheless the total tax (excise and retail sales taxes), about $1.30 per pack, amounts to about 37 percent of the retail price, or about half the rate in the European Union.

What does economics have to say about the appropriate level, and structure, of tobacco taxation?

WHAT COSTS DO SMOKERS IMPOSE ON OTHERS?

The causal link to future health problems from smoking is extremely well documented—smoking is a primary cause of lung cancer, emphysema, chronic bronchitis, and a major cause of heart disease and stroke. Smoking by pregnant women leads to low birth weight babies, neonatal death, and sudden infant death syndrome.

While the health consequences of smoking are important, in principle they are irrelevant to public policy unless the costs imposed are external (that is, imposed on others rather than borne privately by the smoker). The principle of consumer sovereignty implies that a rational person who weighs all the costs and benefits of his actions should be free to smoke as long as he does not impose costs on others and is fully informed about the consequences of his choices.

Virtually all empirical research suggests that the external costs of smoking are relatively small. The burden of medical payments on government due to smoking-related illness is one potential source of external cost. However, this near-term burden is at least partly offset in a life-cycle context, as the average smoker lives a shorter life, which saves on pensions and health–care costs of age-related disease. Bans on smoking in public places have greatly reduced the external costs of environmental or "second-hand" tobacco smoke. However, little has been or can be done about the health problems experienced by children and nonsmoking partners within the family at home. Perhaps economists assume too easily that such costs are largely internalized by the smoker through altruism or negotiation among family members.

INFORMATION AND ADDICTION FAILURES

If smokers, especially teenagers, are poorly informed about the costs of smoking, then to that extent, the costs of smoking are effectively external. However, if inadequate information is the problem, this is best addressed through warning labels and information dissemination programs about health hazards. In fact, evidence suggests that 90 percent of U.S. consumers are aware of the long-term health effects of smoking.

Nonetheless, the fact that nicotine is addictive may undermine the consumer sovereignty argument against government intervention. If smokers behave myopically in choosing to consume an addictive drug, the rationality condition ceases to apply, because the addictive smoker is, to some extent, a different person than the one who decided to start smoking. Furthermore, consumers may excessively discount the longer-term costs of addiction. Consequently, they may therefore have self-control problems, referred to as internal costs, where they continually plan to smoke less in the future than they actually can. In this case, cigarette taxes may help to reinforce a commitment to quit in the future.

In fact, higher taxes seem to be most effective in reducing smoking prevalence among teenagers who are better able to kick the habit, because addiction has not yet taken hold. Evidence suggests that a 10 percent increase in cigarette prices is associated with about a 4 percent reduction in smoking among adults, but an 8 percent reduction among teenagers.

Evidence suggests that tobacco tax levels, even in the United States, are difficult to justify on externality grounds, let alone those levels prevailing in the European Union. High taxes may reflect a form of paternalism, such as a desire to discourage young people from taking up smoking. The internal cost argument for higher taxes has not yet been settled.

WHAT'S THE RIGHT WAY TO TAX TOBACCO?

Tobacco is far from a homogeneous product. The United States and northern European countries tend to produce higher-quality brands than southern European countries. Ad valorem taxes raise the prices of different brands in the same proportion, and therefore they do not distort a consumer's choice between high- and low-quality brands. This makes economic sense, to the extent that the purpose of tobacco taxes is to raise revenue.

Taxing cigarettes according to their external costs leads to a very different conclusion, however. The damage caused by cigarette smoking is independent of the price at which it is sold, so that correction of externalities favors specific over ad valorem taxes. All else equal, the share of specific taxes in total tobacco taxation should be smaller when the importance of raising revenue is greater and the case for correcting externalities correspondingly smaller. To some extent, this reasoning is consistent with the high ad valorem tax element in EU tobacco tax systems and its absence in U.S. structures.

Some variation in specific taxes across different tobacco products may in fact be appropriate. Since health damages are correlated with the tar content of cigarettes, taxes on high-tar cigarettes should be higher too. However, some research shows that addicts smoke low-tar and low-nicotine cigarettes differently, inhaling more to increase the amount of nicotine they ingest. So corrective taxes might not be proportional to tar content, but some differentiation is likely to still be appropriate. Moreover, a "tar tax" would give manufacturers an incentive to develop palatable low-tar cigarettes, which would have long-term health benefits.

A COMPLEX QUESTION

The question of what the right level and structure of tobacco tax should be is a complex one, given the multiple objectives of policymakers. The reasons for levying high taxes on tobacco products are the predictability of the revenue, the desire to discourage youths from taking up smoking, and the belief that smokers should pay for the burden they impose on others. The reasons for moderating the level of tobacco taxes are the principle of consumer sovereignty and the finding that the external costs of smoking may be low. And the choice between specific and ad valorem taxation depends on whether the primary goal of policy is to discourage smoking or raise revenue.

Further Reading

Chossen, Sijbren, and Michael Smart. 2005. Taxation of Tobacco. In *The Theory and Practice of Excise Taxation*, edited by Sijbren Cnossen. Oxford, UK: Oxford University Press.

Manning, Willard G., Emmet B. Keeler, Joseph P. Newhouse, Elizabeth M. Sloss, and Jeffrey Wasserman. 1989. The Taxes of Sin: Do Smokers and Drinkers Pay Their Way? *Journal of the American Medical Association* 261: 1604–1609.

90. HOW ADVERTISING FOR SMOKING-CESSATION PRODUCTS CAN HELP MEET PUBLIC HEALTH GOALS

Donald S. Kenkel
is a professor of policy analysis and management at Cornell University, specializing in the economics of disease prevention and health promotion.

Dean R. Lillard
is a senior research associate at Cornell University, focusing on smoking advertising, education, and empirical methods for retrospective data.

Although progress has been made, smoking remains a leading cause of death in the United States. To what extent do advertisements for smoking-cessation products encourage people to quit smoking, and how might the regulation of such advertising be reformed?

About 20 percent of the U.S. adult population currently smokes cigarettes, and over 400,000 Americans die each year from smoking-related illnesses. Given these stark numbers, it is easy to understand why an ongoing federal public health initiative aims to cut the smoking rate almost in half by 2010. Over the past decade or so, preventing youths from starting to smoke attracted a great deal of media and policy attention. Taxes were raised, antismoking mass media campaigns were launched, and laws restricting the sale of cigarettes to minors were strengthened and enforced.

While it is difficult to know which, if any, of these policies worked, the rate of daily smoking among high school seniors indeed dropped by half from the peak levels reached in the late 1990s. But the remaining gap between the current adult smoking rate and the new goal makes clear what experts have long recognized: large reductions in the smoking rate cannot be achieved unless more of the 45 million adults who currently smoke quit. And as one of the required cigarette warning labels reads: "Quitting smoking now greatly reduces serious risks to your health."

Thinking about smoking cessation as a public health problem naturally focuses attention on public policies such as further cigarette tax hikes, smoking bans, and stronger warning labels. However, it is also a private health issue—the smokers themselves have the most to gain from quitting. There is a healthy private-sector market for products such as nicotine gum that help smokers quit. The pharmaceutical industry's estimated retail sales of smoking-cessation products are nearly $1 billion annually. In recent years, the industry has spent between $100 million and $200 million annually advertising these products. While the pharmaceutical industry is out for higher profits, does the advertising also improve public health? If so, what public policies might encourage more private-sector advertising?

To shed new light on this question, we studied whether pharmaceutical industry advertising affected smokers' decisions to quit. The research team included our colleagues Rosemary Avery and Alan Mathios, as well as undergraduate and graduate research assistants. We linked survey data from individual smokers with an archive of magazine advertisements. With data on these smokers' magazine reading habits, we measured the smoking-cessation ads to which they were exposed. By using the same information about the consumers that the advertisers observe, we tried to control for the potential reverse causality that advertising studies commonly face: are consumers responding to the advertising, or are advertisers responding to the consumer behavior?

After subjecting our results to a battery of checks, we found evidence that, when smokers see more magazine ads for smoking-cessation products, they are more likely to decide to quit. Based on our results, we estimate that if the smoking-cessation product industry increases its average annual expenditures on magazine advertising by about $2.6 million, the average smoker would be exposed to about 2.1 more magazine ads each year. According to our empirical models, the result would be about 225,000 new attempts to quit and 80,000 successful "quits" each year. If an increase of this size in the rate of smoking cessation could be maintained over the years, the adult smoking rate would drop by about a percentage point. Larger increases in advertising budgets could reduce smoking rates by even more. Our study of smoking-cessation product advertising is part of a growing body of economic research finding that direct-to-consumer ads increase consumer demand for a variety of pharmaceutical products.

Interestingly, however, our estimates show that most of the new quit attempts and quits spurred by the ads would not involve the purchase of smoking-cessation products. Other studies find that when smokers attempt to quit, at least two-thirds use a method like going "cold turkey" that does not involve a product purchase. Likewise, our estimates suggest that about two-thirds of smokers who were prompted to quit by the product ads will also go cold turkey.

Firms often worry that their ad expenditures will spill over and help their competitors: does a McDonald's ad prompt a visit to the Golden Arches, or might it help Burger King too? But for smoking-cessation products, the direct competition doesn't cost anything. Because advertising can spur people to quit on their own, some of the public health returns to smoking-cessation product ads are not captured as private profits.

The standard policy prescription is to use subsidies to encourage private-sector activities that generate positive spillovers. For example, the public sector subsidizes education because schooling not only helps the recipients, but also presumably benefits the rest of society. However, instead of subsidizing pharmaceutical ads because of their spillovers, current regulatory policy works to discourage them. The United States and New Zealand are the only countries that allow direct-to-consumer advertising of prescription pharmaceutical products. Even in these two countries, these ads are strictly regulated.

In the United States, this had led to an ironic situation: in some ways, ads for prescription pharmaceutical products for smoking cessation have been more heavily regulated than cigarette ads. Food and Drug Administration (FDA) regulations require magazine ads for prescription smoking-cessation products to include at least an extra page of disclosures about side effects and contraindications, while cigarette ads are required to carry only a short warning label. Easing regulations on ads for smoking-cessation products could exploit more fully the profit incentives to promote public health. Ads for other pharmaceutical products, such as statins to treat high cholesterol, have similar potential. Because the potential gains and harms from advertising vary widely across products, it might make sense for the FDA to adopt a more flexible approach to regulating direct-to-consumer advertising.

More generally, when crafting public policy, it is important to acknowledge private incentives to improve public health. People want to live healthier and longer lives, and private-sector firms can earn profits helping them do so. Public policies should be structured to facilitate, rather than impede, the public health gains enjoyed when firms pursue private profits.

Further Reading

Avery, Rosemary, Donald Kenkel, Dean Lillard, and Alan Mathios. 2007. Private Profits and Public Health: Does Advertising of Smoking Cessation Products Encourage Smokers to Quit? *Journal of Political Economy* 115(3): 447–481.

Avery, Rosemary, Donald Kenkel, Dean Lillard, and Alan Mathios. 2007. Regulating Advertisements: The Case of Smoking Cessation Products. *Journal of Regulatory Economics* 31: 185-208.

Chaloupka, Frank, and Kenneth Warner. 2000. The Economics of Smoking. In *Handbook of Health Economics,* Vol. 1B, edited by Anthony J. Culyer and Joseph P. Newhouse. Amsterdam, Netherlands: North-Holland.

91. MERCURY ADVISORIES FOR COMMERCIAL FISH

Jay Shimshack

is an assistant professor of economics at Tulane University. His research stresses the empirical evaluation of environmental policies, especially applied to information policies and the enforcement and monitoring of environmental laws.

In recent years, environmental policymakers have supplemented traditional pollution regulations with information disclosure programs to better inform the public about the health and other environmental risks of products and firm activities. Mercury advisories are one example of this approach, but the program has had some unintended consequences.

In the last several years, concern has arisen that mercury from commercial fish consumption may pose a significant threat to children's neurological development. In 2001, the FDA responded to increasing risk information by releasing a national advisory. It warned pregnant women, women who may become pregnant, and households with young children to limit their fish consumption. An advisory update was issued in 2004. Both advisories instructed at-risk groups to eliminate consumption of certain types of fish and cap consumption of all seafood, including canned fish.

To better understand this ongoing public health issue, it is useful to provide some context. Levels of mercury circulating in the environment have increased considerably over the last century. Coal-fired power plants are currently the largest source of anthropogenic mercury. When atmospheric mercury is deposited into surface water, bacteria convert the mercury into organic methylmercury. This then enters a fish's bloodstream from water passing over its gills and accumulates in tissues. It also bioaccumulates up the food chain. Even in water where ambient mercury levels are extremely low, methylmercury concentrations may reach high levels in predatory species like tuna, king mackerel, swordfish, and shark.

For the general public, fish consumption is the primary source of exposure to mercury. Cooking and other forms of food preparation do not mitigate the risks. The FDA and other government agencies maintain that even modest mercury concentrations pose a risk of significant harm to the developing neurological systems of fetuses, infants, and young children. Consequences may include reduced IQ, learning and attention disorders, and generally slowed intellectual and behavioral development. Severe neurological illnesses, like cerebral palsy, may result from unusually high exposure. In adults, abnormally high mercury concentrations may contribute to brain damage, heart disease, blurred vision, slurred speech, and other neurological ailments, although such high concentrations are rare.

Conventional economic wisdom tells us that improved information, such as the content of the mercury advisories, will make consumers better off. Indeed, there are theoretical advantages of managing mercury risks with consumption advisories. First, advisories provide flexible risk mitigation. They can directly target at-risk households and do not impose undue costs to society by limiting exposure to consumers that are not susceptible to risk. Second, information policies allow risk mitigation for persistent problems. Even if mercury emissions could be completely eliminated, health risks could not be ruled out in the short run, because mercury persists in the environment. Third, advisories allow risk mitigation for problems that cross boundaries. A complete ban on domestic mercury emissions would still not rule out health risks to American consumers, even in the long run, because the vast majority of seafood consumed in the United States is caught abroad. To complicate matters further, mercury emissions from foreign sources are often deposited in U.S. waters.

Despite the theoretical advantages of mercury advisories for managing risks, the big question is whether those advisories actually work in practice. Recent research suggests there may be serious limitations. Because a moderate amount of fish consumption provides significant health benefits to both adults and children—particularly in the form of IQ, stroke, and heart disease benefits from omega-3 fatty acid intakes—crude advisory responses or overreactions may mitigate advisories' net public health effects. In short, there is a tension between mercury risks and seafood's health benefits. Some members of the scientific community have even speculated that mercury advisories may have caused net harm if at-risk consumers responded to the advisories by reducing consumption of all fish rather than high-mercury fish alone.

A colleague and I have shown that this speculation is justified (Shimshack and Ward 2008). We found that at-risk consumers did reduce mercury intakes in response to the 2001 commercial fish advisory. In isolation, this is positive for public health. However, we also found that at-risk consumers substantially reduced their intake of beneficial omega-3 fatty acids. Further explorations revealed that at-risk consumers did not substitute high-mercury fish with low-mercury fish, nor did they differentially avoid high-mercury fish. They simply reduced consumption of all fish in response to the advisory. When we interpreted our results from a public health perspective, we found that the benefits of mercury reductions were approximately offset by the negative health effects of reduced overall fish consumption. In other words, on net, we found no public health benefits of the mercury advisory.

Other concerns about mercury advisories also exist. Coauthors and I found that advisories affect households differently (Shimshack et al. 2007). Important groups of at-risk consumers, including the least educated, did not seem to react to mercury advisories at all. This may be a notable public health issue, because this group of consumers may be particularly poorly equipped to withstand negative health outcomes. Unintended spillover effects of these advisories are another factor. We found that some consumers not considered at-risk also reduced consumption in response to the advisory—an outcome not consistent with policy goals.

In sum, the evidence justifies strong cautionary notes about commercial fish advisories. While the theoretical advantages of information policies for managing mercury in seafood are significant, the practical realities highlight important disadvantages. More research is needed, but the best available evidence suggests that national commercial fish advisories have no net public health benefits. Advisories must be more carefully crafted and disseminated. Mercury mitigation strategies might also appropriately begin to rely more on emissions reductions than consumption advisories alone.

Further Reading

Cohen, Joshua, et al. 2005. A Quantitative Risk-Benefit Analysis of Changes in Population Fish Consumption. *American Journal of Preventive Medicine* 29(4): 325–334.

Shimshack, Jay P., Michael B. Ward, and Timothy K.M. Beatty. 2007. Mercury Advisories: Information, Education, and Fish Consumption. *Journal of Environmental Economics and Management* 53: 158–179.

Shimshack, Jay P., and Michael B. Ward. 2008. Mercury Advisories and Household Health Trade-offs. Working paper. February. New Orleans: Tulane University.

U.S. National Academies, Food and Nutrition Board. 2005. *Seafood Choices: Balancing the Benefits and the Risks.* Washington, DC: National Academies Press.

92. MEASURING THE BENEFITS OF REDUCED EXPOSURE TO LEAD

Felicia Day

has been the manager of editorial services at Resources for the Future since 2000. A former trade reporter, she has written about environmental and occupational safety issues throughout her career.

For many air pollutants, the most important health hazard is premature mortality. However, in the case of lead emissions, the main health risk is neurological damage to young children. How do economists measure the benefits of reducing lead emissions, and what are the implications for the recent tightening of the lead standard?

Although lead was outlawed from use in gasoline and paint in the 1970s, many children in this country continue to be exposed to lead in dust, soil, and deteriorated paint in housing units. Efforts to cut the use of this neurotoxin in other products—such as foods, cosmetics, folk remedies, and toys—continue because exposure is known to be harmful, particularly in utero and in early childhood.

In fact, thousands of scientific studies over the last two decades have shown that young children suffer neurological harm at much lower blood lead levels than previously recognized, with potentially serious implications for brain development and cognitive abilities as well as noncognitive ones, such as motivation, perseverance, and tenacity. This was a major motivation behind a recent court challenge that resulted in a dramatic tightening in the National Ambient Air Quality Standard for lead (due to take effect by 2017) to 0.15 micrograms per cubic meter. The previous standard, set in 1978, had been 1.5 micrograms per cubic meter.

So is this change justifiable? Do the social benefits from reducing lead emissions outweigh the costs? Economists address these questions by doing the following:

- determining the impact of the control policy on reducing the atmospheric concentration,
- assessing the exposed population that potentially benefits from the reduction in ambient concentrations,
- estimating the reduction in blood lead levels for the affected population,
- evaluating the resulting health benefits, and
- obtaining a monetary measure of these benefits.

The first four steps can be measured by linking emissions/air quality models to local population data, as well as evidence from the scientific literature. The final one is our focus here, as this is perhaps the most contentious.

The benefits of reducing exposure to lead are based on estimated changes in mental ability—usually measured by changes in IQ—in children aged seven and below, and associated changes in their future earnings potential. EPA's regulatory impact assessment for the new lead standard assumed that each 1 percent increase in IQ would increase lifetime earnings by around 1.8 to 2.3 percent. But the reliability of these assumptions is open to question. Would alternative assumptions alter economic assessments of the desirability of previous policies to reduce lead emissions?

The EPA assumption was based on earlier studies, for example by Salkever (1995). The estimates of the IQ premium in those studies were obtained by comparing lifetime earnings of individuals—which depend on their wages and fringe benefits, hours worked, and likelihood of employment—with different IQ levels, holding other factors, like occupation or age, constant.

However, recent analyses appear to cast some doubt on these earlier findings. Heckman et al. (2006) developed better measures to take into account the quality of people's education, finding that, for 30-year-old men, a 1 percent difference in cognitive ability made only a 0.6 percent difference in hourly wages—less than a third of EPA's assumption. (However, this was exclusively for relatively young men, for whom the estimated association between IQ and earnings is somewhat weaker than for older men and for women.) Another study, by Zax and Rees (2002) estimated the wage premium at 0.6 to 1.4 percent for men.

The more recent evidence suggests that the association between cognitive ability and earnings has previously been overstated, and, by implication, the EPA regulatory impact analysis may have overstated the benefits of reducing children's exposure to environmental lead. For example, Grosse et al. (2002) estimated that reductions in lead exposure from the mid-1970s to the late 1990s increased the total lifetime productivity of each year's U.S. birth cohort by $110 billion to $320 billion. Based on the newer Zax–Rees figures, the estimates would fall to $70 billion to $150 billion.

Nonetheless, even these lower benefit figures are large relative to estimates of the annualized costs of phasing out leaded gasoline and paint, and other control measures. Moreover, the benefit estimates would be higher if recent findings were taken into account that link adverse health impacts to relatively low blood lead levels. Furthermore, the Grosse et al. estimate did not account for lead's effects on noncognitive functioning, such as the ability to show up for work and focus on a task. Some studies find that those types of abilities or personality traits may be an even more important determinant of earnings than cognitive ability (Heckman et al. 2006). Nor did the study account for the possible association between lead exposure in childhood and criminal behavior among adults. Interventions in childhood that reduce criminal behavior in adulthood can generate very large economic returns.

As for the recent tightening of the lead standard, cost–benefit analyses are less conclusive, as the results are sensitive to different assumptions, such as the rate at which higher future earnings are discounted. Scaling back the benefits in the EPA regulatory impact assessment (which include some side benefits from related reductions in particulate emissions) to account for the smaller earnings/IQ association leaves an overall net benefit under some range of assumptions and a net loss under others. Therefore, it appears difficult to make a definitive case for or against a tighter standard at this time. Perhaps new assessments will be more positive down the road, if some broader benefits of reduced lead poisoning, noted above, are quantified and taken into account, and if firms develop innovative, lower-cost ways to reduce lead emissions.

Further Reading

Grosse, Scott D., Thomas D. Matte, Joel Schwartz, and Richard J. Jackson. 2002. Economic Gains Resulting from the Reduction in Children's Exposure to Lead in the United States. *Environmental Health Perspectives* 110(6): 563–569.

Heckman, James J., Jora Stixrud, and Sergio Urzua. 2006. The Effects of Cognitive and Noncognitive Abilities on Labor Market Outcomes and Social Behavior. *Journal of Labor Economics* 24: 411–482.

Salkever, David S. 1995. Updated Estimates of Earnings Benefits from Reduced Exposure of Children to Environmental Lead. *Environmental Research* 70: 1–6.

Zax, Jeffrey S., and Daniel I. Rees. 2002. IQ, Academic Performance, Environment, and Earnings. *Review of Economics and Statistics* 84: 600–616.

The author would like to thank Scott Grosse for his thoughtful review of this article.

93. INDOOR AIR POLLUTION AND AFRICAN DEATH RATES

Majid Ezzati

is an associate professor of international health at Harvard School of Public Health. He specializes in the determinants of, and risk factors for, health and disease at the population level, especially environmental risk factors.

Indoor pollution from combustion of traditional cooking and heating fuels is a major health problem in low-income countries. Although there is little prospect of addressing this problem through electrification in the next 20 to 30 years, policy interventions, such as encouraging use of less-polluting fuels and stoves with better ventilation, can bring substantial health benefits in the meantime.

In sub-Saharan Africa, 94 percent of the rural population and 73 percent of the urban population use biomass—wood, charcoal, crop residues, animal dung—and coal as their main sources of energy for cooking and heating. Biomass combustion, particularly in open or poorly ventilated stoves, generates numerous pollutants, including particulate matter, carbon monoxide, and other carcinogens that are potentially harmful to the health of poor adult women and their children (who are carried on their mothers' backs or play by the fire).

Robert Bailis, Daniel Kammen, and I estimated that, for the year 2000, 350,000 sub-Saharan African children who died of lower respiratory infections, and 34,000 adult women who died of chronic obstructive pulmonary disease, would have lived longer had they not been exposed to indoor air pollution caused by burning biomass. Worldwide, studies suggest that exposure to indoor air pollution is responsible for over 1.8 million premature deaths a year, and nearly 3 percent of the global burden of disease. And all these figures may substantially underestimate the true disease burden. Recent evidence suggests an association between exposure to indoor air pollution during pregnancy and low birth weight, which has significant health consequences for adults and children.

Indoor air pollution from solid fuels is now recognized as a major global health concern. For example, solid-fuel use is an indicator for Goal 7 (environmental sustainability) of the UN's Millennium Development Goals. Exposure to indoor air pollution depends critically on household access to, and choice of, energy technology (that is, the choice of fuel and stove). The greatest risk reductions can be achieved by a complete transition to electricity, or even to direct use of fossil fuels like natural gas and kerosene. (Although the health risks of poisoning or burns from kerosene have not been systematically quantified, they are likely much smaller than the health risks from biomass and coal.) In many developing countries, especially in urban areas, high-income households have transitioned to cleaner fuels. There are, however, important exceptions to this: in China, for example, rapid economic growth and infrastructure expansion have contributed to near-universal access to electricity, yet almost 80 percent of households continue to use biomass or coal as their main energy source for cooking and heating.

In fact, for many low-income nations and households, particularly in rural sub-Saharan Africa, transitioning to clean fuels is not a realistic option for the next 20 to 30 years. One reason is the high up-front costs of the infrastructure needed to generate, process, and deliver clean energy. In Kenya, for example, a gas stove and tank costs around \$30–\$50, while a charcoal stove costs \$3–\$5. Another obstacle is the volatility in petroleum-based fuel prices, caused by both instability in international fuel markets and domestic energy policies.

In the meantime, efforts should therefore focus on interventions to modify aspects of the current fuel–stove combinations and energy-use behaviors, and to improve technologies for accessible and clean energy sources. Options include preprocessing biomass and coal to burn more cleanly, and stoves with better ventilation. Separating kitchens or providing additional windows can also reduce pollution exposure. Interventions like these need to take into account local factors like climate and the environment, the purpose of energy use (cooking versus heating), local infrastructure, socioeconomic circumstances, and user behavior.

One particularly important intervention for very low-income societies is greater use of transformed biofuels. Evidence suggests that a substantial portion of the potential health risk reduction from a transition to petroleum-based fossil fuels could still be achieved by shifting toward charcoal. For example, based on current trends in the use of traditional household fuels in sub-Saharan Africa, we projected that, between 2000 and 2030, there would be 8.1 million annual premature deaths among children and 1.7 million premature deaths among adult women. However, about a million of these deaths could be avoided by a gradual transition to the use of charcoal, while a more rapid transition could nearly triple the numbers of premature deaths avoided.

Using charcoal costs no more to households than burning wood, as it avoids the infrastructure requirements of other fossil fuels. Charcoal also has a well-established production and marketing network in many countries and can be more easily scaled up than a transition to fossil fuels.

Greater use of charcoal is not without drawbacks: it would result in much higher emissions of greenhouse gases if the wood is harvested unsustainably and made into charcoal in traditional kilns. And charcoal has implications for forest cover, soil fertility, and biodiversity in ways that have not yet been fully studied. But evidence from Latin America and Asia shows that it is possible to produce charcoal in more environmentally sustainable ways, particularly through changes in land management to ensure sufficient replacement of trees, the use of alternative feedstocks, and the introduction of highly efficient kilns.

Greater use of other transformed biofuels might also produce significant benefits, although these other fuels have received little attention in the health and indoor air pollution literature. Nonetheless, if the technological, funding, and institutional challenges could be met, transitioning to sustainable fuels like charcoal offers a valuable opportunity to promote gender equality and improve environmental sustainability, while also ranking among one of the most cost-effective health interventions in developing countries.

Further Reading

Dherani M., D. Pope, M. Mascarenhas, K.R. Smith, M. Weber, and N. Bruce. 2008. Indoor Air Pollution from Unprocessed Solid Fuel Use and Pneumonia Risk in Children Aged under Five Years: A Systematic Review and Meta-Analysis. *Bulletin of the World Health Organization* 86(5): 390–398C.

Ezzati, M. 2005. Indoor Air Pollution and Health in Developing Countries. *Lancet* 366(9480): 104–106.

Smith, Kirk R., and Majid Ezzati. 2005. How Environmental Health Risks Change with Development: The Epidemiologic and Environmental Risk Transitions Revisited. *Annual Review of Environmental Resources* 30: 291–333.

Smith, Kirk R., Sumi Mehta, and Mirjam Maeusezahl-Feuz. 2004. Indoor Air Pollution from Household Use of Solid Fuels. In *Comparative Quantification of Health Risks: Global and Regional Burden of Disease Attribution to Selected Major Risk Factors*, edited by M. Ezzati, A.D. Lopez, A. Rodgers, and C.J.L. Murray. Geneva, Switzerland: World Health Organization.

PART 7

Environment and Development

This final section touches on some challenging policy problems in developing countries where the institutions for dealing with the adverse side effects of industrialization and population growth are often poorly developed. There are important lessons to be learned – often about what not to do – from how other countries handle problems that defy easy answers. For example, the Washington, DC, metropolitan area regularly earns the third place in having the worst traffic in the nation, and numerous solutions have been implemented, to varying degrees of success, such as expanding the subway system. Mexico City, which is far larger, adopted what looked like a straightforward approach, the "Today Don't Drive" program. But that essentially failed because it didn't address human behavior, specifically the willingness of households to quickly adapt to new government regulations.

Too often, our understanding about other countries or certain phenomenon is based on scarce information or long-held assumptions that have come to be regarded as fact. Several commentaries in this section look at the numbers behind the myths and evaluate possible policy tools. Famines today, for example, are rarely caused by plagues of locusts or totalitarian regimes, like those associated with Stalin and Mao. But the definitions have changed: at present, mass hunger is a far greater challenge to the global community than famine. The "population bomb" once feared a few decades ago basically has been defused, thanks to family planning programs and economic and social progress achieved in many developing nations. But population growth won't be stable for a while, and prospective population increases will continue to power large international migration streams, mainly from the poor areas of Africa, Latin America, and South Asia to the developed nations.

Finally, other commentaries introduce readers to broader development problems such as housing "poverty," green cities, and the need for safe drinking water. Throughout the book, you'll find similar entries, particularly in the Managing Natural Resources, Transportation and Urban Policy, and Public Health Policy sections.

94. DRIVING RESTRICTIONS AND AIR QUALITY IN MEXICO CITY

Lucas W. Davis

is an assistant professor at the University of California, Berkeley's Haas School of Business and a faculty research fellow at the National Bureau of Economic Research. Central to his research and teaching interests are public finance, applied microeconomics, and energy and environmental economics.

Sound economic analysis that sorts out which environmental policies work and which do not is especially important for developing countries where large urban populations are frequently exposed to acute pollution. One environmentally motivated policy that does not seem to be working well, at least for Mexico City, is restricting the number of days people can drive their vehicles.

Whereas U.S. cities have seen dramatic improvements in air quality over the last three decades, Mexico City has been considerably less successful. Levels of major air pollutants in Mexico City routinely exceed the maximum exposure limits established by the World Health Organization (WHO). For example, WHO has warned that eight-hour average ozone levels exceeding 100 micrograms per cubic meter threaten human health, causing respiratory infections, chronic respiratory illness, and aggravation of existing cardiovascular disease. Evidence from monitoring stations in Mexico City indicates that during the period 1986–2005, this guideline was exceeded 92 percent of the time. Extrapolations from U.S. studies suggest that these pollution levels lead to thousands of premature deaths a year in Mexico City.

Nearly 20 years ago, record levels of ozone and other airborne pollutants led the Mexico City government to introduce a program, Hoy No Circula (HNC), which bans most drivers from using their vehicles one weekday per week, based on the last digit of the vehicle's license plate. (For example, vehicles with a license plate ending in 5 or 6 may not be used on Monday.) The restrictions are in place between 5 a.m. and 10 p.m. and affect the vast majority of residential and commercial vehicles, although taxis are excluded. When imposed in 1989, the restrictions applied to 2.3 million vehicles, or 460,000 vehicles per day.

The policy seemed reasonable at the start. After all, vehicle emissions are overwhelmingly the primary source of air pollution in Mexico City. According to a recent emissions inventory, vehicles are responsible for 81 percent of the nitrogen oxides and 46 percent of the volatile organic compounds in the Mexico City atmosphere. However, when hourly air pollution records from monitoring stations were examined, they showed no evidence that the program has improved air quality. While weekend and late-night air pollution increased relative to weekdays, consistent with drivers shifting to hours when the program is not in effect, weekday pollution levels did not change at all.

The primary cause of the program's failure turns out to be human adaptation. While the hope was that drivers would shift to low-emissions forms of transportation, such as the subway or the public or private bus systems, no one got out of their cars. Instead, the evidence indicates that HNC has led to an increase in the total number of vehicles in circulation. What is the easiest way to circumvent the Hoy No Circula program? Buy a second car. A driver with two vehicles can drive every day of the week as long as the last digits of the license plates don't match. Plus, the data shows that most of the new cars are, in fact, used and imported from other parts of the country, and thus tend to be high-emitting.

An additional explanation is the increased use of taxis. There are over 100,000 taxis in Mexico City, or approximately one taxi for every 100 residents. In comparison, New York City has approximately one taxi for every 600 residents, and Beijing has one taxi for every 175 residents. Mexico City's unusually large stock of taxis was well positioned to absorb any increase in demand from HNC. Moreover, from 1986 to

2005, taxis in Mexico City were among the highest-emitting vehicles in circulation; most were Volkswagen Beetles, a vehicle that has not been sold in the United States since 1977.

But given HNC's basic failure to alter driver behavior, Mexico City's highly congested streets are as clogged as ever. Yet the inconvenience of the driving restrictions still imposes costs on vehicle owners; a rough calculation suggests these costs amount to over $300 million per year, or $130 per vehicle owner.

Questions about the effectiveness of this program are relevant to current environmental policy in Mexico City. Air quality remains a severe problem in Mexico City, with ozone levels exceeding WHO standards 79 percent of the time in 2005. Despite the contrary evidence, HNC was actually expanded July 2008 to include Saturday driving restrictions. Some see HNC as the central component of Mexico City's strategy for addressing air pollution, while others would like to replace it with other forms of pollution control. Either way, reliable estimates of the effect of HNC on air pollution are necessary for evaluating these alternatives.

Carrying out such analysis would have implications for air quality and transportation policies throughout the urban developing world. According to the World Bank, the 10 cities with the highest average levels of airborne particulates are all in the developing world. Trends in population and vehicle growth in these urban areas threaten to exacerbate these problems. Between 2000 and 2030, the number of people living in cities in less-developed countries is forecast to increase by 1.96 billion. This represents 97 percent of the projected global population increase during this period.

Driving restrictions are one of the tools available to policymakers as they confront this growing problem. Indeed, since HNC was implemented, similar programs have been started, such as Pico y Placa in Bogota, Restricción Vehicular in Santiago, Rodízio in São Paulo, and restrictions in Beijing in preparation for the 2008 Olympics. In total, over 50 million people live in cities with driving restrictions based on license plates.

Evidence, at least from Mexico City's experience, suggests that these policies to restrict driving are misguided. More effective environmental policies are probably those that have worked best in the United States, namely progressively tighter emissions standards for mobile and stationary sources, as well as better enforcement through, for example, stricter requirements for regular vehicle emissions inspections.

Further Reading

Davis, Lucas W. 2008. The Effect of Driving Restrictions on Air Quality in Mexico City. *Journal of Political Economy* 116(1): 38–81.

Molina, Luisa T., and Mario J. Molina, eds. 2004. *Air Quality in the Mexico Megacity: An Integrated Assessment*. Dordrecht, Netherlands: Kluwer Academic Publishers.

Parry, Ian W.H., and Govinda R. Timilsina. 2008. How Should Passenger Travel in Mexico City Be Priced? Discussion paper 08-17. Washington, DC: Resources for the Future.

World Bank Mexico Air Quality Management Team. 2002. Improving Air Quality in Metropolitan Mexico City: An Economic Valuation. Policy Research Working Paper WPS 2785. Washington, DC: World Bank.

95. DECIPHERING THE DEMAND FOR SAFE DRINKING WATER IN LOW-INCOME COUNTRIES

Michael Kremer

is the Gates Professor of Developing Societies in Harvard University's Economics Department and a senior fellow at the Brookings Institution. His recent work includes evaluation of health and educational programs in developing countries and incentives for research on diseases affecting developing countries.

Edward Miguel

is an associate professor of economics and director of the Center of Evaluation for Global Action at the University of California, Berkeley. He specializes in African economic development.

Clair Null

is a Ph.D. candidate in agricultural and resource economics at the University of California, Berkeley.

Alix Zwane

is a program manager at google.org, the philanthropic arm of Google. She received her Ph.D. from Harvard University in 2002.

Contaminated water is one of the most serious health challenges facing many developing countries. Although a variety of interventions are possible for improving water quality, designing effective policy requires careful study of their health benefits and the willingness of households to adopt them. One such study has been conducted in rural Kenya.

We take water for granted when it flows from our kitchen faucets, but for millions in less-developed countries, safe drinking water remains a matter of life and death. Diarrheal diseases kill around two million children every year, and contaminated water is often to blame. In rural areas where pipe infrastructure is too expensive or too hard to maintain, water collection from sources like wells, streams, or springs can take hours each day, a burden that falls primarily on women and young children. And despite the hours of walking time, the sources they must use are often unsafe.

With so many people relying on the same water sources to collect water for drinking and cooking, wash dishes and clothes, and provide for livestock, it's hard to keep those sources clean. Fecal contamination from surface rainwater runoff makes matters worse. The UN Millennium Development Goal of reducing the under-five child mortality rate by two-thirds can be achieved only if diarrhea-related mortality can be drastically reduced. To do so, expanding access to safe water will be key.

Fortunately, a wide variety of relatively inexpensive technologies for water quality improvement are now at our disposal. Age-old tools like ceramic filters have been improved by modern scientists, and brand-new options—including Procter & Gamble's PUR sachets, which make water visibly clear in addition to disinfecting it—have been added to the arsenal. Solar disinfection requires nothing but empty plastic bottles and the natural UV rays available on a sunny day; but in the high-tech facilities operated by the company WaterHealth International in India and Ghana, UV radiation purifies 20,000 liters of water daily.

The task at hand is to figure out which of these technologies are most useful on the ground in poor countries, recognizing that it is individual women who will ultimately decide whether a particular product is desirable and meets their needs. To that end, we are carrying out the Kenya Rural Water Project, a series of rigorous evaluations that study user responses to water quality improvements in rural western Kenya. Drinking water quality is a major public health issue, with, according to our surveys, nearly 20 percent of young children suffering from diarrhea each week. We focus on the two most commonly used methods for improving drinking water quality in this area: spring protection and treatment with chlorine, both of which are simple and well-established approaches.

In this part of rural Kenya, 90 percent of households have ready access to a naturally occurring local spring. Spring protection entails sealing off the spring's water source and encasing it in concrete so that water flows out from a pipe and directly into a collection bucket—rather than seeping from the ground, where it is vulnerable to contamination from surface runoff. Construction costs are usually around $1,000 but the entire community benefits and protection can last for many years with minimal maintenance. Commercially available dilute chlorine, packaged for retail sale to individual households, is also cheap by Western standards—a month's supply costs about 30 cents per family. As a point-of-use technology, however, each household has to regularly choose whether or not the hassle and expense of using chlorine are worthwhile.

By comparing households that were randomly assigned to have their springs protected or to be given free chlorine (or both)—similarly to the way that drug trials are designed in medical research—we were able to confirm that both approaches are effective. Before the study began, only 14 percent of the surveyed households had drinking water that met EPA safety standards. Spring protection boosted the proportion to almost 20 percent, and distributing free chlorine raised it to above 50 percent. The average drop in fecal contamination (as measured by the presence of *E. coli* bacteria in the water) was even sharper. As a result, both spring protection and chlorine led to statistically significant reductions in child diarrhea—about one-third fewer diarrhea cases among children in households given free chlorine, with somewhat smaller gains for the protected-spring households. In epidemiological terms, these are substantial gains.

We also calculated how much households value these improvements, using what is called a willingness-to-pay analysis. This yielded some surprising and discouraging news. A randomly chosen subset of our rural Kenyan households was given coupons to buy the chlorine at a 50 percent discount after their free supply ran out, but very few were willing to pay even a modest price (roughly 15 cents per month) for a product that resulted in large positive benefits for their children's health. Using the extra travel costs incurred—basically, the time spent walking to the water source—as a measure of how people would value spring protection, we similarly found that most households were willing to pay only slightly more "with their feet" for cleaner water. Some preliminary calculations indicate that most households were willing to pay only between 50 cents and $5 for an annual supply of cleaner water, either from chlorine or access to a protected spring.

The low valuation of clean water is consistent with the fact that both of these technologies have been locally available for many years, and yet few natural springs get protected and very few households choose to purchase chlorine.

A lack of practical health knowledge might help explain the discrepancy between the large, observed health effects and low valuation by households of cleaner water. In baseline surveys, one-third of households did not consider contaminated water as a cause of child diarrhea. It might also be difficult for mothers to discern the benefits of clean water in practice. Over the course of a year, the health benefits from giving away free chlorine translated into about 7 weeks of diarrhea rather than 10 weeks for children whose households lack access to cleaner water. While this is an important medical effect, it might be hard for mothers to detect, especially if children are still sick for a variety of other reasons, such as malaria, malnutrition, and respiratory infections.

Our findings call into question the current model for promoting water quality improvements, which relies on cost-sharing with consumers and promotes retail distribution of treatment technologies as a strategy for sustainability. The subsidies needed to make the retail model work may be so high as to render that approach infeasible. Centralized treatment strategies may be an attractive alternative, and we are exploring this idea in the next phase of the Kenya Rural Water Project. Looking ahead, the challenge for both scientists and policymakers interested in the next generation of safe water technologies will be to identify products and distribution channels that work for people at the local level, and ensure that people will actually use the products.

Further Reading

Ashraf, Nava, James Berry, and Jesse Shapiro. 2007. Can Higher Prices Stimulate Product Use? Evidence from a Field Experiment in Zambia. Working paper 07-034. Boston: Harvard Business School.

Fewtrell, L., R.B. Kaufmann, D. Kay, W. Enanoria, L. Haller, and J.M. Colford Jr. Water, Sanitation, and Hygiene Interventions to Reduce Diarrhoea in Less Developed Countries: A Systematic Review and Meta-Analysis. *Lancet Infectious Diseases* 5(January): 42–52.

Kremer, Michael, Jessica Leino, Edward Miguel, and Alix Peterson Zwane. Spring Cleaning: Rural Water Impacts, Valuation, and Institutions. NBER Working Paper 15280. Cambridge, MA: NBER.

Zwane, Alix Peterson, and Michael Kremer. 2007. What Works in Fighting Diarrheal Diseases in Developing Countries? A Critical Review. *World Bank Research Observer* 22(1): 1–24.

96. ENVIRONMENTAL POLICY INNOVATIONS IN DEVELOPING COUNTRIES

Allen Blackman

is a senior fellow at Resources for the Future. He specializes in the economics of the environment in developing countries, especially Latin America and Asia.

Traditional forms of environmental regulation, such as technology mandates, have not worked particularly well in developing countries because the institutions and political will needed to enforce them have been lacking. Successful policy experiments in industrialized countries have inspired some innovative strategies for developing countries.

After decades of rapid urbanization, population growth, and industrialization, developing countries are now home to many of the world's most severe environmental and natural resource problems. Increasingly, they are crafting regulatory policies to address these problems, relying principally on conventional command-and-control (CAC) approaches: legal mandates requiring firms and farms to take certain actions (such as treating wastewater) and prohibiting them from taking others (like clearing forests). Although some developing countries have made enormous progress, the overall track record is mixed at best. The reasons are well known. Written regulations are often riddled with gaps and inconsistencies. Environmental regulatory agencies lack funding and trained personnel. Public infrastructure needed to control pollution has yet to be built. Difficult-to-monitor small and informal firms abound. And perhaps most important, the political will to enforce regulations is often limited.

Given this conundrum—grave environmental and natural resource problems matched with ineffectual policies—developing countries are increasingly experimenting with innovative regulatory strategies. The hope is that these "leapfrog" policies will sidestep the institutional and political constraints that have undermined CAC.

The popularity of different policy innovations has waxed and waned over the years. These phases reflect a bandwagon effect: an innovative policy is successfully piloted, often in an industrialized country; this experience stirs attention in international policy and academic circles; bilateral and multilateral aid organizations provide funds for new applications; and so forth. In what follows, I'll provide a brief, admittedly impressionistic sketch of the emerging empirical evidence on these experiments. The bottom line is that the overall track record is at least as uneven as that of CAC.

Influenced by the successful debut of the U.S. sulfur dioxide trading program, environmental policy innovation in developing countries 10 to 15 years ago emphasized economic incentive instruments like tradable permits and emissions fees, policies that provide financial incentives for improved environmental performance without dictating whether or how agents make these improvements. The usual argument for applying such policies is that, in theory, they are more cost-effective than CAC, a critical consideration in poor countries.

Several efforts to set up permit programs for air pollution in developing countries died on the vine. The most advanced applications have been in Chile and a handful of Chinese cities, none of which have been particularly successful. Improved air quality in Santiago has been largely due to the construction of new pipelines supplying cheap, clean-burning natural gas. In China, virtually all permit trades have been administratively mandated. Although successful in some regions, Colombia's nationwide liquid effluent discharge fee program—arguably the mostly highly touted emissions fee program in a developing country—has been marred by limited implementation in other regions and widespread noncompliance in key economic sectors.

As calls for using economic incentive instruments in developing countries have waned, attention has shifted to other policy innovations, including public disclosure programs like the U.S. Toxic Release Inventory (TRI), that collect, verify, and disseminate information about facility-level environmental performance in order to heighten pressure for pollution control. A decade after the TRI was established, Indonesia launched its Program for Pollution Control, Evaluation and Rating (PROPER) for major sources of water pollution. Research suggests that the program has spurred significant emissions reductions. Subsequently, multilateral lenders backed efforts to replicate the program in China, India, the Philippines, and Vietnam. Although rigorous evaluations of the impact of these programs have yet to appear, two have not outlasted initial infusions of funding and technical assistance. However, preliminary evaluations of the Green Ratings Project, an independently financed and designed public disclosure program in India, echo those of PROPER.

Voluntary regulation is another innovative environmental strategy now receiving considerable attention. The term refers to programs and policies in which polluters voluntarily commit to environmental performance goals either unilaterally, in the context of an agreement with regulators, or within a program administered by regulators or a third party. Like their counterparts in industrialized countries, developing country policymakers are rapidly putting voluntary programs in place. But evaluations of these programs typically fail to find significant environmental impacts. For example, the Colombian Environment Ministry's 2006 evaluation of 47 voluntary agreements in a wide variety of economics sectors concluded that in only 10 cases did industry keep the bulk of its commitments, most of which were procedural, not substantive. In Mexico, an evaluation of four consecutive agreements with the tanning sector over 13 years showed that the agreements had virtually no substantive impact aside from creating the (less and less credible) appearance of forward progress. The record is not uniformly negative, however. Studies show that voluntary agreements in Chile and a national voluntary audit program in Mexico have spurred significant improvements

In my view, the principal lesson from these policy experiments is that the critical assumption implicit in many environmental policy leapfrog efforts in developing countries—that innovative policies will somehow sidestep the institutional and political constraints that have undermined CAC—has generally turned out to be mistaken. Typically, the same constraints that have bedeviled CAC policies have undercut second- and third-generation policies. For example, tradable permit and emissions fees programs require a strong regulatory institution to reliably measure emissions and either enforce the facility-level caps implied by permit allocations or collect fees. So it is not at all surprising that these programs have foundered in countries and regions with weak regulators.

Perhaps a bit more surprising is that voluntary regulation has also often fallen flat. Upon reflection, however, research on this instrument predicts this outcome. It suggests that a variety of incentives drive compliance with voluntary commitments, including a background threat of mandatory regulation and pressure applied by consumers, capital markets, nongovernmental organizations, and community groups. The problem in many developing countries is that these drivers are relatively anemic.

In several cases where leapfrog experiments have been effective—for example, voluntary agreements in Chile and emissions fees in some parts of Colombia—many of the institutional prerequisites for effective CAC regulation were already in place. Exceptions appear to be Indonesia's public disclosure program and, to a lesser extent, India's Green Ratings Project.

To sum up, the record of environmental policy innovation in developing countries clearly indicates that cutting-edge policies, by themselves, are not a panacea. With the possible exception of well-designed public disclosure programs, the success of environmental management initiatives generally has less to do with the particular type of policy used than the institutional context in which it is implemented, in the same way that a farm's productivity has less to do with the variety of seeds sown than ensuring the soil has sufficient moisture and nutrients.

The take-home message for policymakers is to be wary of indiscriminate applications of newly popular policy innovations (such as payments for ecosystem services) that promise to circumvent chronic institutional problems. The value of such policies largely depends on whether or not they contribute to, or divert attention from, the hard work of building the requisites of effective environmental management, including strong regulatory institutions, clear consistent written regulations, and the political will for diverting scarce resources to environmental protection.

Further Reading

Blackman, Allen. 2008. Can Voluntary Environmental Regulation Work in Developing Countries? Lessons from Case Studies. *Policy Studies Journal* 36(1): 119–141.

Blackman, Allen, and Winston Harrington. 2000. The Use of Economic Incentives in Developing Countries: International Experience with Industrial Air Pollution. *Journal of Environment and Development* 9(1): 5–44.

Russell, Clifford, and William Vaughan. 2003. The Choice of Pollution Control Policy Instruments in Developing Countries: Arguments, Evidence and Suggestions. In *International Yearbook of Environmental and Resource Economics* 2003/2004 edited by H. Folmer and T. Tietenberg. Cheltenham, UK: Edward Elgar.

Sterner, Thomas. 2003. *Policy Instruments for Environmental and Natural Resource Management*. Washington, DC: Resources for the Future.

97. GREEN CITIES AND ECONOMIC DEVELOPMENT

Matthew E. Kahn
is a professor at the UCLA Institute of the Environment, in the Departments of Economics and Public Policy. He blogs at greeneconomics.blogspot.com.

This commentary discusses findings from Green Cities: Urban Growth and the Environment, *a recent book that reviews what economic analysis has to say about the environmental implications of urban development.*

Understanding the relationship between economic development and urban environmental quality is no mere academic exercise. In 2000, 80 percent of the U.S. population lived in a metropolitan area, and worldwide the fraction of people living in cities is projected to rise from 30 percent in 1950 to 60 percent in 2030. Not only are the population numbers large, but the conflicts and conundrums are very real. Some rapidly growing cities, like Beijing, suffer from severe environmental degradation, but others are able to preserve or even enhance their environmental quality. Air quality improved steadily in Los Angeles between 1980 and today, despite an over 85 percent increase in automobile usage.

All cities face "tragedy of the commons" problems. No one individual driver, manufacturer, or institution has sufficient incentive to economize on pollution production. The sheer scale of cities means that when millions of economic actors each pursue their narrow self-interest, the city can turn brown. While population growth scales up this problem, adding millions more polluting producers and consumers to the small geographic area, income growth offers the possibility of both greening and browning the city.

INCOME GROWTH

The main contribution economists have made to sorting out the relationship between income growth and environmental quality is the environmental Kuznets curve (EKC), which models the relationship between economic development and pollution levels over time. By many indicators, environmental quality initially declines as poorer cities develop; for example, as people grow richer, they switch from bikes to cars and demand larger housing units with more energy-using appliances.

However, as growth continues, a turning point is eventually reached, and thereafter, environmental quality improves as incomes rise. Development triggers offsetting effects on pollution, most notably by shifting consumption and production in greener directions and by giving policymakers the mandate and the resources to implement regulation that reduces pollution. Take the case of Los Angeles. Under state law, car companies were required to produce vehicles with lower emissions per mile, which led to an overall decline in air pollution, even as rising affluence caused the total number of miles driven to increase.

But this is one highly conditioned example. If the EKC hypothesis is true, trends in per capita income underestimate overall changes in well-being in rich cities but overestimate such trends in poorer ones. Some World Bank economists have argued that the trade-offs between development and the environment improve over time, though data limitations make it very difficult to confirm this hypothesis. Their optimism is based on the claim that developing countries can adopt greener technologies previously developed in richer nations and learn from the regulatory mistakes of richer nations. If this is true, developing nations can expect to benefit in two ways. First, they are likely to reach the peak of the EKC earlier in their development than other nations have in the past. Second, they will suffer less environmental damage before reaching the turning point.

The stakes in this debate are high. Per capita GDP in 1998 (in purchasing parity dollars) was $1,440 in sub-Saharan Africa, $2,060 in India, and $3,051 in China—nowhere near $8,000 per capita, the figure currently suggested in the empirical literature for when the relationship between environmental quality and economic growth appears to peak and then turn down.

Perhaps the most important problem with the EKC is that it may have little relevance for pollution problems that are borne by others rather than just city residents. The obvious example here is global warming, where greenhouse gases released from one city potentially affect future generations around the globe.

POPULATION GROWTH

Urban population growth, as distinct from per capita income growth, poses additional challenges. By concentrating a large number of people and firms within a small geographic area, pollution levels rise. The greatest problems arise when population growth is unexpected, as in times of war and famine, and the government is not up to the job of responding by scaling up infrastructure. As poor migrants enter a city, they increase the demand for basic services, but typically are incapable of contributing financially to their supply. The resulting water pollution, contagion, and absence of trash removal all raise the risk of serious health epidemics.

Megacity urbanization also weakens the pressure for environmental improvement in a more subtle way. In developed nations, decentralized competition among cities creates an incentive for politicians to adopt green policies; if they do not, residents may "vote with their feet" by relocating to other cities with a better quality of life. While enormous metropolitan areas, such as Los Angeles and New York City, contain less than 5 percent of the U.S. population, elsewhere the percentages are far more imbalanced: for example, in Argentina, 30 percent of the nation's population lives in Buenos Aires, the largest city. When the urban population in a country is concentrated in one or two megacities, local governments are less concerned about losing population to other cities through lax environmental controls.

Of course, cities differ in their ability to absorb population growth without experiencing local environmental degradation. Some of the factors that affect the relationship between growth and sustainability are relatively immutable, such as climate and geography. But the quality of governmental institutions also plays a key role in determining whether a city will be able to successfully cope with population growth. Long-term planning requires resources and expertise. In the best of all possible worlds, urban planners would be able to forecast likely urban growth over the next 20 years, and, anticipating this growth, city leaders would take proactive steps to limit its environmental impact and finance necessary infrastructure upgrades.

Further Reading

Hilton, F., G. Hank, and Arik Levinson. 1998. Factoring the Environmental Kuznets Curve: Evidence from Automotive Lead Emissions. *Journal of Environmental Economics and Management* 35(2): 126–141.

Kahn, Matthew E. 1999. The Silver Lining of Rust Belt Manufacturing Decline. *Journal of Urban Economics* 46(3): 360–376.

Kahn, Matthew E. 2006. *Green Cities: Urban Growth and the Environment.* Washington, DC: Brookings Institution Press.

Moomaw, William R., and Gregory C. Unruh. 1997. Are Environmental Kuznets Curves Misleading Us? The Case of CO_2 Emissions. *Environment and Development Economics* 2(4): 451–463.

98. BUILDING BETTER HOUSING POLICIES FOR THE DEVELOPING WORLD'S POOR

Robert M. Buckley
is the managing director at the Rockefeller Foundation. Previously, he was a lead economist at the World Bank and served as the chief economist of the U.S. Department of Housing and Urban Development.

Jerry Kalarickal
works for the U.S. Department of State. Previously, he was a consultant on urban development issues for the World Bank as well as for the U.S. Department of Housing and Urban Development.

Urban housing in poor countries has seen a dramatic shift away from heavy reliance on state provision and toward a far more market-oriented approach. Nonetheless, unfettered markets do not solve all the problems, and carefully designed policy interventions may still be needed to make the housing market work better.

The photos are always heart-rending: children playing in open sewers, families crowded into filthy apartments, squatters sheltering in tin-and-cardboard tents. They reflect the challenge of rapid urbanization in much of the developing world. By some estimates, more than 50 percent of the world's poor people will live in urban areas by 2035. Little wonder that Target 11 of the UN's Millennium Development Goals is improving the lives of 100 million slum dwellers by 2020.

Once, slums were considered a temporary stage during demographic transition: rural poor people migrated to urban slums in search of work, achieved a better standard of living, and moved up to better housing environments. Today, however, many slum dwellers are no longer immigrants from the villages. Many of the 100,000 pavement dwellers in Mumbai, for instance, are second-generation, as are many of the residents of the *favelas* of Rio de Janeiro. Surveys in India and Brazil find that many slum dwellers are no longer participants in the traditional demographic transition to the middle class.

Though the majority of the world's poor people continue to live in rural areas, poverty is becoming more urban. Most poor people in Brazil, Mexico, and Russia already live in urban areas. In many of India's larger states, the poverty rate is now higher in cities than in rural areas. Urbanization no longer reliably correlates with economic growth and rising incomes, as it did during the urbanization processes in the advanced economies of today.

How to ensure that low-income people have decent housing has concerned policymakers for decades, but the approaches have changed—from intervening in the housing market to letting market mechanisms work on the poor's behalf.

CONTROL AND INTERVENTION

Under interventionist regimes of the past, governments set standards for housing and often undertook its actual construction. Not only was the housing expensive, but its supply was inelastic, and when demand surged, people were pushed into the unregulated informal sector, with its illegal squatting, substandard buildings, and dangerously high occupancy levels. Demolition of squatters' settlements only worsened people's situations.

Rent controls, which discourage private construction, and other public programs that restricted the housing market and building industry also had the effect of decreasing supply elasticity. Another constraint was land suitable for residential construction. Wherever the public sector owned and controlled large amounts of serviced land, as in many developing economies, this major input into housing production was less responsive to increases in demand. Consequently, higher demand was accompanied by rising prices, making it unaffordable for the poor.

MARKETS AND INCENTIVES

Over the past 20 years, housing policy in developing countries has become more market oriented. Possibly the most important reason is the change in perspective on what constitutes effective governance. There are now twice as many democratic governments in the world as two decades ago, and they are overwhelmingly more decentralized. With the fall of the Soviet Union and the general adoption of market-oriented economic policy in China and India, the central planning approach to housing has largely been discarded.

Moreover, most developing economies now have sophisticated and diversified financial sectors. Formal financial institutions, of course, do not serve the very poor who are self-employed or work in the informal sector and cannot show proof of income—a condition for obtaining credit. In these settings, the real promise for assisting low-income families with housing finance is emerging through microfinance institutions, whose financial services let poor people improve their own housing conditions.

Many of the new housing policies adopted in response to the continuing migration to the cities enable, rather than control or displace, the private sector, thereby improving the affordability of housing in general.

After the Soviet Union fell, for example, reforms substituted private incentives for public control over housing production, ownership, design, and allocation. India has rewarded states that eliminate rent controls and urban land-market ownership restrictions. China, Chile, Colombia, Malaysia, and Mexico are letting consumers borrow or use public resources to find the housing they want. Housing vouchers, a market-oriented instrument, are the new form of subsidy. And slum dwellers themselves, who by force of circumstances have always been among the most market-oriented of all consumers because they have no other options, have established the Slum Dwellers International Federation to share experiences and approaches. Policymakers in developing areas are increasingly seeking their views on low-income shelter problems.

CAUTIONS AND CAVEATS

However, despite these improvements in the policy environment, not all the changes have been benevolent, as the recent financial crisis partially spurred by mortgage lending has signaled. Past financial crises have led to capital flight and massive mortgage defaults, as in Mexico in the mid-1990s. In some cases, as in Asia in the late 1990s, overheated real estate markets seem to have precipitated these collapses. In the former Soviet bloc, the government privatized individual apartment units, but the fabric of the buildings, such as roofs and elevators, remained unmanaged, and ambiguous ownership rights to common areas continue to hamper property management.

Governments of developing countries therefore have learned to be cautious in applying sweeping solutions pressed on them by the advocates of free markets. An example is the assertion that clear title to land is the key to productive capitalism. However, in some cases the cost of establishing clear title may outweigh any benefit. And in cases involving squatters, granting amnesty for illegal occupation arguably undermines respect for property rights. Furthermore, many traditional societies have a continuum of degrees of tenure, and a formal title may not be the only viable system for differing cultural, economic, and political environments.

Researchers also warn against an unconditional attack on rent control. Although it is anathema to most economists, those studying housing markets for the poor have come to have more nuanced opinions.

Recent research there has shown that there is no capitalist panacea for improving the shelter conditions for the urban poor. Nevertheless, whereas many old-style interventions exacerbated the housing problems of poor people in developing countries, market-oriented policies by themselves, even without additional resources, can improve their situations. Increased community involvement allows the urban poor to shape their own solutions to the particular challenges of their immediate environments. Circumstances vary widely, and policy must be tailored to local conditions. But where intervention used to be the rule, policymakers are now more inclined to let the market make the decisions.

Further Reading

Angel, Shlomo. 2000. *Housing Policy Matters: A Global Analysis.* New York: Oxford University Press.

Buckley, Robert, and Jerry Kalarickal. 2005. Housing Policy in Developing Countries: Conjectures and Refutations. *World Bank Research Observer* 20(2): 233–257.

Malpezzi, Stephen. 1999. Economic Analysis of Housing Markets in Developing and Transition Economies. In *Handbook of Regional and Urban Economics,* Vol. 3, edited by Paul Cheshire and Edwin S. Mills. Amsterdam, Netherlands: North-Holland.

World Bank. 1993. *Housing: Enabling Markets to Work.* Housing Policy Paper. Washington, DC: World Bank.

This article is based on work the authors did while employed at the World Bank. The views expressed herein do not represent those of the Rockefeller Foundation, the U.S. Department of State, or the World Bank.

99. THE FUTURE OF FAMINE

Cormac Ó Gráda

is a professor of economics at University College Dublin. He specializes in Irish and European economic history, the role of markets during famines, famine demography, and the global history of famine.

How have famines evolved over the past several decades? Once the consequence of natural disasters and plagues, famines today and in the future are more likely to be the result of policy failures and wars.

In the developed world, famines no longer capture headlines like they used to. Billboard images of African infants with distended bellies are less ubiquitous, and the focus of international philanthropy has shifted from disaster relief to more structural issues, especially debt relief, economic development, and democratic accountability in developing countries. Totalitarian famines of the kind associated with Stalin, Mao, in developing countries and their latter-day imitators are on the wane. Even in Africa, the most vulnerable of the seven continents, the famines of the past decade or so have been small by historical standards.

Today, probably for the first time in history, only small pockets of the globe remain truly vulnerable to the threat of major famine. So is it almost time to declare famine "history"? No, if the continuing increase in the number of malnourished people is our guide; yes, perhaps, if we focus instead on their declining share of world population, and on the characteristics of famine in the recent past.

Famines are not easy to measure. Excess mortality is one obvious yardstick, but aside from being hard to calculate, it is as much a function of policy responses to famine, as of the conditions that caused the crisis. In the highly publicized cases of Malawi in 2002 and Niger in 2005, famine deaths were, thankfully, very few; perhaps these are best seen as averted famines. However, the meaning of the word "famine" has also evolved over the centuries. In the recent past, it has been used to refer to events and processes that would not qualify as famine in the apocalyptic, historical sense. Some scholars have argued for a broader definition that would embrace a range, extending from endemic malnutrition to excess mortality and its associated diseases. In support of this view, famine represents the upper end of the continuum whose average is hunger. Malnutrition, which 800 million to 900 million endure every day, might be seen as slow-burning famine. While the absolute numbers have risen, the proportion of malnourished people in the less-developed world has dropped from 29 percent in 1979–1981 to 20 percent in 1990–1992 and to 17 percent today. Progress has been greatest in the Far East and South Asia, two traditionally famine-prone regions. In contrast, in sub-Saharan Africa, famine's chief remaining redoubt, one-third of the population remains malnourished.

Malnutrition and famine are obviously linked. But at present, mass hunger is a far greater challenge to the global community than famine. Perversely, it is much easier to solicit sympathy and funding for one time disaster relief than for alleviating endemic food shortages.

Wars exacerbate economic backwardness and vulnerability to famine. It is no surprise that, in the 18 countries most subject to food emergencies since the mid-1980s, the UN Food and Agriculture Organization (FAO) calculates that current or past armed conflict has been a major factor in 14 cases. Weather, principally drought, was the chief cause in 8 cases, and what the FAO calls "economic problems" in 5. One country, Haiti, has been subject to all of these factors.

The improvements visible in most of the world are the result, of course, of rapid rises in food production as well as falling transport costs. At the global level, food output per head has risen about one-third since the early 1960s. It is particularly reassuring to find agricultural output rising faster than population in former famine black spots such as China and India. Only in sub-Saharan Africa has food output failed to keep pace with population. Since the early 1960s, the decline per capita has been about 10 percent, and as a consequence, reliance on imported food has grown.

As for predictions about the future of famine, it is worth noting that the prognostications of past students of hunger and famine have rarely gotten it right. Stanford University biologist Paul Ehrlich's doomsday forecast in the late 1960s is a notorious case in point. His forecast of global famine in the 1970s—"hundreds of millions of people ... going to starve to death in spite of any crash programs embarked upon now"—got it almost exactly wrong.

Changes in the nature of famine, particularly in recent decades, justify tempered optimism about the future. So does the progress of democracy and relative political stability in much of Africa, where their absence often led to famines in the past. But while the recent examples of famine have occurred in the poorest and most fragile of economies, even much stronger countries would be wise to consider the hazards ahead.

Since the turn of the new millennium, hope for the future has been qualified by increasing concern about the implications of climate change, and the prospect of massive emissions of carbon dioxide leading to accelerated global warming. The challenges of a growing global population, rising living standards, and increasing urbanization are real, with implications in the medium term for soil productivity, the relative price of food, and perhaps political stability. Even more important, any optimism about "making famine history" must be qualified by the realization that the threat of wars between and within nations is never far away. The hope for a famine-free world depends on improved governance and on peace. It is as simple—and as difficult—as that.

Further Reading

Devereux, Stephen. 2007. *The New Famines: Why Famines Persist in an Era of Globalization.* London: Routledge.

Drèze, Jean, and Amartya Sen. 1989. *Hunger and Public Action.* Oxford, UK: Oxford University Press.

Ó Gráda, Cormac. 2007. Making Famine History. *Journal of Economic Literature* 45(1): 5–38.

Ó Gráda, Cormac. 2008. *Famine: A Short History.* Princeton, NJ: Princeton University Press.

100. IS POPULATION STILL AN IMPORTANT POLICY ISSUE?

Warren C. Robinson

is a professor emeritus of economics at the Pennsylvania State University. He has worked on population-related research and policy issues for over 40 years.

Are population control policies still desirable, given that global population is expected to stabilize over the next century? Whereas past population policies and programs have favorably affected the timing and nature of global population stabilization, in the future they must attempt to do the same for the emerging economic and social dimensions of demographic change.

Demographic factors have been the driving force behind much of human history, but for most of the 1960s and 1970s, only one demographic dimension, population growth, dominated the public policy agenda. The sudden rise in population growth rates in Asia, Africa, and Latin America led many development specialists to conclude that rapid population growth made increasing global per capita economic growth difficult if not impossible. As these research findings became clear in the late 1960s, there was an outpouring of alarmist popular works on the "population bomb," with some arguing that it was already too late to reverse these ominous trends. Spaceship Earth might already be doomed.

But governmental policies and programs aimed at reducing human fertility were developed and adopted around the world to nearly universal approval. These family planning programs, together with the economic and social progress achieved in many developing nations, have had an impact. Population growth has fallen sharply, and total world population is now projected to level off toward the end of this century at some 8 billion to 10 billion people, far below previous forecasts. This very success has led some to draw the conclusion that, having defused the population bomb, demographic concerns no longer are important on the public policy agenda. Here I will examine some issues that suggest that such a conclusion may be premature.

WHY POPULATION POLICIES STILL MATTER

First, even accepting the likely prospect of eventual global population stabilization, a considerable amount of further absolute growth will occur in the three to four generations required for a global equilibrium to arise. Due to demographic momentum, this growth will continue to put pressure on employment, education, and health (particularly in urban areas) and require continuing and expanding programs already in place, even if this growth is only temporary.

Second, most of this growth will be in the poorest regions. These policies and programs have barely begun to have an impact on sub-Saharan Africa, parts of South Asia, and the Caribbean. Fertility and potential growth there remain high. Moreover, family planning programs that increase access to contraception are an important component of the reproductive and infant health measures urgently needed to deal with the HIV/AIDS epidemic and related health issues in these same regions. These new threats make these programs more imperative than ever.

Third, large prospective population increases will continue to power large international migration streams, mainly from the poor areas of Africa, Latin America, and South Asia to the developed nations. Even with no population growth, income differentials would cause such movements, but the larger the base population, the greater the migration. These movements will require policy and program reactions at both the sending and receiving ends.

Fourth, sustained low fertility in the developed nations—Europe, North America, and some Asian countries—is leading to a sharp relative increase in the older age groups and will create a growing intergenerational transfer burden to carry out already existing social insurance programs. This problem is exacerbated if fertility remains below replacement level because succeeding cohorts become progressively smaller. Recent policy and program initiatives in some European countries have attempted with some success, through public support to day-care centers and subsidized maternal and child and health programs, to increase fertility. On the other hand, human longevity continues to increase, adding to the retirement burden. These age structure–rooted issues will remain on the public policy agenda for decades to come.

Population—in terms of size, growth, distribution, and composition—will shape many of the issues with which economic and social policymakers will grapple in the decades to come.

ARGUMENTS AGAINST POPULATION POLICIES—PAST AND FUTURE

All the above discussion takes for granted the desirability of public policy and program interventions to affect social and economic outcomes connected with population. But it is also possible to maintain that such interventions interfere with built-in structural adjustment processes that would produce an outcome without public policy or program. This may be thought of as the "invisible hand" solution. The demographic, economic, and social systems may very well tend toward equilibrium if left to their own internal dynamics. From the very outset of family planning programs, some critics have pursued this line of argument and held that family planning programs were unnecessary over the long run.

The great wave of concern over the population bomb in the 1960s and 1970s swept these criticisms aside, but now, with the bomb defused, the critics have returned with a renewed vigor, arguing that population never belonged on the public policy agenda, pointing out that since fertility is typically lower for educated, middle-class couples, birth rates would have fallen naturally with development. These programs, moreover, are further indicted as ethically flawed. After all, fertility is the result of the most intimate and personal interactions imaginable among human couples. Observed outcomes are those desired by the couples involved. Surely public-sector efforts to intervene in these processes are inherently coercive and destructive of human reproductive rights, critics argue.

Ethical issues cannot be settled by debate, but it is worth pointing out that throughout recorded human history, societies operating with a fixed resource base and relatively constant technology have recognized the need to balance population with resources. Fertility decisions made by couples can create externalities—sharp declines in marginal productivity and environmental degradation—that affect the viability of the larger group. Societies have used a variety of measures, ranging from control over access to marriage to infanticide to control population size. Modern family planning programs appear quite benign in comparison.

Would fertility have, indeed, fallen in the developing world with no program intervention? This point cannot be proven one way or the other. But it has been established, beyond any reasonable doubt, that the programs did have an impact. At the very least, they did help lower fertility by supplying information and safe, more effective contraceptive means to couples around the world. Perhaps global population would have eventually stabilized without policy and program intervention, but it would have been at a much larger total and a much lower per capita income level.

Today, a global population of 10 billion may prove manageable, but what about one of 15 billion or 20 billion? Such extremes are not implausible, and population remains the inescapable denominator for all discussions of poverty eradication, global climate change, energy requirements, and ecosystem viability.

Further Reading

Robinson, Warren C., and John A. Ross, eds. 2006. *The Global Family Planning Revolution: Three Decades of Policy and Program.* Washington, DC: World Bank.

Kantner, John F., and Andrew Kantner. 2006. *The Struggle for Consensus on Population and Development.* New York: Palgrave–McMillan.

Sinding, Steven. 2000. The Great Population Debates: How Relevant Are They for the 21st Century? *American Journal of Public Health* 90(12): 1841–1845.

INDEX

Lightning Source UK Ltd.
Milton Keynes UK
17 November 2010

162988UK00001BA/3/P

9 781933 115870